Oracle Data Warehouse Tuning for 10g

Oracle Data Warehouse Tuning for 10g

Gavin Powell

ELSEVIER
DIGITAL PRESS

Amsterdam · Boston · Heidelberg · London · New York · Oxford
Paris · San Diego · San Francisco · Singapore · Sydney · Tokyo

Elsevier Digital Press
30 Corporate Drive, Suite 400, Burlington, MA 01803, USA
Linacre House, Jordan Hill, Oxford OX2 8DP, UK

Library of Congress Cataloging-in-Publication Data
Application Submitted.

British Library Cataloguing-in-Publication Data
A catalogue record for this book is available from the British Library.

ISBN-13: 978-1-55558-335-4

ISBN-10: 1-55558-335-0

For information on all Elsevier Digital Press publications visit our Web site at www.books.elsevier.com

05 06 07 08 09 10 9 8 7 6 5 4 3 2 1

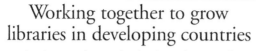

Working together to grow
libraries in developing countries

www.elsevier.com | www.bookaid.org | www.sabre.org

ELSEVIER   BOOK AID
International   Sabre Foundation

Contents at a Glance

Preface		xix
Introduction to Data Warehousing		xxiii
Part I: Data Warehouse Data Modeling		1
	1	The Basics of Data Warehouse Data Modeling	3
	2	Introducing Data Warehouse Tuning	31
	3	Effective Data Warehouse Indexing	49
	4	Materialized Views and Query Rewrite	79
	5	Oracle Dimension Objects	113
	6	Partitioning and Basic Parallel Processing	137
Part II: Tuning SQL Code in a Data Warehouse		161
	7	The Basics of SQL Query Code Tuning	163
	8	Aggregation Using GROUP BY Clause Extensions	215
	9	Analysis Reporting	249
	10	Modeling with the MODEL Clause	281
Part III: Advanced Topics		317
	11	Query Rewrite	319
	12	Parallel Processing	335
	13	Data Loading	351
	14	Data Warehouse Architecture	385
A	New Data Warehouse Features in Oracle Database 10g	423
B.	Sample Schemas	425
C.	Sample Scripting	431
D.	Syntax Conventions	447
E.	Sources of Information	449
Index		451

Contents

Preface   **xix**

Introduction to Data Warehouse Tuning   **xxiii**

Part I: Data Warehouse Data Modeling   **1**

1   The Basics of Data Warehouse Data Modeling   **3**

    1.1   The Relational and Object Data Models   3
        1.1.1   The Relational Data Model   4
                Normalization   4
                    1st Normal Form   4
                    2nd Normal Form   4
                    3rd Normal Form   4
                    4th Normal Form   5
                    5th Normal Form   6
                  Referential Integrity   6
                    Surrogate Keys   7
                  Denormalization   7
                  Data Warehouses—Why Not the Relational Model?   10
        1.1.2   The Object Data Model   10
                Data Warehouses—Why Not the Object Model?   12
        1.1.3   The Object-Relational Data Model   13
    1.2   Data Modeling for Data Warehouses   13
        1.2.1   The Container Shipment Tracking Schema   13
        1.2.2   The Dimensional Data Model   15
                What Is a Star Schema?   18
                    What Is a Snowflake Schema?   19
        1.2.3   Data Warehouse Data Model Design Basics   21
                Dimension Entities   22

			Dimension Entity Types	22
			Fact Entities	24
			Fact Entity Types	25
			Granularity, Granularity, and Granularity	26
			Time and How Long to Retain Data	27
			Other Factors to Consider During Design	27
			Surrogate Keys	27
			Duplicating Surrogate Keys and Associated Names	27
			Referential Integrity	28
			Managing the Data Warehouse	28

2   Introducing Data Warehouse Tuning   31

2.1	Let's Build a Data Warehouse	31
2.1.1	The Demographics Data Model	31
2.1.2	The Inventory-Accounting OLTP Data Model	32
2.1.3	The Data Warehouse Data Model	34
	Identify the Facts	34
	Identify the Granularity	35
	Identify and Build the Dimensions	35
	Build the Facts	36
2.2	Methods for Tuning a Data Warehouse	37
2.2.1	Snowflake versus Star Schemas	37
	Star Schemas	39
	What Is a Star Query?	40
	Star Transformation	40
	Using Bitmap Indexes	43
	Snowflake Schemas	43
	Introducing Oracle Database Dimension Object Hierarchies	44
2.2.2	3rd Normal Form Schemas	44
2.2.3	Introducing Other Data Warehouse Tuning Methods	44

3   Effective Data Warehouse Indexing   49

3.1	The Basics of Indexing	49
3.1.1	The When and What of Indexing	50
	Referential Integrity Indexing	51
	Surrogate Keys	52
	Views and View Constraints in Data Warehouses	53
	Alternate Indexing	53

	3.1.2	Types of Indexes in Oracle Database	54
		BTree Indexes	55
		Types of BTree Indexes	56
		Unique BTree Index	56
		Ascending or Descending BTree Index	56
		Sorted or Unsorted BTree Index	57
		Function-Based BTree Index	57
		Reverse Key Value BTree Index	58
		Compressed Composite Column BTree Index	58
		Bitmap Indexes	58
		Bitmap Index Cardinality	58
		Bitmap Performance	60
		Bitmap Block Level Locking	60
		Bitmap Composite Column Indexes	60
		Bitmap Index Overflow	60
		Bitmap Index Restrictions	60
		Bitmap Join Indexes	61
		Other Types of Indexing	61
	3.2	Star Queries and Star Query Transformations	62
	3.2.1	Star Queries	62
	3.2.2	Star Transformation Queries	69
		Bitmap Join Indexes	70
	3.2.3	Problems with Star Queries and Star Transformations	73
	3.3	Index Organized Tables and Clusters	75
4	**Materialized Views and Query Rewrite**		**79**
	4.1	What Is a Materialized View?	79
	4.1.1	The Benefits of Materialized Views	80
		Related Objects	81
	4.1.2	Potential Pitfalls of Materialized Views	81
	4.2	Materialized View Syntax	82
	4.2.1	CREATE MATERIALIZED VIEW	82
		The REFRESH Clause	82
		ENABLE QUERY REWRITE	85
		What Is Query Rewrite?	85
		Verifying Query Rewrite	86
		Query Rewrite Restrictions	86
		Improving Query Rewrite Performance	86
		ON PREBUILT TABLE	87
		Registering Existing Materialized Views	87
		Compression	87

		Other Syntax Options	88
	4.2.2	CREATE MATERIALIZED VIEW LOG	88
		The WITH Clause	89
		The SEQUENCE Clause	90
	4.2.3	ALTER MATERIALIZED VIEW [LOG]	90
	4.2.4	DROP MATERIALIZED VIEW [LOG]	90
4.3	Types of Materialized Views		91
	4.3.1	Single Table Aggregations and Filtering Materialized Views	91
		Fast Refresh Requirements for Aggregations	93
	4.3.2	Join Materialized Views	94
		Fast Refresh Requirements for Joins	97
		Joins and Aggregations	97
	4.3.3	Set Operator Materialized Views	98
	4.3.4	Nested Materialized Views	98
	4.3.5	Materialized View ORDER BY Clauses	102
4.4	Analyzing and Managing Materialized Views		102
	4.4.1	Metadata Views	102
	4.4.2	The DBMS_MVIEW Package	104
		Verifying Materialized Views	104
		Estimating Materialized View Storage Space	105
		Explaining a Materialized View	105
		Explaining Query Rewrite	106
		Manual Refresh	107
		Miscellaneous Procedures	108
	4.4.3	The DBMS_ADVISOR Package	108
4.5	Making Materialized Views Faster		109
5	**Oracle Dimension Objects**		**113**
5.1	What Is a Dimension Object?		113
		The Benefits of Implementing Dimension Objects	114
		Negative Aspects of Dimension Objects	116
5.2	Dimension Object Syntax		116
	5.2.1	CREATE DIMENSION Syntax	117
		Level Clause	117
		Hierarchy Clause	119
		Dimension Join Clause	120
		Attribute Clause	122
		Extended Attribute Clause	123
	5.2.2	ALTER and DROP DIMENSION Syntax	123
	5.2.3	Using Constraints with Dimensions	123
5.3	Dimension Object Metadata		124

	5.4	Dimension Objects and Performance	125
		5.4.1	Rollup Using Dimension Objects	127
		5.4.2	Join Back Using Dimension Objects	132

6   Partitioning and Basic Parallel Processing   **137**

	6.1	What Are Partitioning and Parallel Processing?	137
		6.1.1	What Is Partitioning?	137
		6.1.2	The Benefits of Using Partitioning	138
		6.1.3	Different Partitioning Methods	139
			Partition Indexing	140
			When to Use Different Partitioning Methods	141
		6.1.4	Parallel Processing and Partitioning	143
	6.2	Partitioned Table Syntax	144
		6.2.1	CREATE TABLE: Range Partition	144
		6.2.2	CREATE TABLE: List Partition	146
		6.2.3	CREATE TABLE: Hash Partition	147
		6.2.4	Composite Partitioning	148
			CREATE TABLE: Range-Hash Partition	148
			CREATE TABLE: Range-List Partition	149
		6.2.5	Partitioned Materialized Views	151
	6.3	Tuning Queries with Partitioning	153
		6.3.1	Partitioning EXPLAIN PLANs	153
		6.3.2	Partitioning and Parallel Processing	154
		6.3.3	Partition Pruning	154
		6.3.4	Partition-Wise Joins	155
			Full Partition-Wise Joins	155
			Partial Partition-Wise Joins	157
	6.4	Other Partitioning Tricks	158
	6.5	Partitioning Metadata	158

Part II: Tuning SQL Code in a Data Warehouse   **161**

7   The Basics of SQL Query Code Tuning   **163**

	7.1	Basic Query Tuning	163
		7.1.1	Columns in the SELECT Clause	164
		7.1.2	Filtering with the WHERE Clause	164
			Multiple Column WHERE Clause Filters	166
		7.1.3	Aggregating	169
			How to Use the HAVING Clause	169
		7.1.4	Using Functions	170

	7.1.5	Conditions and Operators	172
		Comparison Conditions	172
		Equi, Anti, and Range	173
		LIKE Pattern Matching	173
		Set Membership (IN and EXISTS)	174
		Using Subqueries for Efficiency	174
		Groups	175
		Logical Operators	175
		Set Operators	176
	7.1.6	Pseudocolumns	176
		Sequences	176
		The ROWID Pseudocolumn	177
		The ROWNUM Pseudocolumn	178
	7.1.7	Joins	179
		How to Code Joins in SQL Code	179
		How Oracle Joins Tables	181
		How to Tune a Join	183
7.2	How Oracle SQL Is Executed		184
	7.2.1	The Parser	184
	7.2.2	The Optimizer	185
		The Importance of Statistics	186
		Realistic Statistics	186
		Dynamic Sampling	187
		Overriding the Optimizer Using Hints	187
		Classifying Hints	188
		Influence the Optimizer	189
		Change Table Scans	189
		Change Index Scans	189
		Change Joins	190
		Parallel SQL	190
		Changing Queries and Subqueries	190
7.3	Tools for Tuning Queries		191
	7.3.1	What Is the Wait Event Interface?	192
		The System Aggregation Layer	192
		Idle Events	196
		The Session Layer	199
		The Third Layer and Beyond	206
	7.3.2	Oracle Database Wait Event Interface Improvements	208
	7.3.3	Oracle Enterprise Manager and the Wait Event Interface	209

**8   Aggregation Using GROUP BY
Clause Extensions**   **215**

8.1   What Are GROUP BY Clause Extensions?   215
    8.1.1   Why Use GROUP BY Clause Extensions?   215
8.2   GROUP BY Clause Extensions   216
    8.2.1   The ROLLUP and CUBE Clauses   217
        The ROLLUP Clause   217
            ROLLUP Clause Syntax   217
            How the ROLLUP Clause Helps Performance   217
        The CUBE Clause   222
            CUBE Clause Syntax   223
            How the CUBE Clause Helps Performance   223
            The Multiple Dimensions of the CUBE Clause   225
    8.2.2   The GROUPING SETS Clause   225
        GROUPING SETS Clause Syntax   227
        How the GROUPING SETS Clause Helps Performance   227
    8.2.3   Grouping Functions   232
        The GROUPING Function   232
        The GROUPING_ID Function   234
        The GROUP_ID Function   234
8.3   GROUP BY Clause Extensions and
    Materialized Views   235
8.4   Combining Groupings Together   242
    8.4.1   Composite Groupings   243
    8.4.2   Concatenated Groupings   245
    8.4.3   Hierarchical Cubes   246

9   Analysis Reporting   **249**

9.1   What Is Analysis Reporting?   249
    9.1.1   How Does Analysis Reporting
        Affect Performance?   251
9.2   Types of Analysis Reporting   251
9.3   Introducing Analytical Functions   253
    9.3.1   Simple Summary Functions   253
    9.3.2   Statistical Function Calculators   253
    9.3.3   Statistical Distribution Functions   254
    9.3.4   Ranking Functions   255
    9.3.5   Lag and Lead Functions   255
    9.3.6   Aggregation Functions Allowing Analysis   256
9.4   Specialized Analytical Syntax   256

	9.4.1	The OVER Clause	256
		The ORDER BY Clause	257
		The PARTITION BY Clause	257
		The Windowing Clause	260
	9.4.2	The WITH Clause	262
	9.4.3	CASE and Cursor Expressions	266
		CASE Expressions	266
		Cursor Expressions	270
9.5	Analysis in Practice		270
	9.5.1	Rankings and Ratios	271
	9.5.2	Lead and Lag Functionality	275
	9.5.3	Histograms	275
	9.5.4	Other Statistical Functionality	277
	9.5.5	Data Densification	277

10 Modeling with the MODEL Clause   281

10.1	What Is the MODEL Clause?		281
	10.1.1	The Parts of the MODEL Clause	281
	10.1.2	How the MODEL Clause Works	283
	10.1.3	Better Performance Using the MODEL Clause	286
10.2	MODEL Clause Syntax		288
	10.2.1	Cell References	288
	10.2.2	Return Rows	289
	10.2.3	The Main Model	289
		Rules	290
		Assigning Cell Values	291
	10.2.4	MODEL Clause Functions	291
10.3	What Can the MODEL Clause Do?		292
	10.3.1	Materialized Views and the MODEL Clause	292
	10.3.2	Referencing Cells	295
	10.3.3	Referencing Multiple Models	301
	10.3.4	UPDATE versus UPSERT	306
	10.3.5	Loops	308
10.4	Performance and the MODEL Clause		308
	10.4.1	Parallel Execution	308
	10.4.2	Understanding MODEL Clause Query Plans	313

Part III: Advanced Topics   317

11 Query Rewrite   319

11.1   What Is Query Rewrite?   319
   11.1.1   When Does the Optimizer Query Rewrite?   320
   11.1.2   What Can the Optimizer Query Rewrite?   320
11.2   How the Optimizer Rewrites Queries   321
   11.2.1   Matching Entire Query Strings   321
   11.2.2   Matching Pieces of Queries   324
      Join Back   324
      Dimensional Rollups   325
      Aggregation   327
      Filters   328
   11.2.3   Special Cases for Query Rewrite   330
11.3   Affecting Query Rewrite Performance   331

12 Parallel Processing   335

12.1   What Is Parallel Processing?   335
   12.1.1   What Can Be Executed in Parallel?   336
12.2   Degree of Parallelism (Syntax)   336
12.3   Configuration Parameters   337
12.4   Demonstrating Parallel Execution   339
   12.4.1   Parallel Queries   339
   12.4.2   Index DDL Statements   343
   12.4.3   SELECT Statement Subqueries   344
   12.4.4   DML Statements   345
   12.4.5   Partitioning Operations   346
12.5   Performance Views   346
12.6   Parallel Execution Hints   348
12.7   Parallel Execution Query Plans   348

13 Data Loading   351

13.1   What Is Data Loading?   351
   13.1.1   General Loading Strategies   352
      Single Phase Load   352
      Multiple Phase Load   353
      An Update Window   354
         The Effect of Materialized Views   354
      Oracle Database Loading Tools   354

13.2   Extraction   355
    13.2.1   Logical Extraction   355
    13.2.2   Physical Extraction   355
    13.2.3   Extraction Options   356
             Dumping Files Using SQL   356
             Exports   359
             External Tables   359
             Other Extraction Options   361
13.3   Transportation Methods   361
    13.3.1   Database Links and SQL   362
    13.3.2   Transportable Tablespaces   363
             Transportable Tablespace Limitations   365
             Self-Containment   365
             Transporting a Tablespace   367
13.4   Loading and Transformation   368
    13.4.1   Basic Loading Procedures   369
             SQL*Loader   369
                 SQL*Loader Performance Characteristics   369
                 SQL*Loader Architecture   370
                 Input Datafiles   371
                 The SQL*Loader Control File   372
                     Row Loading Options   372
                     Loading Multiple Tables   373
                     Field Definitions   373
                     Dealing with NULL Values   376
                     Load Filters   377
                     Unwanted Columns   377
                     Control File Datatypes   378
                     Embedded SQL Statements   378
                     Adding Data Not in Input Datafiles   379
                 Executing SQL*Loader   379
                     The Parameter File   379
             Plug-Ins   380
                 Partitions   380
                 Transportable Tablespaces   381
                 External Tables   382
             The Import Utility   383
    13.4.2   Transformation Processing   383

14   Data Warehouse Architecture   385

14.1   What Is a Data Warehouse?   385

14.1.1 What Is Data Warehouse Architecture? 385
14.2 Tuning Hardware Resources for
Data Warehousing 386
14.2.1 Tuning Memory Buffers 387
14.2.2 Tuning Block Sizes 388
14.2.3 Tuning Transactions 389
14.2.4 Tuning Oracle Net Services 390
Tuning Net Services at the Server: The Listener 390
Tuning Net Services at the Client 391
14.2.5 Tuning I/O 393
Striping and Redundancy: Types of RAID Arrays 395
The Physical Oracle Database 396
How Oracle Database Files Fit Together 397
Special Types of Datafiles 398
Tuning Datafiles 398
Tuning Redo and Archive Log Files 399
Tablespaces 402
BIGFILE Tablespaces 406
Avoiding Datafile Header Contention 407
Temporary Sort Space 407
Tablespace Groups 407
Automated Undo 408
Caching Static Data Warehouse Objects 408
Compressing Objects 409
14.3 Capacity Planning 409
14.3.1 Datafile Sizes 411
14.3.2 Datafile Content Sizes 412
14.3.3 The DBMS_SPACE Package 412
14.3.4 Statistics 414
Using the ANALYZE Command 414
The DBMS_STATS Package 415
Using Statistics for Capacity Planning 415
14.3.5 Exact Column Data Lengths 419
14.4 OLAP and Data Mining 422

A **New Data Warehouse Features in Oracle Database 10g** **423**

B **Sample Schemas** **425**

C **Sample Scripting** **431**

D **Syntax Conventions** **447**

E **Sources of Information** **449**

Index **451**

Preface

This book focuses on tuning of Oracle data warehouse databases. My previous tuning book, *Oracle High Performance Tuning for 9i and 10g* (ISBN: 1555583059) focused on tuning of OLTP databases. OLTP databases require fine-tuning of small transactions for very high concurrency both in reading and changing of an OLTP database.

Tuning a data warehouse database is somewhat different to tuning of OLTP databases. Why? A data warehouse database concentrates on large transactions and mostly requires what is termed throughput. What is throughput? Throughput is the term applied to the passing of large amounts of information through a server, network, and Internet environment. The ultimate objective of a data warehouse is the production of meaningful and useful reporting. Reporting is based on data warehouse data content. Reporting generally reads large amounts of data all at once.

In layman's terms, an OLTP database needs to access individual items rapidly, resulting in heavy use of concurrency or sharing. Thus, an OLTP database is both CPU and memory intensive but rarely I/O intensive. A data warehouse database needs to access lots of information, all at once, and is, therefore, I/O intensive. It follows that a data warehouse will need fast disks and lots of them. Disk space is cheap!

A data warehouse is maintained in order to archive historical data no longer directly required by front-end OLTP systems. This separation process has two effects: (1) it speeds up OLTP database performance by removing large amounts of unneeded data from the front-end environment, (2) the data warehouse is freed from the constraints of an OLTP environment in order to provide both rapid query response and ease of adding new data en masse to the data warehouse. Underlying structural requirements for OLTP and data warehouse databases are different to the extent that they can conflict with each other, severely affecting performance of both database types.

How can data warehouse tuning be divided up? Tuning a data warehouse can be broken into a number of parts: (1) data modeling specific to data warehouses, (2) SQL code tuning mostly involving queries, and (3) advanced topics including physical architecture, data loading, and various other topics relevant to tuning.

The objective of this book is to partly expand on the content of my previous OLTP database tuning book, covering areas specific only to data warehousing tuning, and duplicating some sections in order to allow purchase of one of these two books. Currently there is no title on the market covering data warehouse tuning specifically for Oracle Database.

Any detail relating directly to hardware tuning or hardware architectural tuning will not be covered in this book in any detail, apart from the content in the final chapter. Hardware encompasses CPUs, memory, disks, and so on. Hardware architecture covers areas such as RAID arrays, clustering with Oracle RAC, and Oracle Automated Storage Management (ASM). RAID arrays underlie an Oracle database and are, thus, the domain of the operating system and not the database. Oracle RAC consists of multiple clustered thin servers connected to a single set of storage disks. Oracle ASM essentially provides disk management with striping and mirroring, much like RAID arrays and something like Veritas software would do. All these things are not strictly directly related to tuning an Oracle database warehouse database specifically but can be useful to help performance of underlying architecture in an I/O intensive environment, such as a data warehouse database.

Data warehouse data modeling, specialized SQL code, and data loading are the most relevant topics to the grass-roots building blocks of data warehouse performance tuning. Transformation is somewhat of a misfit topic area since it can be performed both within and outside an Oracle database; quite often both. Transformation is often executed using something like Perl scripting or a sophisticated and expensive front-end tool. Transformation washes and converts data prior to data loading, allowing newly introduced data to fit in with existing data warehouse structures. Therefore, transformation is not an integral part of Oracle Database itself and, thus, not particularly relevant to the core of Oracle Database data warehouse tuning. As a result, transformation will only be covered in this book explicitly to the extent to which Oracle Database tools can be used to help with transformation processing.

As with my previous OLTP performance tuning book, the approach in this book is to present something that appears to be immensely complex in a simplistic and easy to understand manner. This book will demonstrate by example, showing not only how to make something faster but also demonstrating approaches to tuning, such as use of Oracle Partitioning, query rewrite, and materialized views. The overall objective is to utilize examples to expedite understanding for the reader.

Rather than present piles of unproven facts and detailed notes of syntax diagrams, as with my previous OLTP tuning book, I will demonstrate purely by example. My hardware is old and decrepit, but it does work. As a result I cannot create truly enormous data warehouse databases, but I can certainly do the equivalent by *stressing out* some very old machines as database servers.

A reader of my previous OLTP performance tuning title commented rather harshly on Amazon.com that this was a particularly pathetic approach and that I should have spent a paltry sum of $1,000 on a Linux box. Contrary to popular belief writing books does not make $1,000 a paltry sum of money. More importantly, the approach is intentional, as it is one of stressing out Oracle Database software and not the hardware or underlying operating system. Thus, the older, slower, and less precise the hardware and operating system are, the more the Oracle software itself is tested. Additionally, the reader commented that my applications were *patched* together. Applications used in these books are not strictly applications, as applications have front ends and various sets of pretty pictures and screens. Pretty pictures are not required in a book, such as this book. Applications in this book are scripted code intended to subject a database to all types of possible activity on a scheduled basis. Rarely does any one application do all that. And much like the irrelevance of hardware and operating system, front-end screens are completely irrelevant to performance tuning of Oracle Database software.

In short, the approach in this book, like nearly all of my other Oracle books, is to demonstrate and write from my point of view. I myself, being the author of this particular dissertation, have almost 20 years of experience working in custom software development and database administration, using all sorts of SDKs and databases, both relational and object. This book is written by a database administrator (DBA)/developer—for the use of DBAs, developers, and anyone else who is interested, including end users. Once again, this book is not a set of rules and regulations, but a set of suggestions for tuning stemming from experimentation with real databases.

A focused tutorial on the subject of tuning Oracle database warehouse databases is much needed today. There does not seem to be much in the way of data warehouse tuning titles available, and certainly none that focus on tuning and demonstrate from experience and purely by example.

This book attempts to verify every tuning precept it presents with substantive proof, even if the initial premise is incorrect. This practice will obviously have to exist within the bounds of the hardware I have in use. Be warned that my results may be somewhat related to my insistent use of geriatric hardware. From a development perspective, forcing development on slightly underperforming hardware can have the positive effect of producing better performing databases and applications in production.

People who would benefit from reading this book would be database administrators, developers, data modelers, systems or network administrators, and technical managers. Anyone using an Oracle Database data warehouse would likely benefit from reading this book, particularly DBAs and developers who are attempting to increase data warehouse database performance. However, since tuning is always best done from the word Go, even those in the planning stages of application development and data warehouse construction would benefit from reading a book such as this.

Disclaimer Notice: Please note that the content of this book is made available "AS IS." I am in no way responsible or liable for any mishaps as a result of using this information, in any form or environment.

Once again my other tuning title, *Oracle Performance Tuning for 9i and 10g* (ISBN: 1555583059), covers tuning for OLTP databases with occasional mention of data warehouse tuning. The purpose of this book is to focus solely on data warehouse tuning and all it entails. I have made a concerted effort not to duplicate information from my OLTP database tuning book. However, I have also attempted not to leave readers in the dark who do not wish to purchase and read both titles. Please excuse any duplication where I think it is necessary.

Let's get started.

Introduction to Data Warehouse Tuning

So what is a data warehouse? Let's begin this journey of discovery by briefly examining the origins and history of data warehouses.

The Origin and History of Data Warehouses

How did data warehouses come about? Why were they invented? The simple answer to this question is because existing databases were being subjected to conflicting requirements. These conflicting requirements are based on operational use versus decision support use.

Operational use in Online Transaction Processing (OLTP) databases is access to the most recent data from a database on a day-to-day basis, servicing end user and data change applications. Operational use requires a breakdown of database access by functional applications, such as filling out order forms or booking airline tickets. Operational data is database activity based on the functions of a company. Generally, in an internal company, environment applications might be divided up based on different departments.

Decision support use, on the other hand, requires not only a more global rather than operationally precise picture of data, but also a division of the database based on subject matter. So as opposed to filling out order forms or booking airline tickets interactively, a decision support user would need to know what was ordered between two dates (all orders made between those dates), or where and how airline tickets were booked, say for a period of an entire year.

The result is a complete disparity between the requirements of operational applications versus decision support functions. Whenever you check out an item in a supermarket and the bar code scanner goes beep, a single stock record is updated in a single table in a database. That's operational.

On the contrary, when the store manager runs a report once every month to do a stock take and find out what and how much must be reordered, his report reads all the stock records for the entire month. So what is the disparity? Each sold item updates a single row. The report reads all the rows. Let's say the table is extremely large and the store is large and belongs to a chain of stores all over the country, you have a very large database. Where the single row update of each sale requires functionality to read individual rows, the report wants to read everything. In terms of database performance these two disparate requirements can cause serious conflicts. Data warehouses were invented to separate these two requirements, in effect separating active and historical data, attempting to remove some batch and reporting activity from OLTP databases.

Note: There are numerous names associated with data warehouses, such as Inmon and Kimball. It is perhaps best not to throw names around or at least to stop at associating them with any specific activity or invention.

Separation of OLTP and Data Warehouse Databases

So why is there separation between these two types of databases? The answer is actually very simple. An OLTP database requires fast turnaround of exact row hits. A data warehouse database requires high throughput performance for large amounts of data. In the old days of client server environments, where applications were in-house within a single company only, everyone went home at night and data warehouse batch updates and reporting could be performed overnight. In the modern global economy of the Internet and OLTP databases, end user operational applications are required to be active 24/7, 365 days a year. That's permanently! What it means is that there is no window for any type of batch activity, because when we are asleep in North America everyone is awake in the Far East, and the global economy requires that those who are awake when we are snoozing are serviced in the same manner. Thus, data warehouse activity using historical data, be it updates to the data warehouse or reporting, must be separated from the processing of OLTP, quick reaction concurrency requirements. A user will lose interest in a Web site after seven seconds of inactivity.

At the database administration level, operational or OLTP databases require rapid access to small amounts of data. This implies low I/O activity and very high concurrency. Concurrency implies a lot of users sharing the same data at the same time. A data warehouse on the other hand involves a relatively very small user population reading large amounts of data at once in reports. This implies negligible concurrency and very heavy I/O activity. Another very important difference is the order in which data is accessed. OLTP activity most often adds or changes rows, accessing each row across a group of tables, using unique identifiers for each of the rows accessed (primary keys), such as a customer's name or phone number. Data warehouses on the other hand will look at large numbers of rows, accessing all customers in general, such as for a specific store in a chain of retail outlets. The point is this: OLTP data is accessed by the identification of the end user, in this case the name of the customer. On the other hand, the data warehouse looks at information based on subject matter, such as all items to be restocked in a single store, or perhaps project profits for the next year on airline bookings, for all routes flying out of a specific city.

Tuning a Data Warehouse

A data warehouse can be tuned in a number of ways. However, there are some basic precepts that could be followed:

- Data warehouses originally came about due to a need to separate small highly concurrent activity from high throughput batch and reporting activity. These two objectives conflict with each other because they need to use resources in a different way. Placing a data warehouse in a different database to that of an OLTP database can help to separate the differences to explicitly tailored environments for each database type, and preferably on different machines.

- Within a data warehouse itself it is best to try to separate batch update activity from reporting activity. Of course, the global economy may inhibit this approach, but there are specialized loading methods. Loading for performance is also important to data warehouse tuning.

So when it comes to tuning a data warehouse perhaps the obvious question that should be asked here is: What can be tuned in a data warehouse?

- The data model can be tuned using data warehouse–specific design methodologies.

- In Oracle Database and other databases a data warehouse can implement numerous special feature structures including proper indexing, partitioning, and materialized views.

- SQL code for execution of queries against a data warehouse can be extensively tuned, usually hand-in-hand with use of specialized objects, such as materialized views.

- Highly complex SQL code can be replaced with specialized Oracle SQL code functionality, such as ROLLUP and MODEL clauses, a proliferation of analytical functions, and even an OLAP add-on option.

- The loading process can be tuned. The transformation process can be tuned, but moreover made a little less complicated by using special purpose transformation or ETL tools.

What Is in this Book?

This section provides a brief listing of chapter contents for this book.

Part I. Data Warehouse Data Modeling

Part I examines tuning a data warehouse from the data modeling perspective. In this book I have taken the liberty of stretching the concept of the data model to include both entity structures (tables) and specialized objects, such as materialized views.

Chapter 1. The Basics of Data Warehouse Data Modeling

This first chapter describes how to build data warehouse data models and how to relate data warehouse entities to each other. There are various methodologies and approaches, which are essentially very simple. Tuning data warehouse entities is directly related to four things: (1) time—how far back does your data go, (2) granularity—how much detail should you keep, (3) denormalizing—including duplication in entity structures, and (4) using special Oracle Database logical structures and techniques, such as materialized views.

Chapter 2. Introducing Data Warehouse Tuning

The first part of this chapter builds a data warehouse model that will be used throughout the remainder of this book. The data warehouse model is constructed from two relational data model schemas covering demographics and inventory-accounting. The inventory-accounting database has millions of rows, providing a reasonable amount of data to demonstrate the tuning process as this book progresses. The second part of this chapter will introduce the multifarious methods that can be used to tune a data warehouse data model. All these methods will be described and demonstrated in subsequent chapters.

Chapter 3. Effective Data Warehouse Indexing

This chapter is divided into three distinct parts. The first part examines the basics of indexing, including different types of available indexes. The second part of this chapter attempts to proof the usefulness or otherwise of bitmap indexes, bitmap join indexes, star queries, and star transformations. Lastly, this chapter briefly examines the use of index organized tables (IOTs) and clusters in data warehouses.

Chapter 4. Materialized Views and Query Rewrite

This chapter is divided into three parts covering materialized view syntax, different types of materialized views, and finally tools used for analysis and management of materialized views. We will examine the use of materialized views in data warehouses, benefits to general database performance, and discussions about the very basics of query rewrite. Use of materialized views is a tuning method in itself. There are various ways that materialized views can be built, performing differently depending on circumstances and requirements.

Chapter 5. Oracle Dimension Objects

This chapter examines Oracle dimension objects. In a star schema, dimensions are denormalized into a single layer of dimensions. In a snowflake schema, dimensions are normalized out to multiple hierarchical layers. Dimension objects can be used to represent these multiple layers for both star and snowflake schemas, possibly helping to increase performance of joins across dimension hierarchies.

Chapter 6. Partitioning and Basic Parallel Processing

This chapter covers Oracle Partitioning, including syntax and examples, and some parallel processing as specifically applied to Oracle Partitioning. In general, partitioning involves the physical splitting of large objects, such as tables or materialized views, and their associated indexes into separate physical parts. The result is that operations can be performed on those individual physical partitions, and I/O requirements can be substantially reduced. Additionally, multiple partitions can be executed on in parallel. Both of these factors make partitioning a tuning method, as opposed to something that can be tuned specifically. Any tuning of partitions is essentially related to underlying structures, indexing techniques, and the way in which partitions are constructed.

Part II. Specialized Data Warehouse SQL Code

Chapter 7. The Basics of SQL Query Code Tuning

This chapter begins Part II of this book focusing on aspects of Oracle SQL code provided specifically for the tuning of data warehouse type functionality. In order to introduce aspects of tuning SQL code for data warehouses, it is necessary to go back to basics. This chapter will provide three things: (1) details of the most simplistic aspects of SQL code tuning, (2) a description of how the Oracle SQL engine executes SQL code internally, and (3) a brief look at tools for tuning Oracle Database. It is essential to understand the basic facts about how to write properly performing SQL code and perform basic tuning using Oracle internals and simple tools. Subsequent chapters will progress on to considering specific details of tuning SQL coding for data warehouses.

Chapter 8. Aggregation Using GROUP BY Clause Extensions

This chapter covers the more basic syntactical extensions to the GROUP BY clause in the form of aggregation using the ROLLUP clause, CUBE clause, GROUPING SETS clause, and some slightly more complex combinations thereof. Other specialized functions for much more comprehensive and complex analysis, plus further syntax formats including the OVER clause, the MODEL clause, the WITH clause, and some specialized expression types, will be covered in later chapters. All these SQL coding extensions tend to make highly complex data warehouse reporting more simplified and also much better performing—mostly because of the fact that SQL coding is made easier.

Chapter 9. Analysis Reporting

This chapter describes better performing ways of building analytical queries in Oracle SQL. Oracle SQL, has rich in built-in functionality to allow for efficient analytical query construction, helping queries to run faster and to be coded in a much less complex manner. This chapter examines analysis reporting using Oracle SQL.

Chapter 10. SQL and the MODEL Clause

This chapter describes the Oracle SQL MODEL clause. The use of the MODEL clause is, as in previous chapters, a performance method in itself. The MODEL clause is the latest and most sophisticated expansion to Oracle SQL catering to the complex analytical functionality required by data warehouse databases. Details covered in this chapter include the how and why of the MODEL clause, MODEL clause syntax, and various specialized MODEL clause functions included with Oracle SQL. The second part of this chapter analyzes detailed use of the MODEL clause. Finally, some performance issues with parallel execution and MODEL clause query plans are discussed.

Part III. Advanced Topics

Chapter 11. Query Rewrite

This chapter begins Part III of this book expanding on previous chapters to cover more detail on query rewrite and parallel processing. Additionally, Part III includes details of data warehouse loading and general physical architecture, both as applicable to performance tuning, respectively. This chapter will cover the specifics of query rewrite in detail, rather than why it is used and the tools used for verification. This chapter will examine what query rewrite actually is and how its processing speed and possible use can be improved upon. So this chapter is divided into two parts. The first part explains how the optimizer query rewrites in different situations. The second part examines possibilities for improving query rewrite performance.

Chapter 12. Parallel Processing

This chapter will examine parallel processing. Parallel processing is most beneficial for certain types of operations in very large data warehouses, sometimes in smaller databases for a small number of operations, and rarely in OLTP or heavily concurrent transaction databases.

Chapter 13. Data Loading

This chapter examines the loading of data into an Oracle Database data warehouse. There are various ways in which the loading process can be made to perform better. This chapter will attempt to focus on the performance aspects of what is effectively a three-step process, and sometimes even a four-step process, including extraction, transportation, transformation, and loading. I like to add an extra definitional step to the loading process, called transportation. Transportation methods will also be discussed in this chapter because some methods are better and faster than others and there are some very specific and highly efficient transportation methods specific to Oracle Database.

Chapter 14. Data Warehouse Architecture

This chapter examines general data warehouse architecture and will be divided types of between hardware resource usage, (including memory buffers, block sizes, and I/O usage. I/O is very important in data warehouse databases). Capacity planning will also be covered, so important to data warehousing. The chapter will be completed with brief information on OLAP and data mining technologies.

Sample Databases in This Book

A number of sample databases are used in this book. The best way to demonstrate sample database use is to build the table structures as the book is progressively written by myself and read by you, the reader. Ultimately, the appendices contain general versions of schemas and scripts to create those schemas. The data warehouse schema used in this book is an amalgamation of a number of OLTP schemas, composed, denormalized, and converted to fact-dimensional structures. In other words, the data warehouse database schema is a combination of a number of other schemas, making it into a relatively complex data warehouse schema. The only limitation is the limited disk capacity of my database hardware. However, limited hardware resources serve to performance test Oracle Database to the limits of the abilities of the software, rather than testing hardware or the underlying operating system.

Part I

Data Warehouse Data Modeling

Chapter 1   The Basics of Data Warehouse Data Modeling

Chapter 2   Introducing Data Warehouse Tuning

Chapter 3   Effective Data Warehouse Indexing

Chapter 4   Materialized Views and Query Rewrite

Chapter 5   Oracle Dimension Objects

Chapter 6   Partitioning and Basic Parallel Processing

The Basics of Data Warehouse Data Modeling

This chapter begins Part I of this book, focusing on data warehouse data model tuning techniques. This first chapter describes how to build data warehouse data models and how to relate data warehouse entities to each other. There are various methodologies and approaches, which are essentially very simple. Tuning data warehouse entities is directly related to four things: (1) time—how far back does your data go, (2) granularity—how much detail should you keep, (3) denormalizing—including duplication in entity structures, (4) using special Oracle Database logical structures and techniques, such as materialized views.

- This chapter uses a schema designed for tracking the shipping of containers by sea, on large container vessels.

- The word entity in a data model is synonymous with the word table in a database.

1.1   The Relational and Object Data Models

Before attempting to explain data warehouse data modeling techniques, it is necessary to understand other modeling techniques, and why they do not cater for data warehouse requirements. In other words, it is best to understand the basics of relational data modeling, and perhaps even some object data modeling, in order to fully understand the simplicity of data warehouse data modeling solutions.

1.1.1   The Relational Data Model

The relational model uses a sequence of steps called normalization in order to break information into its smallest divisible parts, removing duplication and creating granularity.

Normalization

Normalization is an incremental process where a set of entities must first be in 1st normal form before they can be transformed into 2nd normal form. It follows that 3rd normal form, can only be applied when an entity structure is in 2nd normal form, and so on. There are a number of steps in the normalization process.

1st Normal Form

Remove repetition by creating one-to-many relationships between master and detail entities, as shown in Figure 1.1.

Figure 1.1
A 1st normal form transformation.

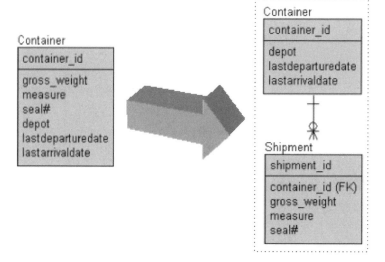

2nd Normal Form

Create many-to-one relationships between static and dynamic entities, as shown in Figure 1.2.

3rd Normal Form

Use to resolve many-to-many relationships into unique values, as shown in Figure 1.3. At and beyond 3rd normal form, the process of normalization

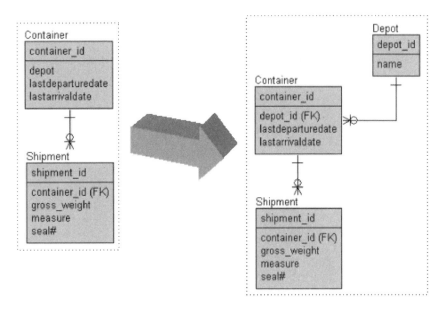

Figure 1.2
A 2nd normal form transformation.

becomes a little fuzzy. Many-to-many join resolution entities are frequently overindulged in by data models and underutilized by applications, superfluous and often created more as database design issues rather than to provide for application requirements. When creating a many-to-many join resolution entity, ask yourself a question: Does the application use the added entity? Does the new entity have meaning? Does it have a meaningful name? In Figure 1.3 the new entity created has a meaningful name because it is called SHIPMENT. SHIPMENT represents a shipment of containers on a vessel on a single voyage of that vessel. If the name of the new entity does not make sense and can only be called Voyage-Container then it might very well be superfluous. The problem with too many entities is large joins. Large, complicated SQL code joins can slow down performance considerably, especially in data warehouses where the requirement is to denormalize as opposed to creating unnecessary layers of normalization granularity.

4th Normal Form

Separate NULL-valued columns into new entities. The effect is to minimize empty space in rows. Since Oracle Database table rows are variable in length this type of normalization is possibly unwise and, perhaps, even unnecessary. Variable length rows do not include NULL-valued columns other than perhaps a pointer. Additionally, disk space is cheap. And once again, too much normalized granularity is not helpful for data warehouse performance.

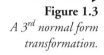

Figure 1.3
A 3rd normal form transformation.

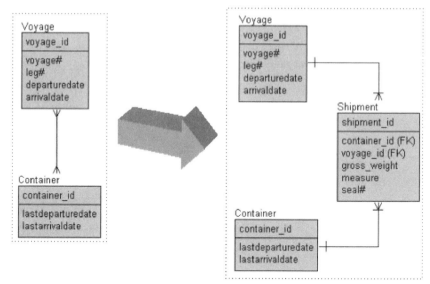

5th Normal Form

The 5th normal form is essentially used to resolve any duplication not resolved by 1st to 4th normal forms. There are other normal forms beyond that of 5th normal form.

Referential Integrity

Referential integrity ensures the integrity or validity of rows between entities using referential values. The referential values are what are known as primary and foreign keys. A primary key resides in a parent entity and a foreign key in a child entity. Take another look at Figure 1.1. On the right side of the diagram there is a one-to-many relationship between the CONTAINER and SHIPMENT entities. There are many shipments for every container. In other words, containers are reused on multiple voyages, each voyage representing a shipment of goods, the goods shipment being the container contents for the current shipment. The resulting structure is the CONTAINER entity containing a primary key called CONTAINER_ID. The SHIPMENT entity also contains a CONTAINER_ID column but as a foreign key. The SHIPMENT.CONTAINER_ID column contains the same CONTAINER_ID column value every time the container is shipped on a voyage. Thus, the SHIPMENT.CONTAINER_ID column is a foreign key. This is because it references a primary key in a parent entity, in this case the CONTAINER entity. Referential integrity ensures that these values are always consistent between the two entities. Referential integrity makes sure that a shipment cannot exist without any containers. There is one small quirk though. A foreign key can contain a NULL value. In this situation a container does not have to be part of shipment because it could be sitting empty on a dock somewhere.

The best method of enforcing referential integrity in Oracle Database is by using primary and foreign key constraints. Other methods are nearly always detrimental for performance. In the case of a data warehouse, referential integrity is not always a requirement, since data is relatively static.

Surrogate Keys

A surrogate key is sometimes called an artificial or replacement key; the meaning of the word surrogate is *a substitute*. Surrogate keys are often used in OLTP databases to mimic object structures when applications are written in SDKs (Software Development Kits) such as Java. In data warehouses, surrogate keys are used to allow unique identifiers for rows with possibly different sources, and very likely different unique key structures. For example, in one source Online Transaction Processing (OLTP) database a customer could be indexed by the name of his company, and in another source database by the name of contact person who works for that same company. A surrogate key can be used to apply the same unique identifying value to what essentially are two separate rows, both from the same customer.

Notice how in Figure 1.1 that the CONTAINER and SHIPMENT entities both have surrogate keys in the form of the CONTAINER_ID and SHIPMENT_ID columns, respectively. Surrogate keys are typically automatically generated integers, using sequence objects in the case of Oracle Database. Before the advent of uniquely identifying surrogate keys, the primary key for the CONTAINER entity would have been a container name or serial number. The SHIPMENT primary key would have been a composite key of the SHIPMENT key contained within the name of the container from the CONTAINER entity, namely both keys in the hierarchy.

Denormalization

By definition denormalization is simply reversing of the steps of the application of 1st to 5th normal forms applied by the normalization process. Examine Figures 1.1 to 1.3 again and simply reverse the transformations from right to left as opposed to left to right. That is denormalization. Denormalization reintroduces duplication and, thus, decreases granularity. Being the reverse of excessive granularity, denormalization is often used to increase performance in data warehouses. Excessive normalization granularity in data warehouse databases can lead to debilitating performance problems.

In addition to the denormalization of previously applied normalization, some relational databases allow for specialized objects. Oracle Database allows the creation of specialized database objects largely for the purpose of speeding up query processing. One of the most effective methods of increasing query performance is by way of reducing the number of joins in queries. Oracle Database allows the creation of various specialized objects just for doing this type of thing. Vaguely, these specialized objects are as follows:

- **Bitmaps and IOTs**. Special index types, such as bitmaps and index organized tables.

- **Materialized Views**. Materialized views are usually used to store summary physical copies of queries, precreating data set copies of joins and groupings, and avoiding reading of underlying tables.

Note: Perhaps contrary to popular belief, views are not the same as materialized views. A materialized view makes a physical copy of data for later read access by a query. On the other hand, a view contains a query, which executes every time the view is read by another query. Do not use views to cater for denormalization, and especially not in data warehouses. Views are best used for security purposes and for ease of development coding. Views can be severely detrimental to database performance in general, for any database type. Avoid views in data warehouses as you would the plague!

- **Dimension Objects**. Dimension objects can be used to create hierarchical structures to speed up query processing in snowflake data warehouse schema designs.

- **Clusters**. Clusters create physical copies of significant columns in join queries, allowing subsequent queries from the cluster as opposed to re-execution of a complex and poorly performing join query.

- **Partitioning and Parallel Processing**. Oracle Partitioning allows physical subdivision of large data sets (tables), such that queries can access individual partitions, effectively allowing exclusive access to small data sets (partitions) contained within very large tables and minimizing I/O. A beneficial side effect of partitioning is that multiple partitions can be accessed in parallel, allowing true parallel processing on multiple-partition spanning data sets.

There are other forms of denormalization falling outside both the structure of normalization and any specialized Oracle Database objects. Some of these methods can cause more problems than they solve. Included are the following:

- **Active and Archived Data Separation**. The most obvious method in this list is separation of active or current from inactive or archived data. Before the advent of data warehouses, archived data was completely destroyed to avoid a drain on current activities. Data warehouses are used to contain and remove archived data from active transactional databases. The data warehouse can then allow for decision forecasting based on extrapolations of old information to future periods of time.

- **Duplication of Columns Into Child Entities**. Duplicating columns across tables to minimize joins, without removing normal form layers. In Figure 1.1 if the CONTAINER.DEPOT column is included much more often in joins between the CONTAINER and SHIPMENT entities than other CONTAINER columns, then the DEPOT column could be duplicated into the child SHIPMENT entity.

- **Summary Columns in Parent Entities**. Summary columns can be added to parent entities, such as adding a TOTAL_GROSS_WEIGHT column to the CONTAINER entity in Figure 1.1. The total value would be a periodical or real time cumulative value of the SHIPMENT.GROSS_WEIGHT column. Beware that updating summary column values, particularly in real-time, can cause hot blocking.

- **Frequently and Infrequently Accessed Columns**. Some entities can have some columns accessed much more frequently than other columns. Thus, the two column sets could be split into separate entities. This method is vaguely akin to 4th normal form normalization, but can have a positive effect of reducing input/output (I/O) by reducing the number of columns read for busy queries.

- **Above Database Server Caching**. If data can be cached off the database server, such as on application servers, Web servers or even client machines, then trips to and from and executions on the database server can be reduced. This can help to free up database server resources for other queries. An approach of this nature is particularly applicable to static application data, such as on-screen pick list. For example, a list of state codes and their names can be read from a database and loaded into a higher-level tier application once. The names of states in the United States and their codes are unlikely to change, don't you think? This kind of practice essentially applies to OLTP databases and not data warehouses. It is unlikely that caching of dimensions would ever be necessary due to the negligible concurrency level present in data warehouse databases. But then again there are circumstances where caching of data warehouse dimensions is sensible.

Data Warehouses—Why Not the Relational Model?

Why does the relational model not cater for data warehouse requirements? Actually, it simply just doesn't make the cut. Why? The relational model is too granular. Like the object model, which we will look at shortly, the relational model introduces granularity by removing duplication. The result is a data model that is nearly always highly effective for front-end application performance, involving small amounts of data accessed frequently and concurrently by many users at once. Data warehouse requirements are in complete opposition to these requirements. Data warehouses require throughput of huge amounts of data by relatively very few users. Where OLTP databases need lightning quick response to many individual users, data warehouses perform enormous amounts of I/O activity over extremely generous amounts of data. Simply put, the requirements of OLTP and data warehouse databases are completely different.

1.1.2   The Object Data Model

The object model is even less appropriate for a data warehouse than the relational model. There is a simple reason for this. The object model is excellent at handling immense complexity. Why? The objective of an object-oriented design approach is to break every part of the model into its smallest self-contained part. Unlike the relational model where dependencies exist between the different parts, the object model allows each part to be autonomous. This is what is meant by self-contained. In other words, there is much less inter-object dependency in the object model than in the relational model. That is even worse than a relational model when considering a data warehouse data model.

Before examining a little of the detail of the object model there are two things that the object model can help to improve on the complexity of the relational model. The object model does not need types or many-to-many relationships. In Figure 1.4 the type of container in the object model is defined by class inheritance. In Figure 1.4 types are defined by the CON-

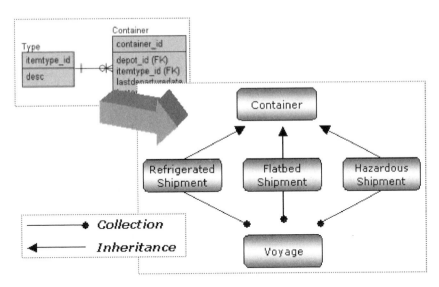

Figure 1.4
The object model does not need types.

TAINER class inherited specializations: REFRIGERATED SHIPMENT, FLATBED SHIPMENT and HAZARDOUS SHIPMENT classes.

In Figure 1.5 three other classes define the many-to-many relationship between the VESSEL and CONTAINER classes. These three other classes are REFRIGERATED SHIPMENT, FLATBED SHIPMENT and HAZ-ARDOUS SHIPMENT.

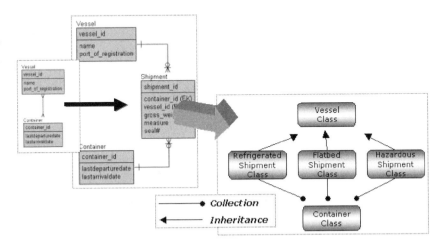

Figure 1.5
The object model automatically includes many-to-many relationships.

Now let's look at some of the detail of the object model. The object model is made up of the following structures, connections, and some of these commonly used terms, without getting too deeply specific about it:

- **Class**. A class is the equivalent of a relational entity or table. It is important to understand that a class is not the same as an object. An object is the instantiation or iteration of a class during execution. Since object structures allow inheritance, the structure and content of an object can be completely different to that of its constructor class. This is because inheritance allows passing of attribute structures, values, and methods up and down through a hierarchy.

- **Attribute**. An attribute is equivalent to a column in a relational entity column or field.

- **Method**. A method is a chunk of code or program executed exclusively on the contents of the object to which it is attached. The relational model does not allow use of methods, using stored procedures instead. Stored procedures are simply stored in the database as database procedures but have no link with specific entities.

- **Inheritance**. Classes are linked together through an inheritance hierarchy; some object databases and SDKs allow multiple inheritance. Multiple inheritance allows a class to inherit from more than one class at a time. Effectively, multiple inheritance allows a hierarchical structure to go in both directions.

- **Multiple Inheritance**. Multiple inheritance allows a class to inherit details from more than one class. Thus, the hierarchy goes both upwards and downwards, such that a class can be both a parent and a child of other classes. In other words a class can inherit properties from parent classes, as well as allowing child classes to inherit attributes from itself.

- **Specialization and Abstraction**. The result of inheritance is that classes can be both specialized and abstracted. Syntactically these two terms could be construed to mean the same thing, but semantically there is a difference. Specialization implies that an inherited class inherits part of a parent class or adds to the parent class, making a special case of the parent class. Abstraction implies an abstraction, or generic form, of a child or more likely a group of child classes.

- **Collection**. A collection is the term applied to a repetition of elements of one object contained within another object. A collection is similar to a relational entity on the many side of a one-to-many relationship.

Data Warehouses—Why Not the Object Model?

Why does the object model not cater for data warehouse requirements? The object model is inappropriate for a data warehouse because there is even more scope for granularity using the object model than with the relational model. In a data warehouse logical granularity in the form of normalized relations or autonomous objects leads to inefficiencies due to a higher reliance on joins between entities, or in the case of the object model, entities become classes and objects.

1.1.3   The Object-Relational Data Model

The object-relational data model simply combines aspects of the relational model with the object model. It could be said that the object-relational model attempts to squeeze parts of the object model into the relational model—unfortunately, only the parts that can be squeezed in. Oracle Database allows inclusion of binary objects into relational entities, either stored inline with the table or as pointers to objects stored externally to the table. Procedural Language/Structured Query Language (PL/SQL) and SQL do allow the construction of new datatypes and methods, but the resulting structures are difficult to build and maintain. These facts are completely contrary to the simplicity of coding using a truly object-oriented database.

1.2   Data Modeling for Data Warehouses

Entity relationship modeling is used for OLTP, or transactional databases, requiring a large number of small operations. Data warehouses, on the other hand, require small numbers of large transactions for data loading and reporting.

Note: A data mart is a term often bandied around in data warehouse terminology. A data mart is simply a subsection of a data warehouse.

1.2.1   The Container Shipment Tracking Schema

Let's take a quick look at the full entity relationship diagram for the container shipment schema used previously in this chapter, as shown in Figure 1.6. This model was built for a customer who ships containers of goods between various countries by sea.

The meanings of the entities in Figure 1.6 are as follows:

Figure 1.6
The relational model container tracking schema.

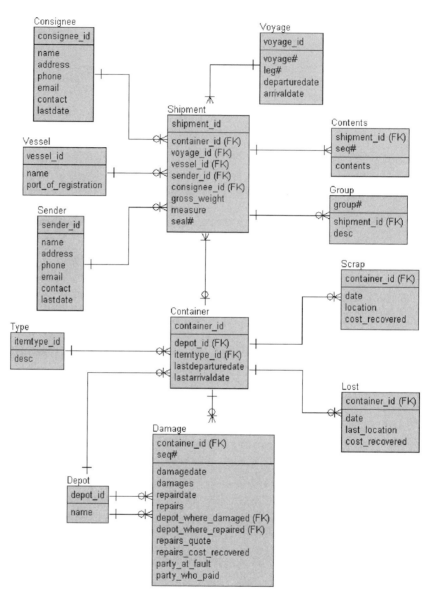

- **CONSIGNEE**. The party receiving the container contents.

- **SENDER**. The party shipping the container contents.

- **VESSEL**. The ship on which the container was transported.

- **VOYAGE**. Ships making voyages can call at multiple ports. Individual containers or groups of containers are transported on all or some legs of the entire voyage.

- **SHIPMENT.** Contents of part of a container, or even one or more containers, are shipped from one port to another. For the sake of simplicity, we assume a shipment as being an individual container shipped from one port to another.

- **CONTENTS.** The contents of a container, or the Bill of Lading.

- **GROUP.** A group of containers is transported from one port to another as a single shipment.

- **CONTAINER.** An individual container.

- **TYPE.** A container can be refrigerated, open-topped, or a flatbed, amongst numerous other types.

- **DEPOT.** A container depot or container port.

- **DAMAGE.** Containers can sustain damage.

- **SCRAP.** Damaged containers can be irreparably damaged and have a scrap value.

- **LOST.** Containers can be stolen or sometimes even lost at sea. In fact, loss of containers at sea happens often. Additionally, these containers, being sealed, can float just below the water, sometimes doing really nasty things to smaller craft.

Now let's convert the relational model to a data warehouse dimensional-fact model.

1.2.2   The Dimensional Data Model

An entity relationship model is inappropriate to the requirements of a data warehouse, even a denormalized one. Another modeling technique used for data warehouses is called dimensional modeling. In layman's terms, a dimensional model consists of facts and dimensions. What is a fact and what is a dimension? A fact is a single iteration in a historical record. A dimension is something used to dig into, divide, and collate those facts into something useful. That isn't really layman's terms, now, is it? Let's try to explain this a little more easily by example.

Let's explain dimensional modeling in small steps. Figure 1.7 shows the same entity relationship as that shown in Figure 1.6, but with a slight difference. Vaguely, facts are the equivalent of transactional entities and dimensions are the equivalent of static data. Therefore, in Figure 1.7, the fact entities are colored gray and the dimensions entities are not. Note how the facts represent historical or archived data and dimensions represent smaller static data entities. It follows that dimension entities will generally be small and fact entities can become frighteningly huge. What does this tell us? Fact entities will always be appended to, and dimension entities can be changed, preferably not as often as the fact entities are appended to. The result is many very small entities related to data in groups from very large entities.

Figure 1.7
Highlighting dimensions and facts.

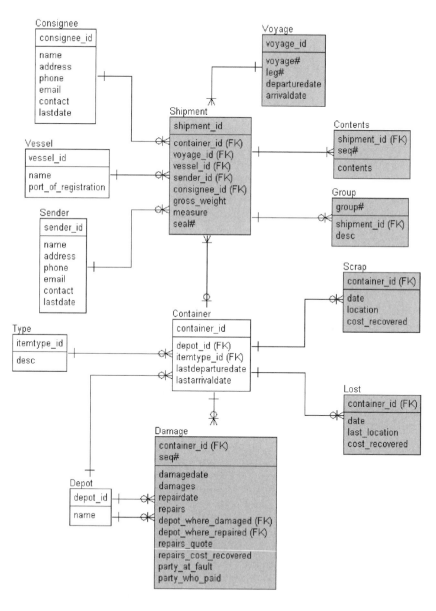

The most desirable result when modeling for a data warehouse using dimensions and facts is called a star schema. Figures 1.8 and 1.9 show slightly modified, pseudo-type star schema versions of the normalized entity relationship diagrams in Figures 1.6 and 1.7. In Figure 1.8 we can see that all dimensions would be contained within a single fact entity, containing shipping history records of containers. Each row in the fact entity would have foreign key values to all related dimension entities.

Figure 1.8
Star schema for containers currently at sea.

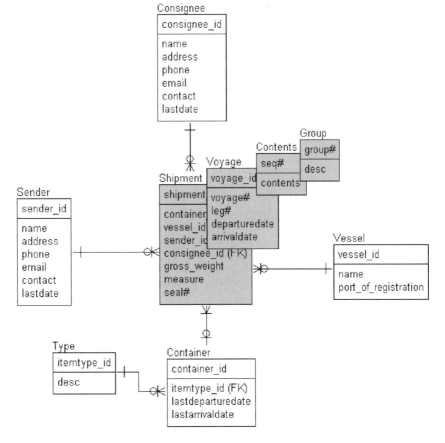

Note: Every star or snowflake schema always has a fact entity. A single data warehouse can consist of multiple fact entities and thus multiple star and/or snowflake schemas.

Figure 1.9 simply contains another fact entity or another subset of the data contained in the normalized entity relationship structure in Figures 1.6 and 1.7. It is quite conceivable that the two fact entity sets in Figures 1.8 and 1.9 should be merged into a single entity, separating used, damaged, scrapped, and lost containers by an appropriate type column.

There could be a small problem with the fact entity shown in Figure 1.9. Damaged, scrapped, and lost containers could either be a fact entity or part of the CONTAINER dimension. This decision would depend on exactly how often containers are damaged, scrapped or lost. It is more than likely that this type of thing occurs frequently in relation to other dimensions, but not necessarily in relation to the high frequency of container shipments.

Figure 1.9
Damaged, scrapped and lost containers star schema.

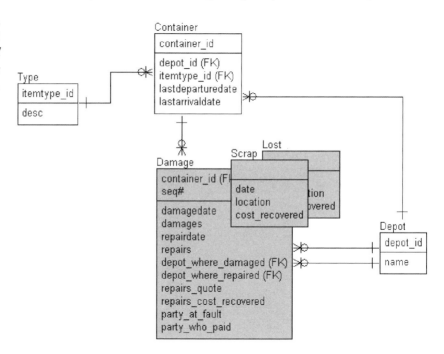

Note: The star schemas shown in Figures 1.8 and 1.9 show that there are two potential fact entities for the relational schema shown in Figures 1.6 and 1.7.

What Is a Star Schema?

A star schema contains one, or at least very few, very large fact entities, plus a large number of small dimensional entities. As already stated, effectively fact entities contain transactional histories and dimension entities contain static data describing the fact entity archive entries. The objective for performance is to obtain joins on a single join level, where one fact entity is joined to multiple small dimension entities, or perhaps even a single dimension entity. Figure 1.10 shows a snowflake schema for the used container portion of the original normalized structure in Figures 1.6 and 1.7, assuming that damaged, scrapped, and lost containers represented in Figure 1.9 are rolled into the CONTAINER dimension.

Figure 1.10
A snowflake schema.

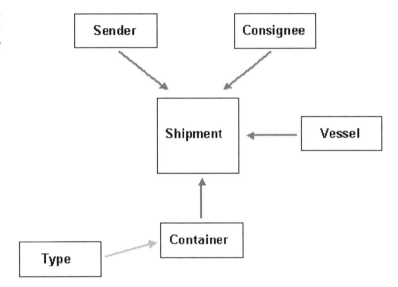

What Is a Snowflake Schema?

A snowflake schema is a normalized star schema such that dimension entities are normalized.

Note: Dimension objects can be used in Oracle Database to represent multiple layers between dimensions, creating dimensional hierarchies. Oracle Database dimensional hierarchies can assist optimizer efficiency and materialized view query rewrite selection.

The schema shown in Figure 1.10 is actually a snowflake schema because the TYPE dimension has been normalized out from the CONTAINER dimension. Figure 1.11 shows a star schema representation of the snowflake schema in Figure 1.10. Figure 1.11 has the TYPE dimension

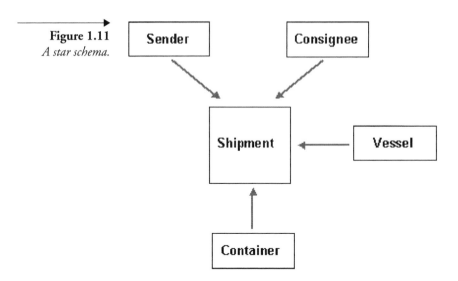

Figure 1.11
A star schema.

included in the CONTAINER dimension. There is no dimensional normalization in a star schema.

Once again let's reinforce the point previously made: the schema representation shown in Figure 1.11 is a star schema of the snowflake schema shown in Figure 1.10. The reason why is because the TYPE entity has been rolled into, or contained within, the CONTAINER entity. Effectively the CONTAINER and TYPE entities have been denormalized, such that TYPE.NAME columns values, the name of the type itself, excluding the TYPE_ID column, are now included with the CONTAINER entity. Denormalization is effective for a data warehouse schema for a number of reasons:

- Nontechnical users, such as sales people, forecasters, and sometimes even executives, often access data warehouse entities. A star schema is very simple to understand without bombarding the user with all the complex entities and intra-entity relationships of a relational data model and multiple dimensional hierarchies. Containers are meaningful to end users. Types of containers may not be as meaningful in a user's mind, perhaps being understood better as *refrigerated* or *flatbed*. If users do not know what something is, it could potentially render the entire structure useless to some people.

- As you can see by the simplicity of the star schema shown in Figure 1.11, a star schema can easily be augmented by adding new dimensions, as long as they fit in with the fact entity.

- From a purely performance tuning perspective, a star schema rolls subset dimensions into single entities from a multiple dimensional hierarchy of a snowflake schema. The number of joins in queries will be reduced. Therefore, queries should execute faster.

Note: A single data warehouse database can contain multiple fact entities and, therefore, multiple star schemas. Additionally, individual dimension entities can point to multiple fact entities. Perhaps more importantly, bear in mind that dimension entities will occupy a small fraction of the storage space that fact entities do. Fact entities in a data warehouse can have billions of rows, whereas dimensions are in the range of tens, hundreds or perhaps thousands. Any larger than thousands and those dimensions could possibly be facts.

As a final note, snowflake schemas help to organize dimensions a little better from a mathematical perspective by saving disk space. Disk space is cheap. Increasing dimension number increases joins in queries. The more joins in queries, the worse a data warehouse will perform, in general.

1.2.3   Data Warehouse Data Model Design Basics

What is the objective of a data warehouse? When asking this question, the primary consideration is for the end users, the people who read reporting produced from a data warehouse, whether they build those reports or not. So think in terms of end users searching for patterns and trying to forecast trends from masses of historical information.

How does one go about designing a data warehouse data model?

- **Business Processes**. What are the business processes? The business processes will result in the source of facts about the business, the fact entities.

- **Granularity**. What is the level of granularity required? Fact entities are appended to at a specific level of granularity or grain. The finer the granularity, the more of your historical data is stored. The lowest level of granularity excludes any summaries of historical data, even though specialized objects such as materialized views can create summaries at a later stage. When you do not know the precise requirements for future use of your data warehouse, to be on the safe side, it is best to store all levels of detail. If you miss a level of detail in any specific area and it is later requested, you are likely to be up the creek without a paddle!

- **Identify Dimensions**. What are your dimensions? Dimensions generally consist of static data such as codes and descriptions, the kind of data that goes into front-end application pick lists. Make sure that the dimensional data conforms to fact data granularity levels.

- **Build Facts**. The last step is to build the fact entities containing all the nonstatic transactional information generated by applications on a daily basis.

When building a data model for a data warehouse database there are various factors to consider. Some of these design factors to consider can be vaguely divided up by dimension and fact entities. Let's begin with dimension entities.

Dimension Entities

Data warehouse dimensions can be loosely classified into various groups. The more generic types are dimensions such as time, product or location dimensions. Obviously, your classifications may vary depending on the data warehouse.

Dimension Entity Types

A time dimension determines how long archived or historical data is to be retained. Figure 1.12 shows an example.

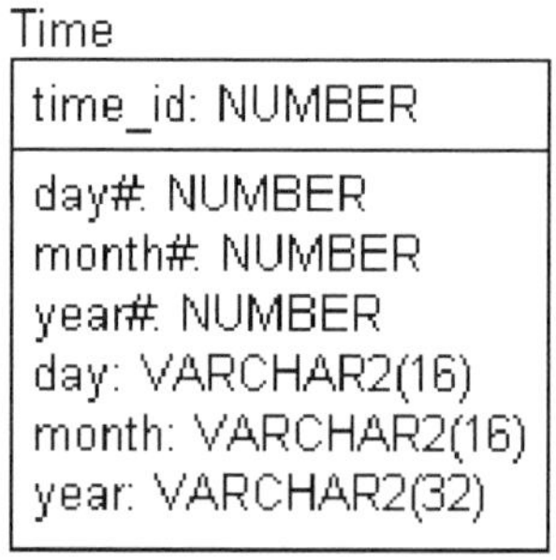

Figure 1.12
A time dimension entity.

Time

time_id: NUMBER
day#: NUMBER month#: NUMBER year#: NUMBER day: VARCHAR2(16) month: VARCHAR2(16) year: VARCHAR2(32)

A product dimension would be used to contain details or products a company produces or deals with in some way, as shown in Figure 1.13.

Figure 1.14 shows what could be an original relational entity set of PRODUCT and CATEGORY entities, with a many-to-one relationship

Figure 1.13
*A product
dimension entity.*

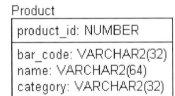

between the PRODUCT and CATEGORY entities. The PRODUCT dimensional entity in Figure 1.14 has the name of the category rolled into the PRODUCT entity, minimizing on joins and ultimately providing for faster performing code in a data warehouse.

Figure 1.14
*Relational to
dimensional star
schema
transformation for
Figure 1.13.*

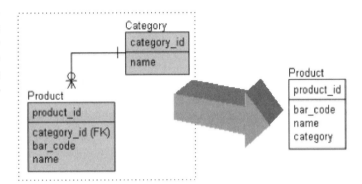

Transactional databases usually have some form of demographic information attached to transactions, either directly or through relations with other entities. The equivalent for a data warehouse is sometimes a location dimension such as that shown in Figure 1.15.

Figure 1.15
*A location
dimension entity.*

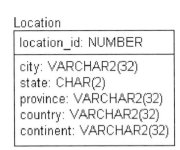

Figure 1.16 shows a transformation between a relational entity location structure design and that of the location dimension entity on the right side of the diagram. Figure 1.16 serves to show the stark difference in complex-

Figure 1.16
Relational to dimensional star schema transformation for Figure 1.15.

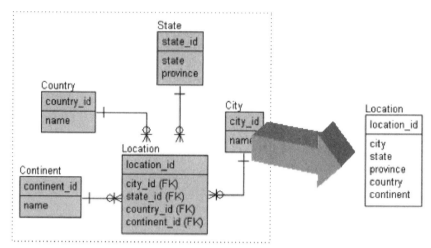

ity between a relational structure and its equivalent denormalized dimensional structure.

Note: Commonly used data warehouse dimensions can also be entities, such as customers, stock items, and suppliers. The star schema in Figure 1.11 shows more specific rather than generic dimensions in the form of senders, consignees, vessels, and containers.

Now let's take a look at factors affecting data warehouse data model design with respect to fact entities.

Fact Entities

In general fact entities contain two column types, namely numeric fact values and foreign key reference attributes, to dimension entities. Figure 1.17 shows a more detailed version of the snowflake schema shown in Figure 1.8. The SHIPMENT, GROUP, CONTENTS, and VOYAGE specific entity columns are named as such simply to indicate their relational entity origins. All of these attributes are measurements of one form or another. The remaining attributes for the SHIPMENT entity shown in Figure 1.17 are all dimensional entity foreign keys.

The two voyage departure and arrival dates could be removed to a time-based entity and replaced with the appropriate foreign keys.

Data warehouse fact entities can be loosely classified into various areas. Once again classifications may vary depending on the data warehouse.

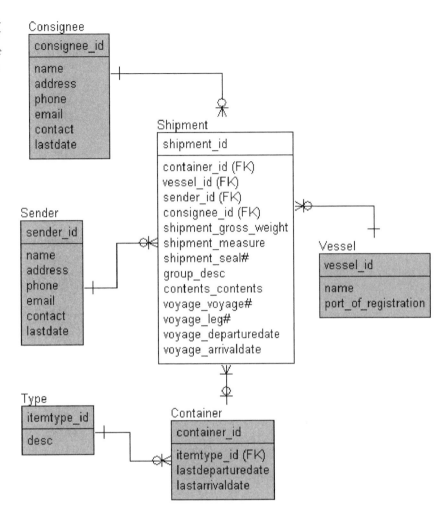

Figure 1.17
A detailed fact table entity.

Fact Entity Types

- Fact tables can contain detailed fact row entries.

- Fact tables can be summary tables, which are aggregations of details. Detail rows are not stored in the data warehouse, probably having been summarized in transportation from transactional databases.

- Fact tables can be simply added to or changed, but are preferably only partially changed, or better still static. The least intrusive method of adding new data is during low usage times and appended to the end of existing data.

Fact Entity Attribute Types

Facts are often known as additive, semi-additive, or nonadditive. For example, accounting amounts can be added together (additive) but averages cannot (nonadditive). Semi-additive facts can be accumulated for some but not all facts.

In Figure 1.17 the SHIPMENT.SHIPMENT_GROSS_WEIGHT is additive across all dimensions. In other words there is a gross weight for a sender (the person or company shipping the container), the consignee (the person or company receiving the container), a vessel, and a container. The SHIPMENT.CONTENTS_CONTENTS attribute is semi-additive because contents are only specific to each container and thus meaningless to sender, consignee or vessel. Multiple senders and consignees can have their individual shipments grouped in a single container or even spread across multiple containers. The SHIPMENT.VOYAGE# and SHIPMENT.VOYAGE_LEG# attributes are nonadditive, since these values simply do not make sense to be accumulated. However, an average number of legs per voyage, per vessel might make some sense as an accumulation.

It is always preferable that fact entities are only added to, and also best appended to. Less desirable situations are fact entities with updatable cumulative columns, such as summaries or even fact entities requiring deletions. Even worse are fact entities containing directly updatable numerical values. For example, if an entity contains a history of stock movements and all prices have increased, it is possible that a large portion of those stock movement entries must be updated. It might be best in a situation such as this to maintain stock item prices outside of the stock movement's entity, perhaps as part of a dimension.

Granularity, Granularity, and Granularity

The most significant factor with respect to fact entities is granularity—how much data to keep, to what level of detail. Do you store every transaction or do you summarize transactions and only store totals for each day, month, per client, and so on?

Granularity is deciding how much detail the data warehouse will need in the future. This is all about requirements. Firstly, do the end users know how much detail they will need? Do you understand and trust that they know what they need? Will they change their minds? Probably. If there is any doubt, and if possible, keep everything! Now there's a simple of rule of thumb. Disk space is cheap unless your data warehouse is truly humongous. If that is the case, you have plenty of other problems to deal with. You also have a good reason why particular details might be missing, say one year down the line when some really irritated executive comes to ask you why the data he wants isn't there. Too much data is your answer.

So the most important design issue with fact entities is the level of granularity. Simply put this means does one should save all the data or summarize it? Storing all data can lead to very large fact entities and, thus, very large databases. However, after data has been deleted from your transactional data sources, it might be costly to discover that all the archived dimensional–fact combinations are required for reports at a later date. From a planning perspective, it might be best to begin by retaining all facts down to the smallest detail if at all possible. Data warehouses are expected to be large, and disk space is cheap.

Time and How Long to Retain Data

How long do you keep data in the data warehouse? Some data warehouses retain data in perpetuity, and others discard data over a few years old. Expired data removed from a data warehouse can always be copied to backup copies. However, remember that if a data warehouse is extremely large, removing older data may cause serious performance problems for appending new data, and most especially for end users. Many modern databases operate on a global 24 hour time scale; there simply is no room for downtime, or even *slow time* for that matter.

Other Factors to Consider During Design

Surrogate Keys

When designing entities for data warehouses use surrogate keys or unique sequential identifiers for entity primary keys. The reason for this is possible multiple data sources from different databases and perhaps even different database vendor software. Additionally, data can originate from flat text files and perhaps from outside purchased data sets. Keys in different data sources could be named differently containing the same values or named the same with different values. The data warehouse needs its own unique key values specific to itself and each of its entities, as a distinct data entity set.

Duplicating Surrogate Keys and Associated Names

When creating composite column keys for child entities, parent key columns could be copied into child entities. Copy not only the key values into the child entities, but also the unique naming values they represent, as shown in Figure 1.18. This will allow access to all details of a multiple hierarchical dimension in all forms.

Figure 1.18
*Duplicate all
composite key
columns.*

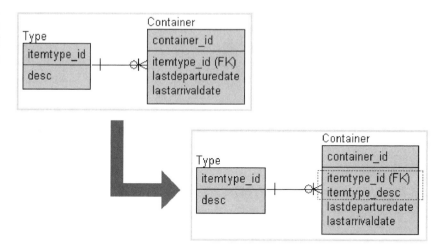

Referential Integrity

This chapter has already described referential integrity in data warehouses. Further comment is necessary. Many data warehouses probably do not have referential integrity implemented at all. If implementing referential integrity, use constraints. If creating foreign key constraints, indexing those foreign keys might be sensible, especially if dimension entity primary key values are to be updated or deleted. Whatever you do, never use triggers. Triggers are ten times slower than constraints for implementing referential integrity. Most importantly, remember that a designer's perspective of constraints being extra overhead pales into insignificance when compared to the cost of not having those constraints for much of the possible functionality required by data warehouse data. Serious problems, particularly performance problems, may result if referential integrity is not implemented using primary and foreign key constraints. Additionally, relying on the idea that data incoming into the data warehouse will always be 100% correct may be foolhardy. If the data warehouse is required to produce correct answers, then data integrity is a must!

Managing the Data Warehouse

Remember that the most important consideration is servicing applications and users. If users need ad-hoc reporting, then the data model must provide for that ad-hoc requirement, even though ad-hoc queries place a heavy load on a database. Additionally, consider aggregations, repetitive data loading, perhaps even complete reloads. Also consider maintenance activities, such as re-indexing or backup and recovery. In other words, build your data warehouse so that it is easily maintainable and usable at an acceptable performance level.

Note: ALWAYS remember that end users and applications are served first!

This chapter has briefly examined the different data models, especially the basics of the data warehouse data model. In the next chapter you will begin the data warehouse tuning process by examining tuning of the data warehouse data model.

2

Introducing Data Warehouse Tuning

The first part of this chapter builds a data warehouse model that will be used throughout the remainder of this book. The data warehouse model is constructed from two relational data model schemas covering demographics and inventory-accounting. The inventory-accounting database has millions of rows, providing a reasonable amount of data to demonstrate the tuning process as this book progresses. The second part of this chapter will introduce the multifarious methods that can be used to tune a data warehouse data model. All these methods will be described and demonstrated in subsequent chapters.

2.1 Let's Build a Data Warehouse

In order to demonstrate how to tune a data warehouse in general, at this stage we need to create a data warehouse data model. The data warehouse model will be a combination of two OLTP data models. The first OLTP data model is a section of an email demographics data model as shown in Figure 2.1, which I built for managing email messages. The second OLTP data model is an inventory-accounting schema as shown in Figure 2.2. The database created from the data model shown in Figure 2.2 contains millions of rows—it is a large database appropriate for data warehouse tuning, giving this book copious amounts of data to work with. The inventory-accounting database is used in a previous book[1] written by myself and also published by Elsevier.

Let's begin by examining the demographics data model.

2.1.1 The Demographics Data Model

The demographics OLTP data model, as shown in Figure 2.1, shows all fact entities. These fact entities are:

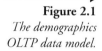

Figure 2.1
*The demographics
OLTP data model.*

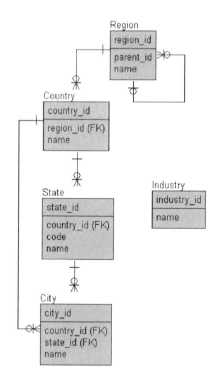

- **REGION**. For example, the continent of Africa.

- **COUNTRY**. A country must be contained within a region based on the COUNTRY.REGION_ID attribute.

- **STATE**. If a country has states then each state must be contained within a country based on the STATE.COUNTRY_ID attribute.

- **CITY**. A city is defined as being part of a country (CITY.COUNTRY_ID), a state (CITY.STATE_ID) or both. Thus the CITY.COUNTRY_ID and CITY.STATE_ID attributes are NULL-valued foreign keys.

- **INDUSTRY**. Customer or supplier industry.

  Now let's take a look at the inventory-accounting OLTP data model.

2.1.2   The Inventory-Accounting OLTP Data Model

The inventory-accounting OLTP data model is shown in Figure 2.2. Rather than detail the contents of all entities, as for the demographics data model in Figure 2.1, I have simply colored all transaction entities as white and all static data entities as gray. As we know from Chapter 1, OLTP transactional entities translate loosely into data warehouse fact entities. Addi-

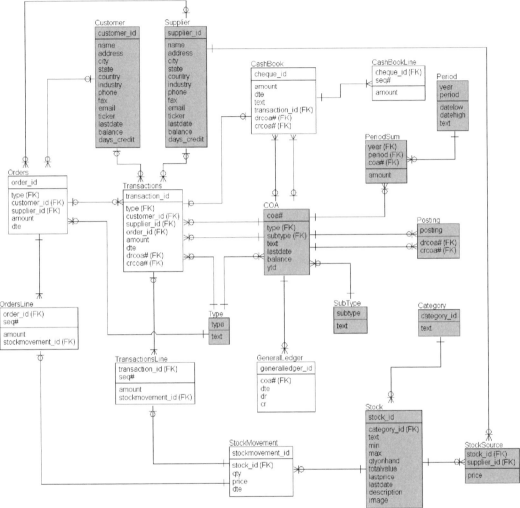

Figure 2.2   *The inventory-accounting OLTP database.*

tionally, OLTP static entities translate roughly into data warehouse dimension entities.

Now let's look at how to combine the two schemas shown in Figures 2.1 and 2.2 into a poorly tuned data warehouse data model.

2.1.3   The Data Warehouse Data Model

Looking at the data models shown in Figures 2.1 and 2.2 it would suffice to say that the resulting data warehouse is going to be quite a monster. So let's do it in small steps, leading up to a data warehouse data model for the entire structure. The resulting data model will consist of a number of fact entity star or snowflake schemas. Parts of the demographics and inventory-accounting schemas will be discarded.

As we saw in Chapter 1 there is a sequence of steps to creating a data warehouse model:

1.   **Business Processes**. What are the business processes? The fact entities or transactions.

2.   **Granularity**. What is the level of granularity required? In our case—everything.

3.   **Identify Dimensions**. What are the dimensions? Dimensions are static. Build the dimensions.

4.   **Build Facts**. The dimensions must be built before the facts because facts depend on dimensions.

Identify the Facts

The demographic schema in Figure 2.1 has no facts. The inventory-accounting schema in Figure 2.2 has the following facts:

- **Sales Orders**. ORDERS and ORDERSLINE entities with TYPE = "S".

- **Sales Transactions**. Invoices and credit notes from the TRANSACTIONS and TRANSACTIONSLINE entities with TYPE = "S".

- **Purchase Orders**. ORDERS and ORDERSLINE entities with TYPE = "P".

- **Purchase Transactions**. Invoices and debit notes from the TRANSACTIONS and TRANSACTIONSLINE entities with TYPE = "P".

- **Payments Made and Received**. CASHBOOK and CASHBOOKLINES entities. Payments and receipts could be split apart.

- **Stock Movements**. These are product movements in and out of inventory from the STOCKMOVEMENTS entity.

- **General Ledger.** This is purely accounting information and is not relevant to this data warehouse.

The list of facts shown above is not the final structure, and it will be refined further. At this point granularity and dimensions should be defined.

Identify the Granularity

As stated above, all rows from all tables will be copied.

Identify and Build the Dimensions

Dimensions are identified based on the facts to be included in the data warehouse. In general each fact entity will become a star or snowflake schema, preferably a star schema. Dimension entities can be used by more than one fact entity. Identified dimensions are:

- **LOCATION.** Construct from the CUSTOMER and SUPPLIER entity COUNTRY, STATE, and CITY attributes. Figure 2.3 shows the LOCATION entity, denormalized from left to right in the diagram.

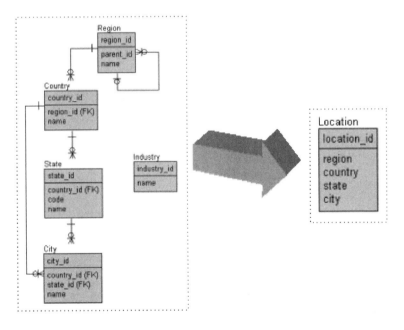

Figure 2.3
Representing locations in the data warehouse.

- **INDUSTRY.** The INDUSTRY entity cannot be denormalized further and is as shown in Figure 2.1.

- **TIME.** Construct from the DTE attributes in the TRANSACTIONS and STOCKMOVEMENT entities. Figure 2.4 shows the TIME entity.

- **PRODUCT.** Construct from the STOCK and CATEGORY entities as shown in Figure 2.5.

Figure 2.4
*Representing times
and dates in the
data warehouse.*

Figure 2.5
*Representing stock
as products in the
data warehouse.*

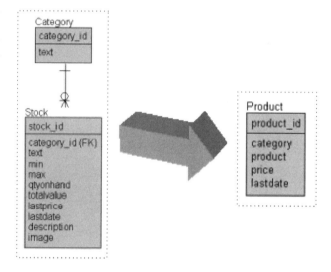

Build the Facts

Facts entities can only be built once all dimension entities have been constructed due to fact dependencies on dimensions. The three fact entities selected are:

- **SALE**. The SALES fact entity will contain attributes from the ORDERS, ORDERSLINE, TRANSACTIONS, TRANSACTION-SLINE, CASHBOOK, and CASHBOOKLINES entities, where the TYPE values are set to the value "S", implying a sale. Additionally, the STOCKMOVEMENTS will be rolled into the SALE fact entity.

- **PURCHASE**. The PURCHASES fact entity will contain attributes from the ORDERS, ORDERSLINE, TRANSACTIONS, TRANS-ACTIONSLINE, CASHBOOK, and CASHBOOKLINES entities, where the TYPE values are set to the value "P", implying a purchase. Additionally, the STOCKMOVEMENTS will be rolled into the PURCHASES fact entity.

Note: Sales must be separated from purchases because positive and negative amounts (AMOUNT) imply different things. For example, both a sales invoice and a purchase invoice have positive amounts in the TRANSAC-TIONS entity, even though these items represent incoming funds and outgoing funds—two different things.

Figure 2.6 shows a general picture of the denormalization process.

Figure 2.7 shows the resulting data warehouse star schemas for the SALE and PURCHASE fact entities. Dates are retained for precision even though the TIME entity caters to periods of time.

2.2   Methods for Tuning a Data Warehouse

Some data warehouses use purely star schemas or snowflake schemas, or a combination of both. Some data warehouses even use 3rd normal form schemas (a relational schema as for an OLTP database). Some data warehouses contain hybrid schemas using a combination of two or even all three data model types, including star schemas, snowflake schemas, and 3rd normal form schemas.

2.2.1   Snowflake versus Star Schemas

How can a data warehouse schema be tuned? Look once again at Figure 2.7 and compare it to the complexity of Figure 2.2. Note how the data warehouse schema shown in Figure 2.7 is so much simpler than the OLTP relational schema structure shown in Figure 2.2. The truth is that other than converting snowflake schemas to star schemas there is not much that can be

Figure 2.6
*The
denormalization
process.*

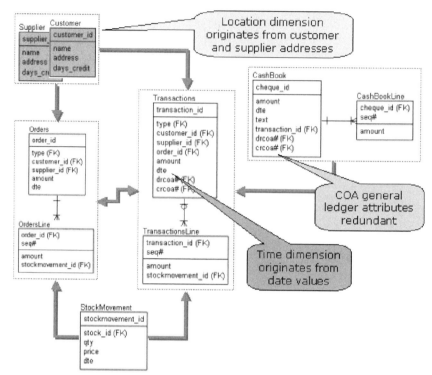

Figure 2.7
*The data
warehouse SALE
and PURCHASE
fact entities.*

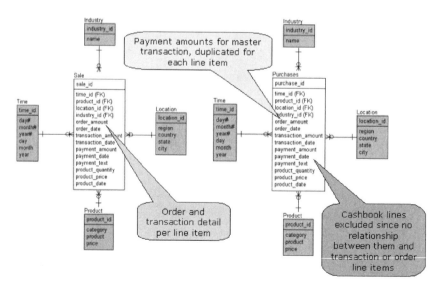

done to tune the individual data warehouse fact and dimension entities, with respect to removal or creation of those entities. As already described in Chapter 1, a snowflake schema can contain multiple hierarchical dimensions. A star schema contains a single hierarchy of dimensions where fact entities are joined directly to each dimension. Examples of two snowflake to star schema denormalization transformations are shown in Figures 2.3 and 2.5, with the snowflake schema on the left and the star schema on the right side of each diagram. Star schemas are better performing than snowflake schemas for one simple reason:

Note: Star schemas minimize on SQL code joins!

Star schemas minimize on SQL code joins. Star schemas contain fewer entities than snowflake schemas. Snowflake schemas contain multiple entity hierarchies of dimensional data (static data). Star schemas denormalize multiple dimensions into single entities. Therefore, star schemas require smaller sized joins simply because there are fewer entities. The smaller the number of entities there are, the smaller and less complex joins will be, and ultimately the faster queries will be. On the contrary, there are some possible odd solutions, such as denormalized views utilizing caching of view results. However, I would not recommend using views for anything other than security or application prototyping. Views can cause too many potential performance problems.

Star Schemas

A star schema is a very simplistic model containing one or more fact entities. Fact entities contain volatile transactional data and are linked to static dimensional entities. Dimensional entities describe the facts in multiple dimensions. The key factor for the efficiency of a star schema is that there is only one level to each dimension, where each dimension is hooked to facts by foreign key constraints and indexes. It is also sensible to create as many dimensions as possible in order to minimize storage of static information in fact entities.

Once again, dimensions must be on a single level. A single-level dimension does not contain links to other dimensions, contained within dimensions. Multiple hierarchical dimensions results in a snowflake schema. A snowflake schema leads to higher numbers of entities in SQL code joins. SQL code joins with more entity joins than necessary become complex inefficient join queries. The more complex joins are, the slower queries will execute, and thus the worse performance will be. With the huge quantities of data in data warehouses, SQL code join performance is paramount.

What Is a Star Query?

Star schemas can be used to execute a special type of query called a star query. A star query joins each dimension to a single fact entity without joining the dimensions to each other. This makes perfect sense when examining the star schemas shown in Figure 2.7.

The Oracle query optimizer can recognize star queries when the STAR_TRANSFORMATION_ENABLED configuration parameter is set to TRUE. Additionally, bitmap indexes for each foreign key dimension must be created in the fact entity. Bitmap indexes are appropriate in this situation for two reasons:

- The relative row counts between fact and dimension entities are such that unique dimensions across fact entities are very small in number. Oracle Database calls this *low cardinality*. Bitmap indexes are most efficient for very small numbers of unique values. In the case of a data warehouse this is generally based on relative row counts between fact and dimension entities.

- The optimizer may execute a star query (star transformation) when fact entity foreign key indexes are bitmap indexes.

Star Transformation

The resulting query is a transparent process called star transformation, where a regularly processed query is transformed into a star query. The optimizer utilizes star transformations to facilitate the performance of joining fact and dimension entities. Star transformations use bitmap indexes on fact entity dimension foreign key column indexes, allowing various highly efficient index lookup and joining methods.

Note: Star transformation requires that the configuration parameter STAR_TRANSFORMATION_ENABLED be set to TRUE in the configuration parameter file, or use of the STAR_TRANSFORMATION hint.

Star queries and star transformations will be scrutinized in greater detail in Chapter 3. There are various restrictions when using star queries, forcing the optimizer to fail when attempting to use a star query transformation. Most of these are fairly logical:

- Any hints must be compatible with bitmap index use. For instance, forcing a full table scan will cause a problem.

- Bind variables are not allowed. Why does this make sense? A data warehouse really requires exact values and items where precise statistics are a necessity, due to huge data volumes. Unlike an OLTP database where high concurrency, and thus sharing of previously executed SQL code using bind variables, is so important, a data warehouse needs throughput for a small number of infrequently executed queries, sometimes even the dreaded ad-hoc query. A data warehouse needs to cater for the unpredictability of end-user reporting requirements. Bind variables require predicable SQL code reuse and are thus completely contrary to unpredictable, nonshareable, low-concurrency SQL code queries in data warehouses.

- If bitmap indexes are created on fact entity foreign key constraints do not leave any of them out. Create bitmap indexes for all the foreign key columns. A star query transformation needs those bitmap indexes. If any foreign key indexes are BTree indexes then the star query transformation will simply not occur.

- Remote fact entities accessed across database links can cause problems. This makes perfect sense, since the bitmap indexes should really exist in the local database. Since bitmap indexes are not essentially required on dimension entities, dimensions can be accessed remotely, but this is not recommended. It is best to have all the entities in one place, in one database.

- Anti-joins of any kind are a serious problem simply because they find what is not there. This type of data access will execute full table scans, avoiding any indexing, thus avoiding any fact entity bitmap indexing, and therefore no star query transformations can occur.

- Do not use views under any circumstances. Views are overlays, not real data. Materialized views, on the other hand, are snapshot copies of data and another thing entirely.

Note: Views and materialized views are two completely different things. A materialized view contains a separate physical copy of data. A view on the other hand, is an overlay that, when accessed, executes a query on underlying table rows. Never, ever, ever use views in a data warehouse!

There are a few more points to note about star transformation queries. Even if you expect a star transformation to occur, even if you use the STAR_TRANSFORMATION hint, the optimizer may not necessarily use a star query. Why?

- If a query accesses more than, say, 10% of a fact table's rows, then the optimizer automatically executes a full table scan of the fact table. A query retrieving more than 10% of a table's rows is automatically faster reading the entire table, according to the optimizer.

- In the past the use of a hint has only been a suggestion to the optimizer and has not forced the optimizer to pick any particular execution plan, especially when the optimizer *thinks* it can do better. Do not assume that the optimizer is *stupid*. The Oracle Database SQL code optimizer is very sophisticated in the latest versions of Oracle Database.

Note: In Oracle Database 10g, hints no longer suggest, but the optimizer tends to blindly follow hints if they are correct syntactically, even when the hints do something severely detrimental to performance.

Figure 2.8 shows hints forcing the optimizer to do exactly the wrong thing—twice!

Figure 2.8
Hints no longer suggest, but force, the optimizer to follow blindly.

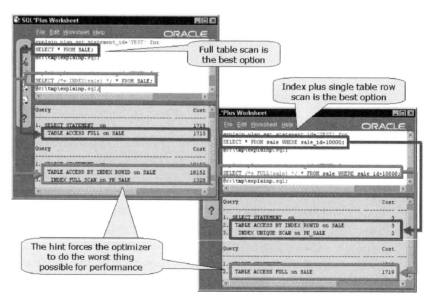

■ An obvious result of the above is that small fact entities will always be full table scanned and star queries will never be used. The optimizer will always assume that a small table is faster read in its entirety rather than reading both index and table rows.

Using Bitmap Indexes

Bitmap indexing can cater not only for a few distinct values but also for thousands of distinct values efficiently. It is possible that bitmap indexes may not be as fast as some Oracle Database texts would lead us to believe. On the contrary, it is possible that the biggest problem with bitmap indexing, and possibly the result of their unfortunate reputation, is consistent use in transactional databases. If frequent DML (Data Manipulation Language) activity occurs on a bitmap index, it can deteriorate to the point of uselessness over time. I have seen one case of a relatively small DML batch procedure being reduced from eight hours to three minutes running time, after the rebuilding of a set of bitmap indexes into BTree indexes. This processing had been running on a regularly scheduled basis for more than a year. It may or may not be possible to state that INSERT activity does not deteriorate bitmap index efficiency as drastically as UPDATE and DELETE activity. I cannot prove either, but I can state with certainty that over time, bitmap indexing and DML activity do not mix well at all.

Note: Oracle Database 10g apparently includes significant improvement with respect to reduction of bitmap index space growth, when subjected to high rates of DML activity. I cannot prove this.

Experimentation with bitmap indexes is suggested prior to implementation.

Snowflake Schemas

A snowflake schema is a contradiction to data warehouse efficiency. Efficiency is best served when using small numbers of entities in star schemas. Smaller numbers of entities reduces the number of entities in SQL code joins. Effectively a star schema is a completely denormalized entity structure, where all duplication is included. A snowflake schema, on the other hand, does attempt to normalize the dimensions of a star schema, creating multiple hierarchies of dimensions, such as that shown on the left side of Figure 2.3. Sometimes use of snowflake schemas is unavoidable.

A snowflake schema removes duplication from star schema dimensions by normalizing dimension entities, either partially or completely. This leads to a higher number of tables in SQL code joins, and thus possibly less efficient queries.

Introducing Oracle Database Dimension Object Hierarchies

Oracle Database dimension objects can be used in Oracle Database to represent multiple layers between dimensions, thereby assisting optimizer efficiency and materialized view query rewrite selection. Implementation of Oracle Database dimension objects will be covered in detail in Chapter 5.

2.2.2 3rd Normal Form Schemas

A 3rd normal form schema is essentially a transactional or OLTP type of entity structure, catering for small amounts of highly concurrently accessed (shareable) data structures. Unlike star and snowflake schemas, 3rd normal form schemas are generally inefficient for data warehouses and are best avoided if possible.

Optimization of 3rd normal form queries is a book in itself, and you can find much detail in my previously published Oracle Database tuning book [1]. Tuning of these types of queries is not covered in detail in this book as this book focuses on data warehouse tuning. However, Chapter 7 discusses the basics of tuning SQL code queries, encompassing SQL code tuning for normalized schemas, tuning tools, and techniques.

2.2.3 Introducing Other Data Warehouse Tuning Methods

There are various tricks, bells, and whistles that can be used to tune data warehouses, which will be covered in this book. So far in this chapter we have introduced the following data warehouse model methods of tuning:

- Star queries, star transformations, and use of bitmap indexes for star schemas

- Oracle Database dimension objects for managing multiple hierarchical dimensions in snowflake schemas

- The folly of using 3rd normal form schemas in a data warehouse, unless absolutely necessary: a typical reason for using 3rd normal form and normalization techniques in data warehouses is often because of limited online disk storage capacity; either the data warehouse is so huge that you simply cannot avoid removal of duplication, or your hardware budget is miniscule

There are numerous other tuning methods and tools for use in data warehouses introduced here, some of which are to be covered in detail in subsequent chapters of this book. These tuning tools and methods are:

- **Bitmap Join Indexes**. Indexing in the form of bitmap indexes, but more importantly bitmap join indexes. A bitmap join index joins a bitmap index with a nonbitmap index. See Chapter 3.

- **Referential Integrity Constraints**. Is referential integrity really needed in your data warehouse? See Chapter 3.

- **Materialized Views and Query Rewrite**. Use materialized views for creating aggregates; often used for data marts.

Note: A data mart is a subsection of a data warehouse, sometimes application-specific, often they are used to build a data warehouse in stages.

Materialized views can be created and maintained in numerous different ways. Many requirements can be catered for. The important factor in utilizing materialized views is that queries can actually be rewritten internally by the optimizer to read smaller physical areas of disk, covered by materialized view aggregations rather than entire fact tables. Obviously, the faster that data content changes, the higher the overhead for refreshing those materialized views. The other factor to consider when using materialized views, is not to create too many, potentially exceeding available storage space. And, obviously, too many materialized view implies too much refresh time. The process of query rewrite allows the optimizer to rewrite or rebuild a query execution plan, accessing a materialized views rather than a table's rows. If a materialized view contains aggregated data then the result is more than likely a much faster query because less I/O is executed on aggregated data.

Note: Query rewrite requires the setting of the QUERY_REWRITE_ENABLED parameter in the configuration parameter file. Also, the OPTIMIZER_FEATURES_ENABLE parameter can be set to the database version in use such as 10.1.0. This enables the best optimization features for that specific version of Oracle Database. The OPTMIZER_FEATURES_ENABLE parameter is described as an "umbrella parameter."

See Chapter 4 for details on materialized views and query rewrites.

- **Indexing and Clustering**. Indexing and clustering are important factors for increased data warehouse performance. BTree indexes are usually best for transactional activities. However, there are a multitude of methods by which BTree indexes can be speeded up for read-only activity, such as using key compression. In addition to bitmap indexes for low cardinality data there are also index-organized tables (IOTs) and clusters for presorting and prejoining tables, respectively. IOTs and clusters are similar to materialized views except that IOTs and clusters are direct copies without refresh or query rewrite capabilities. Materialized views are used for aggregations and transparent optimizer query rewrites. There is immense capacity using specific types of Oracle Database indexing to prejoin, presort, and preclassify data. In a read-only data warehouse–type environment, these specific Oracle Database objects should be utilized to their fullest capabilities. See Chapter 3.

- **Partitioning and Parallel Processing**. Oracle Database is very capable of execution of parallel processing on multiple CPU platforms, especially in combination with partitioning, RAID arrays or physically separated datafiles. Oracle Partitioning allows the physical splitting of large tables into separately, transparently accessible physical I/O chunks. Additionally, Oracle Partitioning is very important, as it not only exceeds parallel processing, but also allows the ability to switch in and out large chunks of data perhaps even allowing access to most of the data while new data is loaded into a single partition or subset of an entire table. For instance, transportable tablespaces can be used to transfer physical Oracle Database datafiles between databases, such as from an OLTP to a data warehouse database, or even an intermediary preprocessing OLTP to data warehouse database structure. See Chapters 6, 12, and 13.

Note: Transportable tablespaces are a very effective method of copying large physical chunks of data between databases. See Chapter 13.

- **Oracle SQL Aggregation, Analysis, and OLAP**. Oracle SQL contains a multitude of aggregation functionality encompassing basic arithmetic through to complex statistical analysis. For instance, the GROUP BY clause can be augmented with the ROLLUP, CUBE, and GROUPING SETS clauses to create multidimensional reports, as well as a MODEL clause, among many other capabilities. The MODEL clause allows creation of spreadsheet-like output. In fact,

Oracle SQL can now function as a more or less complete OLAP analytical set of SQL access commands, even to the point of allowing for user-defined analytical functions. See Chapters 8, 9, and 10.

■ **Other Factors**. These areas will not be covered in this book, as they are only loosely or indirectly connected with data warehouse tuning, being more general approaches to tuning as to specific methods of tuning the structures and processes within a data warehouse database (e.g., data mining of redo logs, server clustering, replication, duplication, and standby databases).

This chapter has briefly demonstrated the building of a relatively simple data warehouse schema from a fairly complex OLTP normalized schema. Additionally, various schema types and Oracle Database tuning tools and methods have been discussed. The next chapter will examine effective indexing in data warehouse databases.

2.3 Endnotes

1. *Oracle Performance Tuning for 9i and 10g* (ISBN: 1555583059)

3

Effective Data Warehouse Indexing

This chapter is divided into three distinct parts. The first part examines the basics of indexing, including different types of available indexes. The second part of this chapter attempts to prove the usefulness, or otherwise, of bitmap indexes, bitmap join indexes, star queries, and star transformations. Lastly, this chapter briefly examines the use of index organized tables (IOTs) and clusters in data warehouses.

3.1 The Basics of Indexing

An index in a database is essentially a copy of a small physical chunk of a table. That index is then used to access the table, because reading the index reads a small portion of what would be read from the table, resulting in much less physical I/O activity. Note that it is sometimes faster to read the entire table rather than both index and table. Sometimes it is best not to create indexes for a specific table at all, such as a table containing a small amount of static data.

Note: Indexes are not always required, and too many indexes can sometimes even hurt performance.

OLTP and transactional databases generally require changes to small amounts of data and benefit greatly from extensive use of precise indexing. Data warehouses often get data from entire tables. Sometimes indexes can be superfluous. However, there are some very specific types of indexes that are useful in data warehouses in particular, such as bitmaps, clusters, and IOTs.

Bitmaps, IOTs, and clusters are not amenable to data changes but are designed to be highly efficient for high-throughput reads common to data warehouses. BTree indexes are efficient for both reading and updating of data, best used for exact hits and range scans common to OLTP databases.

Non-BTree indexes are vulnerable to overflow when updated. Bitmap indexes are particularly vulnerable to overflow and catastrophic degradation in performance over long periods of update activity.

Note: What exactly index overflow is and why it is a performance hindrance will be explained later in this chapter.

Remember one more thing. The more indexes that are created on a table, the more updates occur when a table row is changed. For example, if a single table has five indexes, then a single row insertion involves one table row insertion and five index row insertions—that is six insertions altogether. That is not good for performance!

3.1.1   The When and What of Indexing

It has already been mentioned that one does not always need to create an index for every circumstance that might require an index. What are some specific examples where an index might actually hinder database performance?

- If a table contains a small number of rows the optimizer is likely to perform a full table scan on that table, unless in a highly complex join. In this case any indexing might be ignored.

- Data warehouses are more often than not I/O intensive. This is because they read either large portions of tables or entire tables at once.

Note: In the past many books have stated that the optimizer will generally execute a full table scan by default when more that 10% of a full table is read. On the contrary, the 10% marker will not always be the case, especially since the optimizer gets better with every new version of Oracle Database.

Sometimes in a data warehouse, unless an index is helping in sorting of returned rows, one should consider the implications of including unnecessary indexing. Always check the physical order in which data warehouses create fact tables. Utilities such as SQL*Loader can append rows to the end of files regardless of existing usable block space. Quite often, fact table rows are already in the required physical order as a result of the loading process. Why index?

- Try to keep indexes to a few, if not single, column indexes. Composite indexes consisting of multiple columns can hurt performance simply by being time intensive to build and maintain. Also, the smaller an index is, the faster it will be read. Since most data warehouse queries read large amounts of data, it follows that when indexes are read in data warehouses the indexes will, more often than not, be full scanned either with full index scans or fast fully index scans. As a result, it is probably rare in data warehouses, particularly in fact tables, that unique and range scans will be performed on indexes. This is another factor reducing the effectiveness of indexing in data warehouses.

- Be alert for indexing of columns containing many NULL values. NULL values are included in bitmap indexes—this makes perfect sense if the indexed column contains a small number of unique values. For a BTree index, NULL values are not included in the BTree structure and, thus, not even accessible through the index. Be particularly alert when deleting rows from tables with attached BTree indexes because rows are not removed from an index by deletion, potentially leaving large amounts of empty space in a heavily deleted BTree index.

Referential Integrity Indexing

Referential integrity uses primary and foreign keys to validate relationships between rows in related tables. In the case of a data warehouse, dimension tables contain primary keys referenced as foreign keys in a fact table. Sometimes in OLTP databases referential integrity can be partially or wholly removed. However, since data warehouse fact-dimensional data models can perform star transformations on dimension table primary and related fact table foreign keys, it is ill-advised to remove foreign key constraints or the foreign key indexes from fact tables. There are a number of points to note about referential integrity in data warehouses:

- Oracle Database does not automatically create indexes on foreign keys; it is advisable to do so manually. Star transformation queries require foreign key constraints and foreign key indexes.

- Star queries require fact table foreign key constraint indexes to be created as bitmap indexes.

- Since indexes might have to be frequently rebuilt, it might be effective to remove indexes during batch uploads of the data warehouse, assuming that data being loaded is referentially clean. This point is particularly relevant to bitmap indexing, because major changes to table rows can cause serious performance degradation problems with active bitmap indexes.

- Similarly, data warehouses are subject to large amounts of appended updates. Beware of bitmap overflow potential for fact foreign key bitmap indexes. It might be necessary to perform frequent rebuilds on fact table foreign key indexes in order to prevent skewing in BTrees and overflow in bitmaps.

- BTree indexes can be rebuilt using the ONLINE option. This means that during BTree index rebuild that data in both table and index remains available as normal. In previous versions of Oracle Database bitmap indexes could not be rebuilt with the REBUILD option; instead, they had to be dropped and recreated. In Oracle Database 9*i* (release 2, 9.2), bitmap indexes can be rebuilt using the REBUILD option, but not ONLINE. The ONLINE option allows an index to remain in use. As of Oracle Database production release 10.1.0.2.0 for Win2K, the ONLINE option is still not allowed. The ONLINE option will be available in release 2 of Oracle Database 10*g*, or a later version.

- Index rebuilds might be best catered for in data warehouse appending by recreating indexes at the point of every load. Recreation is likely to be essential in the case of bitmap indexing. Use of bitmap indexes may be determined by the time it takes to recreate those bitmap indexes, and possibly also by how much data is periodically appended, in relation to data warehouse size.

Surrogate Keys

A surrogate key is a substitute for another key, often a unique integer identifier because integer values are the easiest and most efficient datatype to index. Surrogate keys are often used in data warehouses to cater for similar or even the same data with disparate data structures. Data structures for a data warehouse can be absorbed from a multitude of different applications, perhaps even using different formats for the same values. For example, one OLTP application database might include hyphens in phone numbers (212-754-3209) and another may not (2127543209).

Another issue with surrogate key use is that traditional relational database structure assumes use of composite primary and foreign keys. As one descends downwards through a hierarchy of normalized tables, those composite column indexes consist of a greater number of columns, increasing by one column at each level of the hierarchy. Effectively, the usefulness of keys is reduced by too many columns in a composite index, simply because composite column indexes occupy too much space, sometimes almost as much as the table itself, thereby not reducing I/O requirements as the original intention of an index dictates.

Views and View Constraints in Data Warehouses

What about views in data warehouses? A view is not the same thing as a materialized view. A materialized view creates a physical copy of data in tables. A view, on the other hand, overlays tables and executes a query every time the view is accessed. Therefore, views can potentially involve substantial transparent processing overhead, particularly when queries against views are filtered, sorted or aggregated. This is secondary processing on the view and effectively querying data twice. Additionally constraints can be placed on views applying additional overhead to using views. See my other book covering Oracle SQL for details on views and view constraints [1].

Note: There is a simple rule when considering views in a data warehouse—DON'T!

Alternate Indexing

Alternate indexing is sometimes referred to as secondary or additional indexing. Alternate indexing includes any indexes created against tables in a data model, that are not part of referential integrity constraints. Thus, an alternate key is an index created on one or more columns where that key is not a primary or foreign key.

Sometimes the need for alternate indexing is a mismatch between the data model and functionality required by applications. Sometimes unique indexes are required on specific columns in data models other than unique integer identifier surrogate key columns in every table. The application could deal with this particular issue, but it may be best to place unique constraints in the database for the same reasons that referential integrity is not placed into applications or triggers.

Note: Excessive alternate indexing can lead to poor performance, most especially in data warehouses. Often excessive alternate indexing indicates data model problems or simply a mismatch between data model and application requirements.

In short, alternate indexing is not a good thing, especially in data warehouses, for a number of reasons:

- The very existence of alternate indexes in a data warehouse dimensional-fact entity structure contradicts the very simplicity of that data warehouse entity structure.

- A dimensional-fact structure is much closer to the structure of actual business processes than a regular normalized entity structure. Therefore, the deeply nontechnical people running ad-hoc reporting, such as executive level management, should not need alternate indexing.

- Most significantly, with respect to performance, alternate indexes create I/O and additional maintenance overhead. They should not be needed in a data warehouse. If loading procedures require specialized constraints in data warehouse tables, such as verification checks and uniqueness in the form of alternate indexes, then perhaps the loading and transformation processes should be revisited. The primary purpose of a data warehouse is to handle queries by people such as end-user executive management running potentially performance-destructive ad-hoc reporting. The data warehouse should be structurally built for end users by programmers, and not for programmers by programmers. For any type of software it is a simple matter of approach from the right perspective—who is the end user? Well, this is not always the case, but for data warehouses it can be a prudent guideline.

3.1.2   Types of Indexes in Oracle Database

In actuality there are a number of ways to examine index types:

- **The Data Model**. Referential integrity using primary keys and foreign keys, plus use of surrogate keys and alternate indexing. This area of classification is already covered in this chapter.

- **To Index or Not**. Sometimes performance is better served by not creating indexes, usually excluding the removal of primary and foreign key indexing. SQL code optimization will full-scan a table and ignore indexes if more than 10% of an entire table is read. In a data warehouse, that 10% Oracle Database optimizer limit is more often than not exceeded. This area of classification has already been covered in this chapter.

- **Different Index Structures**. In Oracle Database, indexes can be BTrees, bitmaps, IOTs and clusters. A BTree is an upside-down tree structure allowing rapid unique and range scans. A BTree can also have various specific attributes. A bitmap is simply a true or false representation of an existing value. An IOT, or index organized table, includes all the columns of a table in an index. A cluster copies commonly accessed columns, both indexed and nonindexed, into a separate physical copy, with its own indexes. Clusters are typically used to speed up joins. Partitioning allows both indexes local to each partition and global to all partitions across a table. See Chapter 6 for partitioning.

- **BTree Index Attributes**. Index attributes include factors such as composite column indexing, compression, and reverse keys, among others. These factors will be covered later in this chapter.

Now let's examine the different types of indexes provided by Oracle Database focusing on BTree and bitmap indexing. In general, BTree indexes are utilized in OLTP databases and bitmap indexes in data warehouse databases.

BTree Indexes

Figure 3.1 shows the internal structure of a BTree index. Note that there are only three layers. Each separate boxed numbered block node in Figure 3.1 represents a block. A block is the smallest physical unit. Every read of a datafile will read one or more blocks. A unique index scan, reading a single row, will read the index datafile up to three times and the associated table once. Four blocks will be read: the root node index block, the second layer index branch block, the index leaf block, and, finally, the block in the table containing the row using the ROWID pointer stored in the index. Indexes for very small tables may be contained in a single block. All these block references are accessed using ROWID pointers. ROWID pointers allow very fast access to small amounts of data.

Figure 3.1
The internal structure of an Oracle Database BTree index.

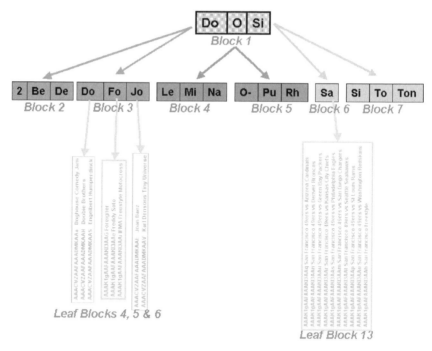

A BTree index does not overflow nearly as drastically as do other index types, such as bitmap indexes and clusters. If a block is filled, a new block is created and branch nodes are changed or added as required. The parent branch and root node contents could even be adjusted to prevent skewing.

BTree indexes do not include NULL values when the entire index value is NULL. In other words, for a composite index, all columns in the composite index must be NULL-valued to exclude the row from the index. NULL values are included in bitmap indexes.

Types of BTree Indexes

BTree indexes can be created in the following ways.

Unique BTree Index

BTree indexes can be specified as unique, where each index value is distinct from every other value in the table.

Ascending or Descending BTree Index

BTree indexes can be specified as sorted in ascending or descending order.

Sorted or Unsorted BTree Index

BTree indexes can be specified as unsorted, assuming table rows have been created in index order.

Function-Based BTree Index

Index values are generated on the result of a function as applied to a table column or columns. For example, an index created on the product of two columns contains the result of the multiplication in the index, not the two column values. Figure 3.2 shows an example of a function-based index.

Figure 3.2
A function-based BTree index.

ROWID	QTY	PRICE
AAAIHgAAJAAAEYKAAA	-1	319.83
AAAIHgAAJAAAEYKAAB	-3	131.66
AAAIHgAAJAAAEYKAAC	-5	1619.3
AAAIHgAAJAAAEYKAAD	-8	141.39
AAAIHgAAJAAAEYKAAE	-10	80.85
AAAIHgAAJAAAEYKAAF	-8	60.71
AAAIHgAAJAAAEYKAAG	-8	51.24
AAAIHgAAJAAAEYKAAH	-6	60.71

```
CREATE INDEX xakfb_sm_amount
ON stockmovement(qty*price)
ONLINE COMPUTE STATISTICS;
```

ROWID	QTY * PRICE
AAAIHgAAJAAAEYKAAA	-319.83
AAAIHgAAJAAAEYKAAB	-394.98
AAAIHgAAJAAAEYKAAC	-8096.35
AAAIHgAAJAAAEYKAAD	-1131.12
AAAIHgAAJAAAEYKAAE	-808.5
AAAIHgAAJAAAEYKAAF	-485.68
AAAIHgAAJAAAEYKAAG	-409.92
AAAIHgAAJAAAEYKAAH	-364.26

The parameters QUERY_REWRITE_ENABLED and QUERY_ REWRITE_ INTEGRITY must be set to TRUE and TRUSTED respectively to allow use of function-based indexes plus execute privileges on any user-defined functions. In past versions of Oracle Database, the QUERY REWRITE system privilege was required. The QUERY REWRITE system privilege is still available but deprecated in Oracle Database 10*g*. In Oracle Database 10*g*, granting the new system privilege GLOBAL QUERY REWRITE to a user will enable query rewrite for any materialized view, regardless of the schema that tables and views are located in.

Reverse Key Value BTree Index

For a reverse key value BTree index the values in the index are reversed. For example, sequences will be stored in reverse order, such that the value 1234 is stored as 4321. Reverse keys have the effect of inserting sequentially generated reverse key values into different blocks, avoiding hot block conflicts. Reverse keys are commonly used in highly concurrent insertion active environments such as Oracle RAC (Real Application Clusters) OLTP databases. Figure 3.3 shows an example of a reverse key value index.

Figure 3.3

A reverse key value BTree index.

ROWID	GENERALLEDGER_ID
AAAIF+AAJAAACuKAAA	344833
AAAIF+AAJAAACuKAAB	344834
AAAIF+AAJAAACuKAAC	344835
AAAIF+AAJAAACuKAAD	344836
AAAIF+AAJAAACuKAAE	344837
AAAIF+AAJAAACuKAAF	344838
AAAIF+AAJAAACuKAAG	344839
AAAIF+AAJAAACuKAAH	344840

Reverse Key Index

ROWID	GENERALLEDGER_ID
AAAIF+AAJAAACuKAAA	338443
AAAIF+AAJAAACuKAAB	438443
AAAIF+AAJAAACuKAAC	538443
AAAIF+AAJAAACuKAAD	638433
AAAIF+AAJAAACuKAAE	738443
AAAIF+AAJAAACuKAAF	838443
AAAIF+AAJAAACuKAAG	938443
AAAIF+AAJAAACuKAAH	48443

Compressed Composite Column BTree Index

For compressed indexes, repeated parent values in composite column indexes are removed from the index, minimizing scanning or repeated index column values. Figure 3.4 shows an example of what index compression does to an index; duplications are removed. A compressed index maintains a prefix key value pointing to ROWID pointers, which point to the table rows. A compressed index saves space. For really large indexes it could potentially save a lot of space.

Bitmap Indexes

A bitmap index stores a value of 0 or 1 for a ROWID. The ROWID points to a row in a table. In Figure 3.5 a bitmap index is created on a column containing codes for states.

Bitmap Index Cardinality

Bitmap indexes work best where a column has low cardinality. Low cardinality means that the value to be indexed has a very small number of distinct values. For example, a column containing M for male and F for female are common columns to be indexed using a bitmap.

Figure 3.4
A compressed composite column BTree index.

ROWID	Country	State	City	Venue
AAACVWAAFAAADGKABT	USA	CA	Modesto	Johanson High School
AAACVWAAFAAADGKABf	USA	CA	Modesto	Modesto Junior College Stadium
AAACVWAAFAAADGKABV	USA	CA	Monterey	Laguna Seca Recreation Area
AAACVWAAFAAADGKABh	USA	CA	Monterey	Monterey Fairgrounds
AAACVWAAFAAADGKABw	USA	CA	Monterey	Pebble Beach Golf Links
AAACVWAAFAAADGLAAH	USA	CA	Monterey	Steinbeck Forum Conference Center
AAACVWAAFAAADGKACU	USA	CA	Mountain View	Shoreline Amphitheatre
AAACVWAAFAAADGKABR	USA	CA	Murphys	Ironstone Winery
AAACVWAAFAAADGKAAS	USA	CA	Oakland	California Ball Room
AAACVWAAFAAADGKAAV	USA	CA	Oakland	Calvin Simmons Theatre

ROWID	Country	State	City	Venue
AAACVWAAFAAADGKABT	USA	CA	Modesto	Johanson High School
AAACVWAAFAAADGKABf				Modesto Junior College Stadium
AAACVWAAFAAADGKABV			Monterey	Laguna Seca Recreation Area
AAACVWAAFAAADGKABh				Monterey Fairgrounds
AAACVWAAFAAADGKABw				Pebble Beach Golf Links
AAACVWAAFAAADGLAAH				Steinbeck Forum Conference Center
AAACVWAAFAAADGKACU			Mountain View	Shoreline Amphitheatre
AAACVWAAFAAADGKABR			Murphys	Ironstone Winery
AAACVWAAFAAADGKAAS			Oakland	California Ball Room
AAACVWAAFAAADGKAAV				Calvin Simmons Theatre

Figure 3.5
A bitmap index.

ROWID	VENUE	CITY	STATE	COUNTRY
AAAHfVAAJAAAK0KAAA	3com Park	San Francisco	CA	USA
AAAHfVAAJAAAK0KAAB	Agenda Lounge	San Jose	CA	USA
AAAHfVAAJAAAK0KAAC	Altamont Raceway Park	Tracy	CA	USA
AAAHfVAAJAAAK0KAAD	Amador Theatre	Pleasanton	CA	USA
AAAHfVAAJAAAK0KAAQ	Caesars	Lake Tahoe	NV	USA
AAAHfVAAJAAAK0KAAR	Caesars Palace	Las Vegas	NV	USA
AAAHfVAAJAAAK0LAAc	Madison Square Garden	New York	NY	USA
AAAHfVAAJAAAK0LAAb	Yankee Stadium	New York	NY	USA

ROWID	STATE='CA'	STATE='NY'	STATE='NV'
AAAHfVAAJAAAK0KAAA	1	0	0
AAAHfVAAJAAAK0KAAB	1	0	0
AAAHfVAAJAAAK0KAAC	1	0	0
AAAHfVAAJAAAK0KAAD	1	0	0
AAAHfVAAJAAAK0KAAQ	0	1	0
AAAHfVAAJAAAK0KAAR	0	1	0
AAAHfVAAJAAAK0LAAc	0	0	1
AAAHfVAAJAAAK0LAAb	0	0	1

Note: In a data warehouse where fact tables become very large, bitmap indexes created on foreign key indexed dimensional values can equate to thousands of values. However, the ratio of fact to dimensional table rows still makes a bitmap index a viable option. Thus, low cardinality is a relative term. In other words, creating a bitmap index on a male or female valued column in a table containing two rows is completely pointless!

Bitmap Performance

In general, a bitmap index occupies less physical space than a BTree index and thus I/O requirements are reduced. Additionally, less physical space implies more index values per block and thus more rows accessed with each read.

Bitmap Block Level Locking

Bitmap indexes are in general better for read-only activity, due to extreme degradation in structure as a result of DML activity and particularly due to the propensity for a bitmap index to require block-level locks, where BTree indexes utilize row-level locks.

Bitmap Composite Column Indexes

Bitmap indexes can be created on more than a single column at once, but this is ill advised. In fact, the Oracle Database SQL optimizer can utilize multiple single column bitmap indexes to perform a query generally more efficiently than a composite column Bitmap index. Of course, this assumes that there has been no deterioration to the bitmap indexes due to DML activity.

Bitmap Index Overflow

One of the most significant factors to remember about bitmap indexes is that they are not conducive to any type of data change (DML) activity. Any changes made to table rows can, over a long period of time, seriously degrade the performance characteristics of bitmap indexes, not only because of block level locking but also as a result of overflow. Unlike a BTree index, where new key values are simply slotted into the tree structure, assuming spare block space, remaining efficient up to a much greater degree than a bitmap index. The problem with adding new rows to a bitmap index is overflow. Within the structure of a bitmap index the focus is on compression of space usage and, thus, any new additions tend to be placed outside the original structure, typically on a different part of the disk. Therefore, any subsequent I/O, after many new additions, can result in queries having the effect of bouncing all over the disk. Overflow can have a profound effect on overall database performance.

Bitmap Index Restrictions

There are some restrictions with respect to the types of indexing that can be created using bitmaps. These restrictions are not nearly as prohibitive as in previous versions of Oracle Database:

- Bitmap indexes cannot be unique and, thus, cannot be used as primary keys. Bitmap indexing is not intended for uniqueness anyway.

- Multiple column bitmap indexes cannot be compressed as BTree indexes can. Each composite value is indexed as a bitmap individually.

- The latest versions of Oracle Database will allow ONLINE rebuilds of bitmap indexes. Versions of Oracle Database prior to 10*g* release 2 will not allow ONLINE rebuilds, and may also not allow rebuilds on bitmap indexes at all, depending on the version.

- DESC and NOSORT options plus reverse key indexing are irrelevant with respect to bitmap indexes due to the structure of a bitmap index.

One benefit of a bitmap index is that NULL values will be indexed, obviously once. A BTree index on the other hand, where all columns in the index are NULL-valued, resulting in a composite values of NULL, would exclude any of those NULL-valued resulting key values from the BTree index altogether.

Bitmap Join Indexes

A bitmap join index is a bitmap containing ROWID pointers of columns or keys used in the join from the tables joined together. The index is created using a SQL join query statement. A bitmap join index is a bitmap index created for a join between two or more tables, where the result of the joined indexes is stored in a bitmap. Bitmap indexes can help performance, since the bitmap join index effectively prejoins two index values into an index usable by a SQL code join query.

Note: A bitmap join index is an optional method of denormalization without denormalizing tables.

Other Types of Indexing

An index organized table (IOT) builds all of a table's rows and columns into a BTree index. A cluster physically copies column values, usually for a join, prejoining values where that cluster can have a cluster-specific indexes created for it. Clusters and IOTs are covered briefly later in this chapter.

Partitions can have indexes created that are global to a set of partitions for a single table or as individual indexes on each local partition. Partitioning and partition indexes are covered in Chapter 6.

3.2   Star Queries and Star Query Transformations

Star queries and star query transformations are used to transparently change the way queries are executed, typically between a single very large fact table and multiple much smaller dimension tables in a data warehouse.

Note: Star queries were introduced many years ago in Oracle Database 7. Star transformation queries, on the other hand, were introduced in Oracle Database 8 and superseded star queries from Oracle Database 7. In the latest versions of Oracle Database, the two terms both seem to describe an Oracle Database 8 introduced star transformation query.

There are a number of ways to optimize in Oracle Database what are called star queries or star transformation queries:

- The STAR_TRANSFORMATION_ENABLED configuration parameter should be set to TRUE.

- Fact table foreign key pointers to dimensional tables should be created as bitmap indexes.

- Where a table is read by more than 10% it is possible that the optimizer will full-table-scan, regardless of index types or hints used.

- When generating subqueries for dimension tables some could be full-scanned or index-scanned using primary key BTree indexes.

3.2.1   Star Queries

A star query simply joins each dimension to a fact table. The process joins all the dimensions together using Cartesian joins on bitmap indexes. After the Cartesian joins have completed, the resulting joined bitmap indexes are joined to the fact table, after which, nonbitmapped column values are pulled from dimension tables. The following query reads all the rows in the SALE fact table, joining to all four of the included dimensions.

```
SELECT l.city, t.monthname, p.product, i.industry
FROM sale s, location l, time t, product p, industry i
WHERE s.location_id = l.location_id AND s.time_id = t.time_id
AND s.product_id = p.product_id AND s.industry_id =
i.industry_id;
```

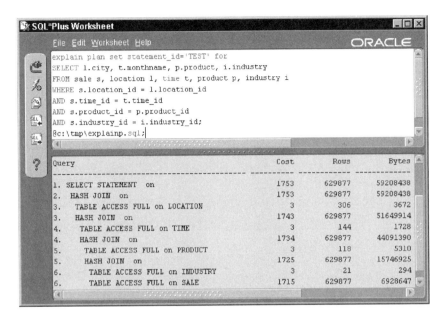

Figure 3.6
A fact-dimensions join using BTree indexes.

Now let's run the query above using the EXPLAIN PLAN command [2]. The query is shown in Figure 3.6.

The query in Figure 3.6 is passed through EXPLAIN PLAN to produce a query plan. There is no star query, star transformation, or bitmap index used in this query. The reasons for this are twofold: (1) all indexes in my star schema are BTree indexes, as shown in Figure 3.7; (2) all the data is retrieved.

Now I will drop some of the dimension table BTree indexes and recreate them as bitmap indexes.

```
DROP INDEX xfx_sale_industry;
DROP INDEX xfx_sale_location;
DROP INDEX xfx_sale_product;
DROP INDEX xfx_sale_time;

CREATE BITMAP INDEX xfx_sale_industry
ON SALE(industry_id) TABLESPACE indx
COMPUTE STATISTICS NOLOGGING;
CREATE BITMAP INDEX xfx_sale_location
ON SALE(location_id) TABLESPACE indx
COMPUTE STATISTICS NOLOGGING;
CREATE BITMAP INDEX xfx_sale_product
```

Figure 3.7

All indexes are BTree indexes.

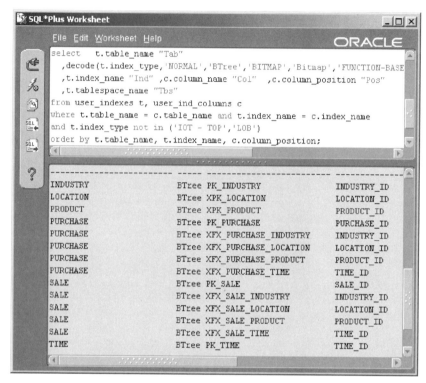

```
ON SALE(product_id) TABLESPACE INDX
COMPUTE STATISTICS NOLOGGING;
CREATE BITMAP INDEX xfx_sale_time
ON SALE(time_id) TABLESPACE indx
COMPUTE STATISTICS NOLOGGING;
```

I also need to disable or drop alternate key unique constraints, plus any other alternate indexes, related or otherwise, that might be used inadvertently.

```
ALTER TABLE industry DROP CONSTRAINT xak_industry_name;
ALTER TABLE location DROP CONSTRAINT xak_region_unique;
ALTER TABLE product DROP CONSTRAINT xak_product_unique;

DROP INDEX xak_industry_name;
DROP INDEX xak_region_unique;
DROP INDEX xak_product_unique;
```

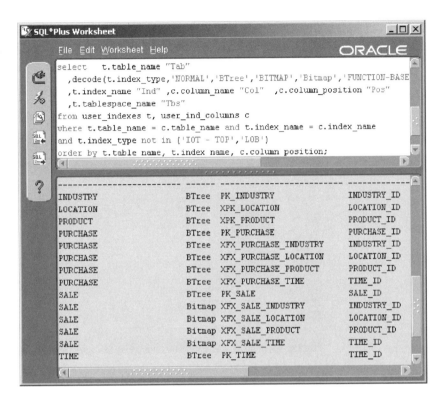

Figure 3.8
*SALE fact table
bitmap indexes.*

As can be seen in Figure 3.8, all the SALE fact table foreign key indexes are now constructed as bitmap indexes.

We should generate statistics:

```
ANALYZE TABLE industry COMPUTE STATISTICS;
ANALYZE TABLE location COMPUTE STATISTICS;
ANALYZE TABLE product COMPUTE STATISTICS;
ANALYZE TABLE time COMPUTE STATISTICS;
ANALYZE TABLE sale COMPUTE STATISTICS;
```

Now I can attempt to run a star query, as shown in Figure 3.9. Note the Cartesian joins between the dimensions and the bitmap conversions and usage.

Note the query cost difference between the queries Figures 3.6 and 3.9. Using the STAR hint to force a star query is definitely not good for performance. Once again, star queries using Cartesian joins on bitmaps were introduced in Oracle Database 7, which is very out-of-date.

Figure 3.9
*SALE fact table
star query using
STAR hint.*

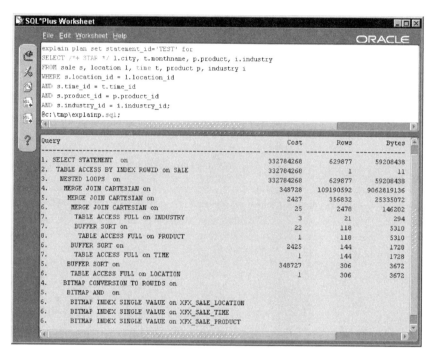

A star query transparently rewrites the SQL code of a query in the following two steps:

1.   Rows are retrieved from the fact table using foreign key bitmap indexes, creating a result set of only the required fact rows.

2.   Resulting fact rows are joined to the dimension table rows of all dimension tables included in the query.

The two steps described above are not as clear cut as they seem. What actually happens is the following (as shown in Figure 3.10):

1.   Dimension tables are Cartesian joined together after filtering has been applied to each dimension.

2.   Fact table bitmap indexes are read based on dimension table requirements. In other words, only bitmap indexes are read for the fact table, not the fact table rows themselves. Additionally, the

rows read from fact table bitmap indexes are dependant on filtering requirements applied to dimension tables.

3. Filtered, dimension Cartesian joined rows are joined to the bitmap resulting row set of the fact table.

4. The final step is reading actual table rows from the fact table using the resulting fact-bitmap to dimension-ROWID join, shown as a nested loop join in Figure 3.10. In Figure 3.10 SALE fact table rows are accessed using the fact table ROWID values found in the previously executed steps.

Figure 3.10

A star query in action.

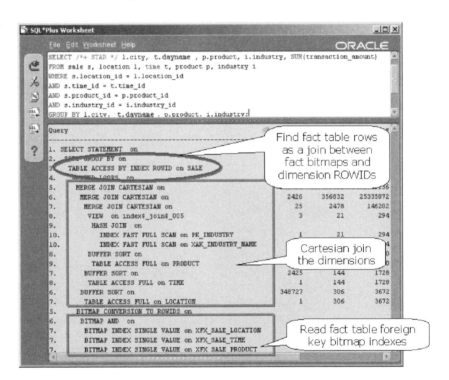

In Figure 3.10 the star transformation query reads and filters each dimension, Cartesian joins all dimensions because dimensions are unrelated to each other, applying results to fact table foreign key bitmap indexes. The star transformation effectively joins all dimensions to fact table indexes before finally retrieving fact table rows.

One more thing with respect to star queries is to compare two queries, both retrieving very small amounts of data, as opposed to the queries in Figures 3.6 and 3.9, which retrieved all possible rows for the join. The query is shown below:

```
SELECT l.city, t.monthname, p.product, i.industry
FROM sale s, location l, time t, product p, industry i
WHERE l.country='Canada' AND l.state='NS'
AND t.year#=2004 AND t.monthname='February'
AND p.category='PDAs' AND i.industry='Aerospace and Defense'
AND s.location_id = l.location_id AND s.time_id = t.time_id
AND s.product_id = p.product_id AND s.industry_id =
i.industry_id;
```

Figure 3.11 shows the nonstar query version. There is no such thing as a NO_STAR hint, not that I can find. The NO_STAR_TRANSFORMATION hint has to be applied and a star transformation query will occur. Remember that a star query is not the same as a star transformation query.

Figure 3.11
A nonstar query with heavy filtering.

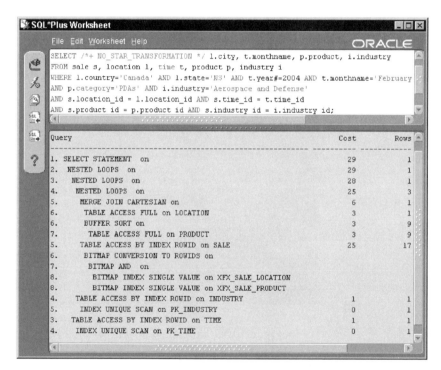

Figure 3.10 shows the star query version of the nonstar query shown in Figure 3.11. Still, the star query is worse.

One small difference between the star queries in Figures 3.9 and 3.12 is, as shown in Figure 3.12, the smaller the amount of data retrieved the fewer

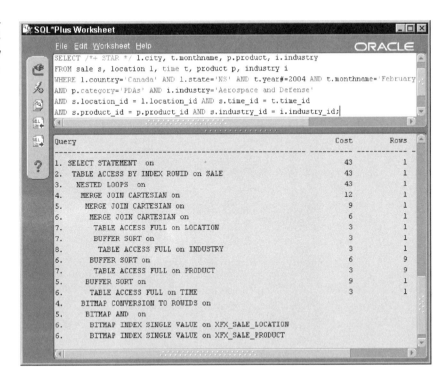

Figure 3.12
A star query with heavy filtering.

Cartesian joins are used. This is because less data is better served without using Cartesian products. A Cartesian product is extremely inefficient.

Next we will examine star transformation queries as opposed to star queries.

3.2.2 Star Transformation Queries

As already stated, star queries were introduced many years ago in Oracle Database 7. Star transformation queries, on the other hand, were introduced in Oracle Database 8 and superseded star queries from Oracle Database 7. In the latest versions of Oracle Database the two terms both seem to describe an Oracle Database 8 introduced star transformation query.

The star transformation query occurs in Figure 3.13 by reading each of the foreign key bitmap indexes on the fact table SALE, with each dimension table. Note how in the star transformation query in Figure 3.13 that the dimension tables are actually full table, scanned twice each.

The cost of the star transformation query is better for performance than all others.

Figure 3.13
*A star
transformation
query.*

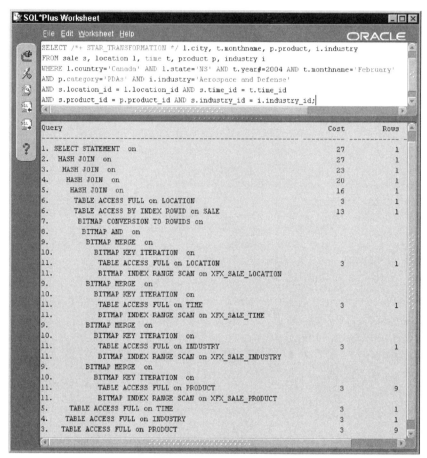

Bitmap Join Indexes

A bitmap join index indexes join results for a join query. The following script creates a bitmap join index on the SALE fact table for all of the foreign key columns, effectively creating a bitmap of the join between the SALE fact table and its four related dimensions:

```
CREATE BITMAP INDEX xbj_sale_1
ON sale(location.location_id,time.time_id
,product.product_id,industry.industry_id)
FROM sale, location, time, product, industry
WHERE sale.location_id = location.location_id
AND sale.time_id = time.time_id
AND sale.product_id = product.product_id
```

```
AND sale.industry_id = industry.industry_id
NOLOGGING COMPUTE STATISTICS TABLESPACE INDX;
```

Where a star transformation query does something like this:

```
SELECT *
FROM sale, location, time, product, industry
WHERE sale.location_id IN (SELECT location_id FROM location)
AND sale.time_id IN (SELECT time_id FROM time)
AND sale.product_id IN (SELECT product_id FROM product)
AND sale.industry_id IN (SELECT industry_id FROM industry);
```

The bitmap join index above will have the effect of changing the previously shown star transformation query with the IN clauses to the following more efficient form:

```
SELECT *
FROM sale, location, time, product, industry
WHERE sale.location_id = location.location_id
AND sale.time_id = time.time_id
AND sale.product_id = product.product_id
AND sale.industry_id = industry.industry_id;
```

Figure 3.14 shows the same query as shown in Figure 3.13, but with the bitmap join index above created.

We could also create four separate bitmap join indexes as four joins between the SALE fact table and each of the four separate dimensions. Bitmap indexes often perform best as single column indexes as opposed to composite column indexes, because there are fewer distinct values to create bitmaps for:

```
DROP INDEX xbj_sale_1;
CREATE BITMAP INDEX xbj_sale_1
ON sale(location.location_id)
FROM sale, location
WHERE sale.location_id = location.location_id
NOLOGGING COMPUTE STATISTICS TABLESPACE indx;

DROP INDEX xbj_sale_2;
```

Figure 3.14
*A star
transformation
query using a
composite bitmap
join index.*

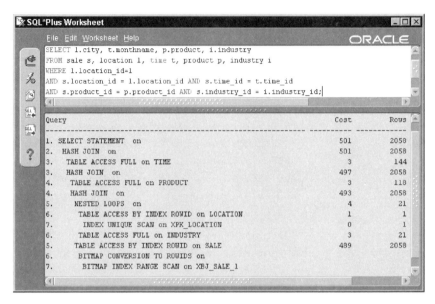

```
CREATE BITMAP INDEX xbj_sale_2
ON sale(time.time_id)
FROM sale, time
WHERE sale.time_id = time.time_id
NOLOGGING COMPUTE STATISTICS TABLESPACE indx;

DROP INDEX xbj_sale_3;
CREATE BITMAP INDEX xbj_sale_3
ON sale(product.product_id)
FROM sale, product
WHERE sale.product_id = product.product_id
NOLOGGING COMPUTE STATISTICS TABLESPACE indx;

DROP INDEX xbj_sale_4;
CREATE BITMAP INDEX xbj_sale_4
ON sale(industry.industry_id)
FROM sale, industry
WHERE sale.industry_id = industry.industry_id
NOLOGGING COMPUTE STATISTICS TABLESPACE indx;
```

Using four single column bitmap indexes for the bitmap join produces
the same result as for Figures 3.13 and 3.14. In Figure 3.15 the single join
index between the SALE fact and LOCATION dimension tables executes
slightly faster than the composite bitmap join index used in Figure 3.14.

Figure 3.15
A star transformation query using multiple single column bitmaps to create a bitmap join index.

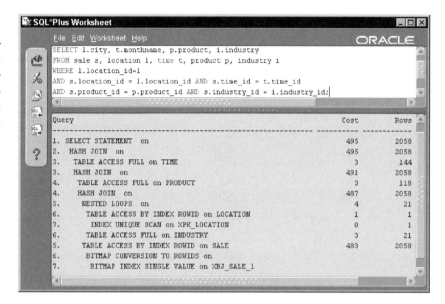

3.2.3 Problems with Star Queries and Star Transformations

The problem is generally not with star queries and star transformations, but more often than not it is related to a misunderstanding of bitmap indexing. When deciding whether to use bitmap indexes or not, there are numerous factors to take into account:

- Converting a BTree index to a bitmap index because a BTree is problematic could quite possibly make your problem worse.

- Bitmap indexes will build faster than BTree indexes since they occupy less physical space. The down side to this is that any type of DML activity will involve access to more index rows for a bitmap than a BTree, since a bitmap is far more compressed.

- One very large factor affecting bitmap index size and, thus, performance and possible optimizer use is data distribution. A bitmap index is likely to be much more effective if like key values are contiguous. In other words, your data is physically ordered in the order required by the bitmap index.

Note: The queries executed in figures shown so far in this chapter show no performance improvement using bitmap indexes and star queries. Data in the generated data warehouse database used for this book is random, and contiguity of data could be an issue for bitmap indexing.

- Bitmap indexes should only be created on individual nonunique columns. Do not create multiple column composite indexes using bitmaps. If multiple columns are required, simply create separate single-column bitmap indexes for each column. The optimizer can then use a WHERE clause in any sequence and still use all of the single column bitmap indexes.

- Overflow and contention have in the past been serious problems with bitmap indexes and can cause catastrophic performance problems over extended periods of time and continuous changes to data. The structure of a bitmap index is fixed and not changeable by data changes. Any additions or alterations could result in overflow. A database overflow is where parts of the same thing are split into separate areas of a storage device such as a disk. This can increase I/O and central processing unit (CPU) costs dramatically.

- When doing any kind of data warehouse batch updates it might be best to drop bitmap indexes before executing the batch, and then regenerating the bitmap indexes afterwards. This is particularly relevant in versions of Oracle Database prior to 10*g*. If data warehouse size and time factors for bitmap index regeneration prohibit this prudent practice, it might be best to avoid bitmap indexing altogether, even in a data warehouse. Benefit must always outweigh cost. The real benefit of multiple single column bitmap indexes is the unpredictability of filtering sequences, so important to BTree indexes in older versions of Oracle Database. Additionally, the advent of new bells and whistles in recent versions of Oracle Database, such as BTree index fast full scans, skip scans, and less reliance on matching WHERE clause sequences with BTree indexes all make bitmap indexes less useful, even multiple single column bitmap indexes.

- Bitmap index cardinality is a relative term and not an absolute. In other words 10,000, distinct dimensional values as compared to 5 billion fact rows is likely to be relatively low cardinality. Similarly, two values of M for male and F for female contains only two distinct values, but if the facts are small in number there is no point in creating a bitmap just because there are only two values.

- Last, but not least, bitmap indexes, bitmap join indexes, star queries, and star transformations were all introduced in previous versions of Oracle Database. It is possible that the optimizer has improved to the point where some of these tricks and techniques are no longer useful.

3.3 Index Organized Tables and Clusters

Are IOTs and clusters used in data warehouses? The answer to that question is yes, but their use is more likely in 3rd normal form data warehouse models than in dimensional-fact models. One of the biggest problems with IOTs and clusters is overflow degradation of performance. Changes to data require occasional rebuilds of IOTs and frequent rebuilds of clusters. Rebuilds are time consuming and can potentially restrict data warehouse database access.

An IOT creates an index of a single table and a cluster physically precreates join column data. Creating an IOT is very simple. It keys off the primary key and looks something like the following:

```
CREATE TABLE SaleIOT (
        sale_id NUMBER NOT NULL
       ,time_id NUMBER NOT NULL
       ,product_id NUMBER NOT NULL
       ,location_id NUMBER NOT NULL
       ,industry_id NUMBER NOT NULL
       ,order_amount NUMBER(10,2)
       ,order_date DATE
       ,transaction_amount NUMBER(10,2)
       ,transaction_date DATE
       ,payment_amount NUMBER(10,2)
       ,payment_date DATE
       ,payment_text VARCHAR2(32)
       ,product_quantity NUMBER
       ,product_price NUMBER(10,2)
       ,product_date DATE
       ,CONSTRAINT pk_sale_IOT PRIMARY KEY (sale_id)
) ORGANIZATION INDEX TABLESPACE data NOLOGGING;
```

It might be sensible to create a cluster for a star join between a fact and multiple dimensional tables, but since clusters are an even more dated option than star queries and star transformations, it is unlikely that clusters are applicable to data warehouses in the latest versions of Oracle Database. However, clusters have been used in data warehouse databases using past versions of Oracle Database because clusters allow for potentially faster read access due to their provision of physically precreated join data spaces.

Note: Materialized views are probably the most up-to-date, powerful, and versatile of options.

Clusters can be created as regular or hash clusters. A hash cluster simply uses a hashing algorithm to split data values into more consistently sized sets. There is also a sorted hash cluster, which builds a hash cluster in a specified order.

In general a cluster is created as an empty definitional container, with a cluster index, as follows:

```
CREATE CLUSTER saleclu(
 sale_id NUMBER
,region VARCHAR2(32)
,industry VARCHAR2(32));
CREATE INDEX xclk_saleclu ON CLUSTER saleclu;
```

Then tables are added to the cluster:

```
CREATE TABLE join_saleclu
CLUSTER saleclu(sale_id, region, industry)
AS SELECT s.sale_id, l.region, i.industry
FROM sale s JOIN location l
ON(l.location_id = s.location_id)
JOIN industry i
ON(i.industry_id = s.industry_id);
```

Not necessarily all columns in all tables are added into a cluster from a join. A cluster is intended to physically group the most frequently accessed data and sorted orders.

Effective indexing in data warehousing is all about choosing the correct type of index, in the form of a BTree or a bitmap index. Choosing which index type to use in a given situation leads to other factors, such as star queries and star transformation. There are other factors to consider in addition to indexing, such as index organized tables and clusters. The next chapter will examine materialized views.

3.4   Endnotes

1.   *Oracle Performance Tuning for 9i and 10g*
      (ISBN: 1555583059)

2.   *Oracle SQL: Jumpstart with Examples* (ISBN: 1555583237)

4

Materialized Views and Query Rewrite

This chapter is divided into three parts covering materialized view syntax, different types of materialized views, and finally tools used for analysis and management of materialized views. We will examine the use of materialized views in data warehouses, identify their benefits to general database performance, and discuss the very basics of query rewrite. Use of materialized views is a tuning method in itself. There are various ways that materialized views can be built, performing differently depending on circumstances and requirements.

4.1 What Is a Materialized View?

A materialized view can be used to create a physical copy of data. The benefit of using the materialized view when reading a database to cater for a query, as opposed to underlying tables,is that it frees up underlying tables for other uses. Materialized views are intended to store the results of aggregated queries. An aggregated query in its most simplistic form is a query containing a GROUP BY clause. The result is that the aggregation part of the query against tables, which is stored physically in the materialized view, does not have to be recomputed when the materialized view is read by a query. The process of reading a materialized view as opposed to underlying tables is handled automatically and transparently by the optimizer, depending on parameter settings, and is called query rewrite.

Note: Materialized views can also be read manually by explicitly specifying a materialized view in a query FROM clause.

Query rewrite transparently *rewrites* a query because the optimizer forces a query to use a materialized view rather than underlying tables when appropriate. This applies at least when the optimizer decides performance is better served by reading a materialized view, namely because the materialized view has already aggregated data.

Note: Query rewrite requires the setting of the QUERY_REWRITE_ENABLED parameter in the configuration parameter file, and the QUERY_REWRITE system privilege.

4.1.1   The Benefits of Materialized Views

Because a materialized view is generally an aggregation, there are a number of benefits to its use:

- Any aggregation processing has already been performed. Aggregation processing can be something as simple as a count or summary. However, aggregation can also be highly complex, requiring intense hardware resources. Materialized views precalculate far less frequently than queries are executed and thus save a lot of processing time by allowing queries to access precalculated values.

- Aggregations generally consist of less data; thus a smaller amount of physical space is occupied. Therefore, less I/O is required. Less I/O means improved performance.

- As a side issue to performance, materialized views can be used as a simple form of master to slave replication.

- Materialized views are automatically refreshed in various different ways, whereas staging tables would require user or administrator intervention.

Note: Materialized views can be used to precalculate aggregations and also to precompute and store joins as an alternative to using clusters. A materialized view can consist of only a join with no aggregation processing at all. However, taking into account the possibility of unfiltered queries on large fact tables, this might not be a prudent option.

Intermediary staging tables could be used to contain precalculated summaries. Materialized views are a better option because they are designed exactly for this purpose and can be accessed by the optimizer transparently, as already mentioned, using query rewrite. Also, they can be set up to refresh from underlying tables automatically. Query rewrite transparently rewrites the code of a query, removing intense aggregation processing from tables to precalculated aggregated rows already stored in a materialized view.

Related Objects

Materialized views can be partitioned, based on partitioned or nonpartitioned underlying tables. Materialized views can also have indexes created against them, allowing for faster access to rows stored in those materialized views.

4.1.2   Potential Pitfalls of Materialized Views

There are a number of potential pitfalls that need to be taken into account:

■ As with indexes, there is always a danger of creating too many materialized views. Not only would large amounts of physical space be used, but also constant refreshing as a result of overzealous utilization of materialized views could kill performance.

■ Materialized views are most commonly accessed transparently, using query rewrite. However, materialized views can be directly accessed and even altered by any SQL code, both application and ad hoc. Either practice should be disallowed, or the content of materialized views should be closely monitored. The real issue is possible future changes to materialized views and escalating to probable application changes as a result. Changing applications is always difficult and usually expensive. Try to retain general materialized view access to transparent query rewrite access only to ensure that materialized views will always be used in the way they have been designed for—to rewrite queries.

■ Probably most importantly materialized views tend to be much more applicable to relatively static data sets. In very large data warehouses it is possible that frequent refreshing on materialized views can cause more problems than are intended to be resolved. It depends wholly on how often refreshing is required and how much is data changed at each refresh. There is no such thing as an incremental refresh, largely due to the nature of aggregation not being dependent on which data in underlying tables is updated. For example, an AVG function applied to an entire fact table requires a recalculation across all the rows, regardless of how many new rows have been added and what the new rows contain. However, in the case of partitioning and calculations within partitions only, the situation might be quite different. Once again, it is all about requirements.

- The sequence by which materialized views are refreshed is highly significant, because a materialized view can be created from another materialized view—an aggregation of an aggregation. If a data warehouse contains a large number of nested materialized views, all built in a hierarchical structure of aggregations, this process could become very complex and difficult to manage.

4.2   Materialized View Syntax

You now have a basic knowledge of materialized views, their benefits, and their potential pitfalls. The next essential step is the boring one and that is to examine syntax. It is essential to have a brief knowledge of syntax elements before jumping into too much detailed example work. At least please read this section lightly before proceeding to the good bits showing example use of materialized views—unless, of course, you already understand all syntactical elements.

In this section there are three primary Data Definition Language (DDL) commands. The first allows you to create a materialized view, the second allows you to change a materialized view, and the third allows you to drop a materialized view. There are three subsidiary DDL commands allowing management of materialized view logs and permitting DML changes to occur.

4.2.1   CREATE MATERIALIZED VIEW

Figure 4.1 shows the syntax for the CREATE MATERIALIZED VIEW statement.

Let's examine some of the different elements of the syntax diagram shown in Figure 4.1, focusing on those relevant to performance tuning.

The REFRESH Clause

The REFRESH clause is comprehensive, so it requires a detailed section of its own. Modifications to tables underlying a materialized view require a refresh to materialized views in order for changes to be reflected in the materialized view.

Figure 4.1
CREATE
MATERIALIZED
VIEW statement
syntax.

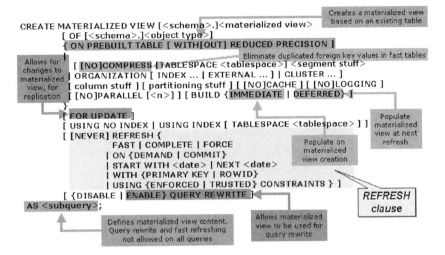

- **NEVER REFRESH**. Creates a static materialized view. Any refresh commands executed against a NEVER REFRESH materialized view will be ignored unless the materialized view is subsequently changed with the ALTER MATERIALIZE VIEW command.

- **REFRESH FAST.** Fast refresh is the best performing type of refresh because it is incremental. An incremental refresh will only refresh what has changed in underlying tables. Fast refresh allows refresh to execute potentially much faster than otherwise. Fast refresh activity is determined by DML changes stored in the associated materialized view log.

Note: See the next section covering the CREATE MATERIALIZED VIEW LOG DDL statement.

There are two possible logs to administer fast refresh incremental changes to materialized views:

1. **Materialized View Log**. Stores DML changes to underlying tables using INSERT, UPDATE, DELETE, and MERGE DML statements. A materialized view log must already exist in order to allow a CREATE MATERIALIZED VIEW statement using the FAST REFRESH option to succeed.

2.   **Direct Loader Log**. Direct path INSERT statements extents such as SQL*Loader direct path loads, append new blocks and to existing tables without slotting new data into usable space in existing blocks. Therefore, direct path loads do not add rows using the SQL engine, as a regular DML INSERT statement would do. As a result, a separate direct loader log is required to implement fast refresh on materialized views. The direct loader log is managed automatically by Oracle Database.

- **REFRESH COMPLETE**. A complete refresh re-executes the entire subquery when the materialized view is refreshed. In other words the materialized view is completely built from scratch whenever it is refreshed, regardless of whether the materialized view allows fast refresh or not.

- **REFRESH FORCE**. This option is the default and forces a fast refresh if possible. Otherwise a complete refresh is performed whenever a refresh occurs.

- **ON DEMAND and ON COMMIT**. ON DEMAND allows refresh by calling of various DBMS_MVIEW refresh procedures. ON DEMAND is the default. ON COMMIT executes a fast refresh whenever a transaction is committed on an underlying table. This approach can be extremely inefficient and somewhat negates the usefulness of materialized views being, semi-static in comparison to transactional tables.

Note: ON COMMIT materialized views can place a strain on high concurrency environments, such as OLTP databases. ON COMMIT is essentially a real-time materialized view refresh.

- **START WITH <date> or NEXT <date>**. These options are obviously completely contrary to ON DEMAND and ON COMMIT, as they execute automatic refresh periodically based on date intervals. START WITH specifies the date and time of the first automated refresh and NEXT the interval between subsequent refresh operations.

- **WITH PRIMARY KEY or WITH ROWID**. WITH PRIMARY KEY is the default and creates a materialized view with a primary key as determined by the primary key constraint on the underlying table. Obviously, this allows some changes to underlying table structure, assuming that primary key constraints are not tampered with. A WITH ROWID materialized view can be restrictive to the point of being more or less useless with respect to refresh, because individual rows cannot be found for refresh. The WITH ROWID option is used when a materialized view does not contain a primary key column from an underlying table.

- **USING ENFORCED CONSTRAINTS or USING TRUSTED CONSTRAINTS**. ENFORCED is the default where all constraints are applied, ensuring that a materialized view is refreshed with referential integrity maintained. The TRUSTED option is likely to perform a little better, as it may not perform as much constraint verification, assuming that constraints are conformed to by data, and it allows use of constraints in a RELY or INVALID state, among other options. When using trusted constraints, a refresh operation might succeed but could result in spurious data contained in a refresh of a materialized view.

ENABLE QUERY REWRITE

The ENABLE QUERY REWRITE clause allows a materialized view to be used for query rewrite. Query rewrite can potentially allow an aggregated row set to replace a detailed row set, increasing query performance. Query rewrite cannot be performed unless all user-defined functions in the materialized view subquery are deterministic and unless all expressions contain repeatable results. For example, SYSDATE is not a repeatable result, because the date is constantly changing. Similarly, a materialized view cannot access NEXTVAL and CURRVAL sequence object pseudocolumns, because they are not guaranteed to always return the same result. However, since a materialized view is based on underlying tables of one form or another, it might be completely silly to access sequence objects from within a materialized view anyway.

What Is Query Rewrite?

Query rewrite is the transparent process used by the optimizer to make an exchange within the processing of a query, changing from reading of one database object for a materialized view. The optimizer typically opts to read data from a materialized view because reading the materialized view will reduce I/O activity, sometimes drastically, therefore increasing query performance. Query rewrite is thus the process of the optimizer rewriting or rebuilding the SQL code text of a query transparently and internally within the database, ultimately speeding up the processing of a query. Query rewrite specifically involves the replacement in a query of a table or even a materialized view with another materialized view.

Verifying Query Rewrite

Not all queries are eligible for query rewrite, and some that you might expect to execute query rewrite on a materialized view might not actually execute query rewrite at all. As a result, we need to have methods of verifying query rewrite.

Note: Query rewrite requires the setting of the QUERY_REWRITE_ ENABLED parameter in the configuration parameter file and the QUERY_REWRITE system privilege. (The QUERY REWRITE privilege is obsolete in Oracle Database 10g.)

There are various methods of verifying the occurrence of query rewrite, such as using the DBMS_MVIEW.EXPLAIN_MVIEW procedure. The DBMS_MVIEW package and other tools will be covered later in this chapter.

Query Rewrite Restrictions

There are restrictions on using query rewrite, such as the obvious one, that only local and not remote database tables apply. Another restriction is that CONNECT BY clauses are not allowed because they link hierarchies. Also, functions can only be applied at the outermost layer, so SUM(<column>) is fine but SUM(SUM(<column>)) will just go nuts. <column> can be found within SUM(<column>) but not within SUM(SUM(<column>)), unless the materialized view stores <column> and SUM(<column>).

Improving Query Rewrite Performance

A constraint such as a primary key in the RELY constraint state assumes that the integrity of newly loaded data is valid with respect to referential integrity. The constraint placed in the RELY state can help to improve query rewrite performance by assuming that data is referentially correct and reducing verification processing.

Related to RELY constraint states is the QUERY_ REWRITE_INTEGRITY configuration parameter, which can be set to ENFORCED, TRUSTED, or STALE_TOLERATED. ENFORCED will guarantee data integrity by adopting the safest path and will not use query rewrite unless a constraint is validated. RELY is not validated, but trusted as validated. TRUSTED assumes data integrity is valid even if it is not. STALE_TOLERATED will allow query rewrite even when Oracle Database is aware that data integrity does not exist, such as when data in a materialized view is inconsistent with underlying data. Chapter 11 contains advanced details of query rewrite.

ON PREBUILT TABLE

This option registers an existing same-name table as a pre-initialized source for a materialized view. WITHOUT REDUCED PRECISION forces the table and materialized view to be matched by columns. The WITH REDUCED PRECISION allows a loss of matched column precision between materialized view and table. The following example creates a prebuilt table for the subsequently created materialized view:

```
CREATE TABLE sales_by_region(
 region VARCHAR2(32)
,amount NUMBER(10,2));

CREATE MATERIALIZED VIEW sales_by_region
    ON PREBUILT TABLE WITH REDUCED PRECISION
    ENABLE QUERY REWRITE
    AS SELECT l.region AS region
, SUM(s.transaction_amount) AS amount
FROM sale s, location l
WHERE s.location_id = l.location_id
GROUP BY l.region;
```

Registering Existing Materialized Views

Older data warehouses may not have been initially built using materialized views. The PREBUILT TABLE option can be used to create a materialized view shell over an already built join or aggregation table, much like a materialized view. Registration of the materialized view with the previously built table is simply a CREATE MATERIALIZED VIEW <materialized view> ON PREBUILT TABLE statement. Registering the materialized view by creating it effectively allows for more up-to-date processing by allowing access to transparent query rewrite, parallel processing, and better refresh methods, such as incremental fast refresh.

Compression

Table compression is important to data warehouses where compression is implemented at the segment level, effectively reducing both disk and memory usage. Segment level in Oracle Database is by definition object level, such as a table—in this case, a materialized view object. Fact tables with lots of dimensions are good candidates for compression. This is because fact tables with lots of foreign keys contain a lot of duplicated foreign key dimensional column values. Compression on tables is very similar to index compression,[1] the physical removal of duplicated values from columns. Obviously, queries are helped by compression, but refresh changes can be slightly adversely affected.

Other Syntax Options

Here are various other materialized view syntax options:

- **CACHE**. Allows placement of a materialized view into the most recently used section of the least recently used (LRU) list in the database buffer cache. This ensures that materialized data is more likely to remain in the buffer cache longer. This allows access of more frequently used objects from RAM.

- **NOLOGGING**. Minimizes logging entries of changes to database objects and their contents. A database with tablespaces and objects set to NOLOGGING is not recoverable.

- **PARALLEL <n>**. Support for parallel operations with a default degree of parallelism, <n>.

- **BUILD IMMEDIATE or BUILD DEFERRED**. By default, a materialized view is populated with data immediately when it is first created. Otherwise, the DEFERRED option allows population at the next refresh, and is unusable until the first complete refresh.

- **USING INDEX**. Allows changing of various storage parameters. This index is internal to the materialized view for fast incremental refresh. If USING NO INDEX, is specified then an index must be specifically created using the CREATE INDEX command only if fast refresh is to be used.

- **TABLESPACE**. It might be useful to create materialized views in a tablespace separate to that of tables, but since query rewrite will read materialized views as opposed to underlying tables, there is not necessarily a chance of conflicting I/O requirements.

4.2.2   CREATE MATERIALIZED VIEW LOG

A materialized view log object is required to allow for incremental fast refresh on materialized views undergoing DML statement changes. Log entries must be referenced by something between underlying tables, materialized view and materialized view log. The WITH clause is used to define the reference.

Note: Fast refresh for a materialized join view obviously requires a materialized view log for all underlying tables. Changes for fast refresh are stored in materialized view logs in much the same way that they are stored in redo logs, allowing for future rebuilding of a materialized view similar to log entry recovery of datafiles.

Figure 4.2
CREATE MATERIALIZED VIEW LOG statement syntax.

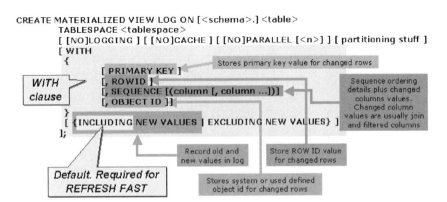

Let's briefly examine a small number of the elements of the syntax diagram shown in Figure 4.2.

The WITH Clause

The WITH clause allows you to specify what is stored in a materialized view log when rows are subjected to DML changes. The following example creates a materialized view of the SALE fact table:

```
CREATE MATERIALIZED VIEW sales_by_country
ENABLE QUERY REWRITE
AS SELECT l.region AS region, l.country AS country
, SUM(transaction_amount) AS amount
FROM sale s, location l
WHERE s.location_id = l.location_id
GROUP BY l.region, l.country;
```

Now we can create a materialized view log storing anything that can change in the underlying SALE fact table, which will affect the materialized view:

```
DROP MATERIALIZED VIEW LOG ON sale;
CREATE MATERIALIZED VIEW LOG ON sale
    WITH PRIMARY KEY, ROWID
, SEQUENCE(location_id, transaction_amount)
INCLUDING NEW VALUES;
```

The materialized view created above is actually a join between the SALE fact table and the LOCATION dimension table. We could create a materialized view log to simply cover the join using the join column as shown below. We would have to drop the existing materialized view log first:

```
DROP MATERIALIZED VIEW LOG ON sale;
CREATE MATERIALIZED VIEW LOG ON sale WITH(location_id);
```

The SEQUENCE Clause

The Oracle Corporation recommends that the SEQUENCE keyword be used in order to add sequencing information to the logs, for individual columns in materialized views. This is important to fast refresh when underlying tables are subject to DML activity using all of INSERT, UPDATE, and DELETE statements.

4.2.3 ALTER MATERIALIZED VIEW [LOG]

Syntax for the ALTER MATERIALIZED VIEW and ALTER MATERIALIZED VIEW LOG statements is shown in Figure 4.3. Most of the syntax is similar to the CREATE MATERIALIZED VIEW statements, apart from annotated items.

4.2.4 DROP MATERIALIZED VIEW [LOG]

Syntax for the DROP MATERIALIZED VIEW and DROP MATERIALIZED VIEW LOG statements is shown in Figure 4.4.

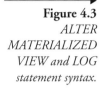

Figure 4.3
ALTER
MATERIALIZED
VIEW and LOG
statement syntax.

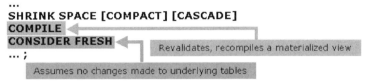

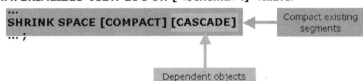

Figure 4.4
DROP
MATERIALIZED
VIEW and LOG
statement syntax.

4.3   Types of Materialized Views

The types of materialized views that can be created are essentially based on a SQL code query. How many different variations of queries can be created? Lots! Generally, materialized views are of the following basic formats:

- Aggregates or filtering, or both aggregation and filtering

- Joins

- Set operator queries using operators such as UNION or INTERSECT

- Nesting where one materialized view contains another materialized view

- Any combination of the above

4.3.1   Single Table Aggregations and Filtering Materialized Views

This is a single table materialized view built using a query containing filtering or aggregation, or both. There is no point in creating a materialized view that excludes both aggregation and filtering, as it would simply mirror the underlying table.

Using a filtered query:

```
CREATE MATERIALIZED VIEW mv_sale1 AS
SELECT * FROM sale
WHERE sale_id < 100000;
```

Note: It is usually sensible to name materialized views with some prefix, such as MV_ or otherwise, that indicates as such.

Using an aggregated query:

```
CREATE MATERIALIZED VIEW mv_sale2 AS
SELECT location_id, COUNT(location_id)
FROM sale
GROUP BY location_id;
```

Using a filtered and aggregated query:

```
CREATE MATERIALIZED VIEW mv_sale3 AS
SELECT location_id, COUNT(location_id)
FROM sale
WHERE sale_id < 100000 GROUP BY location_id;
```

Another form of filtering utilizes the HAVING clause, which applies filtering to aggregated rows. The WHERE clause filters rows as they are retrieved from the table:

```
CREATE MATERIALIZED VIEW mv_sale4 AS
SELECT location_id, COUNT(location_id)
FROM sale GROUP BY location_id
HAVING COUNT(location_id) > 10;
```

Note: A user requires the CREATE MATERIALIZED VIEW privilege to allow creation of materialized views.

Figure 4.5
*Querying the
USER_MVIEWS
metadata view.*

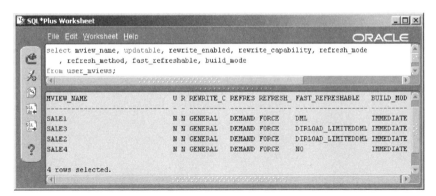

In Figure 4.5, the only materialized view truly capable of fast refresh is the first one. The first materialized view SALE1 has a filter and no aggregation. Fast refresh is sometimes difficult to achieve.

Fast Refresh Requirements for Aggregations

Aggregated materialized views place some restrictions on fast refresh:

- All columns in the GROUP BY clause must be retrieved in the SELECT list.

- All aggregated columns must have both COUNT(*) and COUNT(<column>) on the said column name.

   Let's change the materialized view SALE2 to accommodate all DML with fast refresh:

```
DROP MATERIALIZED VIEW mv_sale2;
CREATE MATERIALIZED VIEW mv_sale2 AS
SELECT location_id, COUNT(location_id), COUNT(*)
FROM sale
GROUP BY location_id;
```

   The same issue applies to materialized view SALE3 created above where COUNT(*) is added.

- All tables in a query must have materialized view logs such that the materialized view logs contain all table columns and are built as in the following example:

```
DROP MATERIALIZED VIEW LOG ON sale;
CREATE MATERIALIZED VIEW LOG ON sale
     WITH ROWID, SEQUENCE(location_id)
INCLUDING NEW VALUES;
```

- Permissible aggregation functions are COUNT, SUM, AVG, VARI-ANCE, STDDEV, MIN, and MAX. No analytical functions are allowed, due to the complexity of on-the-fly calculations with fast refresh.

- Each aggregation, such as SUM(<column>), requires COUNT(<column>) as well. STDDEV and VARIANCE require both COUNT and SUM, due to the nature of standard deviation and variance functions.

4.3.2　Join Materialized Views

Materialized views can contain joins as well as filtering and aggregation. Commonly materialized views are used to store aggregated query results, but they can be used to store joins where no aggregation is involved. A materialized view effectively utilizes all the attributes of table storage in Oracle Database, including indexing, without the potential problems occurring with objects, such as clusters, and overflow. Clusters have been used in the past to store precalculated joins. Additionally, a cluster cannot be automatically updated as a materialized view can.

The benefit of creating a nonaggregated join materialized view is a pre-calculated join. In a data warehouse this can be a significant time-saving factor, and it might even be sensible to create a nonaggregated join-only materialized view as an ON COMMIT materialized view, where any changes made to underlying tables are made to the materialized view within the same transaction. Let's experiment with this by creating a join for all dimensions with the SALE fact table. All the tables in the materialized view join must have materialized view logs containing ROWIDs:

```
CREATE MATERIALIZED VIEW LOG ON location WITH ROWID;
CREATE MATERIALIZED VIEW LOG ON time WITH ROWID;
CREATE MATERIALIZED VIEW LOG ON product WITH ROWID;
CREATE MATERIALIZED VIEW LOG ON industry WITH ROWID;
DROP MATERIALIZED VIEW LOG ON sale;
CREATE MATERIALIZED VIEW LOG ON sale WITH ROWID;
```

Now create the materialized view with both FAST REFRESH and ON COMMIT to allow reflection of changes at the same time that changes are made to underlying fact and dimension tables. All ROWID values from all tables must be retrieved, and it is best to create explicit indexes on both fact and dimension table ROWID columns in the materialized view.

```
CREATE MATERIALIZED VIEW mv_sale
PARALLEL NOLOGGING BUILD IMMEDIATE
REFRESH FAST ON COMMIT
ENABLE QUERY REWRITE
AS SELECT s.ROWID "sROWID"
, l.ROWID "lROWID", t.ROWID "tROWID"
, p.ROWID "pROWID", i.ROWID "iROWID"
, s.order_amount,s.order_date
, s.transaction_amount,s.transaction_date
, s.payment_amount,s.payment_date,s.payment_text
, s.product_quantity,s.product_price,s.product_date
, l.region,l.country,l.state,l.city
, t.month#,t.monabbrev,t.monthname,t.quarter#,t.year#
, p.category, p.product, p.price
, i.industry
FROM sale s, location l, time t, product p, industry i
WHERE s.location_id = l.location_id
AND s.time_id = t.time_id
AND s.product_id = p.product_id
AND s.industry_id = i.industry_id;


CREATE UNIQUE INDEX mv_sale_1 ON mv_sale("sROWID")
TABLESPACE indx COMPUTE STATISTICS NOLOGGING;
CREATE INDEX mv_sale_2 ON mv_sale("lROWID")
TABLESPACE indx COMPUTE STATISTICS NOLOGGING;
CREATE INDEX mv_sale_3 ON mv_sale("tROWID")
TABLESPACE indx COMPUTE STATISTICS NOLOGGING;
CREATE INDEX mv_sale_4 ON mv_sale("pROWID")
TABLESPACE indx COMPUTE STATISTICS NOLOGGING;
CREATE INDEX mv_sale_5 ON mv_sale("iROWID")
TABLESPACE indx COMPUTE STATISTICS NOLOGGING;
```

One of the biggest performance issues with data warehouses is that of joins across facts and dimensions where fact tables have truly enormous amounts of data. The materialized view created above could turn out to be a little bit of a problem, perhaps taking an acceptable time to update but an unacceptable amount of time and resources to create initially. In the next example, the materialized view is only altered if the SALE fact table is altered. It seems sensible, since dimensional data is static in nature, that it is unlikely to be updated. Additionally, using the REFRESH FORCE option will make the materialized view fast refresh for changes to the fact table and not the dimensions—a perfectly sensible and perhaps more attainable scenario. However, dimensional changes will cause a complete refresh to occur, and that is a possibility that one might want to avoid with respect to performance.

```
DROP MATERIALIZED VIEW LOG ON location;
DROP MATERIALIZED VIEW LOG ON time;
DROP MATERIALIZED VIEW LOG ON product;
DROP MATERIALIZED VIEW LOG ON industry;

DROP MATERIALIZED VIEW mv_sale;
CREATE MATERIALIZED VIEW mv_sale
PARALLEL NOLOGGING BUILD IMMEDIATE
REFRESH FORCE
ENABLE QUERY REWRITE
AS SELECT s.ROWID "sROWID"
, s.order_amount,s.order_date
, s.transaction_amount,s.transaction_date
, s.payment_amount,s.payment_date,s.payment_text
, s.product_quantity,s.product_price,s.product_date
, l.region,l.country,l.state,l.city
, t.month#,t.monabbrev,t.monthname,t.quarter#,t.year#
, p.category, p.product, p.price
, i.industry
FROM sale s, location l, time t, product p, industry i
WHERE s.location_id = l.location_id
AND s.time_id = t.time_id
AND s.product_id = p.product_id
AND s.industry_id = i.industry_id;

CREATE UNIQUE INDEX mv_sale_1 ON mv_sale("sROWID")
TABLESPACE INDX COMPUTE STATISTICS NOLOGGING;
```

Essentially, using materialized views to pre-create join queries on facts and dimensions in data warehouses is a trade-off between initial creation performance and the capacity for refresh, in terms of refresh requirements—how often and how much? Initial materialized view creation may depend on available resources and the size of the data warehouse at the time of materialized view creation. An extreme scenario could involve, for example, a spare computer for building a materialized view that could perhaps be plugged back into the main data warehouse as a transportable tablespace at a later date.

Fast Refresh Requirements for Joins

There are restrictions, of which most are sensible or already listed for other types of materialized views. There is one point to note, which I should stress as being a matter of personal opinion or preference—in other words, other database administrators (DBAs) might not agree with me on this one. Outer joins can be included in materialized view joins. However, when using a star schema, the occurrence of outer joins could possibly indicate an entity structural problem. In a star schema it makes sense that the only potential for outer joins is NULL-valued foreign key dimensions in the fact table. If that is the case, then outer joins are unavoidable. Then again, do you really want NULL-valued foreign key columns in enormous fact tables?

Joins and Aggregations

The most sensible use of a materialized view is in a data warehouse, and in a situation where I/O is reduced by reading aggregated data. The additional factor of reading information from a preconstructed join as a materialized view can help to reduce SQL code performance in join execution but not necessarily I/O activity. Therefore, materialized views should never be created from the perspective of what can be speeded up but from what end users most commonly require in terms of reporting performance. It might be adequate at this stage of the book to state that construction of materialized views is not a data model design issue, but more likely a reaction to general SQL code use in a production environment. Therefore, this chapter will not go too deeply into the creation and maintenance of example materialized views; that will wait for later chapters covering various aspects of SQL code aggregation and analysis in data warehouse databases. It may even be found in later chapters that specific types of newly introduced SQL code bells and whistles might be in the process of making materialized views partially redundant.

4.3.3   **Set Operator Materialized Views**

Materialized views can even be used to pre-create physical structures for unions between tables, such as the following example:

```
DROP MATERIALIZED VIEW LOG ON sale;
CREATE MATERIALIZED VIEW LOG ON sale WITH ROWID;
CREATE MATERIALIZED VIEW LOG ON purchase WITH ROWID;

CREATE MATERIALIZED VIEW mv_transactions
PARALLEL NOLOGGING BUILD IMMEDIATE
REFRESH FAST ON COMMIT
ENABLE QUERY REWRITE
AS (
SELECT s.ROWID "sROWID", s.transaction_amount "Amount"
, 1 marker FROM sale s
UNION ALL
      SELECT p.ROWID "pROWID", p.transaction_amount "Amount"
,  2 marker FROM purchase p
);
```

Fast refresh is only supported for UNION ALL when there is a distinct UNION ALL column marker to enable unique identification of each block of rows on either side of the set operator.

Note that the cost and execution time produced by the above query could be catastrophic to database performance in general. Perhaps use of the MINUS and INTERSECT operators would be more performance friendly, but these are unlikely to be useful in a star or snowflake schema data model unless set operations were required between separate fact tables– a highly unlikely scenario in a properly designed fact-dimensional entity structured data warehouse data model. In other words, using UNION ALL to merge fact tables together may indicate that perhaps those separate fact tables should be a single table in the first place. Perhaps a better use would be to extract multiple separate row sets from a single fact table, which may create data mart materialized view row sets. In this case, perhaps simple filtering would suffice anyway.

4.3.4   **Nested Materialized Views**

Materialized views can be nested such that one materialized view can access another materialized view or views and other objects, apart from itself, of course. When examining why nested materialized views make sense, it also leads us to understand that the use of join and single table aggregation materialized views are not simply complete folly. Quite often in a data warehouse with multiple dimensions, and even multiple layers within each dimension, there are a multitude of requirements for aggregation across all the different dimensions and all the layers within those dimensions. What nesting of materialized views can help to do is to effectively pass the I/O read access processing on up through a chain of successively aggregated materialized views, allowing for less and less I/O activity to occur as the aggregation level required becomes more and more aggregated.

The down side to this approach is obviously a layered refresh capacity on materialized views that can lead to complex refresh requirements, and an overload of materialized views, perhaps leading to a situation where there is simply too much to update at once. The other question is, when the optimizer is overwhelmed with choices will it make the most appropriate choice? Yet another issue is storage space. Even though disk space is now relatively cheap, data warehouses can get big enough for overzealous use of materialized views to easily exceed reasonable capacity.

Perhaps one the most effective tricks of materialized view nesting is to create a single join materialized view between a single fact table and its related dimensions (a single star schema) and create single table aggregation materialized views on the join materialized view. This type of approach is perfect for a star schema, allowing the join materialized view to be processed independently of its dependent single table materialized views, thus not requiring the overhead of join queries in aggregations. Effectively, the separate join and single table aggregation materialized views can be tuned individually, allowing for both rapid read access and refresh tuning possibilities due to their separation.

The first step is to use the first version of the SALE fact table join view we created. Since that particular join view has been replaced, it has to be rebuilt, along with the dimension table logs, which were also dropped:

```
CREATE MATERIALIZED VIEW LOG ON location WITH ROWID;
CREATE MATERIALIZED VIEW LOG ON time WITH ROWID;
CREATE MATERIALIZED VIEW LOG ON product WITH ROWID;
CREATE MATERIALIZED VIEW LOG ON industry WITH ROWID;

DROP MATERIALIZED VIEW mv_sale;
CREATE MATERIALIZED VIEW mv_sale
PARALLEL NOLOGGING BUILD IMMEDIATE
```

```
REFRESH FAST ON COMMIT
ENABLE QUERY REWRITE
AS SELECT s.ROWID "sROWID"
, l.ROWID "lROWID", t.ROWID "tROWID"
, p.ROWID "pROWID", i.ROWID "iROWID"
, s.order_amount,s.order_date
, s.transaction_amount,s.transaction_date
, s.payment_amount,s.payment_date,s.payment_text
, s.product_quantity,s.product_price,s.product_date
, l.region,l.country,l.state,l.city
, t.month#,t.monabbrev,t.monthname,t.quarter#,t.year#
, p.category, p.product, p.price
, i.industry
FROM sale s, location l, time t, product p, industry i
WHERE s.location_id = l.location_id
AND s.time_id = t.time_id
AND s.product_id = p.product_id
AND s.industry_id = i.industry_id;

CREATE UNIQUE INDEX mv_sale_1 ON mv_sale("sROWID")
TABLESPACE INDX COMPUTE STATISTICS NOLOGGING;
CREATE INDEX mv_sale_2 ON mv_sale("lROWID")
TABLESPACE INDX COMPUTE STATISTICS NOLOGGING;
CREATE INDEX mv_sale_3 ON mv_sale("tROWID")
TABLESPACE INDX COMPUTE STATISTICS NOLOGGING;
CREATE INDEX mv_sale_4 ON mv_sale("pROWID")
TABLESPACE INDX COMPUTE STATISTICS NOLOGGING;
CREATE INDEX mv_sale_5 ON mv_sale("iROWID")
TABLESPACE INDX COMPUTE STATISTICS NOLOGGING;
```

The above scripting gives us a fast refresh on commit materialized view. This structure allows filtering into the materialized view of any changes in the SALE fact table or any of the four related dimension tables.

The second step is to create a materialized view log of the materialized view join as if it were a table. Additionally, any columns to be included in the single table aggregation materialized view must be stored in the materialized view log for the aggregation materialized view, plus the old and new values must be recorded in the log, for the purposes of correct updating in the aggregated materialized view in the event of changes to underlying tables being passed through the join materialized view.

```
CREATE MATERIALIZED VIEW LOG ON mv_sale
WITH ROWID(region, year#, quarter#, product, price
, transaction_amount) INCLUDING NEW VALUES;
```

And now we could create a single table aggregation as follows:

```
CREATE MATERIALIZED VIEW mv_income_by_region
PARALLEL NOLOGGING BUILD IMMEDIATE
REFRESH FAST ON COMMIT
ENABLE QUERY REWRITE
    AS SELECT region, year#, quarter#, product
,COUNT(transaction_amount − price),COUNT(*)
,SUM(transaction_amount − price)
    FROM mv_sale
    GROUP BY region, year#, quarter#, product;
```

At this stage, the obvious point to make is that further materialized views can be created, such as the following:

```
CREATE MATERIALIZED VIEW mv_revenue_by_region
PARALLEL NOLOGGING BUILD IMMEDIATE
REFRESH FAST ON COMMIT
ENABLE QUERY REWRITE
AS SELECT region, year#, quarter#, product
,COUNT(transaction_amount),COUNT(*)
,SUM(transaction_amount)
FROM mv_sale
GROUP BY region, year#, quarter#, product;
```

Any requirements not fitting in with existing materialized view logs obviously would require creation of additional materialized view logs if the most up-to-date capabilities of fast refresh are to be maintained throughout a data warehouse.

Note: Don't forget that overuse of materialized views can lead to heavy refresh load on resources and, perhaps, an oversized and even very large and scary database.

4.3.5 **Materialized View ORDER BY Clauses**

A materialized view creation query can contain an ORDER BY clause. The ORDER BY clause will help to physically sequence data. However, materialized views are maintained by underlying tables, and underlying tables are not necessarily sorted in the sequence of the ORDER BY clause. Also, the materialized view ORDER BY clause sort order is not used during refresh. It should suffice to state that if the materialized view initial creation ORDER BY clause matches sorting requirements when queries execute query rewrite operations through the materialized view, that ORDER BY sorting will certainly help query performance, especially in a situation where sorting actually performs clustering of duplicated values, such as for dimension foreign key column values in fact tables.

4.4   **Analyzing and Managing Materialized Views**

There are a number of methods of analyzing and managing materialized views:

- Syntax management using DDL commands for materialized view and materialized view logs; relevant DDL commands are already covered in this chapter

- Metadata views

- DBMS_MVIEW package, allowing access to details and features of materialized views and materialized view logs

- DBMS_ADVISOR.TUNE_MVIEW procedure, returning tuning advice on changes advantageous to fast refresh and query rewrite

4.4.1 **Metadata Views**

The most obvious method of analyzing materialized views is by accessing metadata and performance views, as shown in Figure 4.6. Note that there are no V$ performance views returned for materialized views. Tuning of materialized views is performed using various DBMS packages, which we will get to shortly. However, the objective of materialized view creation is generally for the purposes of better query performance through query rewrite. Query rewrite is a more advanced topic and requires coverage of all aspects of data warehouse SQL code first, covered in all chapters after this chapter. Query rewrite itself is detailed further in Chapter 11.

Figure 4.6
Materialized view metadata and performance views.

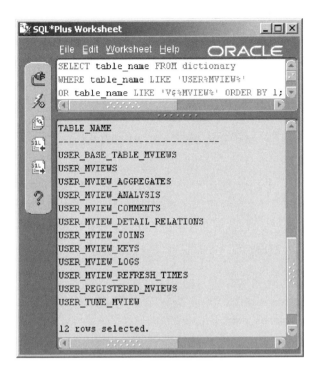

Let's examine the metadata views shown in Figure 4.6 one by one, elucidating where detail is necessary:

- **USER_MVIEWS**. Shows syntax details of materialized views. A sample is shown in Figure 4.5.

- **USER_MVIEW_LOGS**. Simple syntax details of materialized view logs used to record DML activity for later refresh application.

- **USER_BASE_TABLE_MVIEWS**. This view contains a listing of materialized views that contain materialized view logs.

- **USER_REGISTERED_MVIEWS**. A registered materialized view is a view registered as eligible to be accessed for query rewrite, either as a created materialized view or on an existing table (PREBUILT).

- **USER_MVIEW_REFRESH_TIMES**. When materialized views were last refreshed.

- **USER_MVIEW_KEYS**. Content and sequence of elements in the SELECT list of materialized view queries.

- **USER_MVIEW_AGGREGATES.** Content and sequence of GROUP BY clauses for materialized view queries.

- **USER_MVIEW_JOINS**. WHERE clause join details for materialized view join queries.

- **USER_MVIEW_ANALYSIS**. Detailed information with respect to the ability of a materialized view for query rewrite potential.

- **USER_MVIEW_DETAIL_RELATIONS**. FROM clause list details for materialized view queries.

- **USER_TUNE_MVIEW.** Contains results of the DBMS_ADVISOR.TUNE_MVIEW procedure. See later section in this chapter.

4.4.2   The DBMS_MVIEW Package

The DBMS_VIEW package is purpose-built for materialized views, allowing access to details on capabilities, rewrite potential, manual refresh, and materialized view log purging.

Verifying Materialized Views

The procedures DBMS_VIEW.BEGIN_TABLE_REORGANIZATION and DBMS_VIEW.END_TABLE_REORGANIZATION are shown in Figure 4.7. In Figure 4.7, the only error returned indicates that the SALES_BY_REGION materialized view contains no materialized view log, which, of course, it is not supposed to.

Figure 4.7
The
DBMS_MVIEW.
TABLE_REORG-
ANIZATION
procedures.

Estimating Materialized View Storage Space

If a materialized view is created not based on a prebuilt table then it will occupy physical space on disk. A DBMS_MVIEW package procedure called ESTIMATE_MVIEW_SIZE can be used to accurately estimate

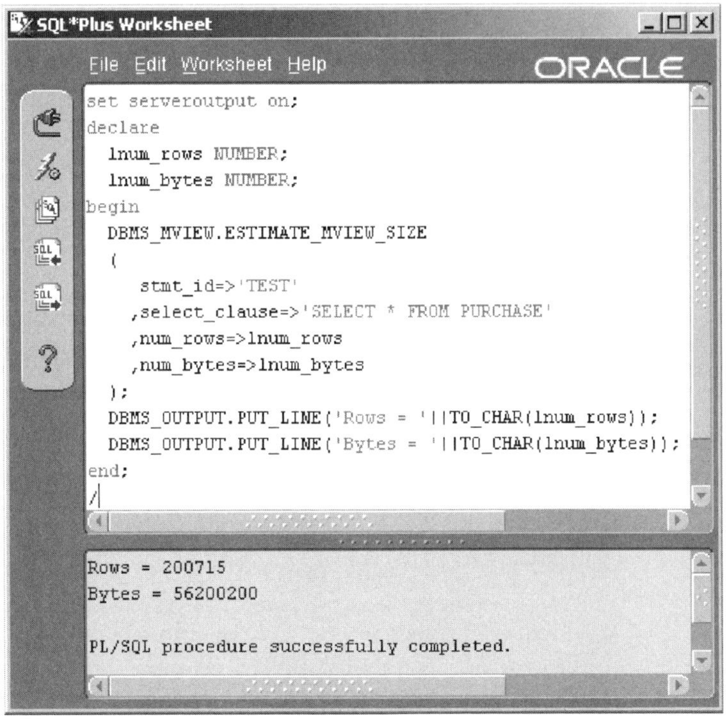

Figure 4.8
The DBMS_VIEW. ESTIMATE_ MVIEW_SIZE procedure.

physical uncompressed space, an example execution of which is shown in Figure 4.8.

Explaining a Materialized View

The EXPLAIN_MVIEW procedure can be used to examine the potential of a materialized view, the output of which can be sent to a table called MV_CAPABILITIES_TABLE object.

Note: The MV_CAPABILITIES_TABLE table can be created using the utlxmv.sql script.

Figure 4.9
The
DBMS_VIEW.
*EXPLAIN_*
MVIEW
procedure.

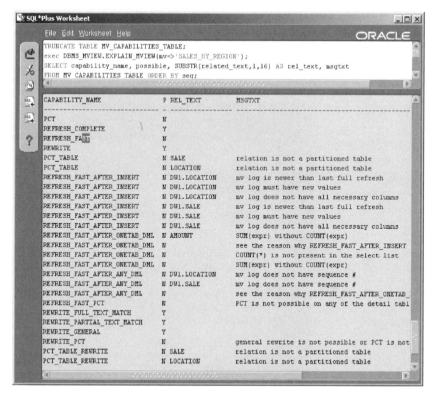

Figure 4.9 shows an example execution of the EXPLAIN_MVIEW procedure on an existing materialized view, including subsequent output from the MV_CAPABILITIES_TABLE.

Explaining Query Rewrite

The EXPLAIN_REWRITE procedure can be used to help explain details of optimizer materialized view choice, or the lack thereof, when rewriting a query, or if query rewrite failed altogether. Output from the EXPLAIN_REWRITE procedure can be sent to a table called REWRITE_TABLE.

Note: The REWRITE_TABLE table can be created using the utlxrw.sql script.

Figure 4.10 shows an example execution of the EXPLAIN_REWRITE procedure on an existing materialized view, including subsequent output

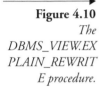

Figure 4.10
*The
DBMS_VIEW.EX
PLAIN_REWRIT
E procedure.*

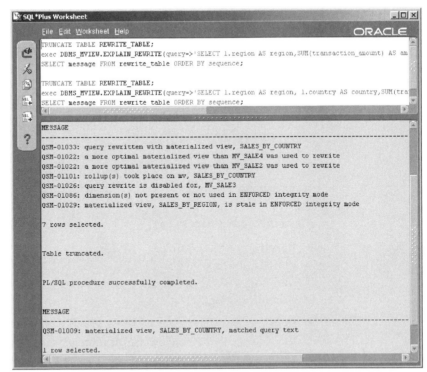

from the REWRITE_TABLE object. The queries are examined; both have
materialized views created for them.

Manual Refresh

There are three DBMS_MVIEW procedures used to manually refresh one
or more materialized views:

- **REFRESH**. Refreshes one or more specified materialized views, as in
  the following example where **c** indicates a complete refresh and **f** a
  fast refresh:

  ```
  exec DBMS_MVIEW.REFRESH
  (list=>'SALES_BY_COUNTRY,SALES_BY_REGION',method=>'cf');
  ```

- **REFRESH_DEPENDENT**. Refreshes dependent materialized views.

- **REFRESH_ALL_MVIEWS**. Attempts to refresh all materialized
  views in a schema where refresh is required. This one is, of course, self-

explanatory and could take a very, very, very long time to complete. So be sure you want to run something like this before you do so.

> **Note:** Both REFRESH and REFRESH_DEPENDENT have a NESTED flag that, if set to TRUE, will refresh all dependent objects from the bottom of the hierarchy upwards. One would expect this, of course. If refreshing manually, remember to start at materialized views generated from tables; otherwise you could get a real mess.
>
> The NESTED flag is a new addition to Oracle Database 10g.

Miscellaneous Procedures

- **Purging Materialized View Logs**. The procedures PURGE_DIRECT_LOAD_LOG, PURGE_LOG and PURGE_MVIEW_FROM_LOG can be used to purge various types of materialized view logs.

- **Registration**. The REGISTER_MVIEW and UNREGISTER_MVIEW procedures allow registration management of materialized views.

4.4.3　The DBMS_ADVISOR Package

The DBMS_ADVISOR package has numerous procedures used to make tuning strategies as part of a set of expert tools in Oracle Database.

> **Note:** As an experienced database administrator, I would recommend testing any advisory results. Additionally, any automated features should absolutely be tested on a test platform before being thrown into a production environment.

The DBMS_ADVISOR.TUNE_MVIEW procedure is stated in the manual to be capable of showing a potential materialized decomposition, which should allow for better fast refresh and query rewrite performance. When executing the TUNE_MVIEW procedure, results are sent to the USER_TUNE_MVIEW view. Scripts to get results look something like this:

```
DECLARE
    mvname VARCHAR2(30) := 'SALES_BY_CITY';
```

```
BEGIN
    DBMS_ADVISOR.TUNE_MVIEW(mvname, 'CREATE MATERIALIZED
VIEW sales_by_city ENABLE QUERY REWRITE AS SELECT l.region AS
region,l.country AS country,l.city AS
city,SUM(transaction_amount) AS amount FROM sale s, location
l WHERE s.location_id = l.location_id GROUP BY
l.region,l.country,l.city');
END;
/
SELECT * FROM USER_TUNE_MVIEW;
```

Note: The ADVISOR system privilege is required to access the DBMS_ADVISOR package.

Details have not been provided in this situation, because in the past I have had lackluster results from Oracle Database expert tuning advisory tools. They are primitive at best, and dangerous at worst. In my experience, memory advisors in Oracle Database 9*i* give advice that is perhaps dated, sparse, and generally useless, and I often do not agree with it. These tools will obviously get better in current and future versions of Oracle Database. I simply do not recommend blind faith in anything new. Test everything first!

4.5   Making Materialized Views Faster

Materialized view performance gains boil down to a number of things:

- Can you use query rewrite? If so, definitely do so.

- Fast refresh and concurrent commit requirements will hurt performance. Do not create materialized view logs unless they are actually needed by fast incremental refresh.

- Can refresh wait, or can it be removed altogether? The best query performance of query rewrite against materialized views comes when minimizing the updateable aspects of materialized views. Set NEVER REFRESH for static materialized views and USING NO INDEX for materialized views not requiring fast refresh.

- Do not forget to use the NOLOGGING, COMPRESS, PARALLEL, and TABLESPACE <tablespace> options, where appropriate.

In this chapter so far we have created a number of materialized views, one of which is called MV_SALE, a materialized view join between all dimension tables and the SALE fact table. In its most recently created form, the MV_SALE materialized view caters for fast refresh on the SALE fact table only. Additionally, I will create another materialized view to aggregate revenues by month, based on the MV_SALE join materialized view:

```
CREATE MATERIALIZED VIEW mv_revenue_by_month
PARALLEL NOLOGGING BUILD IMMEDIATE
REFRESH FORCE
ENABLE QUERY REWRITE
    AS SELECT year#, quarter#, month#
,COUNT(transaction_amount),COUNT(*)
,SUM(transaction_amount)
    FROM mv_sale
    GROUP BY year#, quarter#, month#;
```

Figure 4.11 shows a cost of 2 with a byte count read of 3432 bytes.

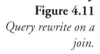

Figure 4.11
Query rewrite on a join.

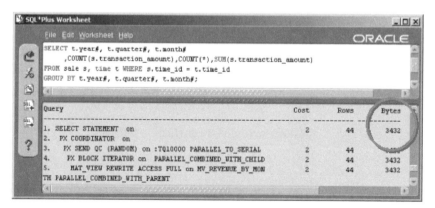

Now let's attempt to make the processing using query rewrite and our materialized views a little faster. Drop all the materialized view logs:

```
DROP MATERIALIZED VIEW LOG ON industry;
DROP MATERIALIZED VIEW LOG ON location;
DROP MATERIALIZED VIEW LOG ON product;
DROP MATERIALIZED VIEW LOG ON purchase;
DROP MATERIALIZED VIEW LOG ON sale;
DROP MATERIALIZED VIEW LOG ON time;
```

Drop the aggregated materialized view created on the materialized view join:

```
DROP MATERIALIZED VIEW mv_revenue_by_month;
```

And now drop and recreate the materialized view join as well, using highlighted options:

```
DROP MATERIALIZED VIEW mv_sale;
CREATE MATERIALIZED VIEW mv_sale
PARALLEL NOLOGGING TABLESPACE MVDATA COMPRESS
USING NO INDEX NEVER REFRESH
ENABLE QUERY REWRITE
AS SELECT s.order_amount,s.order_date
, s.transaction_amount,s.transaction_date
, s.payment_amount,s.payment_date,s.payment_text
, s.product_quantity,s.product_price,s.product_date
, l.region,l.country,l.state,l.city
, t.month#,t.monabbrev,t.monthname,t.quarter#,t.year#
, p.category, p.product, p.price, i.industry
FROM sale s, location l, time t, product p, industry i
WHERE s.location_id = l.location_id
AND s.time_id = t.time_id
AND s.product_id = p.product_id
AND s.industry_id = i.industry_id;

CREATE MATERIALIZED VIEW mv_revenue_by_month
PARALLEL NOLOGGING TABLESPACE MVDATA COMPRESS
USING NO INDEX NEVER REFRESH
ENABLE QUERY REWRITE
    AS SELECT year#, quarter#, month#
,COUNT(transaction_amount),COUNT(*)
,SUM(transaction_amount)
    FROM mv_sale
    GROUP BY year#, quarter#, month#;
```

And compute statistics on both materialized views:

```
ANALYZE TABLE mv_sale COMPUTE STATISTICS;
ANALYZE TABLE mv_revenue_by_month COMPUTE STATISTICS;
```

Now we can run the EXPLAIN PLAN command again on the same query used in Figure 4.11. The result is shown in Figure 4.12. There is little difference between Figures 4.11 and 4.12, except that the bytes read has dropped to nearly a fourth of what it was. That is quite a sharp drop. If the database were much larger, there would ultimately be a cost difference. It is not necessary to demonstrate further at this stage, but suffice it to say that in data warehouses, a difference in I/O activity of this magnitude could result in a substantial cost saving. The byte count has probably changed due to the introduction of compression using the COMPRESS keyword.

Figure 4.12
Improving query rewrite from Figure 4.11.

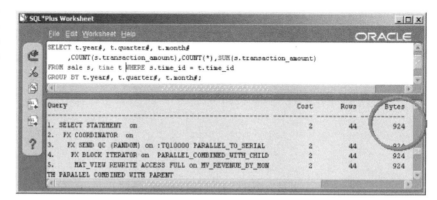

Materialized views are certainly very useful in data warehousing environments, and their use is a tuning method in itself. Perhaps an important conclusive point to note is that, like many other types of database objects, most restrictions on materialized views all make perfect sense, especially with respect to fast refresh and on commit.

The next chapter will look at Oracle Dimension objects, which can be used to alleviate performance issues occurring in the multiple level dimensional entity hierarchies of star and snowflake schemas. A snowflake schema is a less purely dimensional-fact version of a star schema, such that dimensions are normalized.

4.6   Endnotes

1.   Chapter 7 in *Oracle Performance Tuning for 9i and 10g*
         (ISBN: 1555583059)

5

Oracle Dimension Objects

This chapter examines Oracle dimension objects. In a star schema, dimensions are denormalized into a single layer of dimensions. In a snowflake schema, dimensions are normalized out to multiple hierarchical layers. Dimension objects can be used to represent these multiple layers for both star and snowflake schemas, possibly helping to increase performance of joins across dimension hierarchies.

Note: This chapter uses a number of example dimensional structure hierarchies in order to demonstrate the widely variable applicability of dimensional objects.

5.1   What Is a Dimension Object?

In a data warehouse a dimension, is one of two types of entities in a fact-dimensional entity schema. A star schema is a denormalized version of a fact-dimensional structure, such that all dimensions relate directly to fact entities, where there is only a single dimensional level as shown in Figure 5.1.

Figure 5.2, on the other hand, shows a snowflake schema version of the schema shown in Figure 5.1. A snowflake schema is a normalized form of a star schema. In Figure 5.2, the container dimension consists of a two-level hierarchy in which the two separate levels are comprised of the container and container-type dimensions.

A dimension object is used to represent multiple-level hierarchical structured dimensions, as shown by the container and container-type dimensions shown in Figure 5.2. Dimension objects can be used to represent multiple dimensional arrays of dimensions.

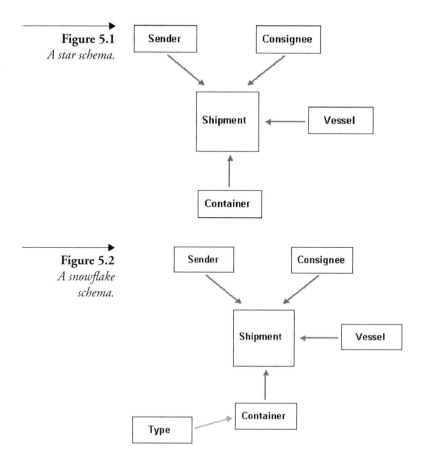

Figure 5.1
A star schema.

Figure 5.2
A snowflake schema.

The Benefits of Implementing Dimension Objects

The most significant factor, with respect to using dimension object hierarchies, is that of a more understandable model from a business perspective. Since many data warehouse query types, at least at the beginning of the application life cycle, are ad hoc, it is extremely likely that most queries are constructed (if not actually executed) by end users.

Typically, end users of data warehouses are business people, or even researchers, and not necessarily computer technical personnel. After all, a data warehouse is built for end users. The end-user perspective is on analysis of information. In other words, data warehouses are built by coders and database administrators from a purely technical perspective, but the requirements are very distinctly defined by the end users. This situation is perhaps far more prevalent with data warehouse databases than with OLTP transactional databases. In an OLTP database back end for an Internet site, the user population is so incredibly large that database access is nearly always very tightly controlled by front-end applications. Therefore, the computer programmers and database administrators building those applications control the applications. The opposite is often the case for data warehouse databases, where direct access to raw data sets is more immediate for the end-user population. The result is that an easily understandable business model applicable structure is very important in data warehouse databases. Using dimensional objects in an Oracle database data warehouse can help to represent, utilize, and enforce the dimensional hierarchies that are so important to the only real reason for the existence of data warehouses—analysis of data by the people who can put the results to good use. Those people are the end users.

That is a lot of waffle. How does all this make sense from a technical perspective? After all, readers of a book like this might be end users, but are also likely to be people like myself—experienced developers and database administrators.

- **Easily Understandable Structure**. Dimensions can be used to create structure in the form of multiple dimensional hierarchies.

- **Easy Access to Granularity**. This is so important in data warehouses, where end-user requirements on granularity can be determined based on aggregation and drill down requirements. Dimensions are linked in a business perspective structure from the most general to the most granular. End users do not need to see every level of detail, at least not at first.

- **Easy Application of Aggregation**. Multiple layers in a dimensional hierarchy can be used to aggregate at specific layers, avoiding extra processing down to layers that are not required for a particular query.

- **Connecting Hierarchical Levels**. Connections between levels in a hierarchy are made obvious by multiple dimensional structures, where each element is connected to a parent and a child dimension.

- **Drill Down**. It follows that since we can access data down to a specific point in a dimensional hierarchy, that we can also use that hierarchical structure to perform drill down into successive layers. Drill down is very important, because it allows filtering not only at each layer but also within each layer, into lower layers or levels. End users are most likely to start at the top of a hierarchy, drilling their way down into successive levels depending on what results they dig up.

- **Improved Performance**. Using dimensional object hierarchies can help to improve query, query rewrite, and optimizer performance.

We will attempt to demonstrate all of the factors in this list later on in this chapter.

Note: When building dimensional hierarchies with dimension objects, always attempt to build hierarchical structures from a business requirements perspective. Business people need to use the data in your data warehouse. Programmers and database administrators only build data warehouses; they do not actually use the data to retrieve real-world applicable results.

Let's take a brief look at the negative perspective of using dimension objects in data warehouses.

Negative Aspects of Dimension Objects

The danger when using dimension objects is that not completely satisfying all the dimensional relationships in a schema can result in the return of spurious results. One very obvious example of this situation is shown in Figure 5.6, where some countries are not listed with state names; thus, the state exists for the United States, or the province for Canada, but states as such do not exist for European countries. Some countries do not have states or provinces but, perhaps, other structures, such as counties or even principalities. The obvious confusion that results can also confuse query rewrite and ultimately the optimizer, resulting in potentially spurious results from queries submitted by end users.

Before experimenting with the performance aspects of using Oracle Dimension objects, we need to examine the syntax details and descriptive explanations of dimension object syntax, allowing a clearer understanding of exactly what dimension objects are and what they can be used to achieve.

5.2   Dimension Object Syntax

Syntax for managing dimension objects is shown in Figure 5.3 in the form of the CREATE DIMENSION, ALTER DIMENSION, and DROP DIMENSION statements.

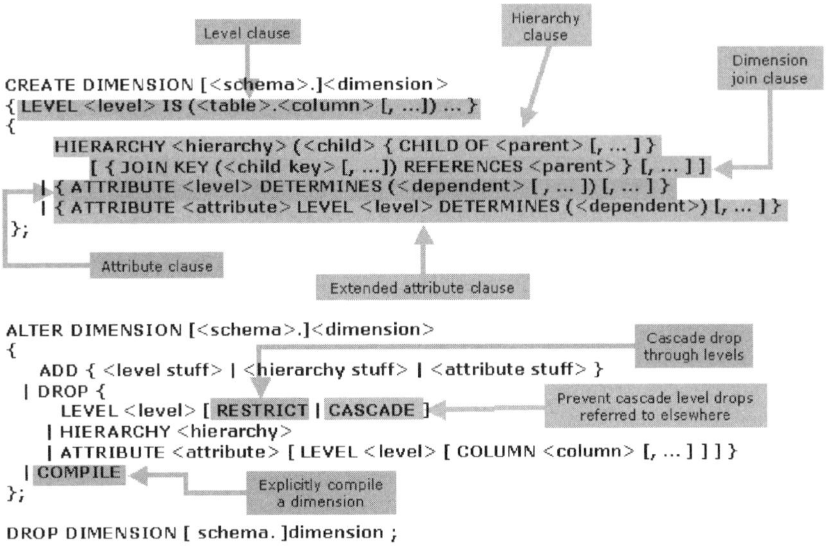

Figure 5.3
Dimension object syntax.

5.2.1 **CREATE DIMENSION Syntax**

The CREATE DIMENSION statement allows creation of dimension objects. The idea is to link normalized dimensions in separate entities into hierarchies of level separated dimensions. The point of using the dimension object is that the optimizer can use query rewrite using the dimension objects, in much the same way that it can use materialized views to rewrite queries: to read more compact physical data sets.

Note: The CREATE DIMENSION system privilege is required to create Oracle Dimension objects.

Let's examine each section of Oracle Dimension object DDL statement syntax.

Level Clause

Dimensions are constructed in hierarchies. This hierarchical structure is somewhat akin to an upside-down tree, except with fewer branches than a BTree index. The level clause allows definition of the level of a dimension within a hierarchy. The level of a dimension within a hierarchy is the layer in which the dimension resides, between or including the root or primary parent, down to the lowest layered child dimension objects.

There are a number of restrictions, which, as usual, are basic common sense. Generally, dimension objects are used to identify relationships between completely normalized or different dimensional entities. Figure 5.4 shows a denormalized version on the left of the diagram, and the nor-

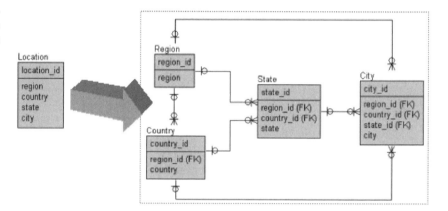

Figure 5.4
Normalizing a dimension.

malized structure on the right of the diagram, using the data warehouse LOCATION table.

Let's begin creating a dimension object by identifying normalizable relationships within a single dimensional entity, the LOCATION entity shown in Figure 5.4:

```
CREATE DIMENSION dm_location
LEVEL city IS (location.city)
LEVEL state IS (location.state)
LEVEL country IS (location.country)
LEVEL region IS (location.region);
```

Now let's create a dimension object for the normalized structure in Figure 5.4:

```
DROP DIMENSION dm_location;
CREATE DIMENSION dm_location
LEVEL city IS (city.city_id)
LEVEL state IS (state.state_id)
LEVEL country IS (country.country_id)
LEVEL region IS (region.region_id);
```

The definition of each level must stem from only one table, and you cannot duplicate a table column across levels. In other words, each level represents a single dimension, be it in one or more tables. Additionally, there is no sense in attempting to place the same dimension into different levels.

Hierarchy Clause

A hierarchy defines a parent-child linear structure between the object accessed in a dimension. In other words, for the normalized structure in Figure 5.4, a city is contained within a state, which is in turn contained within a country, which is contained within a region of the world as a whole. So REGION is a parent of COUNTRY and COUNTRY is a child of REGION. Hierarchies must match existing levels already declared by the level clause. Let's examine a more simplistic normalization, shown in Figure 5.5.

Figure 5.5
Normalizing another dimension.

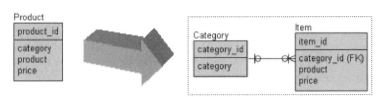

As the columns are all from the same dimension entity, we can define a hierarchy for the structure shown in Figure 5.5 as follows:

```
CREATE DIMENSION dm_product
LEVEL product IS (product.product)
LEVEL category IS (product.category)
HIERARCHY products(
product CHILD OF category);
```

Similarly, for the more complex example shown in Figure 5.4 we can do the following:

```
DROP DIMENSION dm_location;
CREATE DIMENSION dm_location
LEVEL city IS (location.city)
LEVEL state IS (location.state)
LEVEL country IS (location.country)
LEVEL region IS (location.region)
HIERARCHY locations(
    city CHILD OF state CHILD OF country CHILD OF region);
```

Dimension Join Clause

The dimension join clause is a subset syntactical enhancement to the hierarchy clause. When columns in different levels originate from separate tables, those different levels must be joined. Joins are performed using the dimension join clause section of the hierarchy clause, as shown in the following example using the structure shown in Figure 5.5:

```
DROP DIMENSION dm_product;
CREATE DIMENSION dm_product
LEVEL product IS (item.item_id)
LEVEL category IS (category.category_id)
HIERARCHY products(
product CHILD OF category
JOIN KEY (item.category_id) REFERENCES category);
```

Now let's go on to the more complex structure, as shown in Figure 5.4. Note that this particular statement will cause an error because the hierarchy requires a connection between each level, not across levels.

```
DROP DIMENSION dm_location;
CREATE DIMENSION dm_location
LEVEL city IS (city.city_id)
LEVEL state IS (state.state_id)
LEVEL country IS (country.country_id)
LEVEL region IS (region.region_id)
HIERARCHY locations(
    city CHILD OF state
    CHILD OF country
    CHILD OF region
JOIN KEY(city.region_id) REFERENCES region
JOIN KEY(city.country_id) REFERENCES country
JOIN KEY(city.state_id) REFERENCES state
JOIN KEY(state.region_id) REFERENCES region
JOIN KEY(state.country_id) REFERENCES country
JOIN KEY(country.region_id) REFERENCES region
);
```

The schema diagram in Figure 5.4 could have to change as shown in Figure 5.6 in order to properly represent LOCATION as a hierarchy.

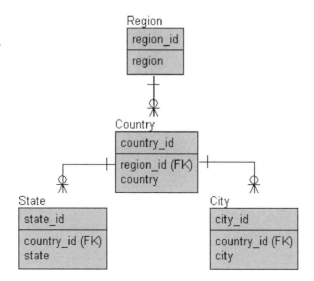

Figure 5.6
Normalizing locations.

There is a problem with the schema shown in Figure 5.6 in that it does not properly represent a hierarchy. The only way to represent this particular structure is by using two hierarchies, because NULL-valued and non NULL-valued states cannot be represented by a single structure, see Figure 5.7.

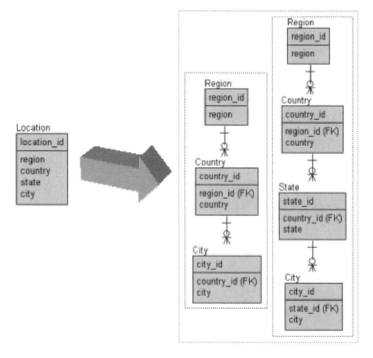

Figure 5.7
There are two options for a hierarchy.

There will now be two CREATE DIMENSION statements in order to cater for locations, as shown below:

```
DROP DIMENSION dm_location;
CREATE DIMENSION dm_location
LEVEL city IS (city.city_id)
LEVEL country IS (country.country_id)
LEVEL region IS (region.region_id)
HIERARCHY locations(
city CHILD OF country
    CHILD OF region
JOIN KEY(city.country_id) REFERENCES country
JOIN KEY(country.region_id) REFERENCES region
);

DROP DIMENSION dm_location;
CREATE DIMENSION dm_location
LEVEL city IS (city.city_id)
LEVEL state IS (state.state_id)
LEVEL country IS (country.country_id)
LEVEL region IS (region.region_id)
HIERARCHY locations(
city CHILD OF state
    CHILD OF country
    CHILD OF region
JOIN KEY(city.state_id) REFERENCES state
JOIN KEY(state.country_id) REFERENCES country
JOIN KEY(country.region_id) REFERENCES region
);
```

Note: A single dimension can be built based on multiple hierarchies.

Attribute Clause

The attribute clause allows allocation of attributes specific to each entity. Returning to the PRODUCT dimension, shown in Figure 5.5, the PRICE column is an attribute of each product, as shown by the CREATE DIMENSION statement below:

```
DROP DIMENSION dm_product;
CREATE DIMENSION dm_product
LEVEL product IS (item.item_id)
LEVEL category IS (category.category_id)
HIERARCHY products(
product CHILD OF category
JOIN KEY (item.category_id) REFERENCES category)
ATTRIBUTE product DETERMINES(price);
```

Extended Attribute Clause

The extended attribute allows extension of the attribute clause by allowing assignment of a specific name to an attribute, shown below in the CREATE DIMENSION statement for the PRODUCT entity:

```
DROP DIMENSION dm_product;
CREATE DIMENSION dm_product
LEVEL product IS (item.item_id)
LEVEL category IS (category.category_id)
HIERARCHY products(
product CHILD OF category
JOIN KEY (item.category_id) REFERENCES category)
ATTRIBUTE product_detail LEVEL product DETERMINES(price);
```

5.2.2 ALTER and DROP DIMENSION Syntax

Within the ALTER DIMENSION statement levels can be both added and dropped, including cascading drops. The RESTRICT option is the default and restricts level drops referred to elsewhere.

5.2.3 Using Constraints with Dimensions

Primary and foreign key constraints should be enabled to allow for proper performance of query rewrite processing. If constraint checking is best switched off for performance data warehouse data loading, then use NOV-ALIDATE RELY as a constraint state. The RELY state allows query rewrite to be enabled on nonvalidated (NOVALIDATE) constraint values, such that RELY assumes that all referential integrity is valid.

Validation of dimensions is therefore important, because dimension syntax on dimension object creation is declarative only and not enforced in terms of the enforcement of referential integrity on values within hier-archical structures. The VALIDATE_DIMENSION procedure in the

DBMS_DIMENSION package can be used to validate data referential integrity for dimension objects. If dimensions are not periodically validated, and referential integrity is violated, then spurious results could be returned by queries, as dimension DDL statement syntax is only declarative and not absolute.

Note: It is best to maintain data referential integrity using validated (VALID) constraints if performance is not adversely affected.

5.3   Dimension Object Metadata

The state of dimensions can be viewed using the USER_DIMENSIONS metadata view. Additionally, the DBMS_DIMENSION package contains a procedure called DESCRIBE_DIMENSION, which allows viewing of the details of a dimension as shown in Figure 5.8.

Figure 5.8
*Using the DBMS_
DIMENSION.
DESCRIBE_
DIMENSION
procedure.*

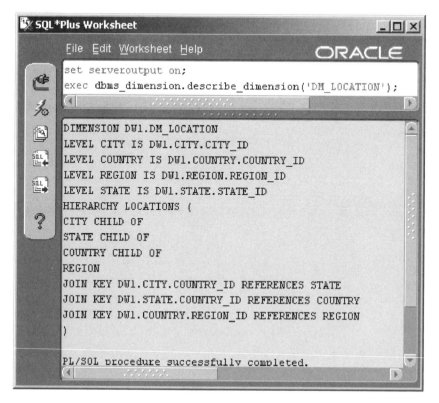

5.4   Dimension Objects and Performance

When attempting to demonstrate performance improvements using dimensional object hierarchies, we should first reiterate the list of benefits described earlier in this chapter. These are the reasons why dimensional hierarchies should be used in data warehouses:

- Easily understandable structure

- Easy access to granularity

- Easy application of aggregation

- Obvious connections between hierarchical levels

- Drill down

- Improved performance

One of the easiest types of structures to demonstrate multiple dimensional hierarchies is that of time. Figure 5.9 shows the structure of the TIME dimension entity as it now exists for the SALE and PURCHASE fact entities within the large data warehouse used in this book.

Figure 5.9
The TIME dimensional entity.

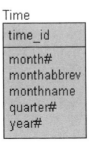

Time

time_id
month# monthabbrev monthname quarter# year#

Now let's make use of the TIME dimensional entity shown in Figure 5.9 to demonstrate in more detail how the list of benefits as detailed above can be realized. Is the TIME dimension shown in Figure 5.9 easy to understand from a business perspective? Yes, this is probably the case, but it could be improved upon. Figure 5.10 shows a multiple dimensional hierarchy of the TIME dimensional entity.

The only problem is we have now lost the crucial TIME_ID primary key link into the fact tables. Therefore, since our data warehouse database is already constructed and the TIME_ID column is essential, we cannot

Figure 5.10
A TIME dimensional hierarchy.

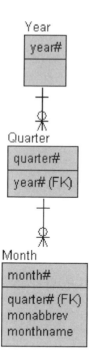

change the TIME entity itself. However, we can create a multiple dimensional structure on the TIME dimension as it stands.

```
CREATE DIMENSION dm_time
LEVEL month IS (time.month#)
LEVEL quarter IS (time.quarter#)
LEVEL year IS (time.year#)
HIERARCHY time(month CHILD OF quarter CHILD OF year)
ATTRIBUTE month DETERMINES(monabbrev, monthname);
```

Now we will test using the EXPLAIN PLAN command and timing tests. First, we should clean up all dimensions and materialized views in order to obtain a clean slate, using commands such as the following:

```
SQL> select 'drop dimension '||dimension_name||';' from
user_dimensions;

'DROPDIMENSION'||DIMENSION_NAME||';'
------------------------------------------------
drop dimension DM_LOCATION;
```

```
drop dimension DM_PRODUCT;
drop dimension DM_TIME;

SQL> select 'drop materialized view '||mview_name||';' from
user_mviews;

'DROPMATERIALIZEDVIEW'||MVIEW_NAME||';'
-----------------------------------------------------
drop materialized view MV_JOIN_SALE;
```

5.4.1   Rollup Using Dimension Objects

Now let's execute an EXPLAIN PLAN and timing test on base tables using an aggregation on a join. Figure 5.11 shows the EXPLAIN PLAN and the timing test result.

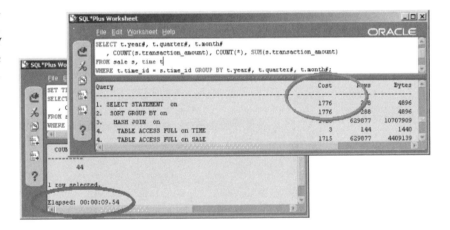

Figure 5.11
EXPLAIN PLAN and timing test on a base table join.

Now we will create the materialized view join, joining all dimensions and the SALE fact table. We can adjust the DDL statement, building the materialized view with all possible beneficial query performance options as highlighted in the statement shown below:

```
CREATE MATERIALIZED VIEW mv_join_sale
PARALLEL NOLOGGING TABLESPACE MVDATA COMPRESS
USING NO INDEX NEVER REFRESH
ENABLE QUERY REWRITE
AS SELECT s.order_amount,s.order_date
, s.transaction_amount,s.transaction_date
, s.payment_amount,s.payment_date,s.payment_text
```

```
, s.product_quantity,s.product_price,s.product_date
, l.region,l.country,l.state,l.city
, t.month#,t.monabbrev,t.monthname,t.quarter#,t.year#
, p.category, p.product, p.price, i.industry
FROM sale s, location l, time t, product p, industry i
WHERE s.location_id = l.location_id AND s.time_id = t.time_id
AND s.product_id = p.product_id AND s.industry_id =
i.industry_id;
```

Let's gather statistics:

```
ANALYZE TABLE mv_join_sale COMPUTE STATISTICS;
```

Now let's do another EXPLAIN PLAN with the same query against the SALE and TIME tables as in Figure 5.11. The result is shown in Figure 5.12.

Figure 5.12
*Query rewrite
using the join
materialized view.*

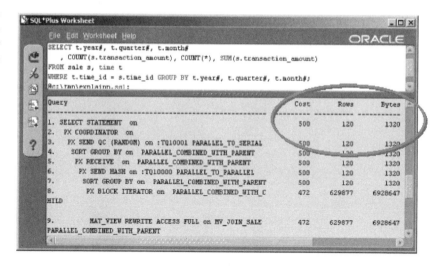

Now let's create an aggregated materialized view on the join materialized view just created:

```
CREATE MATERIALIZED VIEW mv_revenue_by_month
PARALLEL NOLOGGING TABLESPACE MVDATA COMPRESS
USING NO INDEX NEVER REFRESH
ENABLE QUERY REWRITE
    AS SELECT year#, quarter#, month#
```

```
,COUNT(transaction_amount),COUNT(*)
,SUM(transaction_amount)
     FROM mv_join_sale
     GROUP BY year#, quarter#, month#;
```

And gather statistics:

```
ANALYZE TABLE mv_revenue_by_month COMPUTE STATISTICS;
```

Once again, let's do another EXPLAIN PLAN with the same query against the SALE and TIME tables as in Figures 5.11 and 5.12. The result is shown in Figure 5.13, including a timing test. The substantial, or should I say astronomical, increase in speed between Figures 5.11 and 5.13 is obvious.

Figure 5.13
Query rewrite using the materialized view nesting.

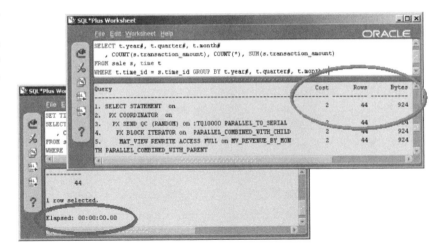

Now supposedly an Oracle Dimension object can be used to cater for hierarchical rollup. For example, a query grouping to quarters can be rolled up to from a materialized view grouped at the next layer down, in this case months. The way to demonstrate this process is to execute the table join query without the dimension, create the dimension, execute the query again, and see if there is a difference. So Figure 5.14 shows the EXPLAIN PLAN result for the table join query grouped to quarters, as opposed to months.

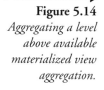

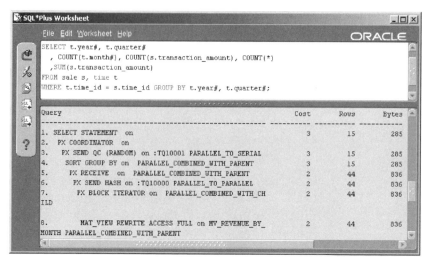

Unfortunately in Figure 5.14 it is shown that the optimizer does not need an Oracle Dimension object to figure out the obvious. Now let's create the appropriate dimension against the materialized view join:

```
DROP DIMENSION dm_time;
CREATE DIMENSION dm_time
LEVEL month IS (time.month#)
LEVEL quarter IS (time.quarter#)
LEVEL year IS (time.year#)
HIERARCHY time_rollup(month CHILD OF quarter CHILD OF year)
ATTRIBUTE month DETERMINES(time.monabbrev, time.monthname);
```

Note: The ALTER DIMENSION statement could have been used here.

By connecting the TIME dimension between year, quarter, and month, as shown in the above CREATE DIMENSION statement, that dimension is supposed to permit access to a materialized view on a lower level, namely the MV_REVENUE_BY_MONTH materialized view, created earlier in this chapter. As we have already seen in Figure 5.14, the existence of the Oracle Dimension object makes no difference to the optimizer, but we will go through the motions to see if we can spot any EXPLAIN PLAN differences. Therefore, Figure 5.15 is a re-execution of the query shown in Figure 5.14, with the dimension object now included.

Figure 5.15
Aggregating a level above available materialized view aggregation, utilizing a dimension object.

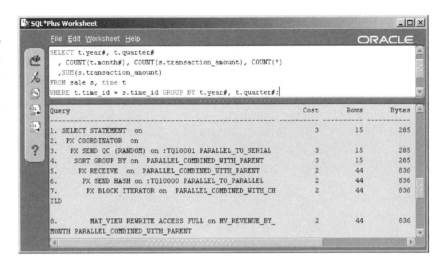

As you can see in Figure 5.15, there is no difference in cost, or even the details, of the EXPLAIN PLAN when including an appropriate dimension object. Essentially, the dimension object is supposed to prevent the need to create another aggregated materialized view, as shown below, aggregating by quarters rather than months:

```
CREATE MATERIALIZED VIEW mv_revenue_by_quarter
PARALLEL NOLOGGING TABLESPACE MVDATA COMPRESS
USING NO INDEX NEVER REFRESH
ENABLE QUERY REWRITE
    AS SELECT year#, quarter#
        , COUNT(month#), COUNT(transaction_amount), COUNT(*)
        , SUM(transaction_amount)
FROM mv_join_sale
GROUP BY year#, quarter#;
```

Note: The materialized view above could be created from the months aggregation materialized view, but multiple layers of aggregation will severely restrict refresh capabilities.

And, always gather statistics:

```
ANALYZE TABLE mv_revenue_by_quarter COMPUTE STATISTICS;
```

5.4.2   Join Back Using Dimension Objects

Another useful feature of dimension objects is the ability to allow for an operation known as join back. Join back is a term applied to the reprocessing of a join back to an already joined table (already joined in a materialized view, for instance) where a query requires columns in base tables but not added into the materialized join view. Does this affect performance? Yes, because joining the base tables all over again does not have to be re-executed. Joins can be expensive and are usually one of the most significant factors with respect to data warehouse performance.

So how can dimension objects help with join back? The DETER-MINES clause of a dimension can be used to define what is known as a functional dependency between a materialized view and a column that is missing in the materialized view, but accessible through a dimension. In the case of the materialized view MV_JOIN_SALE, created earlier in this chapter, the MONABBREV and MONTHNAME columns in the TIME table were deliberately omitted from the definition of the materialized view MV_JOIN_SALE:

```
CREATE MATERIALIZED VIEW mv_join_sale
PARALLEL NOLOGGING TABLESPACE MVDATA COMPRESS
USING NO INDEX NEVER REFRESH
ENABLE QUERY REWRITE
AS SELECT s.order_amount,s.order_date
, s.transaction_amount,s.transaction_date
, s.payment_amount,s.payment_date,s.payment_text
, s.product_quantity,s.product_price,s.product_date
, l.region,l.country,l.state,l.city
, t.month#,t.quarter#,t.year#
, p.category, p.product, p.price, i.industry
FROM sale s, location l, time t, product p, industry i
WHERE s.location_id = l.location_id AND s.time_id = t.time_id
AND s.product_id = p.product_id AND s.industry_id =
i.industry_id;
```

Additionally, the dimension object was deliberately created using the ATTRIBUTES clause and the DETERMINES clause defines the two missing columns as part of the TIME table, and effectively accessible from the MV_JOIN_SALE materialized view through the DM_TIME dimension object:

```
DROP DIMENSION dm_time;
CREATE DIMENSION dm_time
    LEVEL time IS (time.time_id)
LEVEL month IS (time.month#)
LEVEL quarter IS (time.quarter#)
LEVEL year IS (time.year#)
HIERARCHY time_rollup(
time       CHILD OF
month      CHILD OF
quarter    CHILD OF year)
ATTRIBUTE time DETERMINES time.monabbrev
ATTRIBUTE time DETERMINES time.monthname;
```

In the script above, the dimension object has been altered from its previous appearance in this chapter in order to include and accommodate the TIME table primary key. In other words, any join query rewrites can find the two missing month definition columns based on the primary key.

Now the optimizer should be able to access the TIME columns missing in the materialized view using a process called join back, such that rows are retrieved from the TIME table without having to re-execute the join between the TIME dimension table and the enormous SALE fact table. The example query in Figure 5.16 shows quite clearly that the optimizer and query rewrite simply cannot execute the query rewrite using join back and the dimension object. Figure 5.16 fails miserably at query rewrite, reading the underlying SALE fact table. In short, it does not work. Oops!

The query shown below is the kind of thing that the query rewrite join back process should have done, joining the materialized view to the TIME

Figure 5.16
Query rewrite join back.

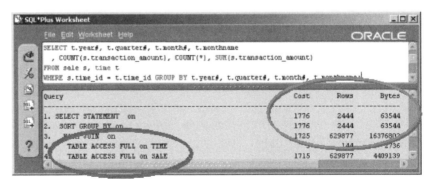

dimension table and not full table scanning the SALE fact table as shown in Figure 5.16. The EXPLAIN PLAN for this query is shown in Figure 5.17.

```
SELECT mv.year#, mv.quarter#, mv.month#
, iv.monabbrev, iv.monthname
        , COUNT(mv.transaction_amount), COUNT(*)
        ,SUM(mv.transaction_amount)
FROM mv_join_sale mv
,(SELECT DISTINCT month#, monabbrev
, monthname FROM time) iv
WHERE mv.month# = iv.month#
GROUP BY mv.year#, mv.quarter#, mv.month#
, iv.monabbrev, iv.monthname;
```

Figure 5.17
Manual join back when query rewrite fails.

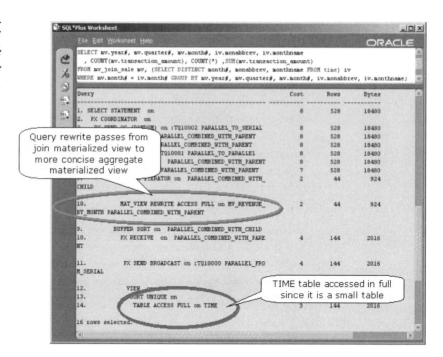

Figure 5.18 shows an example using a much larger SALE fact table containing five million rows, simply to show the larger difference between no query rewrite and query rewrite, showing the enormous potential benefit of query rewrite in general.

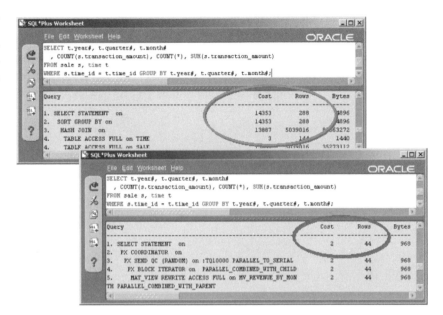

Figure 5.18
*Querying the large
database without
and with
materialized views.*

The only interesting point I did manage to determine with respect to the disappointing result of no join back in Figure 5.18 is as follows. When removing all nested materialized views and retaining only the materialized join view and the DM_TIME dimension object, query plan costs were drastically increased when accessing columns in the TIME table outside of the MV_SALE materialized join view. The query plan consistently showed access to the MV_SALE materialized join view only. This indicated that perhaps an extremely inefficient form of join back was occurring, but that it was not generated by the EXPLAIN PLAN command into the PLAN_TABLE, and thus not visible in the query plan.

This chapter has discussed Oracle Dimension objects, their application and their potential performance improvement factors. It is possible to state that general implementation of dimension objects is perhaps more of a design than a performance tuning issue. It is also a possibility that the creation of additional database objects could even hurt performance—materialized views being the obvious exception. In fact, it is even likely that since dimension objects were introduced in Oracle Database 8*i* that dimension objects might have become redundant in the latest releases of Oracle Database in the same way that clusters and bitmap indexes have become much less useful than they were originally intended. The optimizer is getting more intelligent all the time and simply needs less and less help. Essentially, the only quantifiable potential performance factor for using dimension objects is that the optimizer and query rewrite mechanism can manage more complex query rewrites when appropriate dimension objects are created.

The next chapter will examine another Oracle optional feature that is so significant to Oracle Database data warehouse performance: Oracle Partitioning and the basics of parallel processing.

6

Partitioning and Basic Parallel Processing

This chapter covers Oracle Partitioning, including syntax and examples, and some parallel processing as specifically applied to Oracle Partitioning. In general, partitioning involves the physical splitting of large objects, such as tables or materialized views, and their associated indexes into separate physical parts. The result is that operations can be performed on those individual physical partitions, resulting in a substantial reduction in I/O requirements. Additionally, multiple partitions can be executed on in parallel. Both of these factors make partitioning a tuning method, as opposed to a thing that can be tuned specifically. Any tuning of partitions is essentially related to underlying structures, indexing techniques, and the way in which partitions are constructed.

6.1 What Are Partitioning and Parallel Processing?

Partitioning is a process or methodology of splitting physical data sets into smaller physical parts. Each of the subset physical parts can be operated on individually or as parallel processing on multiple partitions at the same time.

6.1.1 What Is Partitioning?

Oracle Partitioning is the splitting of data sets, usually into separate physical files using separate partition tablespaces. However, partitions can actually coexist in the same physical file. Separating partitions into separate datafiles is not essential with certain types of RAID array architectures. Separate partitions are accessible in parallel, individually or in groups. Why is partitioning relevant to tuning? Partitioning can be used to break large objects into smaller subsets. Processing of smaller subsets of data-separately and in parallel, is potentially much faster than serial processing on very large data sets. Partitioning and parallelism generally only applies to very large databases on high end multiple CPU server platforms. Figure 6.1 illustrates how partitioning can be used to split a physical datafile containing a table into multiple physical datafiles, mapped individually to separate partitions within that table.

Figure 6.1
Physical partitioning.

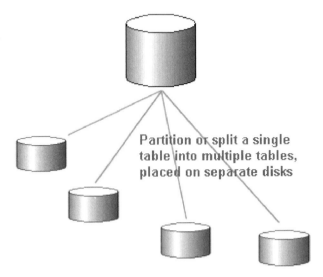

Partition or split a single table into multiple tables, placed on separate disks

6.1.2   **The Benefits of Using Partitioning**

Oracle Partitioning is beneficial usually in very large database environments and sometimes in smaller databases. But it is most beneficial for data warehouse databases (depending on applications) for the following reasons:

- **Physical Separation**. Parallel processing by way of splitting of data into separately located physical files. Separating table and index datafiles onto separate disks in a nonpartitioned database is a form of partitioning. Table and index physical spaces are often read more or less in parallel. In older versions of Oracle Database, this practice could have been highly beneficial, reading data from separate locations at the same time. Partitioning can enhance the benefits of splitting datafiles. However, in the latest version of Oracle Database, Oracle Database 10*g*, the SAME (Stripe and Mirror Everything for protection and performance) method is recommended as the best approach. The SAME methodology is best used in tandem with ASM (Oracle Automatic Storage Management). Storage arrays such as RAID arrays are effective underlying physical hardware structures.

- **Storage Structures**. Different partitions within the same table can have different physical storage structures. Different partitions within a table can even be both read-write and read only, perhaps allowing separation of archived and current data.

- **Backup, Recovery, and Utilities**. These programs can utilize parallel processing and perform activities on individual partitions. Examples of utilities are SQL*Loader, Data Pump Export, and Import.

- **Partition Pruning**. The Optimizer can access individual partitions when processing SQL code. This process is termed Partition Pruning, since only partitions required by a query will be read and other partitions ignored. Additionally, the optimizer can execute against multiple partitions using parallel processing, generally on high-end multiple CPU server platforms, with datafiles spread across multiple disks.

Note: Rows can also be accessed by partition name, effectively allowing manual partition pruning.

- **Parallel Processing**. Parallel processing, with or without multiple CPUs and Oracle Partitioning, applies to both DML and DDL commands.

Note: Parallel processing can be achieved on a single CPU platform by executing multiple server processes.

6.1.3 Different Partitioning Methods

Partitions can be created on single or multiple columns of a table. A table can be divided up into separate partitions based on three methods. These methods are ranges of values, values in lists, and hashing algorithms on columns. Additionally, partitions can be one of two composites of the already mentioned three partitioning methods. Therefore, there are five different types of partitions:

- **Range Partitioning**. Divides up rows based on ranges of values. For example, split a table of transactions into periods or quarters derived from a transaction date.

- **List Partitioning**. Divides up rows based on sets of literal values. For example, divide large population samples into separate partitions based on M for male and F for female.

- **Hash Partitioning**. Uses a hashing algorithm to divide rows, resulting in consistently sized partitions. Sometimes ranges and lists can result in skewed numbers of values spread across separate partitions. For example, a retailer with 90% of its sales during the Christmas period might not find good performance benefits with parallel processing dividing up data based on quarters.

Note: Do not misunderstand the term "consistent" as used above. A hash algorithm uses a single consistent value to calculate lots of other values. Thus, the original values calculated into hash values by the single value are retrievable, simply by reversing the calculation. Rows will be divided consistently where hashed values are unique. Applying a hashing algorithm to nonunique values WILL result in a skewed (unbalanced) distribution. As a general rule, it is unwise to apply hashing algorithms to anything but unique values.

- **Composite Partitioning**. Contains subpartitions within each separate partition. Partitions can contain subpartitions of two types. First, a range partition can contain multiple hash subpartitions and second, a range partition can contain multiple list subpartitions:
  - **Range-Hash Partitioning**. A range partition containing hash subpartitions within each range partition.
  - **Range-List Partitioning**. A range partition containing list value subpartitions within each range partition.

Partition Indexing

A partition is divided based on what is called a Partition Key. This key is internal to Oracle Database: effectively, the data definition splits table rows into separate partitions. For example, a range partition on a table could have rows separated into different partitions based on a date for each row, perhaps dividing financial data into quarters. Both the partition key and other columns can be indexed. There are two types of partitioning indexes:

- **Local Index**. These indexes have the same structure as their relative table partitions. Local indexes are preferred due to more automated maintenance.

- **Global Index**. These indexes are created on partitioned tables, but are not the same structure as the partitioning key. Oracle Database 10*g* includes a new type of global partition index called a hash partitioned global index. It allows for an even spread of index values.

When to Use Different Partitioning Methods

Different partitioning methods have different applications:

- **Range Partitioning**. Range partitioning is traditionally used to split active and historical information, based on dates or derivations of dates such as month, quarter, or year numbers. The majority of queries should access data by some form of temporal filtering and sorting. Additionally, managing the removal of archived information becomes easier when partitions falling outside of required ranges can simply be dropped. Data from previous years too old to be useful can be removed simply by dropping out-of-date individual partitions. There is no effect on active partitions.

- **List Partitioning**. Like range partitioning, list partitioning splits data based on values making visible sense. A classic example of list partitioning is the splitting of a table into separate partitions based on what in a relational database is called a type. For example, a population database could contain M for male and F for female as types. In this case we could create two partitions, one with males and one with females. Another example would be to split location data based on state codes in the United States. In this case each list partition can be created for a single or multiple states. For example, the Northeast could contain states such as NY, NJ, and CT.

- **Hash Partitioning**. Range and list partitioning split data based on specific values. This usually provides a real-world business perspective, which makes visible sense. The result of range and list partitioning is that different partitions can have widely varying numbers of rows and thus widely varying physical sizes, potentially skewing numbers of rows across partitions. Hash partitioning, on the other hand, uses an algorithm to equally divide all rows into separate physical partitions, regardless of actual column values. Thus, hash partitioning is more or less guaranteed to give an equal physical split among partitions. Since hash partitioning does not provide a business perspective split, it is more useful in terms of improving internal I/O performance, such as when processing multiple partitions in parallel. Good uses for hash partitioning include very large, unmanageable tables; tables requiring frequent reindexing; unevenly distributed range or list values creating skewing across partitions sizes; or any situation where an even physical spread is important. Hash partitioning is often most useful in getting good performance for partitioning pruning and partition-wise joins (see later in this chapter) where that processing is performed on the partition key.

Note: The partition key is the column (or list of columns) used to split a partition for all partition types. For a hash partition, the partition key is used to generate the hashing algorithm result for each row.

Partition pruning is limited to = (equality) and IN operator lists for hash partitions. A hash algorithm is not sorted or rapidly accessible by any externally visible value, being internally generated, and thus only exact items can be found, allowing only = (equality) and IN operator lists.

- **Range-Hash Composite Partitioning**. Creating hash subpartitions within range partitions identifies each range partition as having range limitations, where hash subpartitions divide data within each range equally, helping to spread data evenly within partitions. The disadvantage is that each partition is identified by range as a whole and not within each range partition. Thus, hash query restrictions apply within each range partition.

The result of range-hash composite partitions provides a lesser degree of benefit than both range partitioning and hash partitioning, but provides the benefits of both methods. For example, it is suited to situations where temporal data is best divided into partitions, but the data within each partition is unmanageable or skewed within each range. In other words, composite range-hash partitioning is beneficial for extremely large tables not only requiring some type of business-visible split, such as archived data, but also needing parallel processing capabilities. Also, the primary range partitions allow partition pruning and partition-wise joins both when using and when not using the partition key.

■ **Range-List Partitioning**. Implementing range-list partitioning, as opposed to range-hash partitioning, provides the same benefits, except that parallel processing might be somewhat less efficient for somewhat skewed data. However, separation by list values gives a visible business perspective, as opposed to range-hash partitioning, which only allows a visible perspective split at the partition level, not within each hash subpartition.

6.1.4   Parallel Processing and Partitioning

Parallel processing is the concurrent processing of more than one thing at the same time, either on separate CPUs or using multiple server processes, or both.

One of the most effective applications of parallel processing in Oracle Database is the processing of I/O activity on multiple partitions at once—typically when partitions are physically split with separate datafiles across separate storage devices. When a query is executed, if the query processes a filtered or sorted order matching the partition key, effectively splitting the partitioned table, then each partition can have the same query executed on it simultaneously. Parallel processing of separate partitions can provide enormous performance improvements when executed against partitions based on the structure of those partitions.

The most significant performance gains for parallel processing and multiple partitions are:

■ **Parallel Full Scans**. Any kind of full scan on large tables or indexes, including single table scans and multiple table joins. Scans of partitioned indexes, not nonpartitioned indexes.

■ **Parallel Index Creation**. Large index creations and rebuilds.

■ **SQL*Loader and Import Parallelism**. Bulk DML operations using certain DML commands and utilities, such as SQL*Loader and Import.

■ **Materialized View Creation**. Aggregating and copying of data, such as when creating materialized views.

Note: Implementing parallel execution can be beneficial, but sometimes it can be detrimental to performance. In general, parallel processing requires greater hardware resources, such as multiple CPU platforms and large amounts of RAM. However, there is definite, if limited, performance improvement using multiple server processes for parallel processing on single CPU platforms—even on a Windows 2000 box!

6.2   Partitioned Table Syntax

Partitioned tables are part and parcel of an add-on option called Oracle Partitioning. Oracle Partitioning, working in concert with parallel processing and separate disk spindles or RAID arrays, can provide fairly substantial performance improvements. The syntax diagrams listed in this section on Oracle Partitioning do not contain all available table creation partitioning syntax, but merely pseudo-like syntax structures. There is simply too much detail to include in this book. Examples will suffice to get you started syntactically. Refer to Oracle documentation for more information.

Note: CREATE TABLE partition syntax is shown in Figures 6.2 to 6.6. These syntax diagrams are cumulative with respect to annotations. In other words, annotations present in Figure 6.2 still apply to Figure 6.6, but may not be present in Figure 6.6 for the sake of avoiding "busy" diagrams.

6.2.1   CREATE TABLE: Range Partition

Figure 6.2 shows CREATE TABLE syntax for a range partition. The specification RANGE(<column>) specifies the column as the partition key. Rows are partitioned by placing them into separate partitions, called <partition>,

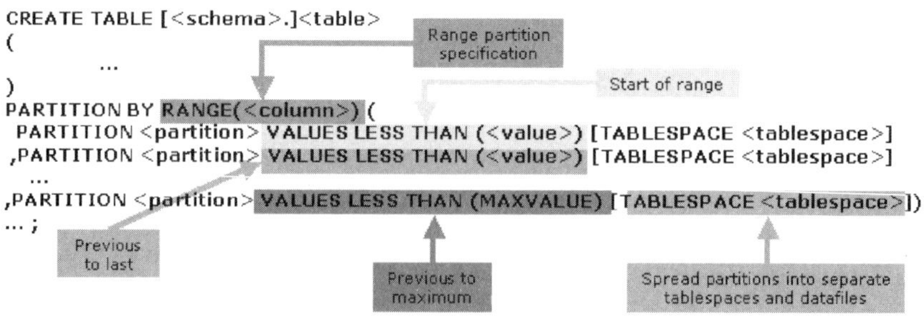

Figure 6.2
CREATE TABLE syntax for range partitions.

based on where column values of <value> fit in. Note how the specifications of VALUES LESS THAN and VALUES LESS THAN (MAXVALUE) allow for all possible values of <column> to be accounted for.

The data warehouse SALE table is a good example for range partitioning based on a date value, such as the TRANSACTION_DATE column:

```
CREATE TABLE psale_year
PARTITION BY RANGE(transaction_date)
(
  PARTITION sale_to_2003 VALUES LESS THAN
(TO_DATE('2003-01-01','YYYY-MM-DD'))
TABLESPACE pdata1
, PARTITION sale_to_2004 VALUES LESS THAN
(TO_DATE('2004-01-01','YYYY-MM-DD'))
TABLESPACE pdata2
, PARTITION sale_after_2003
VALUES LESS THAN (MAXVALUE)
TABLESPACE pdata3
  )
AS SELECT * FROM sale;
```

We could also create a partition index where indexing is local to each partition:

```
CREATE INDEX lkx1_psale_year ON psale_year
(industry_id, location_id, product_id) LOCAL
(
  PARTITION sale_to_2003 TABLESPACE pindx1
, PARTITION sale_to_2004 TABLESPACE pindx2
, PARTITION sale_after_2003 TABLESPACE pindx3
);
```

And we could create an index global to the entire partition:

```
CREATE INDEX gkx1_psale_year ON psale_year
(time_id) TABLESPACE INDX;
```

Note: Global partition indexing is more difficult to maintain, especially if entire partitions are exchanged, added or removed.

Now generate statistics:

```
ANALYZE TABLE psale_year COMPUTE STATISTICS;
```

6.2.2   CREATE TABLE: List Partition

Figure 6.3 shows CREATE TABLE syntax for a list partition. The specification LIST(<column>) specifies the column as the partition key. Rows are partitioned by placing them into separate partitions called <partition> based on where column values of <list> fit in.

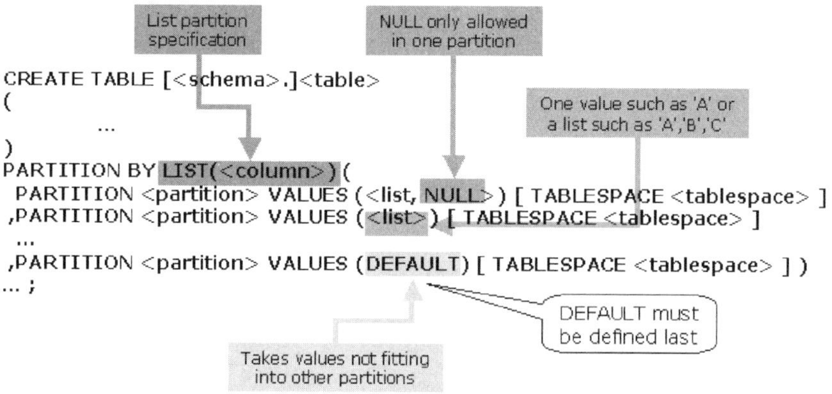

Figure 6.3
CREATE TABLE
syntax for list
partitions.

The following example makes a list partition for industry values in the SALE table:

```
CREATE TABLE psale_ind
PARTITION BY LIST(industry_id)
(
   PARTITION sale_ind_1_7 VALUES (1,2,3,4,5,6,7)
TABLESPACE pdata1
, PARTITION sale_ind_8_14 VALUES (8,9,10,11,12,13,14)
TABLESPACE pdata2
, PARTITION sale_ind_15_21 VALUES (15,16,17,18,19,20,21)
TABLESPACE pdata3
```

```
)
AS SELECT * FROM sale;
```

And we could create an index global to the entire partition:

```
CREATE INDEX gkx1_psale_ind
ON PSALE_IND (industry_id) TABLESPACE indx;
```

Now generate statistics:

```
ANALYZE TABLE psale_ind COMPUTE STATISTICS;
```

6.2.3 CREATE TABLE: Hash Partition

Figure 6.4 shows CREATE TABLE syntax for a hash partition. The specification HASH(<column>) specifies the column as the partition key. Rows are partitioned and spread evenly into <n> partitions as defined by the hashing algorithm.

Figure 6.4
*CREATE TABLE
syntax for hash
partitions.*

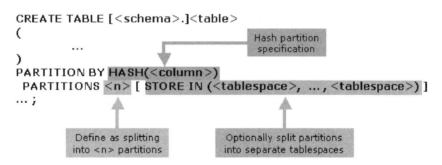

The following example makes a hash partition for industry values in the SALE table:

```
CREATE TABLE psale_revenue
PARTITION BY HASH(transaction_amount)
PARTITIONS 2 STORE IN (pdata1, pdata2)
AS SELECT * FROM sale;
```

> **Note:** Oracle Corporation recommends calculating hash algorithms as powers of 2 (exponents of 2). Thus, hash partitions should be numbers of 2, 4, 8, and beyond. 2 is 2^1, 4 is 2^2, and 8 is 2^3.

Local partition indexing could apply in this case, but this is not necessarily meaningful or useful:

```
CREATE INDEX lkx1_psale_revenue ON psale_revenue
(transaction_amount) LOCAL
(
  PARTITION sale_rev_1 TABLESPACE pindx1
, PARTITION sale_rev_2 TABLESPACE pindx2
);
```

Now generate statistics:

```
ANALYZE TABLE psale_revenue COMPUTE STATISTICS;
```

6.2.4 Composite Partitioning

Composite partitions can be of two forms. Those two forms are a range partition containing hash subpartitions, or a range partition containing list subpartitions. How composite partitioning is used is dependent on requirements. A range-hash composite could be used where equal division within large range sets is useful, perhaps to prevent skewing and aid in parallel processing. A range-list composite could be useful in dividing archival data into usable regions.

CREATE TABLE: Range-Hash Partition

Figure 6.5 shows CREATE TABLE syntax for a range-hash partition where range partitions are subdivided into hash subpartitions.

The following example makes hash subpartitions for each range partition of the SALE fact table:

```
CREATE TABLE psale_yrrev
PARTITION BY RANGE(transaction_date)
SUBPARTITION BY HASH(transaction_amount) SUBPARTITIONS 2
(
```

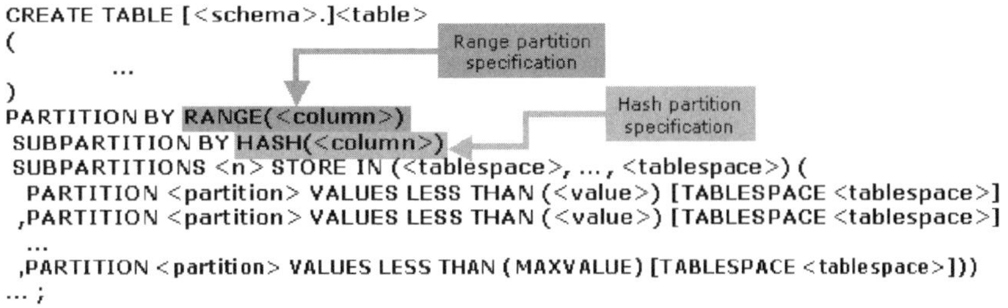

Figure 6.5
CREATE TABLE
syntax for range-
hash partitions.

```
CREATE TABLE [<schema>.]<table>
(
        ...
)
PARTITION BY RANGE(<column>)
 SUBPARTITION BY HASH(<column>)
 SUBPARTITIONS <n> STORE IN (<tablespace>, ... , <tablespace>) (
  PARTITION <partition> VALUES LESS THAN (<value>) [TABLESPACE <tablespace>]
 ,PARTITION <partition> VALUES LESS THAN (<value>) [TABLESPACE <tablespace>]
  ...
 ,PARTITION <partition> VALUES LESS THAN (MAXVALUE) [TABLESPACE <tablespace>]))
 ... ;
```

Range partition
specification

Hash partition
specification

```
    PARTITION sale_to_2003 VALUES LESS THAN
(TO_DATE('2003-01-01','YYYY-MM-DD'))
TABLESPACE pdata1
, PARTITION sale_to_2004 VALUES LESS THAN
(TO_DATE('2004-01-01','YYYY-MM-DD'))
TABLESPACE pdata2
, PARTITION sale_after_2003 VALUES LESS THAN
(MAXVALUE) TABLESPACE pdata3
)
AS SELECT * FROM sale;
```

Let's create a global index:

```
CREATE INDEX gkx1_psale_yrrev
ON psale_yrrev(industry_id) TABLESPACE indx;
```

Now generate statistics:

```
ANALYZE TABLE psale_yrrev COMPUTE STATISTICS;
```

CREATE TABLE: Range-List Partition

Figure 6.6 shows CREATE TABLE syntax for a range-list partition where range partitions are subdivided into list subpartitions.

The following example makes a list subpartition for each range partition of the SALE fact table:

```
CREATE TABLE psale_yrind
   PARTITION BY RANGE(transaction_date)
   SUBPARTITION BY LIST(industry_id)(
      PARTITION sale_to_2003 VALUES LESS THAN
```

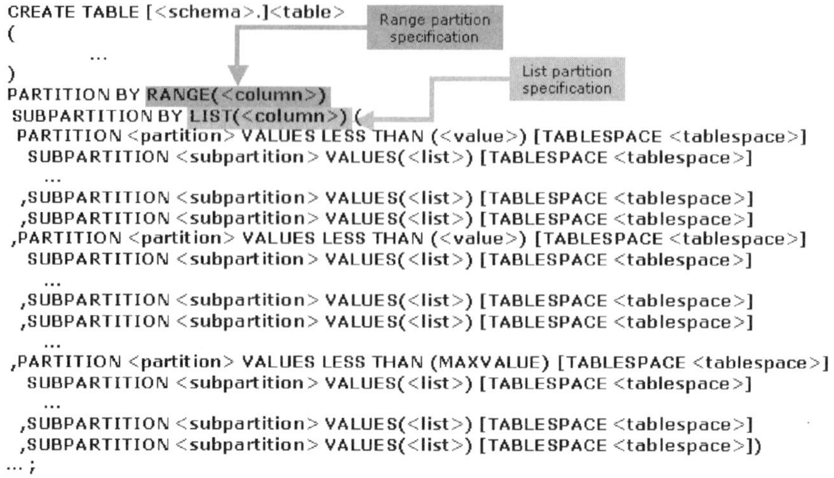

Figure 6.6
*CREATE TABLE
syntax for range-list
partitions.*

```
CREATE TABLE [<schema>.]<table>     Range partition
(                                    specification
    ...
)                                                    List partition
PARTITION BY RANGE(<column>)                         specification
    SUBPARTITION BY LIST(<column>) (
    PARTITION <partition> VALUES LESS THAN (<value>) [TABLESPACE <tablespace>]
        SUBPARTITION <subpartition> VALUES(<list>) [TABLESPACE <tablespace>]
        ...
    ,SUBPARTITION <subpartition> VALUES(<list>) [TABLESPACE <tablespace>]
    ,SUBPARTITION <subpartition> VALUES(<list>) [TABLESPACE <tablespace>]
    ,PARTITION <partition> VALUES LESS THAN (<value>) [TABLESPACE <tablespace>]
        SUBPARTITION <subpartition> VALUES(<list>) [TABLESPACE <tablespace>]
        ...
    ,SUBPARTITION <subpartition> VALUES(<list>) [TABLESPACE <tablespace>]
    ,SUBPARTITION <subpartition> VALUES(<list>) [TABLESPACE <tablespace>]
        ...
    ,PARTITION <partition> VALUES LESS THAN (MAXVALUE) [TABLESPACE <tablespace>]
        SUBPARTITION <subpartition> VALUES(<list>) [TABLESPACE <tablespace>]
        ...
    ,SUBPARTITION <subpartition> VALUES(<list>) [TABLESPACE <tablespace>]
    ,SUBPARTITION <subpartition> VALUES(<list>) [TABLESPACE <tablespace>])
    ... ;
```

```
            (TO_DATE('2003-01-01','YYYY-MM-DD'))
                (SUBPARTITION sale_ind_2003_1_7 VALUES (1,2,3,4,5,6,7)
                ,SUBPARTITION sale_ind_2003_8_14 VALUES
        (8,9,10,11,12,13,14)
                ,SUBPARTITION sale_ind_2003_15_21 VALUES
        (15,16,17,18,19,20,21))
            ,PARTITION sale_to_2004 VALUES LESS THAN
            (TO_DATE('2004-01-01','YYYY-MM-DD'))
                (SUBPARTITION sale_ind_2004_1_7 VALUES (1,2,3,4,5,6,7)
                ,SUBPARTITION sale_ind_2004_8_14 VALUES
        (8,9,10,11,12,13,14)
                ,SUBPARTITION sale_ind_2004_15_21 VALUES
        (15,16,17,18,19,20,21))
            ,PARTITION sale_after_2003 VALUES LESS THAN (MAXVALUE)
                (SUBPARTITION sale_ind_2005_1_7 VALUES (1,2,3,4,5,6,7)
                ,SUBPARTITION sale_ind_2005_8_14 VALUES
        (8,9,10,11,12,13,14)
                ,SUBPARTITION sale_ind_2005_15_21 VALUES
        (15,16,17,18,19,20,21))
            )  AS SELECT * FROM sale;
```

Local and global indexes are accounted for with partition and subpartition keys. We could however, generate statistics:

```
ANALYZE TABLE psale_yrind COMPUTE STATISTICS;
```

6.2.5 **Partitioned Materialized Views**

The main benefit of partitioning materialized views is that of parallel processing of DML refresh operations in parallel, on multiple partitions. Partition Change Tracking (PCT) is a feature of partitioning on materialized views, most obviously beneficial, where only a specific partition is processed. For example, when exchanging or dropping a partition, only the rows in the partition concerned are updated. Therefore, only a small part of a materialized view is subject to refresh.

There are various restrictions, most of which are logical. Obviously, the materialized view must have sufficient content in order to refer back to base tables adequately, as with other types of materialized views. Other factors are joins, which can make PCT complicated, if not impossible. Additionally, the structure of the partition key should enable access between materialized view rows and base tables.

Note: The partition key or partitioning factor must consist of a single column.

A partition marker can be stored as a column within a materialized view SELECT statement using a function called DBMS_VIEW.PMARKER. The CREATE MATERIALIZED view statement below shows a partitioned materialized view:

```
drop MATERIALIZED VIEW mv_revenue_by_quarter;
drop MATERIALIZED VIEW mv_revenue_by_month;
drop MATERIALIZED VIEW mv_join_sale;

CREATE MATERIALIZED VIEW mv_join_sale
    PARALLEL NOLOGGING
    PARTITION BY RANGE(transaction_date)
    (
      PARTITION sale_to_2003 VALUES LESS THAN
    (TO_DATE('2003-01-01','YYYY-MM-DD'))
    TABLESPACE pdata1
    , PARTITION sale_to_2004 VALUES LESS THAN
    (TO_DATE('2004-01-01','YYYY-MM-DD'))
    TABLESPACE pdata2
    , PARTITION sale_after_2003 VALUES LESS THAN
    (MAXVALUE)
```

```
        TABLESPACE pdata3
        )
        BUILD IMMEDIATE REFRESH FORCE
ON COMMIT ENABLE QUERY REWRITE
AS SELECT s.ROWID "sROWID"
        , l.ROWID "lROWID", DBMS_MVIEW.PMARKER(s.ROWID) "tROWID"
        , p.ROWID "pROWID", i.ROWID "iROWID"
    , s.order_amount,s.order_date
        , s.transaction_amount,s.transaction_date
        , s.payment_amount,s.payment_date,s.payment_text
        , s.product_quantity,s.product_price,s.product_date
        , l.region,l.country,l.state,l.city
        , t.month#,t.quarter#,t.year#
        , p.category, p.product, p.price, i.industry
FROM sale s, location l, time t, product p, industry i
WHERE s.location_id = l.location_id
AND s.time_id = t.time_id
AND s.product_id = p.product_id
AND s.industry_id = i.industry_id;
```

In order to allow refresh in this situation, materialized view logs would have to be created for any tables allowing refresh DML updates into the materialized view.

The DBMS_MVIEW.PMARKER function returns a partition-specific identifier that effectively locates each materialized view row within a specific partition. This function will not affect query rewrite in any way whatsoever, as it granularizes a materialized view at the partition level rather than the row level. This obviously helps when performing operations on entire partitions, such as dropping a partition. A partition marker can be used to identify a row for fact or dimension table columns, using a ROWID identifier from an underlying base table, which allows partition level granularity on refresh.

Note: The syntax for creating materialized view partitions is identical to creating partitions on tables. Refer to syntax sections earlier in this chapter and to Chapter 4. Even prebuilt table materialized views can be partitioned.

One of the most significant benefits of partitioning materialized views in data warehouses is partitioning by time, in which out-of-date archived data can be removed from the data warehouse by dropping entire partitions.

6.3   Tuning Queries with Partitioning

This section examines how queries behave when using Oracle Partitioning. The four areas to be discussed are: understanding EXPLAIN PLAN command results, parallel processing as applied to partitioning, partition pruning, and partition-wise joins.

6.3.1   Partitioning EXPLAIN PLANs

The EXPLAIN PLAN command produces an assessment of the way in which a query could be executed by the optimizer,[1] generating results into a table called PLAN_TABLE, more commonly known as the query plan table. The four columns OTHER_TAG, PARTITION_START, PARTITION_STOP, and PARTITION_ID will contain details of query execution against a partitioned object.

To demonstrate, let's begin by querying a nonpartitioned table. We can check partitioning on tables and materialized views by executing the query as shown in Figure 6.7.

Figure 6.7
Which tables and materialized views are partitioned?

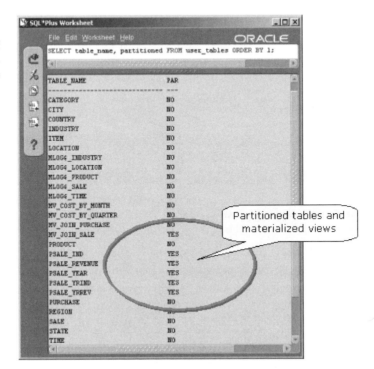

Figure 6.8
*A full table scan on
a nonpartitioned
table.*

Now query a nonpartitioned table as shown in Figure 6.8.

6.3.2   Partitioning and Parallel Processing

Parallel processing using partitions is very simple to understand. Partitioning can be used to split a table or materialized view into separate physical chunks. Earlier in this chapter, we created a range partition table of the SALE table called PSALE_YEAR. The partition key is the TRANSACTION_DATE column. Figure 6.9 shows the same query statement, but executed against the partitioned table PSALE_YEAR. The query plan in Figure 6.9 is thus vastly different to that of Figure 6.8.

Figure 6.9
*Parallel processing
against multiple
partitions.*

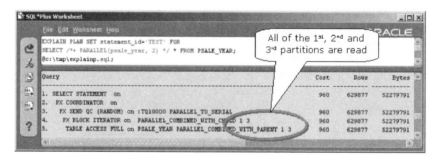

6.3.3   Partition Pruning

Partition pruning is a fancy name applied to a very simple process in which a query reads a subset of partitions in a table, quite often a single partition, as a result of a filter. In other words, the use and definition of partition pruning is really no big deal. However, the difference in performance can be phenomenal. Figure 6.10 shows partition pruning in action, using a filter to reduce the query to reading a single partition.

Figure 6.11 shows the same query as in Figure 6.10, but using the parallel hint once again.

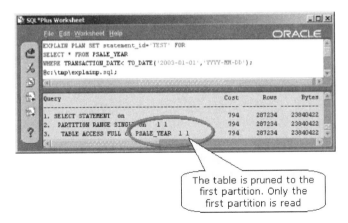

Figure 6.10
Partition pruning to read individual partitions.

Figure 6.11
Partition pruning to read individual partitions.

6.3.4 Partition-Wise Joins

A partition-wise join is a join across partitions where one or both tables in the join are partitioned. This leads to the possibility that there is potential for both full partition-wise joins and partial partition-wise joins. Before examining some example partition-wise joins it is essential to have something for comparison. Figure 6.12 shows a join between the two nonpartitioned tables SALE and TIME.

Full Partition-Wise Joins

A full partition-wise join can be selected by the optimizer when both tables are partitioned on the same matching column. Now, for the purposes of demonstration, we will partition both the SALE and TIME tables on the TIME_ID column:

```
CREATE TABLE psale_time
PARTITION BY RANGE(time_id)
```

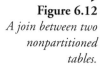

Figure 6.12
*A join between two
nonpartitioned
tables.*

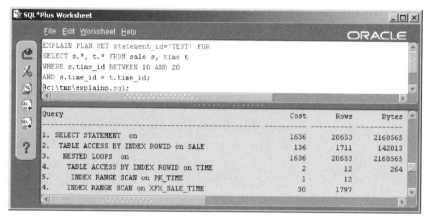

```
(
  PARTITION ptime_1 VALUES LESS THAN (51)
TABLESPACE pdata1
, PARTITION ptime_2 VALUES LESS THAN (101)
TABLESPACE pdata2
, PARTITION ptime_3 VALUES LESS THAN (MAXVALUE)
TABLESPACE pdata3
)
AS SELECT * FROM sale;

CREATE TABLE ptime
PARTITION BY RANGE(time_id)
(
  PARTITION ptime_1 VALUES LESS THAN (51)
TABLESPACE pdata1
, PARTITION ptime_2 VALUES LESS THAN (101)
TABLESPACE pdata2
, PARTITION ptime_3 VALUES LESS THAN (MAXVALUE)
TABLESPACE pdata3
)
AS SELECT * FROM time;
```

And create indexes global to entire partitions:

```
CREATE INDEX gkx1_psale_time ON psale_time(time_id)
TABLESPACE indx;
CREATE INDEX gkx1_ptime ON ptime(time_id) TABLESPACE indx;
```

And generate statistics:

```
ANALYZE TABLE psale_time COMPUTE STATISTICS;
ANALYZE TABLE ptime COMPUTE STATISTICS;
```

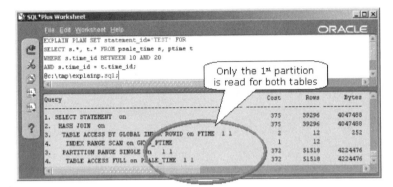

Figure 6.13
A full partition-wise join.

The query plan in Figure 6.13 demonstrates a full partition-wise join, because both tables have only their first partitions read. In other words, the join is performed on the pruned partitions as opposed to the entire tables.

Partial Partition-Wise Joins

A partial partition-wise join can be selected by the optimizer when only one of the tables in a join is partitioned on the joining column. The partitioned table or materialized view is usually the fact entity. We can demonstrate this by joining the PSALE_TIME partitioned sales fact table and the nonpartitioned TIME table, as shown in Figure 6.14.

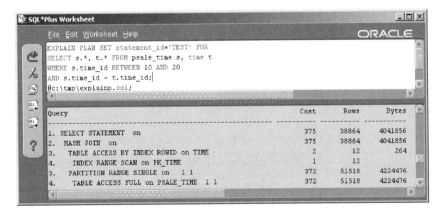

Figure 6.14
A partial partition-wise join.

6.4　Other Partitioning Tricks

There are numerous interesting possibilities that use partitioned objects and cannot be accomplished with nonpartitioned objects. In general, each of these tricks can be performed on or with individual partitions, avoiding the need to access entire table data sets. Partitioning tricks that potentially help database performance are:

- **DML Operations**. DML operations apply to individual partitions, where, for example, a DELETE command executed as a filter against a specific partition would only require access to rows in partitions indicated by the WHERE clause filter.

- **Add, Drop, and Truncate**. Individual partitions can be added, dropped or even truncated without affecting the rest of the partitions in a table.

- **Split and Merge**. A partition can be split into two partitions, or two partitions can be merged into a single partition. Once again, there is no effect on rows outside of the partitions being split or merged.

- **Rename**. Individual partitions can be renamed.

- **Move**. A partition can be moved into a different tablespace. No costly SQL code is involved in transferring data between tablespaces. Physical blocks must still be moved.

- **Exchange**. Partitions and subpartitions can be converted into tables and vice versa. Again, no costly SQL code is involved in transferring data.

6.5　Partitioning Metadata

Figure 6.15 shows the various metadata views giving access to partitioned metadata structures.

Some of the most basic and most useful views are:

- **USER_PART_TABLES**. Table partitioning details of tables at the table, rather than the individual partition, level.

Figure 6.15
Oracle Partitioning metadata.

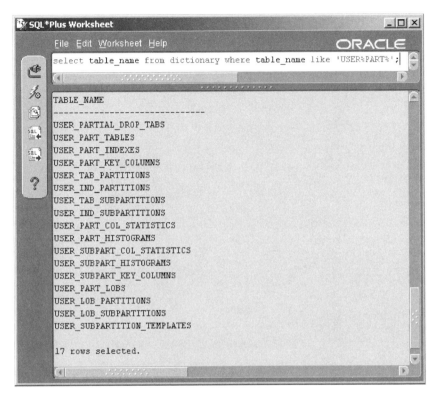

- **USER_TAB_PARTITIONS** and **USER_TAB_SUBPARTITIONS**. Table partition and subpartition structures, as per individual partitions within parent tables.

This chapter has examined the various basic aspects of using Oracle Partitioning. Oracle Partitioning is a tuning method in itself, and also one of the most appropriate and effective approaches to performance tuning of data warehouse databases.

The next chapter will begin the second part of this book, which will cover SQL coding for data warehouses. Before getting into the detail of aggregating and summarizing data warehouse data, we will take a brief look at the very basics of tuning Oracle SQL coding.

6.6   Endnotes

1.   Chapter 9 in *Oracle Performance Tuning for 9i and 10g* (ISBN: 1555583059)

Part II

Tuning SQL Code in a Data Warehouse

Chapter 7   The Basics of SQL Query Code Tuning

Chapter 8   Aggregation Using GROUP BY Clause Extensions

Chapter 9   Analysis Reporting

Chapter 10   Modeling with the MODEL Clause

7

The Basics of SQL Query Code Tuning

The chapter begins Part II of this book, which focuses on aspects of Oracle SQL code provided specifically for tuning of data–warehouse type functionality. In order to introduce aspects of tuning SQL code for data warehouses, it is necessary to go back to basics. This chapter will provide three things: (1) details of the most simplistic aspects of SQL code tuning, (2) a description of how the Oracle SQL engine executes SQL code internally, and (3) a brief look at tools for tuning Oracle Database. It is essential to understand the basic facts about how to write properly performing SQL code and perform basic tuning using Oracle internals and simple tools. Subsequent chapters will progress to considering specific details of tuning SQL coding for data warehouses.

Perhaps one of the most important rules of thumb for coding well performing SQL code statements—and particularly queries, those most subject to tuning—is what is commonly known as the *KISS* rule: *Keep It Simple, Stupid!* The simpler your SQL statements are, the faster they will be. There are two reasons for this. First, simple SQL statements are much more easily tuned by a programmer: second, the optimizer will function a lot better when assessing less complex SQL code. The negative effect of this is granularity, but this negative effect depends on how applications are coded. For instance, connecting to and disconnecting from a database for every SQL code statement is extremely inefficient.

7.1   Basic Query Tuning

This section examines the following topic areas:

- SELECT clause columns
- WHERE clause filtering

- Aggregating
- Functions
- Conditions and Operators
- Pseudocolumns
- Joins

7.1.1   Columns in the SELECT Clause

It is always faster to SELECT exact column names, as shown in Figure 7.1, as opposed to simply selecting all columns, because Oracle has to resolve columns in metadata before execution. For large tables, the difference is likely to be negligible, as shown in the following query:

```
SELECT * FROM sale;
```

Figure 7.1
Selecting the entire table.

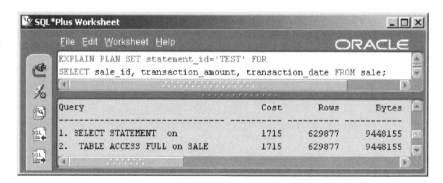

If there is an index, then use it. Reading column values directly from an index without reading a table at all is faster, because the index occupies less physical space. There is, therefore, less I/O. In the example shown in Figure 7.2, only the index is read.

7.1.2   Filtering with the WHERE Clause

The WHERE clause can be used to either include wanted rows or exclude unwanted rows, or both. The WHERE clause can be used to tune SQL statements simply by attempting to match WHERE clause specifications to indexes, sorted orders, and physical ordering in tables. In other words, filter according to how the metadata is constructed.

Figure 7.2
Selecting index columns only.

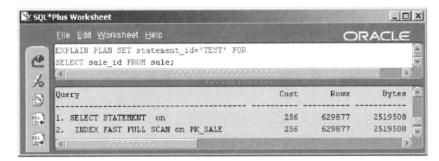

Note: The optimizer in the latest versions of Oracle Database is capable of using indexes when columns are not ordered, such that index column order no longer needs to precisely match WHERE clause column sequencing. However, good programming practice is best in the long run for application stability. Portability between different programmers is also important.

Figure 7.3 shows a query with a WHERE clause not matching an index such that a full table scan is executed. Only 14 rows are retrieved from the table. That amounts to about one thousandth of 1% of all the rows in the table. However, there is no usable index containing the TRANSACTION_AMOUNT column; thus, the entire table is read.

Figure 7.3
WHERE clause filtering on table only.

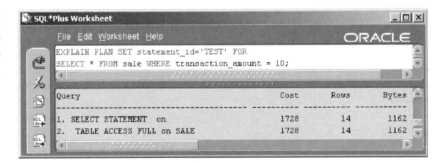

Figure 7.4 shows an index and the table being read, as opposed to the table alone. The index is used to rapidly find the index row; then the ROWID is used to rapidly access the unique row in the table. Whereas in Figure 7.3 all the blocks in the table are read, in Figure 7.4 only a few block reads in both the index and the table are required to find the required row. This demonstrates how a very simple change to a WHERE clause filter can make an immense difference in performance.

Figure 7.4
*WHERE clause
filtering matching
an index.*

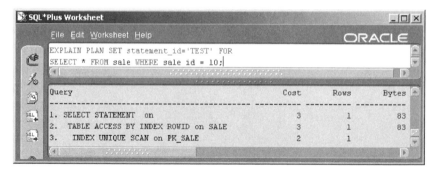

Note: Remember that when reading a small table, even if an index is indicated in a WHERE clause, it is quite possible that the optimizer will full scan the table, as reading the entire table could be faster than reading both index and table.

The optimizer may even opt to full table scan a large table if the cost is estimated at being less than reading index and table. It depends on how many rows are being read. It is all about cost!

Multiple Column WHERE Clause Filters

Multiple column WHERE clauses can also match indexes and perform better. In most recent versions of Oracle Database, the sequence of column comparisons within a WHERE clause is less important, but still significant to performance.

Note: Oracle Database 10*g* optimization has less stringent requirements for SQL code case sensitivity than previous versions of Oracle Database.

There are a number of possibilities for index use with WHERE clauses containing multiple column comparisons. Separate column comparisons do not have to be coded in the order of indexed column sequence to use the index. The table PSALE_YEAR is created in Chapter 6 as a partitioned table. This table has a three-column local partition composite index on INDUSTRY_ID, LOCATION_ID, and PRODUCT_ID columns, in that order. Figure 7.5 shows a query with a WHERE clause matching the index with both columns in the index and the sequence of columns in the index.

Figure 7.5
*Reading a
composite index
with a matching
WHERE clause.*

Figure 7.5
*Reading a
composite index
with a matching
WHERE clause.*

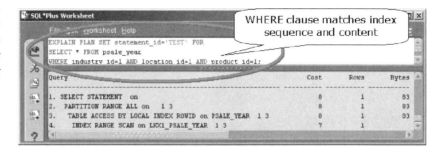

Figure 7.6 uses a WHERE clause containing all the columns in the index, but with the sequence of the columns reversed and thus not the same as the index. However, the optimizer can still read the index in the same way as in Figure 7.5.

Figure 7.6
*Reading a
composite index
without a
matching WHERE
clause.*

The optimizer will decide on index use depending on how many rows are accessed by the WHERE clause filter. If the percentage of rows in the table becomes too great, then the optimizer will revert to a full table scan as in Figure 7.7.

Figure 7.7
*Using too few
columns in a
composite index.*

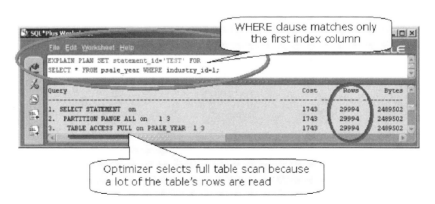

Figure 7.8 shows the same query as in Figures 7.6 and 7.7, but with the first two prefix columns for the index. The index is used even though the third column is omitted from the WHERE clause. The optimizer considers using the index the best option, because much fewer rows are read than for the query in Figure 7.7, where only a single column of the index was used.

Figure 7.8
Using enough composite index prefix columns.

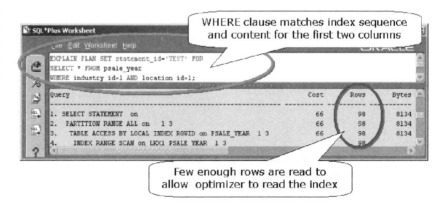

An index skip scan is used in Figure 7.9, where prefix index columns can be skipped. An index skip scan is a special type of index read that can utilize subset columns of composite indexes, where perhaps the first column in a multiple column composite index is not required in order for that index to be used by the optimizer.

Figure 7.9
A skip scan index read on a composite index.

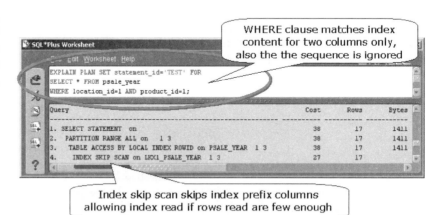

When coding WHERE clauses, try to match comparison condition column sequences with the existing index column sequences, although it is not always strictly necessary. Also try to use unique, single column indexes wherever possible. A single column unique index is much more likely to produce exact hits. An exact hit finds a single row and is, therefore, the fastest access method, because it performs unique row matches (finds a single row) rather than range scans of multiple rows.

7.1.3 Aggregating

Aggregation involves use of the GROUP BY clause, application of functions, and various other extensions such as ROLLUP, CUBE, and MODEL clauses, to be covered in detail in later chapters.

How to Use the HAVING Clause

The only thing to remember about the HAVING clause is that it applies to the aggregated results returned by the GROUP BY clause. In other words, the HAVING clause is used to filter aggregated rows. A common mistake is to use HAVING in place of a WHERE clause, or vice versa. The WHERE clause filters rows at the source; in other words, it can potentially decrease I/O activity by reading fewer rows. Reading fewer rows is always good for performance. The HAVING clause will be applied to aggregated results produced by a GROUP BY clause. In other words, the HAVING clause is executed after all I/O activity is completed. Therefore, replacing WHERE clause filtering with HAVING clause filtering can hurt performance, since I/O activity could be increased. Figure 7.10 shows the inappropriate use of the HAVING clause replaced with a more appropriate WHERE clause, clearly showing the resulting improvement in performance.

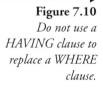

Figure 7.10
Do not use a HAVING clause to replace a WHERE clause.

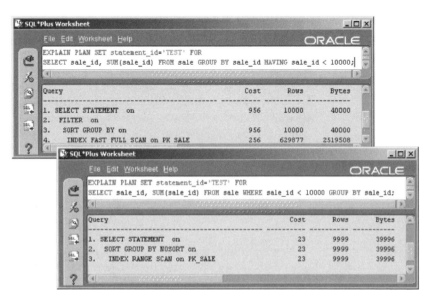

Figure 7.11 shows an appropriate use of the HAVING clause, such that the HAVING clause filters the result of the GROUP BY clause, the aggregation, and the expression SUM(SALE_ID). Also note the significant decrease in cost between Figures 7.10 and 7.11, where Figure 7.11 has a much smaller amount in the Bytes column, thus much less I/O activity.

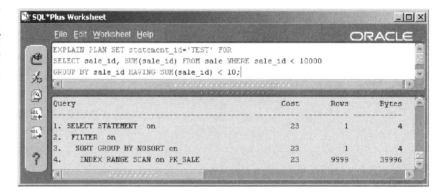

Figure 7.11
The HAVING clause filters aggregated groups.

The HAVING clause filter can help performance because it filters. Filtering allows the processing and return of fewer rows. The HAVING clause filtering, shown in the query plans in Figures 7.10 and 7.11, shows that HAVING clause filtering is always executed after the GROUP BY sorting process.

In general, the GROUP BY clause can perform some sorting if it matches indexing. Filtering aggregate results with the HAVING clause can help increase performance by filtering aggregated results of the GROUP BY clause.

7.1.4   **Using Functions**

The most relevant thing to say about functions is that they are best not used where you expect a SQL statement to use an index. Let's begin by creating a new index on the TRANSACTION_DATE column of the SALE table as follows:

```
CREATE INDEX xak_sale_tran_date ON SALE(transaction_date)
TABLESPACE indx COMPUTE STATISTICS NOLOGGING;
```

Now examine Figure 7.12 and note how the first query does not use the index and the second does use the index. In the first query, the function forces the optimizer to ignore the index on the TRANSACTION_DATE

Figure 7.12
*Functions and
index use in
queries.*

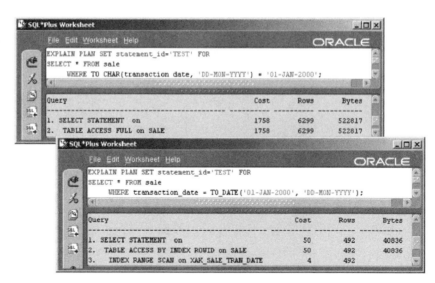

column, and a full table scan results because the function is applied to the table column. In the second query, the function is not applied to the table column but to the literal string, allowing index access for the table column.

The significance of the two queries shown in Figure 7.12 is which side of a comparison to place a function. The function is best placed on the side of the comparison not working with the table column.

One solution for using functions in SQL code is function-based indexes, of course. However, the more indexes created for a table, the slower DML activity will be. A function-based index contains the resulting value of an expression. Let's recreate the previously created index as a function-based index:

```
DROP INDEX xak_sale_tran_date;
CREATE INDEX xak_sale_tran_date
ON SALE(TO_CHAR(transaction_date, 'DD-MON-YYYY'))
TABLESPACE indx COMPUTE STATISTICS NOLOGGING;
```

An index search against that function-based index will search the index for the value of the expression, as shown in Figure 7.13.

Figure 7.13
Function based indexing.

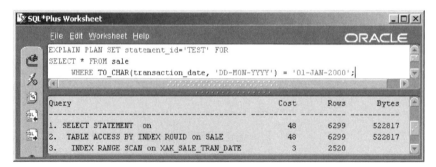

Note: Use of function-based indexing requires up-to-date statistics, the QUERY_REWRITE system privilege (obsolete in Oracle Database 10*g*), and execute privileges on any user-defined functions. Additionally, the configuration parameters QUERY_REWRITE_ENABLED = TRUE and QUERY REWRITE_INTEGRITY = TRUSTED must be set. (Setting these parameters is not required to allow function-based indexes to operate when using Oracle Database 10*g*).

7.1.5   Conditions and Operators

A condition measures a state between two expressions, such as whether two expressions are equal to each other. If the two expressions are equal, then the condition is said to be true. An operator combines expressions, allowing multiple conditional results to be verified together. This section will cover:

- Comparison conditions, such as equality, inequality, and ranges

- Pattern matching using LIKE

- Set membership with IN and EXISTS

- Logical operators, such as AND and OR

- Set operators, such as UNION and INTERSECT

Comparison Conditions

Comparison conditions are used in SQL statements, most commonly in WHERE and HAVING clause filters. Different comparison conditions can sometimes have vastly different effects on the performance of SQL statements. Let's examine each in turn with various options and recommendations for potential improvement.

Equi, Anti, and Range

The syntax of equi, anti, and range comparison conditions is as follows:

```
<expression> { [!]= | > | < | <= | >= } <expression>


<expression> [ NOT ] BETWEEN <expression> AND <expression>
```

Using an equals sign (equi) is the fastest comparison condition if a unique index exists, potentially finding a single row as an exact row hit. Any type of anti comparison, such as != or NOT, is looking for what is not in a table and thus must read the entire table regardless; sometimes full index scans can be used.

LIKE Pattern Matching

The syntax of the LIKE pattern matching condition is:

```
<expression> [ NOT ] LIKE <expression>
```

Anything but a precise string pattern match, using wild card characters, will often result in a full table scan. Patterns beginning with wild card characters are likely to prohibit string searches through indexes. In other words, the following query could use an index search:

```
SELECT * FROM location WHERE region LIKE 'North America%';
```

On the contrary, a query such as the following will use a full table scan, as it cannot really do otherwise:

```
SELECT * FROM location WHERE region LIKE '%North America';
```

Obviously the number of rows accessed can help determine whether the optimizer opts for a full table scan.

Set Membership (IN and EXISTS)

The syntax of the IN and EXISTS set membership comparison conditions is:

```
<expression> [ NOT ] IN <expression>
```

```
<expression> [ NOT ] EXISTS <expression>
```

Traditionally IN is used to test against a list of literal values, as in the query:

```
SELECT * FROM location WHERE region IN
('Asia','Europe','Africa');
```

EXISTS, on the contrary, is used to check against a dynamic set of values, such as that produced by a subquery, as in the example:

```
SELECT * FROM location WHERE EXISTS
(SELECT region FROM region WHERE region = location.region);
```

In the above example the REGION column is passed down from the calling query into the subquery. This is called a correlated query because the two queries are correlated or associated together by the passed expression. A correlated query allows the checking of row against row, as opposed to the complete execution of the subquery for every row of the calling query. Additionally EXISTS is more likely to make use of index links between calling query and subquery.

Note: IN and EXISTS were introduced in a previous version of Oracle Database. In the most recent versions of Oracle Database, the advantages of EXISTS rather than IN, particularly for correlated queries, are becoming somewhat blurred and EXISTS probably no longer exists.

Using Subqueries for Efficiency

Up to Oracle Database version 9*i*, multiple nesting of subqueries using IN, EXISTS, and inline views sometimes allowed for fairly successful tuning of highly complex join queries [1]. Other than providing performance improvements, multiple-layered nesting of subqueries can help simplify the coding and testing of highly complex joins. In Oracle Database 10*g*, the optimizer appears to have largely caught up with this approach, making it effectively redundant as far as performance is concerned. Data warehouses are usually denormalized and simplified structures in terms of entity numbers, and highly complex join queries are less prevalent.

Note: Multiple layers of nested subqueries can greatly simplify the coding of highly complex joins of more than five tables. Breaking complex problems into small problems simplifies the smaller problems, and as a result, the entire problem is simplified. Performance may not necessarily be affected other than that the SQL code can be written more easily and efficiently. I have seen joins of more than fifteen tables, that if they had not been broken down into smaller chunks, would have needed a brain the size of a planet just to figure out what they were doing, let alone performance-tune them!

Groups

The syntax of the grouping comparison condition is as follows:

```
<expression> [ = | != | > | < | >= | <= ] [ ANY | SOME | ALL ]
<expression>
```

ANY, SOME, and ALL comparisons are generally not very conducive to SQL tuning. In some respects they are best not used.

Logical Operators

Logical operators in Oracle SQL are AND, OR, and NOT. Logical operators allow for Boolean logic when comparing expressions, such as in WHERE clause filtering tests. Mathematically, the sequence of precedence is NOT, followed by AND, and finally OR. Precedence can be altered using parentheses.

With respect to tuning, it makes sense that the more logical operators in a WHERE clause, the more complex it becomes for the optimizer to make an informed decision. In extreme cases it may be expedient to substitute a set of AND operators with case statements, DECODE functions or even an IN or EXISTS operator. Additionally, OR can be substituted for with set operators such as the UNION set operator, although this method is not recommended. There are nearly always better ways to recode complexity than resorting to set operators, quite often using subqueries.

Set Operators

There is not really any effective way to tune queries containing set operators. Sometimes set operators can be substituted for with some other type of equivalent functionality, such as using subqueries. The most significant tuning factor is to tune the two individual queries merged by a set operator. Set operators are used to combine two separate queries into a composite or merged query. Both queries must have the same datatypes for each column in the column select list:

- **UNION ALL**. UNION ALL retrieves all rows from both queries, including duplicates. Duplicate rows are rows returned by both queries.

- **UNION**. UNION is as UNION ALL, but duplicate rows are only returned once.

- **INTERSECT**. INTERSECT returns distinct rows occurring in both queries. An intersection is a little like an inner join.

- **MINUS**. MINUS returns one query less the other, a little like a left outer join where only distinct rows in the first query and not in the second query are returned.

7.1.6 Pseudocolumns

In this section we will briefly discuss sequences, ROWID and ROWNUM pseudocolumns.

Sequences

Sequences are used in Oracle Database as automated counters. Sequences are the most efficient way of creating sequentially incrementing numbers. Sequences are accessed by the two pseudocolumns <sequence>.CURRVAL and <sequence>.NEXTVAL, most commonly the latter. Sequences are often used to create unique integer identifiers, such as surrogate key primary key values for tables.

As shown in Figure 7.14, the cost of accessing a sequence, as opposed to a maximum value from a large table, is slightly lower. The real performance difference when using sequences is that each sequence is accessed as a separate object in the database. In the old and dirty days before the advent of Oracle sequence objects and automated counters, items such as unique surrogate keys were either not used or stored in a single central system meta-

Figure 7.14
Using sequences as auto counters.

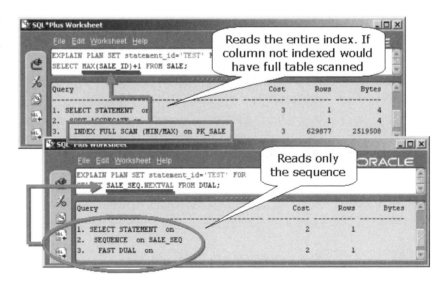

data table. This was potentially disastrous in a highly concurrent environment and often lead to serious hot block issues. In fact, even in modern applications, these central tables are quite common when design is approached from the application level alone, and quite often when older data models are copied.

Note: Use sequences where appropriate.

The ROWID Pseudocolumn

A ROWID is, in programming terms, a logical address in a Oracle Database. ROWID values point to rows in tables. Accessing rows using ROWID pointers is probably the fastest row access method in Oracle Database, since it is a direct pointer to a database-wide unique address. The down side of ROWID pointers is that they do not necessarily point at the same rows in perpetuity, because they are relative to datafile, tablespace, block, and row. These values can change, sometimes even unexpectedly. Never store a ROWID in a table column as a pointer to other tables or rows if data or structure will be changing in the database. If ROWID pointers can be used for data access they can be blindingly fast, but is not recommended by Oracle Corporation. Any type of restructuring operation can and will alter ROWID pointer values to rows in a database. If ROWID values were stored and their row locations change, immense quantities of data can become orphaned, perhaps even irretrievably, depending on table structure.

Note: Then again, accessing rows using ROWIDs can be leaps and bounds faster than any other access method. Static data or read-only data warehouses are most certainly a possibility. Be aware of anything that might cause changes to ROWID values—namely, anything making up the ROWID, such as tablespace or datafile. I have experimented with ROW-IDs. Once again, it is not a recommended practice, so I can't be held responsible if your implementation goes completely nuts. I would suggest experimenting with purely static databases. And the operative term is I think database-wide, not tablespace–wide, or even table-wide, but an entire database. And nothing but a single instance local database please. This practice is not recommended or supported!

The ROWNUM Pseudocolumn

A ROWNUM is a row number or a sequential counter representing the order in which a row is returned from a query. ROWNUM can be used to restrict the number of rows returned. There are numerous interesting ways in which ROWNUM can be used. For instance, the example following allows creation of a table from another, including all constraints but excluding any rows. This is a useful and fast method of making an empty copy of a very large table.

```
CREATE TABLE tmp AS SELECT * FROM sale WHERE ROWNUM < 1;
```

One point to note is as in the following example. A ROWNUM restriction is applied in the WHERE clause. Since the ORDER BY clause occurs after the WHERE clause, the ROWNUM restriction is not applied to the sorted output. The solution to this problem is the second example.

```
SELECT * FROM sale WHERE ROWNUM < 25 ORDER BY
transaction_date;

SELECT * FROM
(SELECT * FROM sale ORDER BY transaction_date)
WHERE ROWNUM < 25;
```

7.1.7 Joins

Tuning joins in data warehouses is mostly about the simplification of data warehouse entities using star schemas and fewer entities, leading to less complex joins. Besides the structural details there are two approaches to tuning SQL code joins. The first approach is deciding how to join tables from a purely SQL code perspective. The second approach is how the Oracle Database optimizer executes joins.

How to Code Joins in SQL Code

The easiest approach when building SQL code is to attempt to divide joins into two sections: (1) potentially efficient joins and (2) potentially inefficient joins.

What is an efficient join? An efficient join is a join SQL query that can be tuned to an acceptable level of performance. Certain types of join queries are inherently easily tuned and, thus, can give good performance. In general a join is efficient when it can use indexes on large tables or is reading only very small tables.

Note: Any type of join will be inefficient if coded improperly.

What types of joins are inherently efficient?

- **Intersection**. Intersections using equality.
- **Self Join**. Self joins using equality between separate hierarchical levels.
- **Range Join**. Range joins are dubious. I have never understood the advantage of joining two tables based on a row in one being both equal to and not equal to multiple differing rows in another table. I am thus inclined to ignore range joins as being potentially meaningless in the real world.

Note: A range join is not the same as an index range scan. An index range scan reads a chunk of an index. A range join attempts to join something like: <expression> >= <expression>.

What is an inefficient join? An inefficient join is a SQL query that joins tables; it is difficult to tune or cannot be tuned to an acceptable level of performance. Certain types of join queries are inherently both poor performers and difficult, if not impossible, to tune. Inefficient joins are best avoided. In data warehouse databases avoiding these types of joins is sometimes not possible. However, using GROUP BY clause extensions, the MODEL clause, and OLAP (Online Analytical Processing) features can help, as shown in subsequent chapters of this book.

What types of joins are inherently inefficient?

- **Outer Join**. Outer joins can sometimes be a problem. Tuning an outer join requires the same approach to tuning as with an inner join. Even though outer joins are applicable to reporting and data warehouse type structures, a need for their profligate use could indicate potential data model problems, such as a data model being too granular. In a data warehouse, this can cause serious performance problems. On the other hand, outer joins are not always inefficient. To a certain extent, performance depends on the ratio of rows retrieved from the intersection to rows retrieved outside the intersection. The more rows retrieved from the intersection the better. The more rows retrieved outside the intersection, the more likely there could be a data modeling issue.

- **Cross Join**. A cross join, or Cartesian Product, joins every row in one table to every row in another table. If two tables have one million rows each the result would be 10^{12} rows. That's a lot of rows! Data warehouses sometimes use Cartesian Product joins.

- **Anti Join**. An anti join is a little like a range join, and it might seem a little silly even to mention it. An anti join finds nonmatching rows between tables. Why do this? Additionally, a negative will always full table scan because it searches for what does not exist rather than what does exist.

Note: The larger the number of tables and columns involved in a join, the less likely the optimizer will be able to assess an optimal query plan. Additionally, the more complex a join is, the more time and effort in terms of people hours required to tune that SQL code.

Join types are not always efficient or inefficient, because a lot depends on coding quality, index quality, and structural design. Structural design equates to both entity structures and underlying physical structure—determining I/O efficiency.

How Oracle Joins Tables

The other approach to joins is the way that Oracle Database and the optimizer execute joins. The optimizer will execute a join as a nested loop join, a hash join or a sort merge join.

- **Nested Loop Join.** A nested loop is the most efficient and is generally selected by the optimizer when joining a small and a large row set. A nested loop join is relatively small because a relatively small number of rows are joined. For example, in a data warehouse a nested loop is often applied between a small dimension table and a large fact table, as shown in Figure 7.15.

Figure 7.15
A nested loop join between very small and large row sets.

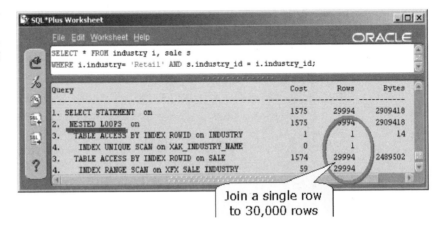

Join a single row to 30,000 rows

Hash Join. A hash join is usually applied to two row sets with similar row counts, with both row sets having a large number of rows. The optimizer selects a hash join when it is cheaper than either a nested loop or a

Figure 7.16
*A hash join
between small and
large row sets.*

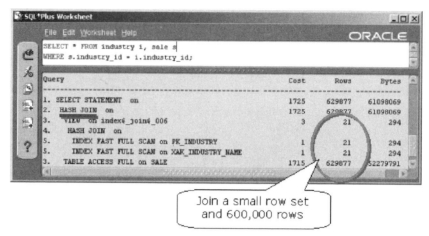

> Join a small row set
> and 600,000 rows

sort merge join. A hash join effectively full scans both data sources, where selection of a hash join over that of a nested loop join has more to do with retrieval of rows by the inner loop of the nested loop join. One again the number of rows joined is the deciding factor. A hash join creates a hash table for one of the tables in memory, usually the smaller of the two, in order to join the other table with a fast access hash table. The two sets of rows are joined using a hash join. A hash join has the overhead of creating a hash table first, where as a nested loop join just joins the row sets. A hash join is shown in Figure 7.16.

- **Sort Merge Join**. A sort merge join is used by the optimizer to join two very large row sets in cases when neither a nested loop or hash

Figure 7.17
*A sort merge join
between very large
row sets.*

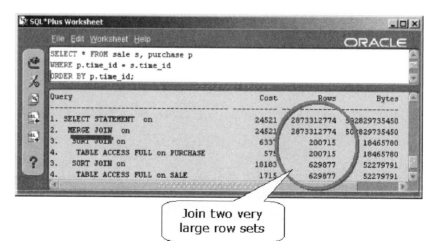

> Join two very
> large row sets

join will suffice. A sort merge join sorts each row set first and then merges the two sorted results into a merged sorted result. Sort merge joins are slow in comparison to nested loop and hash joins and could indicate that a join query is simply joining too many rows. Perhaps it is best to examine filtering before trying to do anything else to tune the query. A sort merge join is shown in Figure 7.17.

How to Tune a Join

So how can a join be tuned? There are a number of factors to consider:

- **Equality**. Use equality first.
- **Ranges**. Use range operators where equality does not apply. However, range operators are dubious with joins, because results might be meaningless.
- **Avoid Searching for What Is Not Present**. Avoid use of negatives in the form of != or NOT.
- **LIKE**. Avoid LIKE pattern matching.
- **Small Row Counts**. Try to retrieve specific rows and in small numbers.
- **Apply Largest Filters First**. Filter from large tables first to reduce rows joined. Retrieve tables in order from the most highly filtered table downwards, preferably the largest table has the most filtering applied.

Note: It is essential to reduce row numbers from large tables as much as possible before joining them to other tables.

The most highly filtered table is the table with the smallest percentage of its rows retrieved, preferably the largest table is filtered the most.

- **Use Indexes**. Use indexes wherever possible, except for very small tables, as the optimizer might decide it is more efficient to full table scan small static tables. However, full table scans become less likely, even for small tables, when joins include large numbers of tables.
- **The Optimizer Is Very Capable**. Let the optimizer do its job. The optimizer in the latest version of Oracle Database is highly effective, but still not completely infallible.

- **Nested Subquery Semi-Joins**. As already mentioned earlier in this chapter, it is possible to tune joins or at least simplify their coding, by using nested layers of subqueries. However, this type of tuning is more likely to apply in highly normalized OLTP transaction data model structures, not data warehouse data models.

7.2   How Oracle SQL Is Executed

What happens when an Oracle SQL statement is sent to the database? A portion of memory is allocated to store the results of a SQL statement. This chunk of memory is called a cursor. Among other things, a cursor contains a pointer to the row in an index or table currently being fetched from the database. Unless a cursor is declared explicitly in a tool, such as PL/SQL, then a cursor is implicitly created for every SQL SELECT statement submitted to Oracle Database. When a SQL statement has finished executing, the cursor can either be left in memory as a reusable, already allocated chunk of memory or it can be removed from memory altogether.

After parsing is complete, if a previously calculated query plan is not found, the optimizer will create a query plan for the submitted query. The purpose of the optimizer is to optimize the performance of SQL statements.

Let's begin with a brief explanation of the parser.

7.2.1   The Parser

A SQL statement is parsed when submitted to the query engine. What is parsing? The meaning of the word "parsing" is that of syntactical and perhaps grammatical or semantic analysis of a sentence. In programming terms, parsing is a syntax check on a line of program code and between related lines. SQL statements are lines of program code. So the parser is effectively a compiler of SQL statements, much like a C compiler is a compiler or syntax analyzer of C programming language commands.

The Oracle SQL parser does a few other things. There is a portion of memory or a buffer in the Oracle Database configuration called the shared pool. The shared pool is used to store parsed execution plans for previously executed SQL statements. These previously parsed execution plans can be used to re-execute the SQL statement if exactly, and I mean *exactly*, the same string is executed once again.

Thus, the optimizer does not have to do its work all over again. The result is that if the parser finds an existing SQL code statement in the shared pool it does not have to call the optimizer and recalculate the execution plan for the SQL statement.

Parses can be split into two categories:

- **Hard parse**. No match is found in the shared pool for a SQL statement never before submitted to the database engine.
- **Soft parse**. A match is found for a SQL statement perhaps submitted to the database engine by a different session.

Hard parses are more expensive in system resources than soft parses, but re-parsing is best avoided altogether if possible.

7.2.2   The Optimizer

The optimizer determines the best way to execute a SQL code statement in the fastest way possible, based on information available to it. The optimizer can use various methods of assessing the best path of performance for a SQL code statement. These methods include:

- Statistics
- Hints
- Histograms

Indexes against tables may or may not be used as the better option to execute a SQL statement. Sometimes the optimizer will decide that reading an entire table is more efficient than reading a small part of an index to access a ROWID pointer accessing a small number of table rows.

Through the years and various versions of Oracle Database, the optimizer has become more and more intelligent. In Oracle Database 10*g*, it can be relied on fairly heavily to produce the best performance for SQL code.

In general, the capabilities of the optimizer will deteriorate as the complexity of SQL code increases and particularly as the the quality of SQL code decreases. The optimizer should not be affected by database size unless SQL code or data model are poorly tuned and constructed. Database size merely exacerbates problems caused by poor design. Unfortunately these circumstances happen often. In OLTP systems, SQL code can sometimes become so complex and convoluted that the optimizer simply cannot cope and executes full table scans on all tables. In data warehouses, tables are sometimes so large sometimes that special attention is needed, because scale and poor coding are simply way beyond the capabilities of the optimizer.

Statistics are very important to the optimizer and the cost-based approach.

Note: Rule-based optimization is redundant and no longer supported.

The more up-to-date statistics are, the more accurately the optimizer can predict the best way to execute a SQL statement. In very large, or very active, databases, continual update of statistics is impractical, time consuming, and possibly a cause for contention. However, the more out of date statistics are the less accurate the optimizer will be.

The Importance of Statistics

Statistics are a computation or estimation of the exact size and placement of data in tables and indexes. Statistics can be used by the optimizer to make a better assessment of actual data, thus producing better query plans, more accurately matching the data as it actually is in the database.

Note: The accuracy of statistics is much more important in data warehouses as compared to OLTP databases, due to increased accuracy requirements and the enormous volumes of data in data warehouses.

Realistic Statistics

The SQL code Optimizer uses statistics to compile the most efficient methods of executing SQL statements. Statistics are measurements of the data itself, such as how large a table is and how useful an index is. When an SQL statement accesses a table, both table and index states are important. States of database objects, such as tables and indexes, are contained within statistics. If the statistics are out-of-date, the optimizer is not functioning realistically. Out-of-date statistics would have the same effect on all types of databases. In a data warehouse this is doubly important due to the high level of accuracy required when searching through enormous volumes of data.

Dynamic Sampling

For statistics to be realistic and effective, they must be frequently generated. In any type of database, data could be changing all the time; even a data warehouse can change substantially on a daily basis. Statistics can rapidly become redundant. Optimization against redundant statistics can sometimes cause as big a performance problem as not having those statistics at all, depending, of course, on how relatively out-of-date statistics are. If statistics are out-of–date, or not present, then dynamic sampling may be used. Dynamic sampling reads a small number of blocks in a table to make a best guess at actual statistical values.

Note: The configuration parameter controlling dynamic sampling is OPTIMIZER_DYNAMIC_SAMPLING and is set on by default, at a value of 2.

The OPTIMIZER_DYNAMIC_SAMPLING parameter sets dynamic sampling of data, substituting for cost-based statistics, from between a setting of 0 and 10. Set to 0 dynamic sampling is disabled, and set to 10 the entire table is read. Settings in between simply change the number of blocks read for the sample.

Overriding the Optimizer Using Hints

Hints can be used to force an alteration to the way that the optimizer creates a query plan for a query [2]. OLTP databases rarely require use of hints if statistics can be regularly maintained. Data warehouses, on the other hand, can benefit substantially from using hints quite often due to large data quantities and difficulty in maintaining up-to-date statistics.

In fact, hints are more commonly used in large data warehouse or reporting databases, rule-based databases, or those lacking current or any statistics. Generating statistics can be time consuming. Using the DBMS_STATS package instead of the ANALYZE command may help alleviate some potential problems by executing statistics generation procedures in parallel. Hints can be used to control the optimizer and, to a certain extent, freeze execution plans, in much the same way as outlines were used in older versions of Oracle Database.

The syntax of a hint is such that it is placed after a DML command between comments as shown, including the plus (+) sign.

```
SELECT /*+ <HINT> */ * FROM sale;

INSERT /*+ <HINT> */ INTO sale( … ) VALUES( … );

UPDATE /*+ <HINT> */ sale SET … ;

DELETE /*+ <HINT> */ FROM sale … ;
```

Note: If an alias is used in a SQL statement, then any hints must refer to the alias and not the table.

It is always a good idea to check query plans for SQL statements, if only to ensure that hints are coded in a syntactically correct manner. Incorrectly coded hints do not produce SQL code parser errors and may never be detected. The following SQL statement will execute without error:

```
SELECT /*+ STUPIDHINT */ * FROM customer;
```

Classifying Hints

There are all sorts of hints for suggesting that the optimizer do things differently. This chapter contains a list of hints. This list does not include all available hints, just the interesting ones. See Chapter 8 in *Overriding the Optimizer Using Hints: Oracle Performance Tuning for 9i and 10g* (ISBN: 1555583059) for extensive examples using of hints. This book simply does not have enough pages to include all the detail from my previous OLTP tuning title.

I like to categorize hints as:

- Influence the optimizer
- Change table scans
- Change index scans
- Change joins
- Parallel SQL
- Change queries and subqueries
- Other hints

Influence the Optimizer

- **ALL_ROWS**. Suppresses indexes and favors full table scans to find all rows.

- **FIRST_ROWS(n)**. More likely to use indexing, because the query plan should assume that only the first *n* rows for a query will be retrieved.

- **CPU_COSTING**. Default mode, persuades the optimizer to estimate query execution time based on CPU cycles and I/O activity. This hint fills a column in the PLAN_TABLE called CPU_COST, based on CPU cycles and I/O operations.

- **NO_CPU_COSTING**. Ignores CPU cycles, basing query execution time estimation on I/O activity only.

- **CURSOR_SHARING_EXACT**. Overrides behavior of configuration parameter CURSOR_SHARING=FORCE, which changes literal values to bind variables.

- **DYNAMIC_SAMPLING**. On the fly sampling, if statistics are not present or are out-of-date.

Change Table Scans

- **FULL**. Suggests a full table scan. Typically, the FULL hint could be used on small static tables, since it might sometimes be faster to read the entire table rather than read both the index and the table.

Change Index Scans

- **INDEX[_ASC | _DESC]**. Forces use of an index where if multiple indexes are specified then the lowest cost index is selected. The selected index is scanned as it is sorted, or as specified in ascending or descending order.

- **INDEX_FFS**. Forces a fast full index scan, reading the index in physical block order, not key order.

- **NO_INDEX**. Ignores the named indexes.

- **INDEX_COMBINE**. Typically, combines use of single column bitmap indexes.

- **INDEX_JOIN**. Suggesting a join between indexes alone.

- **INDEX_SS_ASC and INDEX_SS_DESC**. Suggests an index skip scan.

- **NO_INDEX_FFS and NO_INDEX_SS**. Suggest the optimizer does not use index fast full scans or index skip scans, respectively.

- **USE_NL_WITH_INDEX**. Suggests that a query use a specific table as the inner loop of a nested loops join, with the option of using a particular index.

Note: Index hints include index names or table names with column lists. TABLE.COLUMN name settings can also be used, even with columns in separate tables, for join indexes.

Change Joins

- **ORDERED**. Makes the optimizer join tables in the sequence in which the tables appear in the FROM clause of an SQL statement, among other uses (refer to the section on DISTINCT earlier in this chapter).

- **LEADING**. Makes the optimizer use a named table as the first table in the join, regardless of which table occurs first in the FROM clause.

- **USE_NL, USE_HASH, and USE_MERGE**. Suggest nested loops, hash join, or sort merge join, respectively.

- **NO_USE_NL, NO_USE_HASH, and NO_USE_MERGE**. Suggest that the optimizer not use nested loops, hash joins, or sort merge joins, respectively, in a particular query.

Parallel SQL

- **[NO_]PARALLEL**. Parallel executes on multiple CPUs or servers.

- **PQ_DISTRIBUTE**. Improves a parallel join.

- **[NO_]PARALLEL_INDEX**. Processes index scans for partitions in parallel.

Changing Queries and Subqueries

- **[NO]CACHE**. CACHE can be used to suggest that data be forced into a Most Recently Used list (MRU). NOCACHE pushes data to a Least Recently Used list (LRU).

- **ORDERED_PREDICATES**. Preserves SQL statement precedence of evaluation, such as the sequence of comparisons in a WHERE clause.

- **[NO_]UNNEST**. Undoes subquery layers by allowing the optimizer to attempt to merge subqueries into a calling query. This is probably contrary to performance tuning of multiple layered SQL statements.

- **[NO_]PUSH_SUBQ**. Resolves subqueries first or last (NO_).

Note: The most important thing to remember about using hints is that a hint is only a suggestion to the optimizer, not an instruction. In other words, the optimizer will ignore the hint if it thinks the hint is inappropriate.

7.3 Tools for Tuning Queries

This chapter would be seriously lacking without a solution as to how to tune queries from the perspective of a production environment. This section fills that need. There are various tools for tuning queries:

- **EXPLAIN PLAN**. The EXPLAIN PLAN command and the PLAN_TABLE have already seen extensive use in this book. For explanation of the details returned by the EXPLAIN PLAN command, see Oracle documentation, or you can read my other tuning book.

- **SQLTrace and TKPROF**. SQLTrace allows generation of trace files and TKPROF is used to format those trace files into a readable format. Personally, I find using these tools to be overkill. Far too much superfluous information is produced.

- **STATSPACK**. STATSPACK is extremely useful in identifying potential problems between snapshots, but it does produce a lot of information. Too much information can often confuse the issue when searching for a bottleneck under pressure. STATSPACK can also be used to analyze individual queries [3].

- **V$ Performance Views**. There are a large number of performance views. Using these views to tune any type of database can become extremely complex and time consuming.

- **Oracle Database 10g Tools**. There are numerous tools introduced or, perhaps, simply repaired and renamed in Oracle Database 10g.

The advisory tools are one set of new tools. I have not found advisory tools particularly useful compared to other tools.

- **The Wait Event Interface**. This is the tuning tool I like. The wait event interface consists of a large set of V$ performance views. However, a small number of specific views can be used to find bottlenecks and, particularly, to help locate problem SQL code statements. The best way to access these views is by using the graphical drill-down capabilities in Oracle Enterprise Manager software. I have more or less copied this entire section from my previous tuning book, because this approach to tuning is by far the best when searching for a bottleneck. My apologies to those who have purchased both books.

7.3.1   What Is the Wait Event Interface?

The Wait Event Interface is a group of Oracle Database performance views that allow drilling down into various areas of activity occurring in an Oracle database installation. These activities are either summarized from the most recent database startup or maintained for the life of each session. The simplest way to present those views and their interrelated structure is to present them in steps. It should also be noted that drilling into wait events not only includes waits on events but deeper layers, such as latches and otherwise.

I like to divide the Wait Event Interface performance views into three sections: the system aggregation layer, the session layer, and the third layer and beyond. The first I call the *system aggregation* layer because in its simplest form, it contains a record of statistics collected by what I like to call the *session layer*. The session layer contains statistics about sessions during the life of those sessions. There is a deeper layer of the Wait Event Interface, which involves hooks through to many other performance views. I like to call this deeper layer the *crazy about V$ views* layer or *the third layer and beyond*. This third layer will not be examined in detail.

The System Aggregation Layer

A brief overview of the system aggregation layer of the Wait Event Interface is shown in Figure 7.18. The V$EVENT_NAME view gives a list of all possible events. The V$SYSTEM_EVENT view contains an aggregation of existing wait events and total wait times for each. V$SYSTEM_EVENT view is cleared on database restart. In other words, V$SYSTEM_EVENT contains statistics on all wait events since the previous database startup.

> **Note:** The TIMED_STATISTICS parameter must be set to TRUE for V$SYSTEM_EVENT to contain information. Setting the TIMED_STATISTICS parameter has minimum performance impact.

The V$SYSTEM_EVENT view can be joined to the V$EVENT_NAME view using the EVENT and NAME columns, respectively, as shown in Figure 7.18.

Figure 7.18
The system aggregation layer of the Wait Event Interface.

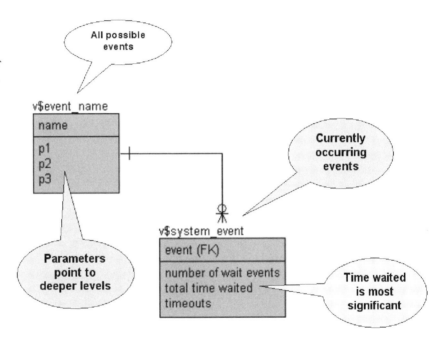

The V$EVENT_NAME view has information about hooks to drill down into the third layer, mentioned above, of potential bottleneck problems using the parameter columns: PARAMETER1, PARAMETER2, and PARAMETER3. These parameter columns contain information as to what event parameters in third layer views, such as the V$LATCH view, will be pointed to from the V$SESSION_WAIT view.

> **Note:** V$EVENT_NAME view parameter columns do not contain actual values, only descriptions of what values are. The parameter values are contained in the session layer in the V$SESSION_WAIT performance view.

Some of the values in the V$EVENT_NAME view parameter columns are as shown. There are a lot of them:

```
SELECT DISTINCT(parameter1) FROM v$event_name
WHERE parameter1 LIKE '%#%';


PARAMETER1
------------------------------------------------------------
block#
branch#
buffer#
by thread#
circuit#
copy latch #
end-point#
event #
file#
log#
segment#
session#
thread#
undo seg#|slot#
undo segment#


SELECT DISTINCT(parameter2) FROM v$event_name
WHERE parameter2 LIKE '%#%';


PARAMETER2
------------------------------------------------------------
#bytes
block#
chain#
our thread#
process#
wrap#


SELECT DISTINCT(parameter3) FROM v$event_name
WHERE parameter3 LIKE '%#%';
```

```
PARAMETER3
------------------------------------------------------------
process#
set-id#
```

For instance, the combination of FILE# in PARAMETER1 and BLOCK# in PARAMETER2 can be used to drill down into extents to find an offending segment—in other words, a table. The diagram shown in Figure 7.18 is appropriately adjusted in Figure 7.19.

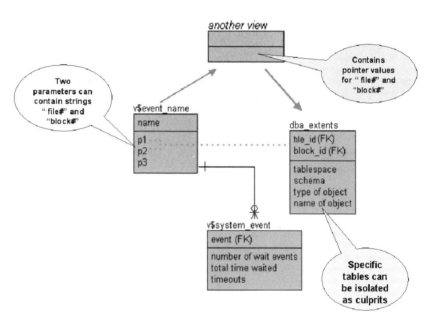

Figure 7.19
Isolating segments using event parameters.

The next query shows how to join the various views for existing wait events, and will not be executed in this chapter. A demonstration later on using Oracle Enterprise Manager will suffice:

```
SELECT de.segment_name, sw.event
FROM dba_extents de, (
    SELECT sw.event, sw.p1 AS file_id, sw.p2 AS block_id
    FROM v$session_wait sw WHERE IdleEvent(event) IS NOT NULL
AND sw.sid IN
(SELECT sid FROM v$session
 WHERE username = 'ACCOUNTS')
    AND sw.event != 'null event') sw
WHERE de.owner = 'ACCOUNTS'
AND de.file_id = sw.file_id AND de.block_id = sw.block_id;
```

> **Note:** The IDLEEVENT function filters events on the V$SESSION_ WAIT view.

A faster result is possible for the above query by joining DBA_EXTENTS.FILE_ID and DBA_EXTENTS.BLOCK_ID, retrieving only wait events for extent headers as follows:

```
sw.block_id BETWEEN de.block_id AND de.block_id + blocks -1
```

Idle Events

An idle event is idle because nothing is happening. An idle event is a result of a process that is busy waiting for something else to respond. Idle events are generally insignificant as far as performance is concerned, although they can sometimes show a distinct lack of activity, a lack of use of resources or simply overconfiguration. High idle times in specific areas, such as SQL*Net network usage, are quite normal. However, high idle times on SQL*Net configuration could indicate overconfiguration of shared servers, for instance, or a client process waiting for submission of a command to the database. Overconfiguration is not really a performance problem except that hardware resources are wasted and could be better used elsewhere.

All possible database events are listed in the V$EVENT_NAME view. This view contains a lot of entries. Events in this view are applicable to all Oracle Database software options, such as Oracle Replication and Oracle Real Application Clusters. This book covers only Oracle Database tuning and does not delve into Oracle optional applications and architectures other than Oracle Partitioning. This query finds a lot of idle events:

```
SELECT name FROM v$event_name
WHERE name LIKE '%null%' OR name LIKE '%timer%'
OR name LIKE '%SQL*Net%' OR name LIKE '%rdbms ipc%'
OR name LIKE '%ispatcher%' OR name LIKE '%virtual circuit%'
OR name LIKE '%PX%' OR name LIKE '%pipe%' OR name LIKE
'%message%'
OR name LIKE 'jobq%';
```

This is the code for the IDLEEVENT function:

```
CREATE OR REPLACE FUNCTION IdleEvent(pEvent IN VARCHAR2
DEFAULT NULL)
RETURN VARCHAR2 IS
    CURSOR cIdleEvents IS
        SELECT name FROM v$event_name
        WHERE name LIKE '%null%' OR name LIKE '%timer%'
        OR name LIKE '%SQL*Net%' OR name LIKE '%rdbms ipc%'
        OR name LIKE '%ispatcher%' OR name LIKE '%virtual
circuit%'
        OR name LIKE '%PX%' OR name LIKE '%pipe%'
        OR name LIKE '%message%' OR name LIKE 'jobq%';
BEGIN
    FOR rIdleEvent in cIdleEvents LOOP
        IF pEvent = rIdleEvent.name THEN
        RETURN NULL;
        END IF;
    END LOOP;
    RETURN pEvent;
EXCEPTION WHEN OTHERS THEN
    DBMS_OUTPUT.PUT_LINE(SQLERRM(SQLCODE));
END;
/
ALTER FUNCTION IdleEvent COMPILE;
/
```

Note: If using STATSPACK, the STATS$IDLE_EVENTS table can be used.

Examining the DBA_EXTENTS view in detail from this perspective, we can see the different segment types:

```
SELECT DISTINCT(segment_type) FROM dba_extents;

SEGMENT_TYPE
------------------
CACHE
CLUSTER
INDEX
INDEX PARTITION
```

```
LOBINDEX
LOBSEGMENT
NESTED TABLE
ROLLBACK
TABLE
TABLE PARTITION
TYPE2 UNDO
```

From another perspective, we can see table and index names:

```
SELECT DISTINCT(segment_name) FROM dba_extents
WHERE segment_type IN ('TABLE','INDEX') AND owner='ACCOUNTS';


SEGMENT_NAME
--------------------------------------------------------
AK_GL_DTE
AK_SP_ZIP
AUDITSIM
CASHBOOK
CASHBOOKLINE
CATEGORY
COA
CUSTOMER
GENERALLEDGER
ORDERS
ORDERSLINE
PERIOD
PERIODSUM
PLAN_TABLE
POSTING
...
```

So we should be able see from the various queries already shown that potential wait event issues can be isolated to specific objects in the database. Let's look at some details. First, let's list the top currently occurring wait events:

```
COL event FORMAT a32;
COL percentage FORMAT 9999999990;
SELECT * FROM(
```

```
SELECT event "Event", total_waits "Waits", time_waited "Total
Time"
    ,TO_CHAR(
        (time_waited /
            (SELECT SUM(time_waited) FROM v$system_event
            WHERE IdleEvent(event) IS NOT NULL)
    )*100, 990.99) "Percentage"
FROM v$system_event WHERE IdleEvent(event) IS NOT NULL
ORDER BY 3 DESC) WHERE ROWNUM <= 10;
```

These are my top ten wait events, based on the total amount of time
the system spends waiting for each event. The only thing to decide at this
point is what is a significant event? Which event in this list is the most
significant and can have the most profound effect on performance? Some
knowledge of applications might be required at this stage, because high
incidence of some wait events could be normal and thus acceptable,
depending on applications:

Event	Waits	Total Time	Percent
db file sequential read	623840	7542616	71.59
buffer busy waits	259455	2330819	22.12
enqueue	1944	566381	5.38
latch free	3996	49586	0.47
control file parallel write	4956	21016	0.20
db file parallel write	1102	7472	0.07
library cache pin	112	6666	0.06
control file sequential read	2156	6371	0.06
log file parallel write	1559	1621	0.02
library cache load lock	8	714	0.01

The real problem with the preceding query is that the information
obtained is a little too vague at this point. The *db file sequential read* event
could indicate hot block issues, but could also be normal. The same applies
to *buffer busy waits*. The *enqueue, latch free,* and wait events in the library
cache could have more significant impact on performance.

The Session Layer

The session layer uses various performance views, such as
V$SESSION_EVENT and V$SESSION_WAIT. These session views only

Figure 7.20
*Session level event
and wait views.*

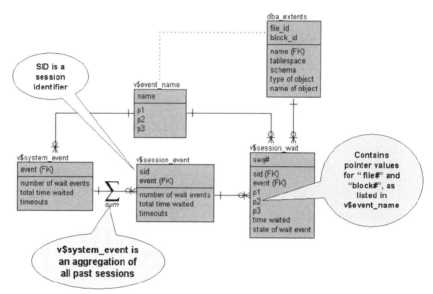

contain information on a session for as long as that session exists, and are shown in Figure 7.20.

Note: The V$SYSTEM_EVENT contains an accumulated aggregation, or summation, of values in the V$SESSION_EVENT view, aggregated on termination of a session.

It is important to stress that using session-level performance views only finds wait events as they occur. If sessions are application-controlled, or connections are shared, then session level wait event detection may be awkward to decipher without deeper analysis.

Note: Snapshots may have to be taken over specified time periods, as is possible using STATSPACK.

In OLTP database environments-sessions are often shared between connections in one form or another. The net result is that the specific nature of session-level wait event tracking can become somewhat blurred, possibly less useful, and perhaps even more akin to that of system-level event tracking. Session-level wait event detection may often be more appropriate to tracking down bad SQL code executed in ad hoc environments. Ad hoc

SQL code is rare in mission-critical OLTP-type databases. Most OLTP databases are controlled by applications.

The V$SESSION_EVENT performance view provides wait events for sessions for the entire life of the session. The V$SESSION_WAIT performance view provides the same information, but as the wait events are occurring; it also provides access to deeper layers using parameter pointer values as shown in Figure 7.20. The V$SESSION_EVENT view is effectively an accumulation of wait events for sessions during the life of those sessions. Thus, V$SESSION_EVENT could be used to isolate sessions causing specific problems. Here are the worst ten events by session:

```
COL event FORMAT a32;
SELECT * FROM (
SELECT sid, event, total_waits "Waits", time_waited "Total Time"
FROM v$session_event WHERE IdleEvent(event) IS NOT NULL
ORDER BY 4 DESC) WHERE ROWNUM <= 10;
```

```
       SID EVENT                                Waits Total Time
---------- -------------------------------- ---------- ----------
        50 db file sequential read               8826      91390
         4 db file sequential read               3204      33929
        17 enqueue                                  94      28399
        19 enqueue                                  94      28398
        25 enqueue                                  93      28255
        35 db file sequential read               6791      28112
        40 buffer busy waits                      3857      21593
        45 buffer busy waits                      3811      21338
         3 control file parallel write            2383      20054
        37 db file sequential read               1493      17461
```

This query shows events causing the highest wait times, which is more significant than those occurring most frequently. The most frequently occurring events would be found by summing the number of waits:

```
COL event FORMAT a32;
SELECT * FROM (
SELECT event, SUM(time_waited) "Total Time"
FROM v$session_event WHERE IdleEvent(event) IS NOT NULL
GROUP BY event ORDER BY 2 DESC) WHERE ROWNUM <= 10;
```

```
EVENT                              Total Time
-------------------------------    ----------
db file sequential read                489236
enqueue                                360328
buffer busy waits                      292884
control file parallel write             20653
db file parallel write                  10501
control file sequential read             6169
latch free                               3959
log file parallel write                  2306
LGWR wait for redo copy                   165
log file sequential read                   52
```

Examining the V$SESSION_WAIT performance view will not only show wait events as they occur, but also allow us to use parameter value pointers to find specific details, such as database objects, as shown in the DBA_EXTENTS view query previously shown in this chapter. An accumulation on the V$SESSION_WAIT view is useful to get a better overall picture, as shown by using the procedure called TMP following.

Note: This type of cumulative processing can be performed easily using a tool, such as STATSPACK. At this stage, the objective is to explain and teach the basics rather than the syntax of a tool such as STATSPACK.

In the following procedure we try to find offending segments by using the FILE# and BLOCK# pointers, as found in the V$EVENT_NAME view:

```
DROP TABLE tmp;
CREATE TABLE tmp
  (sid NUMBER, event VARCHAR2(64), file_id NUMBER, block_id
NUMBER,
   wait_time NUMBER, seconds_in_wait NUMBER);
BEGIN
 FOR counter IN 1..1000 LOOP
   INSERT INTO tmp
     SELECT sw.sid, sw.event AS event, sw.p1 AS file_id,
       sw.p2 AS block_id, sw.wait_time, sw.seconds_in_wait
     FROM v$session_wait sw WHERE IdleEvent(sw.event) IS NOT
NULL
```

```
    AND sw.event IN (SELECT name FROM v$event_name
    WHERE parameter1 = 'file#' AND parameter2 = 'block#');
    COMMIT;
  END LOOP;
END;
/


COL event FORMAT a32;
SELECT * FROM (
SELECT sid, event, SUM(seconds_in_wait) "Current Wait Time"
FROM tmp
WHERE IdleEvent(event) IS NOT NULL
GROUP BY sid, event ORDER BY 2 DESC) WHERE ROWNUM <= 10;


EVENT                              Current Wait Time
-----------------------------      -----------------
db file sequential read                         2670
buffer busy waits                                617
db file sequential read                          163
buffer busy waits                                 43
control file sequential read                       0
```

Now take a step back and try to find the worst performing sessions in the V$SESSION_EVENT view:

```
COL event FORMAT a32;
SELECT * FROM (
SELECT sid, SUM(time_waited) "Total Time"
FROM v$session_event WHERE IdleEvent(event) IS NOT NULL
GROUP BY sid ORDER BY 2 DESC) WHERE ROWNUM <= 10;


       SID Total Time
---------- ----------
        50     124491
        17      54034
        19      54027
        25      52969
        40      52958
        45      52933
         4      41486
        35      40264
```

                    41   34010
                    29   33403

That query does not really tell us much. What is session identifier (SID) 50? We can find more information about SID 50 using the V$SESSION performance view. The real value of the session-level part of the Wait Event Interface, other than searching for offending database objects in the DBA_EXTENTS view, is the way in which the session identifier can be connected to sessions in the V$SESSION view and, ultimately, to other views including SQL code and optimizer query execution plans. Figure 7.21 shows the drill-down path of session-level executed SQL code and query plans. One of the primary factors causing database performance problems is poorly built SQL code.

Note: Sometimes data model problems can be isolated as a result of finding poorly performing SQL code.

Figure 7.21
Hooking wait events to sessions.

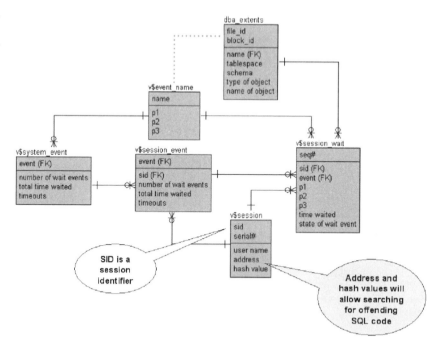

So we could find the usernames (schemas) of offending sessions by joining the V$SESSION_EVENT or V$SESSION_WAIT views with the V$SESSION performance view:

```
COL event FORMAT a32;
SELECT * FROM (
SELECT s.username, SUM(se.time_waited) "Total Time"
FROM v$session_event se, v$session s
WHERE IdleEvent(se.event) IS NOT NULL
GROUP BY s.username ORDER BY 2 DESC) WHERE ROWNUM <= 10;
```

USERNAME	Total Time
ACCOUNTS	69680468
	24120162
SYS	5360036

Now let's add some of the various SQL code views, as shown in Figure 7.22.

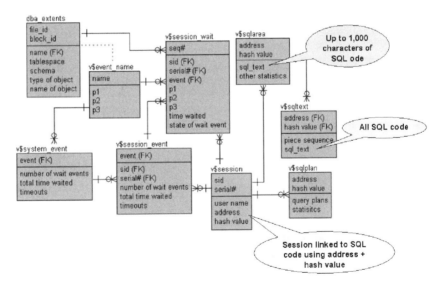

Figure 7.22
Find SQL code for sessions.

The following query simply joins sessions and SQL code statements to find the SQL code that is currently executing the most often:

```
SELECT * FROM (SELECT s.username, a.sql_text, a.executions
FROM v$session s, v$sqlarea a
WHERE s.sql_address = a.address
AND s.sql_hash_value = a.hash_value
ORDER BY 3 DESC) WHERE ROWNUM <= 10;


USERNAME    SQL_TEXT
----------  ----------------------------------------------------------
            SELECT to_number(to_char(SYSTIMESTAMP,'FF3'))+1 from dual
            SELECT to_number(to_char(SYSTIMESTAMP,'FF3'))+1 from dual
ACCOUNTS    INSERT into transactions
values(transactions_seq.nextval,'S'
ACCOUNTS    INSERT into transactions
values(transactions_seq.nextval,'S'
ACCOUNTS    INSERT into transactions
values(transactions_seq.nextval,'S'
ACCOUNTS    INSERT into transactions
values(transactions_seq.nextval,'S'
ACCOUNTS    INSERT into transactions
values(transactions_seq.nextval,'S'
ACCOUNTS    SELECT min(order_id),max(order_id) from orders
ACCOUNTS    SELECT min(order_id),max(order_id) from orders
ACCOUNTS     SELECT min(order_id),max(order_id) from orders
```

Similar join queries can be used to access both entire SQL code statements from the V$SQLTEXT view and stored query execution plans from the V$SQL_PLAN view, joined using the ADDRESS and HASH_VALUE columns.

The Third Layer and Beyond

From examination of the system aggregation and session layers you should have noticed two general paths of drill down that can be followed. First, drilling into the parameters allows access to details about events and why they are causing issues. Second, SQL code can be accessed directly using address and hash values. These two wait event drill-down access paths can be joined together because the SQL views are linked to a session, and a session is linked to session wait events in the V$SESSION_WAIT performance view.

Let's take a look at a specific example of drilling down into the third layer before we go on to show how Oracle Enterprise Manager does all this stuff! Let's examine latch-free wait events. Figure 7.23 shows a pseudo-type structure for latch V$ performance views. There are numerous views, but we will simply look at the topmost part of the third layer, for latches only.

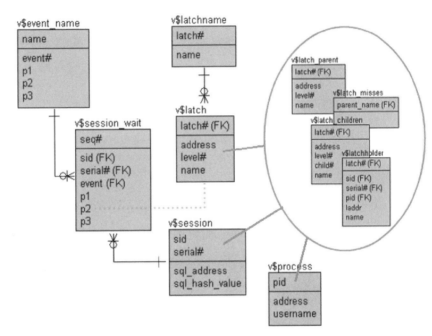

Figure 7.23
Drilling down into latches.

For latch-free wait events, the LATCH# column on the V$LATCH-NAME view is contained in the PARAMETER2 column of the V$SESSION_WAIT view, allowing direct or indirect drill-down access into all the various latch performance views. Let's take a look at current latch wait problems to demonstrate parameter-level drill-down into the third layer of the Oracle Database Wait Event Interface.

First check the parameter values:

```
SELECT parameter1||' '||parameter2||' '||parameter3
FROM v$event_name WHERE name = 'latch free';

PARAMETER1||''||PARAMETER2||''||PARAMETER3
-------------------------------------------
address number tries
```

PARAMETER2 contains a latch number, the equivalent of the LATCH# column in the V$LATCH performance view. The following query will not really tell us much, but it joins the V$LATCH and V$SESSION_WAIT performance views:

```
SELECT sw.sid, sw.event, sw.wait_time, sw.seconds_in_wait
,l.name, l.gets, l.misses, l.sleeps
FROM v$session_wait sw, v$latch l WHERE sw.p2 = l.latch#;
```

It would obviously be more efficient to filter down to latch events only:

```
SELECT sw.sid, sw.event, sw.wait_time, sw.seconds_in_wait
,l.name, l.gets, l.misses, l.sleeps
FROM v$session_wait sw, v$latch l
WHERE sw.event LIKE '%latch%'
AND sw.p2 = l.latch#;
```

We could quite obviously drill into the latches further, as can be seen in Figure 7.23, linking through to sessions, processes, SQL code, query execution plans, and the list goes on. The point to make now is as follows: there is a much easier way of drilling down into the Oracle Database Wait Event Interface, using Oracle Enterprise Manager. Similar functionality is available in Spotlight and STATSPACK. Before going on to using Oracle Enterprise Manager to drill down into the Oracle Database Wait Event Interface, we should digress a little.

7.3.2 Oracle Database Wait Event Interface Improvements

These V$ performance views have been added to:

- V$EVENT_NAME. Class information is added, allowing classification and links to other V$ performance views containing class columns. A class is a classification or category for a wait event or statistic, as can be seen in the following query:

```
SQL> SELECT DISTINCT(class) FROM v$event_name;
```

```
CLASS
-----------------------------------------------------------
Administrative
Application
Archival Process Scheduling
Cluster
Commit
Concurrency
Configuration
Idle
Managed Recovery Processing Scheduling
Network
Other
Scheduler
System I/O
User I/O
```

- V$SESSION. Has a lot more information in it, including class and parameter details for direct hooks to the third layer and beyond, of the Oracle Database Wait Event Interface:

These V$ performance views are new to Oracle Database 10*g*:

- V$SYSTEM_WAIT_CLASS. Aggregation layer wait times for classes.

- V$SESSION_WAIT_CLASS. As above, but in the session layer.

- V$EVENT_HISTOGRAM. Waits and wait times event histogram.

- V$FILE_HISTOGRAM and V$TEMP_HISTOGRAM. Single block read histograms for datafiles and temporary files.

7.3.3   Oracle Enterprise Manager and the Wait Event Interface

Oracle Enterprise Manager is an excellent tool for drilling down visually into the Oracle Database Wait Event Interface. Spotlight is best for real-time monitoring of a busy production database, since it places all the important monitoring information in one place. However, Oracle Enterprise Manager might be more visually palatable and easier to use as a drill-down tool. We now have a basic understanding of the underlying V$ performance views allowing access into Oracle Database Wait Event Interface statistics.

On that basis I have abandoned any deeper layer drill down into the Oracle Database Wait Event Interface using the V$ performance views, because Oracle Enterprise Manager is so much easier to use in this respect. Why make it difficult?

What I am going to do is to connect to my very busy database in the console and execute the Diagnostic, Performance Overview. Then I will see if there are any problems with my database. If there are, I will drill down into the problem areas, attempting to locate something I can tune.

In Figure 7.24, there is something odd. The database buffer cache hit ratio is going up and down, vacillating between 60% and 90%. Depending on the application, this may not be a problem.

Figure 7.24
Database memory health.

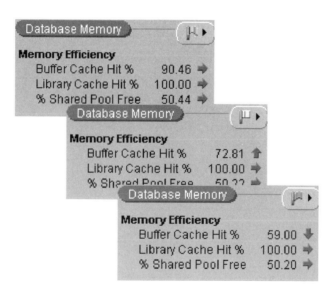

I am certainly not going to make my database buffer cache larger. Bumping the database buffer cache size is an outdated solution, which never solves underlying problems, such as poorly coded SQL statements. Another clue is noticeable latch-free wait events, as well as scattered reads being much more prominent than sequential reads, when the red flag is up, as seen in Figure 7.25.

A large transaction is probably forcing highly used blocks out of the buffer; consequently, those highly used blocks will probably be loaded back

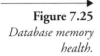

Figure 7.25
Database memory health.

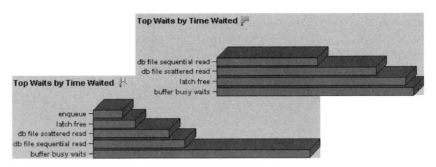

into the buffer. Let's drill down. In Figure 7.26, I drill down into Top Objects and Top SQL. These two drill downs tell me a lot:

- The CASHBOOK table is at the top of both database objects and SQL in terms of data reads.

- The number of executions for the top SQL statement is relatively low.

- The physical reads for the CASHBOOK table are double compared to the next object down on the list, the ORDERS table primary key index.

- The really obvious part is that the CASHBOOK table is shown as being heavily active. An index on the CASHBOOK table is not being used.

Examining Figure 7.26 a little further, do I know what to look for yet? Yes, I do. The CASHBOOK table is probably being full table scanned when it should not be. Why? The SQL code statement on the CASH-BOOK table has a where clause against a foreign key index. I check foreign key indexes on the CASHBOOK table. I find that the foreign key index on the CASHBOOK table TRANSACTION_ID column foreign key relation, to the TRANSACTIONS table, was missing. The chances are I dropped the index in error sometime during the course of writing this book. Or it was never created. Let's create that index:

```
CREATE INDEX XFK_CB_TRANS ON cashbook(transaction_id)
TABLESPACE INDX ONLINE;
```

Figure 7.26
Top Objects and
Top SQL.

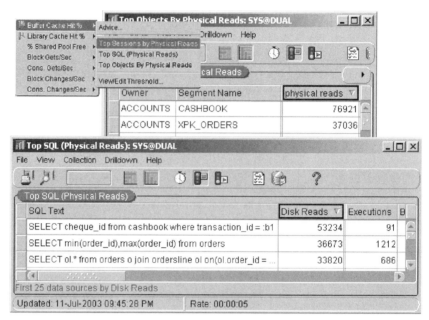

I then drilled down into the Top SQL and Top Objects tools again and found that the CASHBOOK table was not even in the top ten for both tools, as was evident in Figure 7.26. The problem was solved.

Any type of wait event can be drilled down into to the lowest level of detail with a multitude of iterations of each tool using the Oracle Database Wait Event Interface, as implemented in the Oracle Enterprise Manager GUI. I would not recommend using the Oracle Database Wait Event Interface in any other way.

This chapter has examined the most simplistic aspects of SQL code tuning, the ways that the Oracle SQL engine executes SQL code internally, and looked at tools for tuning Oracle Database. This chapter has introduced the basics of SQL code tuning, essential for a deeper understanding of material to be covered in subsequent chapters. The next chapter will begin the SQL code tuning process for data warehouses by discussing in detail aggregation using the GROUP BY clause and various standard extensions, such as the ROLLUP and CUBE clauses, so important to simplifying highly complex data warehouse queries.

7.4   Endnotes

1.   Chapter 8 in *Overriding the Optimizer Using Hints: Oracle Perfor-mance Tuning for 9i and 10g* (ISBN: 1555583059)

2.   Chapter 6 in *Replacing Joins with Subqueries: Oracle Performance Tuning for 9i and 10g* (ISBN: 1555583059)

3.   Chapter 22 in *Oracle Performance Tuning for 9*i *and 10*g (ISBN: 1555583059)

8

Aggregation Using GROUP BY Clause Extensions

This chapter covers the more basic syntactical extensions to the GROUP BY clause in the form of aggregation using the ROLLUP clause, CUBE clause, GROUPING SETS clause, and some slightly more complex combinations thereof. Other specialized functions for much more comprehensive and complex analysis, plus further syntax formats including the OVER clause, the MODEL clause, the WITH clause, and some specialized expression types, will be covered in later chapters. All these SQL coding extensions tend to make highly complex data warehouse reporting more simplified and also much better performing—mostly because of the fact that SQL coding is made easier.

8.1   What Are GROUP BY Clause Extensions?

The ROLLUP, CUBE, and GROUPING SETS clauses can be used to create breaks and subtotals for groups. The GROUPING SETS clause can be used to restrict the results of ROLLUP and CUBE clauses. Before the advent of ROLLUP and CUBE, producing the same types of results would involve extremely complex SQL statements, possibly with the use of temporary tables or perhaps even PL/SQL as well.

8.1.1   Why Use GROUP BY Clause Extensions?

The GROUP BY clause extensions should be used because they simplify SQL coding massively, and they enhance performance. Both of these factors are highly significant, both in relation to the complexity of data warehouse reporting requirements and due to the enormous amounts of data. In its most basic form, the GROUP BY clause aggregates or summarizes data into smaller packets. The ROLLUP, CUBE, and GROUPING SETS extensions empower simplification of further calculations and extrapolation of aggregations. These summaries are sometimes called super aggregates, as they are in actuality aggregations of aggregations, or summaries of summaries.

- **The ROLLUP Clause**. The ROLLUP clause is best suited to build two-dimensional summaries over multiple hierarchical layers.

- **The CUBE Clause**. The CUBE clause is best suited to production of multiple dimensional summaries from a two-dimensional structure of dimension and fact entities.

- **The GROUPING SETS Clause**. The GROUPING SETS clause is effectively a filter, allowing selection of only required groupings produced by the ROLLUP and CUBE clauses.

- **Grouping Functions**. There are three specialized grouping functions allowing access to ROLLUP and CUBE calculated aggregates. The three grouping functions cater to NULL values, the level of an aggregation in a hierarchy (across a single dimension), and, finally, a set identifier for multiple sets in a single level.

GROUP BY clause extensions are SQL tuning tools for data warehousing simply because they exist. These extension clauses allow for better performance because they will execute faster than building highly complex SQL statements to cope with this type of functionality. Obviously, simplification of coding saves time and places the burden of performance on the optimizer, not the programmer. Additionally, where complex SQL code might be executed across a network between client and server machines as a highly complex GROUP BY clause, GROUP BY extensions place the processing burden squarely on the shoulders of the server. And, obviously, creating special objects, such as materialized views, provides for reduced I/O activity and lower concurrency requirements.

8.2   GROUP BY Clause Extensions

The GROUP BY clause in its most basic form consists of the GROUP BY clause, any columns or expressions not subjected to aggregation in the query, plus an optional HAVING clause. The HAVING clause allows the filtering out of rows from the resulting aggregated row set. In other words, the HAVING clause allows retention of specific summary rows and exclusion of others.

GROUP BY clause extensions allow operations on aggregations produced by a query with a GROUP BY clause. Let's begin with the easiest extension clauses, the ROLLUP and CUBE clauses.

8.2.1   The ROLLUP and CUBE Clauses

The ROLLUP clause builds two-dimensional structures, and the CUBE clause builds multiple-dimensional structures.

The ROLLUP Clause

The ROLLUP clause is best suited to build two-dimensional summaries over multiple hierarchical layers. In simple terms, the ROLLUP clause lets you create multiple layers of subtotals within subtotals for all rows in a row set. The result also includes a grand total for all subtotal layers.

ROLLUP Clause Syntax

Figure 8.1 highlights the syntax of the ROLLUP clause.

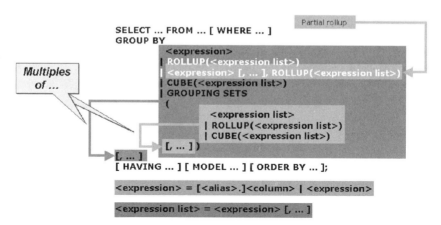

Figure 8.1
GROUP BY clause
ROLLUP
extension clause
syntax.

How the ROLLUP Clause Helps Performance

The ROLLUP clause is very simple. All it does is accept the nonaggregated columns selected in a query, producing multiple hierarchical totals for each column grouping layer. The following query, as shown below and in Figure 8.2, executes a rollup summation aggregation over three separate dimensions:

```
SELECT l.city, i.industry, p.category
,SUM(s.transaction_amount) AS Amount
```

```
FROM sale s, location l, industry i, product p
WHERE l.city IN('New York','Los Angeles')
AND s.time_id=8
AND s.location_id = l.location_id
AND s.industry_id = i.industry_id
AND s.product_id = p.product_id
GROUP BY ROLLUP(l.city, i.industry, p.category);
```

Figure 8.2
A simple ROLLUP clause example across three dimensions.

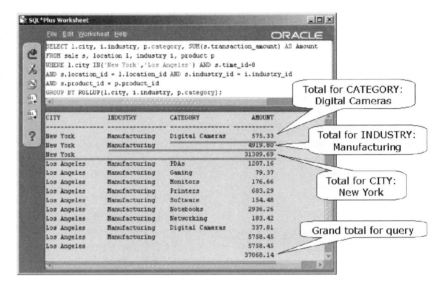

The point to make about why using the ROLLUP clause enhances performance is as follows. Producing a query, such as that shown in Figure 8.2, would require a UNION ALL of multiple queries, each with an aggregation for each separate dimension in the hierarchy.

Note: It is possible to use the SQL*Plus BREAK and COMPUTE commands to produce results similar to those in Figure 8.2. However, execution from an application written in a language such as Java cannot use SQL*Plus BREAK and COMPUTE commands, as these commands apply to the SQL*Plus interface only, and not the Oracle SQL processing engine.

So the query in Figure 8.2 would need the following separate queries. This first query finds the totals for each category:

```
SELECT l.city, i.industry, p.category
,SUM(s.transaction_amount) AS Amount
FROM sale s, location l, industry i, product p
WHERE l.city IN('New York','Los Angeles')
AND s.time_id=8
AND s.location_id = l.location_id
AND s.industry_id = i.industry_id
AND s.product_id = p.product_id
GROUP BY l.city, i.industry, p.category;
```

This second query finds the total for each industry within each city:

```
SELECT l.city, i.industry, NULL AS Category
,SUM(s.transaction_amount) AS Amount
FROM sale s, location l, industry i, product p
WHERE l.city IN('New York','Los Angeles')
AND s.time_id=8
AND s.location_id = l.location_id
AND s.industry_id = i.industry_id
AND s.product_id = p.product_id
GROUP BY l.city, i.industry;
```

This third query finds the total for each city:

```
SELECT l.city, NULL AS Industry, NULL AS Category
,SUM(s.transaction_amount) AS Amount
FROM sale s, location l, industry i, product p
WHERE l.city IN('New York','Los Angeles')
AND s.time_id=8
AND s.location_id = l.location_id
AND s.industry_id = i.industry_id
AND s.product_id = p.product_id
GROUP BY l.city;
```

And, finally, we also need a fourth query to find the grand total for the entire row set to be returned:

```
SELECT NULL AS City, NULL AS Industry, NULL AS Category
,SUM(s.transaction_amount) AS Amount
FROM sale s, location l, industry i, product p
```

```
WHERE l.city IN('New York','Los Angeles')
AND s.time_id=8
AND s.location_id = l.location_id
AND s.industry_id = i.industry_id
AND s.product_id = p.product_id;
```

That is much more complicated, involved, and quite simply convoluted in comparison to using the ROLLUP clause. Additionally, we have to sort it all in the required sorted order as shown in Figure 8.2. The result of the union of all the aggregated queries would have to be sorted in the required multiple dimensional hierarchical sorted order. Therefore, the final multiple UNION ALL query would look as shown below. Yikes!

```
SELECT l.city, i.industry, p.category
,SUM(s.transaction_amount) AS Amount
FROM sale s, location l, industry i, product p
WHERE l.city IN('New York','Los Angeles')
AND s.time_id=8
AND s.location_id = l.location_id
AND s.industry_id = i.industry_id
AND s.product_id = p.product_id
GROUP BY l.city, i.industry, p.category
UNION ALL
SELECT l.city, i.industry, NULL AS Category
,SUM(s.transaction_amount) AS Amount
FROM sale s, location l, industry i, product p
WHERE l.city IN('New York','Los Angeles')
AND s.time_id=8
AND s.location_id = l.location_id
AND s.industry_id = i.industry_id
AND s.product_id = p.product_id
GROUP BY l.city, i.industry
UNION ALL
SELECT l.city, NULL AS Industry, NULL AS Category
,SUM(s.transaction_amount) AS Amount
FROM sale s, location l, industry i, product p
WHERE l.city IN('New York','Los Angeles')
AND s.time_id=8
AND s.location_id = l.location_id
AND s.industry_id = i.industry_id
AND s.product_id = p.product_id
```

```
GROUP BY l.city
UNION ALL
SELECT NULL AS City, NULL AS Industry, NULL AS Category
,SUM(s.transaction_amount) AS Amount
FROM sale s, location l, industry i, product p
WHERE l.city IN('New York','Los Angeles')
AND s.time_id=8
AND s.location_id = l.location_id
AND s.industry_id = i.industry_id
AND s.product_id = p.product_id
ORDER BY 1 DESC NULLS LAST, 2 DESC NULLS LAST
, 3 DESC NULLS LAST;
```

The result of this horribly complex query is shown in Figure 8.3, verifying the identical result as Figure 8.2 when using the ROLLUP clause.

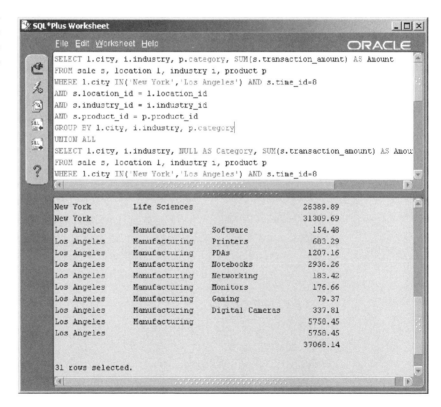

Figure 8.3
Doing a rollup without the ROLLUP clause.

The entire query is not displayed in Figure 8.3 because there is simply too much of it. Let's take this a step further and execute EXPLAIN PLAN

Figure 8.4
*Query plan and
timing cost for
ROLLUP clause
query in Figure
8.2.*

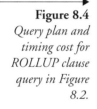

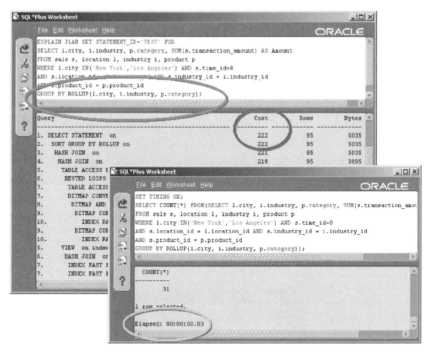

commands and timing for both the non-ROLLUP clause query shown in Figure 8.3 and the ROLLUP clause query shown in Figure 8.2. Figure 8.4 shows the query plan and timing cost for the ROLLUP clause query shown in Figure 8.2.

Figure 8.5 shows the query plan and timing cost for the non-ROLLUP clause, UNION ALL query shown in Figure 8.3.

Examining Figures 8.4 and 8.5, it is plain to see that using the ROLLUP clause reduced the expected cost in the query by a factor of about four, and the actual query execution cost performs twice as fast. The ROLLUP clause definitely helps performance.

The CUBE Clause

The CUBE clause is best suited to production of multiple-dimensional summaries from a two-dimensional structure of dimension and fact entities. The CUBE clause is more comprehensive than the ROLLUP clause; it allows not only totals of totals up through layered groupings, but cross calculations of totals within totals. In other words, it allows all combinations across groupings, regardless of the layer of the group in the hierarchy. What does "all combinations" imply? All combinations means that in addition to

Figure 8.5
Query plan and timing cost for non-ROLLUP clause, UNION ALL query in Figure 8.3.

summarizing within a single dimension, the CUBE clause allows summarizing between multiple dimensions. The effect of the CUBE clause is multiple-dimensional summaries, as opposed to the two dimensions of the ROLLUP clause or cross-tabulation reporting.

CUBE Clause Syntax

Figure 8.6 shows the syntax for the CUBE clause.

How the CUBE Clause Helps Performance

Below is the same query used for Figure 8.2, except the ROLLUP clause has been changed to a CUBE clause:

```
SELECT l.city, i.industry, p.category
,SUM(s.transaction_amount) AS Amount
```

Figure 8.6
*GROUP BY clause
CUBE extension
clause syntax.*

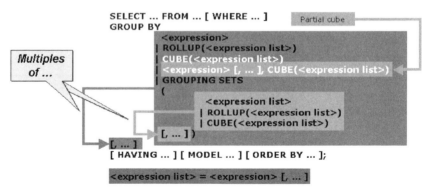

```
FROM sale s, location l, industry i, product p
WHERE l.city IN('New York','Los Angeles')
AND s.time_id=8
AND s.location_id = l.location_id
AND s.industry_id = i.industry_id
AND s.product_id = p.product_id
GROUP BY CUBE(l.city, i.industry, p.category);
```

Figure 8.7 shows the result of the above query.

Figure 8.7
*The CUBE clause
produces totals for
all combinations of
all dimensions.*

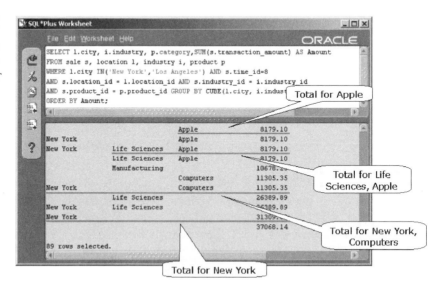

The CUBE clause helps performance for the same reasons that the ROLLUP clause helps performance. As with the ROLLUP clause, the CUBE clause helps to reduce the extreme complexity of the SQL code for certain types of queries. The CUBE clause is even more extreme than the ROLLUP clause, because many more aggregations are produced by the CUBE clause. Moreover, the more complex a SQL code query is, the higher its performance cost is likely to be.

There is no need to go further with examples for the CUBE clause as was presented for the ROLLUP clause. The CUBE clause in regular Oracle SQL would be even more involved and overindulgent than the UNION ALL equivalent of the ROLLUP clause described previously. In other words, the CUBE clause conversion would produce even more queries to merge together with UNION ALL set operators.

The Multiple Dimensions of the CUBE Clause

Let's examine what exactly is meant by cubic data. Figures 8.8 to 8.11 show pictorial representations of CITY, INDUSTRY, and CATEGORY dimensions from the query in Figure 8.7. These four figures show the way that multidimensional cubic data is used by different departments of a company, for instance, beginning with the entire set of cubic data represented in Figure 8.8.

Figure 8.8
All sales revenues.

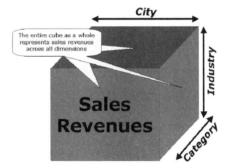

Figures 8.8 to 8.11 show that data can be analyzed from a cube of multiple dimensions, either as single dimensional slices or as multiple dimensions across some or all of the dimensions in the query-generated cube. Data is retrieved depending on where dimensional intersections are located, or at those dimensional intersections. There is really nothing complicated about cubic data, so there is no need for further explanation.

8.2.2 **The GROUPING SETS Clause**

The GROUPING SETS clause is effectively a summary filter, allowing selection of only required groupings produced by the ROLLUP and

Figure 8.9
Sales revenues by category.

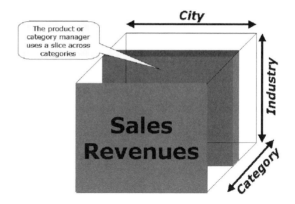

Figure 8.10
Sales revenues by region.

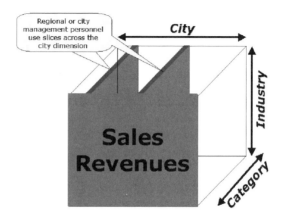

Figure 8.11
Sales revenues by industry.

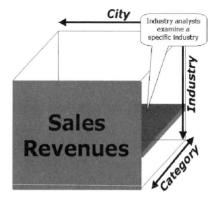

CUBE clauses. The GROUPING SETS clause allows you to remove some of the subtotals from the result set, in much the same way that the

HAVING clause can be used to filter out aggregated groups from an aggregated row set.

GROUPING SETS Clause Syntax

Figure 8.12 highlights the syntax of the GROUPING SETS clause. Note how both ROLLUP and CUBE clauses can be subset parts of the GROUPING SETS clause.

Figure 8.12
GROUP BY clause GROUPING SETS extension clause syntax.

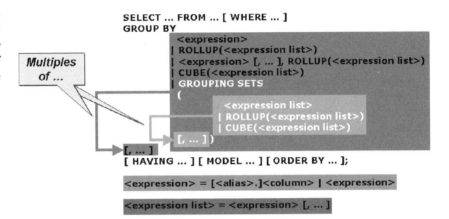

```
SELECT ... FROM ... [ WHERE ... ]
GROUP BY
        <expression>
      | ROLLUP(<expression list>)
      | <expression> [, ... ], ROLLUP(<expression list>)
      | CUBE(<expression list>)
      | GROUPING SETS
        (
                <expression list>
              | ROLLUP(<expression list>)
              | CUBE(<expression list>)
          [, ... ])
[, ... ]
[ HAVING ... ] [ MODEL ... ] [ ORDER BY ... ];

<expression> = [<alias>.]<column> | <expression>

<expression list> = <expression> [, ... ]
```

Multiples of ...

How the GROUPING SETS Clause Helps Performance

The ROLLUP clause creates aggregates for each group it encounters in a hierarchy, effectively creating lots and lots of totals within totals. That can be a lot of aggregations. The CUBE clause is even more intensive than the ROLLUP clause, because, in addition to rolled-up aggregates, it also generates aggregates across multiple dimensions, calculating far more aggregations than even the ROLLUP clause. What the GROUPING SETS clause does is to create sets of groups, therefore, filtering out or retaining only specified aggregates produced when, for example, a CUBE operation is performed.

First, let's look at an example GROUPING SETS clause in action; then we will attempt to prove various performance precepts, perhaps justifying its use. A basic GROUPING SETS clause allows computation of cubic cross-dimensional aggregations without calculating all the aggregations in the cube. The following query is the same query as that used in Figure 8.7, returning a total of 89 rows.

Note: The GROUPING SETS clause helps performance by preventing unspecified totals from being calculated in ROLLUP and CUBE clauses.

```
SELECT l.city, i.industry, p.category
,SUM(s.transaction_amount) AS Amount
FROM sale s, location l, industry i, product p
WHERE l.city IN('New York','Los Angeles')
AND s.time_id=8
AND s.location_id = l.location_id
AND s.industry_id = i.industry_id
AND s.product_id = p.product_id
GROUP BY CUBE(l.city, i.industry, p.category);
```

I can reduce the row set returned by the query above by reducing the number of aggregations in the CUBE clause:

```
SELECT l.city, i.industry, p.category
,SUM(s.transaction_amount) AS Amount
FROM sale s, location l, industry i, product p
WHERE l.city IN('New York','Los Angeles') AND s.time_id=8
AND s.location_id = l.location_id
AND s.industry_id = i.industry_id
AND s.product_id = p.product_id
GROUP BY GROUPING SETS((l.city, i.industry)
, (l.city, p.category));
```

The result of the above query is shown in Figure 8.13.

The GROUPING SETS clause can now be explained more clearly. Additionally, we can now also prove wheter the GROUPING SETS clause helps performance, specifically for the ROLLUP and CUBE clauses, by removing some aggregations.

```
GROUP BY CUBE(l.city, i.industry, p.category)
```

The CUBE on city, industry, and category is equivalent to every combination in the following:

Figure 8.13
*GROUPING
SETS can filter out
unwanted
aggregates.*

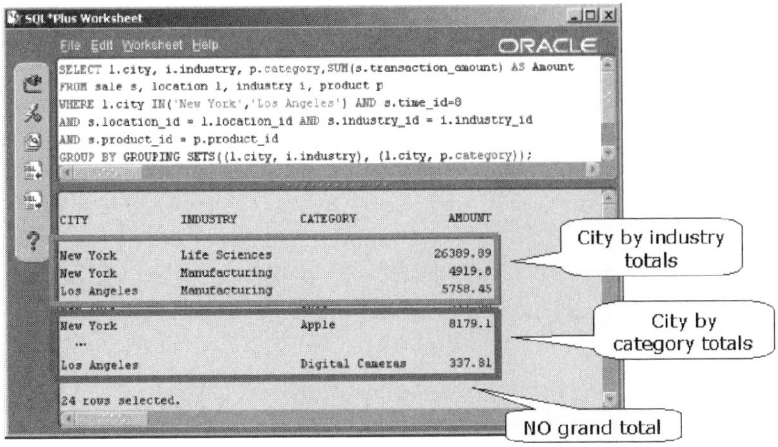

```
GROUP BY GROUPING SETS
(
  (l.city, i.industry, p.category)
,(l.city, i.industry)
,(i.industry, p.category)
,(l.city, p.category)
,(l.city)
,(i.industry)
,(p.category)
)
```

Therefore, the query shown in Figure 8.13 (GROUPING SETS) is bound to perform better than the query shown in Figure 8.7 (CUBE), simply because it is finding a lot fewer rows and calculating fewer totals. Then again, examine Figure 8.14 and you can see that the CUBE clause executes faster than the GROUPING SETS clause. One can only assume it depends on what one is pulling using the GROUPING SETS clause. However, during experimentation, no matter what combinations I tried, GROUPING SETS performed poorly compared to CUBE and ROLLUP clauses.

Note: Let's rephrase the note mentioned previously: The GROUPING SETS clause "is supposed to" help performance by preventing unspecified totals from being calculated in ROLLUP and CUBE clauses. Unwanted aggregations are supposed to be removed before they are calculated. At least that is how I understood the function of the GROUPING SETS clause. Due to performance testing results described here, it is highly probable that totals are removed after calculation, and that is why the GROUPING SETS clause is slower than the ROLLUP or CUBE clauses.

Figure 8.14
GROUPING SETS is not always faster than CUBE.

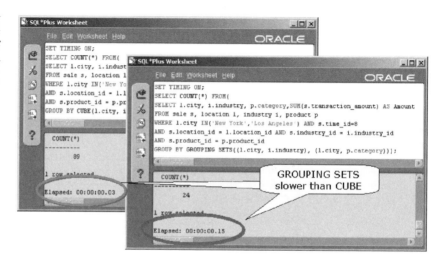

The processing behind the GROUPING SETS clause is complex and convoluted, and appears to produce temporary tables when viewed using the EXPLAIN PLAN command, shown in Figure 8.15.

Here are some equivalence expressions for CUBE and GROUPING_SETS clauses:

```
GROUP BY CUBE(l.city, i.industry)
```

is equivalent to every combination as:

```
GROUP BY GROUPING SETS
(
  (l.city, i.industry)
,(l.city)
```

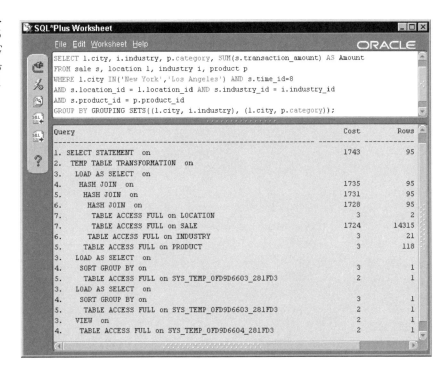

Figure 8.15
*GROUPING
SETS is not always
faster than CUBE.*

```
,(i.industry)
)
```

It also follows that:

```
GROUP BY ROLLUP(l.city, i.industry)
```

is equivalent to:

```
GROUP BY GROUPING SETS
(
 (l.city, i.industry)
,(l.city)
)
```

The ROLLUP and CUBE clauses perform internal UNION ALL set operations between multiple query group aggregations. The GROUPING

SETS clause minimizes on the internal UNION ALL operations produced by the ROLLUP and CUBE clauses. Therefore:

```
GROUP BY GROUPING SETS
(
 (l.city, i.industry)
,(l.city)
,(i.industry)
)
```

is actually:

```
SELECT . . . GROUP BY l.city, i.industry
UNION ALL
SELECT . . . GROUP BY l.city
UNION ALL
SELECT . . . GROUP BY i.industry
```

That is the essence of the ROLLUP, CUBE, and GROUPING SETS clauses—they make some types of coding a lot easier to build. Highly complex code can result when not using the GROUP BY clause extensions. Complicated code is more difficult to tune. The real crux of the matter is that there is only so much that programmers and database administrators can do in a reasonable amount of time. Using options such as ROLLUP, CUBE, and GROUPING SETS clauses simplifies complex SQL coding tasks.

8.2.3 Grouping Functions

Three grouping functions are used for doing various interesting things with the ROLLUP, CUBE, and GROUPING SETS clauses. These functions are the GROUPING function, the GROUPING_ID function, and the GROUP_ID function. Once again, these functions are more likely to help simplify SQL code, helping performance indirectly rather than directly.

The GROUPING Function

The GROUPING function returns a 1 for a ROLLUP or CUBE aggregation having a NULL value. The syntax is:

```
SELECT . . ., GROUPING(<dimension>), . . .
GROUP BY <extension> (<dimension>)
```

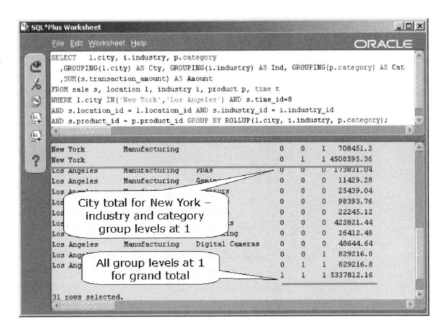

Figure 8.16
Using the GROUPING function.

Figure 8.16 clearly shows applicable use of the GROUPING function.

Figure 8.17 shows a more useful interpretation of the query in Figure 8.16.

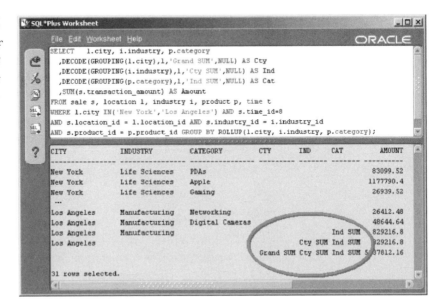

Figure 8.17
Making sense of GROUPING function parent totals.

Figure 8.18
Filtering
GROUPING
function results
with the HAVING
clause.

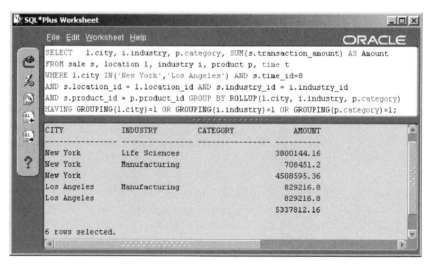

We can also use the GROUPING function to filter out rows with the HAVING clause, as shown in Figure 8.18.

The GROUPING_ID Function

The GROUPING_ID function returns a single number determining the GROUP BY level of an aggregation layer, or a group level for a particular row returned. The syntax is:

```
GROUPING_ID(<expression> [, … ])
```

Effectively the GROUPING_ID function concatenates the 0 or 1 result of the GROUPING function for all aggregations of all rows. A bit vector value returns a decimal equivalent of the binary value of the concatenated bit values, as shown in Figure 8.19 (see GROUPING function results in Figure 8.15).

Query results equivalent to Figures 8.15 and 8.19 are shown in Figure 8.20.

The GROUP_ID Function

The GROUP_ID function returns a group-level identifier starting at 0 and counting upwards for multiple row sets in a given aggregation level. It can be used to filter duplicate aggregations from a query result set. The syntax is:

Figure 8.19
Bit vector concatenations and GROUPING_ID function results.

Aggregation	Bit Vector	GROUPING_ID
Category	000	0
Industry	001	1
	010	2
City	011	3
	100	4
	101	5
	110	6
Grand total	111	7

Figure 8.20
GROUPING and GROUPING_ID function results.

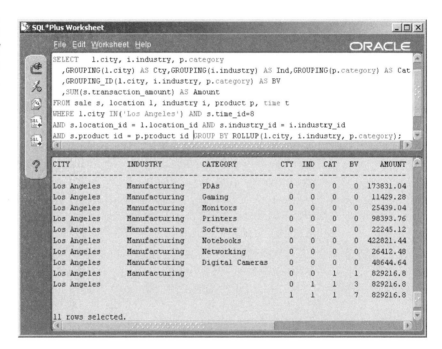

GROUP_ID( )

Figure 8.21 shows a 1 for the GROUP_ID function for each of the city totals for both New York and Los Angeles.

8.3 GROUP BY Clause Extensions and Materialized Views

ROLLUP and CUBE SQL clauses can benefit materialized views, such that multiple nested layers of materialized views do not have to be created for

Figure 8.21
Using the
GROUP_ID
function.

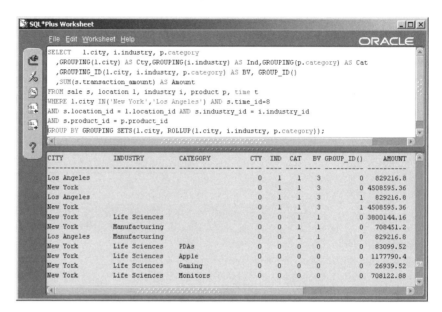

each hierarchical dimensional layer. How does this help performance? ROL-LUP and CUBE clauses can help performance and maintenance of materialized views because there are fewer layers to maintain. On the contrary, because rows of multiple nested materialized views are merged, perhaps into fewer materialized views or even a single materialized view, rollups and cubes might actually be detrimental to query performance, particularly where a query only requires higher aggregation layers. A materialized view higher in the hierarchy could contain many fewer rows. Let's attempt to verify these points. In a previous chapter, we created a materialized view called MV_JOIN_PURCHASE, as shown below. This materialized view is not partitioned, in order to reduce current complexity.

```
CREATE MATERIALIZED VIEW mv_join_purchase
     PARALLEL NOLOGGING TABLESPACE MVDATA
COMPRESS USING NO INDEX NEVER REFRESH
     ENABLE QUERY REWRITE
AS SELECT pu.order_amount,pu.order_date
, pu.transaction_amount,pu.transaction_date
, pu.payment_amount,pu.payment_date,pu.payment_text
, pu.product_quantity,pu.product_price,pu.product_date
, l.region,l.country,l.state,l.city
, t.month#,t.quarter#,t.year#
, p.category, p.product, p.price, i.industry
```

```
FROM purchase pu, location l, time t, product p, industry i
WHERE pu.location_id = l.location_id
AND pu.time_id = t.time_id
AND pu.product_id = p.product_id
AND pu.industry_id = i.industry_id;
ANALYZE TABLE mv_join_purchase COMPUTE STATISTICS;
```

Let's go and create separate, successive, super-aggregation layers as materialized views for CATEGORY, INDUSTRY, and CITY:

```
CREATE MATERIALIZED VIEW mv_cost_by_category
    PARALLEL NOLOGGING TABLESPACE mvdata
COMPRESS USING NO INDEX NEVER REFRESH
    ENABLE QUERY REWRITE
AS SELECT city, industry, category
    ,COUNT(transaction_amount),COUNT(*)
    ,SUM(transaction_amount)
FROM mv_join_purchase
GROUP BY city, industry, category;
ANALYZE TABLE mv_cost_by_category COMPUTE STATISTICS;

CREATE MATERIALIZED VIEW mv_cost_by_industry
    PARALLEL NOLOGGING TABLESPACE mvdata
COMPRESS USING NO INDEX NEVER REFRESH
    ENABLE QUERY REWRITE
AS SELECT city, industry
    ,COUNT(transaction_amount),COUNT(*)
    ,SUM(transaction_amount)
FROM mv_join_purchase
GROUP BY city, industry;
ANALYZE TABLE mv_cost_by_industry COMPUTE STATISTICS;

CREATE MATERIALIZED VIEW mv_cost_by_city
    PARALLEL NOLOGGING TABLESPACE mvdata
COMPRESS USING NO INDEX NEVER REFRESH
    ENABLE QUERY REWRITE
AS SELECT city
    ,COUNT(transaction_amount),COUNT(*)
    ,SUM(transaction_amount)
FROM mv_join_purchase
GROUP BY city;
```

```
ANALYZE TABLE mv_cost_by_city COMPUTE STATISTICS;
```

Now let's execute a query plan against the MV_JOIN_PURCHASE materialized view, but aggregating up to CITY (the top layer). The result is shown in Figure 8.22. Note the low cost, the small number of rows, and the materialized view query rewrite all the way to the top layer using the MV_COST_BY_CITY materialized view, reading only 302 rows, one for each city.

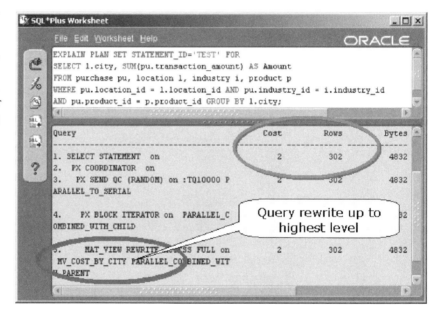

Figure 8.22
A query plan without a ROLLUP clause, against the top layer of a set of nested materialized views.

Figure 8.23 shows a ROLLUP clause in the query also executing query rewrite in the same way as for the non-ROLLUP clause query in Figure 8.22.

Now let's alter the nested materialized view structure into a single ROLLUP clause materialized view sitting on top of the join materialized view. This new materialized view will contain the same rows as all three of the MV_COST_BY_CATEGORY, MV_COST_BY_INDUSTRY, and MV_COST BY_CITY materialized views:

```
DROP MATERIALIZED VIEW mv_cost_by_city;
DROP MATERIALIZED VIEW mv_cost_by_industry;
DROP MATERIALIZED VIEW mv_cost_by_category;
```

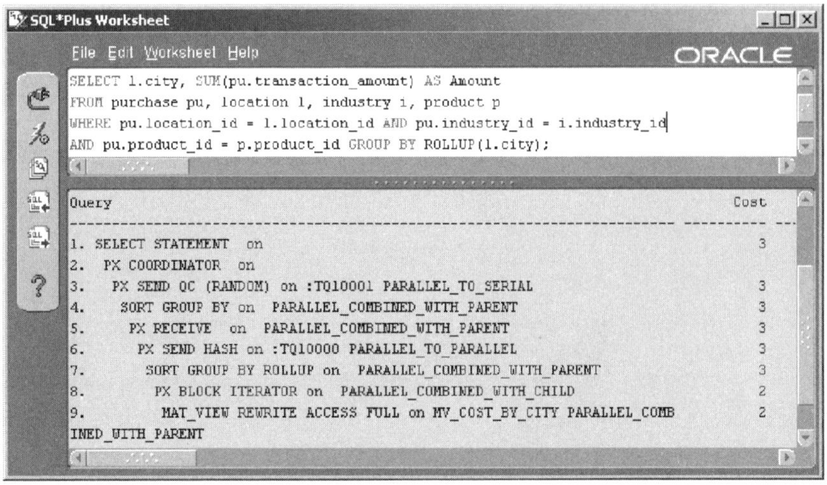

Figure 8.23
Executing ROLLUP and query rewrite through nested materialized views.

```
CREATE MATERIALIZED VIEW mv_rollup_cost
    PARALLEL NOLOGGING TABLESPACE mvdata
COMPRESS USING NO INDEX NEVER REFRESH
    ENABLE QUERY REWRITE
AS SELECT city, industry, category
    ,COUNT(transaction_amount),COUNT(*)
    ,SUM(transaction_amount)
FROM mv_join_purchase
GROUP BY ROLLUP(city, industry, category);
ANALYZE TABLE mv_rollup_cost COMPUTE STATISTICS;
```

Figure 8.24 shows that query rewrite is actually not allowed up to the second nested materialized view. This is probably caused by the presence of the ROLLUP clause.

A possible solution to the lack of nested query rewrite shown in Figure 8.24 is to create only a single layer and transform the MV_JOIN_PURCHASE materialized view itself into a rollup.

```
DROP MATERIALIZED VIEW mv_cost_by_city;
DROP MATERIALIZED VIEW mv_cost_by_industry;
DROP MATERIALIZED VIEW mv_cost_by_category;
ALTER MATERIALIZED VIEW mv_join_purchase
DISABLE QUERY REWRITE;

DROP MATERIALIZED VIEW mv_rollup_cost ;
```

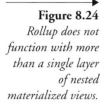

Figure 8.24
Rollup does not function with more than a single layer of nested materialized views.

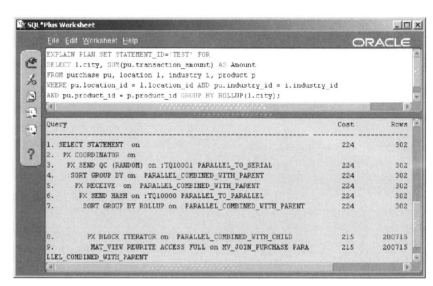

```
CREATE MATERIALIZED VIEW mv_rollup_cost
    PARALLEL NOLOGGING TABLESPACE mvdata
COMPRESS USING NO INDEX NEVER REFRESH
    ENABLE QUERY REWRITE
AS SELECT l.city, i.industry, p.category
    ,COUNT(pu.transaction_amount),COUNT(*)
    ,SUM(pu.transaction_amount)
FROM purchase pu, location l, time t, product p, industry i
WHERE pu.location_id = l.location_id
AND pu.time_id = t.time_id
AND pu.product_id = p.product_id
AND pu.industry_id = i.industry_id
GROUP BY ROLLUP(l.city, i.industry, p.category);
ANALYZE TABLE mv_rollup_cost COMPUTE STATISTICS;
```

Unless the query executed against the join creating the MV_ROLLUP_COST materialized view is matched for the ROLLUP clause precisely, no query rewrite will occur. The following query will query rewrite to the MV_ROLLUP_COST materialized view:

```
SELECT l.city, i.industry, p.category
    ,COUNT(pu.transaction_amount),COUNT(*)
    ,SUM(pu.transaction_amount)
FROM purchase pu, location l, time t, product p, industry i
```

```
WHERE pu.location_id = l.location_id
AND pu.time_id = t.time_id
AND pu.product_id = p.product_id
AND pu.industry_id = i.industry_id
GROUP BY ROLLUP(l.city, i.industry, p.category);
```

The following three non-ROLLUP and partial ROLLUP clause queries will not query rewrite at all, at least not using the MV_ROLLUP_COST materialized view:

```
SELECT l.city, SUM(pu.transaction_amount) AS Amount
FROM purchase pu, location l, industry i, product p
WHERE pu.location_id = l.location_id
AND pu.industry_id = i.industry_id
AND pu.product_id = p.product_id
GROUP BY l.city;

SELECT l.city, i.industry, p.category
    ,COUNT(pu.transaction_amount),COUNT(*)
    ,SUM(pu.transaction_amount)
FROM purchase pu, location l, time t, product p, industry i
WHERE pu.location_id = l.location_id
AND pu.time_id = t.time_id
AND pu.product_id = p.product_id
AND pu.industry_id = i.industry_id
GROUP BY l.city, ROLLUP(i.industry, p.category);

SELECT l.city, i.industry, p.category
    ,COUNT(pu.transaction_amount),COUNT(*)
    ,SUM(pu.transaction_amount)
FROM purchase pu, location l, time t, product p, industry i
WHERE pu.location_id = l.location_id
AND pu.time_id = t.time_id
AND pu.product_id = p.product_id
AND pu.industry_id = i.industry_id
GROUP BY l.city, i.industry, ROLLUP(p.category);
```

There is a solution! The way it is done is to utilize the GROUPING_ID function. Remember that the GROUPING_ID function returns a single number determining the GROUP BY level of an aggregation layer, or a group level for a particular row returned. In other words, the GROUPING_ID function can be used to tell your query where in a ROLLUP or CUBE aggregation the current row is.

Note: In Oracle Database 10*g* Release 2 it is mandatory for materialized views containing GROUP BY clause extensions, to contain the GROUPING_ID function executed on all columns in the GROUP BY clause extension ROLLUP, CUBE, or GROUPING SETS clause. Without the appropriate GROUPING_ID functionality, the DBMS_MVIEW.EXPLAIN_ REWRITE procedure will produce an error: (QSM-01295: no suitable grouping_id found in materialized view with grouping sets).

Including the GROUPING_ID function, as shown in the query below (and shown in Figure 8.25), will cause multiple nested layers of materialized views to be accessible for query rewrite. All the combinations shown above will query rewrite as well.

```
DROP MATERIALIZED VIEW mv_rollup_cost ;
CREATE MATERIALIZED VIEW mv_rollup_cost
     PARALLEL NOLOGGING TABLESPACE mvdata
COMPRESS USING NO INDEX NEVER REFRESH
     ENABLE QUERY REWRITE
AS SELECT l.city, i.industry, p.category
     ,COUNT(pu.transaction_amount),COUNT(*)
     ,SUM(pu.transaction_amount)
     ,GROUPING_ID(l.city, i.industry, p.category)
FROM purchase pu, location l, time t, product p, industry i
WHERE pu.location_id = l.location_id
AND pu.time_id = t.time_id
AND pu.product_id = p.product_id
AND pu.industry_id = i.industry_id
GROUP BY ROLLUP(l.city, i.industry, p.category);
ANALYZE TABLE mv_rollup_cost COMPUTE STATISTICS;
```

8.4   Combining Groupings Together

There are three factors to deal with when trying to understand the more complex aspects of basic GROUP BY clause extensions. These factors are composites of multiple groups, concatenation of multiple groups, and finally hierarchical cubes. Essentially, these methods in this section simply

Figure 8.25
*GROUP BY
extensions function
in nested
materialized views
when the
GROUPING_ID
function is
included.*

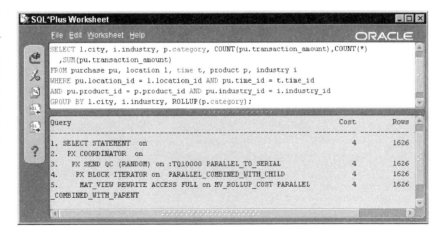

show other ways of making SQL code easier to write, and, thus, easier to tune for performance.

8.4.1 Composite Groupings

A simple ROLLUP expression rolls up aggregations across individual columns in a query. A composite grouping allows creation of groups such that the following syntax applies:

```
GROUP BY ROLLUP
(
  <expression>
, (<expression>, <expression>)
, <expression>
)
```

What this means is that we limit the number of rolled up aggregations. Thus, where the following query produces aggregations for each city, industry, and category:

```
SELECT  l.city, i.industry, p.category
     , SUM(s.transaction_amount) AS Amount
FROM sale s, location l, industry i, product p, time t
WHERE l.city IN('New York','Los Angeles')
AND s.time_id=8
AND s.location_id = l.location_id
AND s.industry_id = i.industry_id
```

```
AND s.product_id = p.product_id
GROUP BY ROLLUP(l.city, i.industry, p.category);
```

Another query on the other hand will limit aggregations to cities and categories, omitting industry aggregations as shown in Figure 8.24.

```
SELECT   l.city, i.industry, p.category
       , SUM(s.transaction_amount) AS Amount
FROM sale s, location l, industry i, product p, time t
WHERE l.city IN('New York','Los Angeles')
AND s.time_id=8
AND s.location_id = l.location_id
AND s.industry_id = i.industry_id
AND s.product_id = p.product_id
GROUP BY ROLLUP(l.city, (i.industry, p.category));
```

In Figure 8.26, the industries and categories have been handled as a single unit and, thus, no aggregation for city and industry is returned. Simi-

Figure 8.26
Using composite groupings to filter out aggregates.

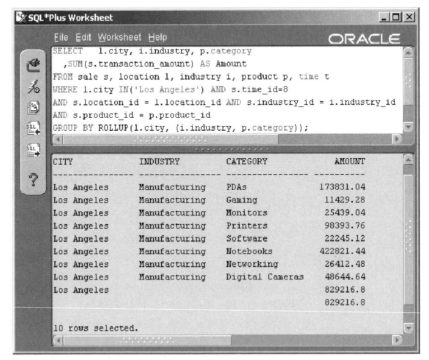

larly, the following query would produce an aggregation for each category, each industry within each city, but no city aggregations:

```
SELECT  l.city, i.industry, p.category
, SUM(s.transaction_amount) AS Amount
FROM sale s, location l, industry i, product p, time t
WHERE l.city IN('Los Angeles')
AND s.time_id=8
AND s.location_id = l.location_id
AND s.industry_id = i.industry_id
AND s.product_id = p.product_id
GROUP BY ROLLUP((l.city, i.industry), p.category);
```

The same approach can apply to ROLLUP, CUBE, and GROUPING SETS clauses.

8.4.2 Concatenated Groupings

We can also concatenate groupings together as in the following syntax:

```
GROUP BY GROUPING SETS(<expression>,<expression>)
, GROUPING SETS(<expression>,<expression>)
```

This has the effect of combining each element in the first expression list with each element in every other expression list.

The following query:

```
SELECT  l.city, i.industry, t.year#, t.quarter#
, SUM(s.transaction_amount) AS Amount
FROM sale s, location l, industry i, time t
WHERE l.city IN('Los Angeles')
AND s.time_id BETWEEN 10 AND 50
AND s.location_id = l.location_id
AND s.industry_id = i.industry_id
AND s.time_id = t.time_id
GROUP BY GROUPING SETS(l.city, i.industry)
, GROUPING SETS(t.year#, t.quarter#);
```

will produce aggregations as follows:

```
l.city, t.year#
l.city, t.quarter#
i.industry, t.year#
i.industry, t.quarter#
```

The result will be the equivalent of:

```
GROUP BY l.city, t.year#
UNION ALL
GROUP BY l.city, t.quarter#
UNION ALL
GROUP BY i.industry, t.year#
UNION ALL
GROUP BY i.industry, t.quarter#
```

Therefore, we get aggregations for each city by both year and quarter, and each industry by year and quarter. We do not, however, get other aggregations, such as city by industry by year. The result of the above query is shown in Figure 8.27.

8.4.3 **Hierarchical Cubes**

Factors, such as composite and concatenated groupings, can allow avoiding generating too many aggregations. This is particularly the case for cubic aggregations where superfluous and very costly cross dimensional aggregations can be avoided. Cubic multiple dimensional aggregations can take up an inordinate, and often unacceptable, amount of processing time. In short, fully calculated cubes are often far too complex to be worth their processing time and, thus, simplification can offer substantial performance improvements.

Rollups calculate aggregations throughout a hierarchy. Cubes, on the other hand, create multiple dimensional structures by calculating aggregations across different dimensions and producing combinations of aggregations across those dimensions. The most effective result is a combination of rollups and cubes leading to a combination of hierarchical and multiple dimensional aggregations. The result is a hierarchical cube or a multiple dimensional hierarchy. What else could it be? Duh!

The advantage of performing all these calculations in Oracle SQL is that you do not get the overhead of producing the same types of calculations either by using highly complex SQL code, or front-end application tools,

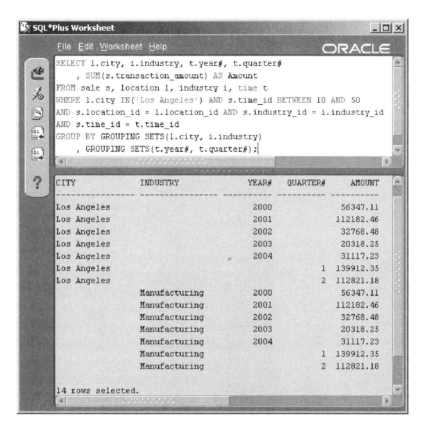

Figure 8.27

Using concatenated groupings to filter out aggregates.

generating possibly even less efficient, nondatabase vendor specific generic, really nasty, complicated SQL code statements.

This chapter has examined the three basic GROUP BY clause extensions in the form of the ROLLUP clause, the CUBE clause, and the GROUP-ING SETS clause. Additionally, the three grouping functions GROUP-ING, GROUPING_ID, and GROUP_ID have been covered. More complex aspects of the creation of combination hierarchical cubes using composites and concatenations were also discussed. The next chapter will examine the rich functionality provided in Oracle SQL for building better-performing, complex analytical queries.

9

Analysis Reporting

This chapter describes better-performing ways of building analytical queries in Oracle SQL. Oracle SQL is rich in built-in functionality that allows efficient analytical query construction, helps queries run faster, and makes codeing much less complex. This chapter examines analysis reporting using Oracle SQL.

9.1 What Is Analysis Reporting?

A simple nonanalytical report retrieves one or more rows from one or more tables, and sends the rows back to the user as the row set that has been retrieved, a straightforward two dimensional array of rows and columns. Figure 9.1 shows a simple row set returning nonanalytical query.

As shown in Figure 9.1, the rows are returned showing data as it is in the database. The ROLLUP clause allows a rollup of totals for all aggregations in the GROUP BY clause, namely totals for all cities, industries, and categories, plus a grand total for the entire report.

Analytical reporting allows processing and reporting across rows and columns returned by a query, or even multiple queries. Figure 9.2 shows a simple analytical query, such that a cumulative total is produced over all category aggregated amounts. Figure 9.2 also shows cross row-calculations in which the sum of all categories is accumulated for each category summary encountered.

The objective of analytical reporting is ultimately to provide for predictive analysis based on existing data—usually, large amounts of archived data. Typically, a data warehouse contains huge volumes of archived data. The goal of analytical reporting is to provide support for general budgeting forecasts, planning provision, looking for trends—by extrapolating analysis of past data warehouse fact entries activity into future *guesstimates*. The

Figure 9.1
*A simple row set
returning query.*

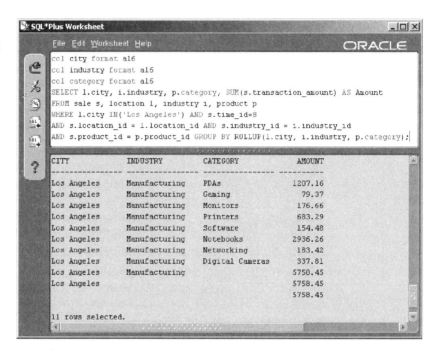

Figure 9.2
*A simple analytical
query.*

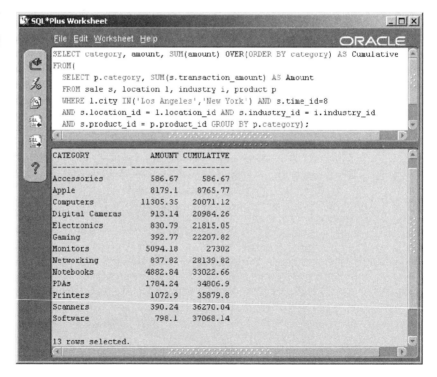

more comprehensive and granular data warehouse data is, the more accurate predictive analytical reporting will be. The downside to this is that the larger the data warehouse becomes, the longer reporting will take to produce results, and the more development and maintenance person-hours are required.

9.1.1   How Does Analysis Reporting Affect Performance?

In general, Oracle SQL includes a slew of functionality and specialized SQL expressions and syntax that can be used to make analytical queries much simpler. Provided functionality is built into, and executed within, the Oracle Database query engine in compiled form, or in provided functional libraries. Performance and development times are improved because coders do not have to write as much code, reducing performance tuning complexity and programming time. The more complex SQL code statements are, the more difficult they are to tune. There is only so much even the most brilliant of programmers can do.

9.2   Types of Analysis Reporting

Analysis, or analytical, reporting can generally be divided into the following categories:

- **Rankings**. The rank of a value within a group of values, where a rank is the position a value takes relative to a set of values. Professional golfers are ranked as to their most recent historical winnings, depending on the competition. The top ranked player is currently the best player in the world, and the tenth ranking player is the tenth best.

- **Moving Windows**. The windowing clause syntax allows placement of a window, or subset picture, onto a set of data, and applies analysis to that data window subset only. The window becomes a subset of rows within a query. The window can be moved across the row set as the query executes. Aggregations within the window can be computed against the data set contained in the window.

- **Lag and Lead**. These functions access rows in row sets behind or ahead of a current row, in relation to a current row position within the row set, and are used when the relative position of one row to another is unreliable.

- **First and Last**. These functions allow access to highest or lowest ranking rows in a row set within a ranked row set.

- **Linear Regressions**. Linear regression functions fit a least-squares regression line to two expressions. Linear regression is used to make predictions about values.

- **Inverse Percentiles**. Find the probability that a variable is less than or equal to a given value, or vice versa—compute a value for a given probability.

- **Hypothetical Ranks and Distributions**. These are what-if scenarios, such as what happens if row x is added to row set y, and how are results affected?

- **Frequent Itemsets**. This represents the frequency of a set of items. How often a group of events occur, as opposed to how often a single event occurs, can be analyzed using the DBMS_FREQUENT_ ITEMSETS PL/SQL package. Using frequent itemset calculations, you can compare the frequency of the same event recurring or even recurrence of multiple different events happening simultaneously. For instance, how often do customers buy both milk and cream at the local grocery store, as opposed to only milk or only cream? This type of analysis can help with forecasting potential distribution requirements for goods.

- **Specialized Expressions**. CASE expressions allow more efficient inline DECODE functionality. Cursor expressions allow easy embedding of SQL statements inside other SQL statements.

- **Equiwidth Histograms**. An equiwidth histogram is a histogram created in which all histogram intervals contain a similar number of entries, using the WIDTH_BUCKET function.

- **Data Densification and Time Series Calculations**. Usually, data is stored in sparse form, such that not all dimensional entries in a star schema structure have related fact entries. Data densification uses partitioned outer joins—an inherent or automated outer join, basically. The result is densified data, such that inter- and cross-row calculations do not occur between existing and nonexisting rows, making these types of queries more efficient. Time series calculations deal with calculations across a time dimension, as in when a transaction occurred. Time series calculations are made considerably more efficient using data densification, because a time dimension is often a larger dimension, depending, of course, on how much granularity is stored with respect to time.

- **Highly Specialized Statistical Functions**. Various types of highly complex and unusual statistical functionality exist in Oracle SQL as compiled procedures. Additionally, the DBMS_STAT_FUNCS package contains a specialized set of statistical functions.

The next task is to examine analysis function syntax. After introducing appropriate functions and methods, we will examine various specialized syntactical elements. The details of how these functions and specialized syntax elements are applied will be discussed later in this chapter.

9.3 Introducing Analytical Functions

What are the available aggregate functions, and how are they used? Let's go through the definitions. Functions are divided into different sections.

9.3.1 Simple Summary Functions

- **AVG(<expression>)**. The average.

- **COUNT(*|<expression>)**. The number of rows in a query.

- **MIN(<expression>)**. The minimum.

- **MAX(<expression>)**. The maximum.

- **SUM(<expression>)**. The sum.

9.3.2 Statistical Function Calculators

- **STDDEV(<expression>)**. The standard deviation is the average difference from the mean. The mean is similar to the average.

- **VARIANCE(<expression>)**. The variance is the square of the standard deviation and, thus, the average squared difference from the mean, or the squared average deviation from the mean.

- **STDDEV_POP(<expression>)**. The population standard deviation.

- **STDDEV_SAMP(<expression>)**. The sample standard deviation.

- **VAR_POP(<expression>)**. The population variance, excluding NULL values.

- **VAR_SAMP(<expression>)**. The sample variance, excluding NULL values.

- **COVAR_POP(<expression>, <expression>)**. The population covariance of two expressions. The covariance is the average product of differences from two group means.

- **COVAR_SAMP(<expression>, <expression>)**. The sample covariance of two expressions.

- **CORR(<expression>, <expression>)**. The coefficient of correlation of two expressions. A correlation coefficient assesses the quality of a least squares fitting to the data. The least squares procedure finds the best fitting curve to a given set of values.

- **REGR_[SLOPE | INTERCEPT | COUNT | R2 | AVGX| AVGY | SXX | SYY | SXY](<expression>, <expression>)**. Linear regression functions fit a least-squares regression line to two expressions. Linear regression is used to make predictions about a single value. Simple linear regression involves discovering the equation for a straight line that most nearly fits the given data. The discovered linear equation is then used to predict values for the data. A linear regression curve is a straight line through a set of plotted points. The straight line should get as close as possible to all points at once—a best fit!

- **CORR_{S | K}**. This function calculates Pearson's correlation coefficient, measuring the strength of a linear relationship between two variables. Plotting two variables on a graph results in a lot of dots plotted from two axes. Pearson's correlation coefficient can tell you how good the straight line is.

- **MEDIAN**. A median is a middle or interpolated value. Quite literally, a median is the value in the middle of a set of values. If a distribution is discontinuous and skewed, or just all over the place, then the median will not be anywhere near a mean or average of a set of values. A median is not always terribly useful.

- **STATS_{BINOMIAL_TEST | CROSSTAB | F_TEST | KS_TEST | MODE | MW_TEST | ONE_WAY_ANOVA | STATS_T_TEST_* | STATS_WSR_TEST}**. These functions provide various statistical goodies. Explaining what all these very particular statistics functions do is a little bit more of statistics than Oracle SQL for this book.

9.3.3 Statistical Distribution Functions

- **CUME_DIST(<expression> [, <expression> . . .]) WITHIN GROUP (ORDER BY <expression> [, <expression>])**. The cumulative distribution of an expression within a group of values. A cumulative frequency distribution is a plot of the number of observations falling within or below an interval, a histogram. The cumulative distribution function is the probability that a variable takes a value less than or equal to a given value.

- **PERCENTILE_{ CONT | DISC }(<expression>) WITHIN GROUP (ORDER BY <expression>).** The percent point function or the inverse distribution function for a **CONT**inuous or **DISC**rete distribution. Since the percent point function is an inverse distribution function, we start with the probability and compute the corresponding value for the cumulative distribution.

9.3.4 Ranking Functions

- **RANK(<expression> [, <expression> . . .]) WITHIN GROUP (ORDER BY <expression> [, <expression>]).** The rank of a value in a group of values.

- **DENSE_RANK(<expression> [, <expression> . . .]) WITHIN GROUP (ORDER BY <expression> [, <expression> . . .]).** The rank of a row within an ordered group of rows.

- **PERCENT_RANK(<expression> [, <expression> . . .]) WITHIN GROUP (ORDER BY [, <expression> . . .]).** Similar to a cumulative distribution function, where the rank produced is a percentage of the current value's rank in relation to the rank of the highest ranked value.

- **NTILE(<expression>) OVER . . .** Split a sorted row set into equally sized groups or buckets.

- **ROW_NUMBER() OVER . . .** Adds a unique integer to each row in a row set.

- **FIRST | LAST (<expression> [, <expression> . . .]) WITHIN GROUP (ORDER BY <expression> [, <expression> . . .]).** Works with only the first and last ranking rows in a sorted group of rows.

9.3.5 Lag and Lead Functions

- **LAG | LEAD (<expression> [, <offset>] [, <default>]) OVER (<expression> (ORDER BY <expression> [, <expression> . . .]).** Access to rows at an offset count from the current row.

9.3.6　**Aggregation Functions Allowing Analysis**

Analytics is used to calculate cumulative, moving, centered, and reporting summary aggregate values often used in data warehouse environments. Unlike aggregate functions, analytical functions return multiple rows for each group. Each grouping of rows is called a *window* and is effectively a variable group, comprising of a range of rows. The number of rows in a window can be based on a specified row count or an interval, such as a period of time. Apart from the ORDER BY clause, analytical functions are always executed at the end of a query statement. The following functions allow analysis and thus analytics, using tools such as the windowing clause:

- COUNT, SUM, AVG, MIN, and MAX.

- FIRST_VALUE and LAST_VALUE. (return moving window first and last row values).

- STDDEV, VARIANCE, and CORR.

- STDDEV_POP, VAR_POP, and COVAR_POP.

- STDDEV_SAMP, VAR_SAMP, and COVAR_SAMP.

9.4　**Specialized Analytical Syntax**

Areas of specialized Oracle SQL syntax that implement and assist in the construction of analytical queries are the OVER clause, the WITH clause, and inline expressions, such as CASE and cursor expressions.

9.4.1　**The OVER Clause**

The OVER clause allows the application of specific functionality in separate groupings by splitting with partitions. For example, you can build a sorted result set where sorting is performed exclusively within each group or partition, not across all returned rows. Thus, you can sort within each partition, regardless of sort order, across all rows returned by the query. Obviously, a query containing an OVER clause with no PARTITION BY clause simply applies the sorted order to the entire row set returned by the query.

The syntax for the OVER clause is shown in Figure 9.3.

We have already seen use of the OVER clause in Figure 9.2. The OVER clause is used to create an analysis across a specific expression. In the case of Figure 9.2 a cumulative total, summed up line by line, is created to contain

Figure 9.3
*OVER clause
syntax.*

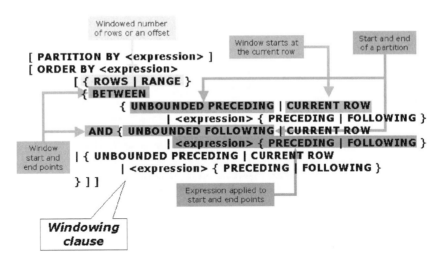

```
[ PARTITION BY <expression> ]
[ ORDER BY <expression>
      [ { ROWS | RANGE }
        { BETWEEN
              { UNBOUNDED PRECEDING | CURRENT ROW
                | <expression> { PRECEDING | FOLLOWING }
          AND { UNBOUNDED FOLLOWING | CURRENT ROW
                | <expression> { PRECEDING | FOLLOWING }
        | { UNBOUNDED PRECEDING | CURRENT ROW
            | <expression> { PRECEDING | FOLLOWING }
        } ] ]
```

*Windowing
clause*

a running total as each category is listed. Now let's describe each syntax element shown in Figure 9.3.

The ORDER BY Clause

The ORDER BY clause sorts the contents of rows within partitions. Figure 9.4 shows a query sorted in descending order by TRANSACTION_AMOUNT, each row has a ranking within the descending order of TRANSACTION_AMOUNT.

The PARTITION BY Clause

The PARTITION BY clause can be used to break the query into groups. Otherwise, a single partition encompassing all rows is created. Figure 9.5 uses the same query as in Figure 9.4, but adds the partition on the city. This has the effect of sorting ranks within separate cities, sorted by cities.

How can the example shown in Figure 9.5 be demonstrated without using the analytical OVER clause and resorting to straight Oracle SQL? Perhaps the biggest issue is that the RANK function will only accept a constant value expression to evaluate, so you cannot embed a subquery into the RANK function. Therefore, a PL/SQL procedure is an option. Figure 9.6 shows the result of executing the following script:

```
SET SERVEROUTPUT ON;
EXEC DBMS_OUTPUT.ENABLE(1000000);
DECLARE
  ranking FLOAT;
```

Figure 9.4
Sorting in the OVER clause.

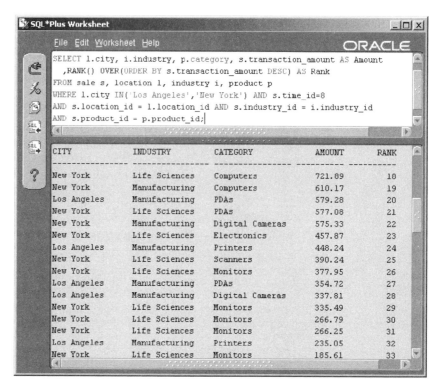

Figure 9.5
Partitioning the OVER clause.

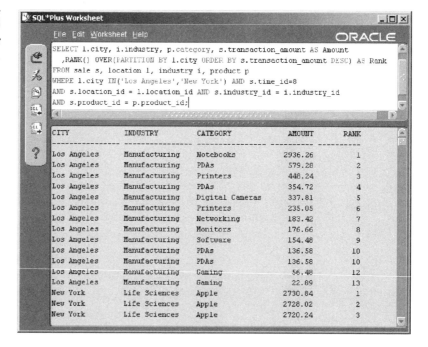

```
        CURSOR CAmounts IS
          SELECT s.transaction_amount AS Amount
          FROM sale s, location l, industry i, product p
          WHERE l.city IN('Los Angeles','New York')
          AND s.time_id=8
          AND s.location_id = l.location_id
          AND s.industry_id = i.industry_id
          AND s.product_id = p.product_id;
    BEGIN
      FOR RAmount IN CAmounts LOOP
        SELECT RANK(RAmount.amount) WITHIN GROUP
          (ORDER BY s.transaction_amount) "Rank" INTO ranking
        FROM sale s, location l, industry i, product p
        WHERE l.city IN('Los Angeles','New York')
        AND s.time_id=8
        AND s.location_id = l.location_id
        AND s.industry_id = i.industry_id
        AND s.product_id = p.product_id;
        DBMS_OUTPUT.PUT_LINE
          (TO_CHAR(ranking)||' '||TO_CHAR(RAmount.amount));
        END LOOP;
    END;
    /
    EXEC DBMS_OUTPUT.DISABLE;
    SET SERVEROUTPUT OFF;
```

You can see from the script above in relation to the query in Figure 9.6 that complexity is most certainly an issue, and very likely to be a problem. Also, note how in the script that in order to find the ranking value for each row in the row set, the query is essentially executed twice—once to find all the amounts for the entire row set and a second time to find the ranking of each amount within all the amounts. That is what I mean by use of Oracle SQL analytics helping performance. Additionally, the PL/SQL procedure above only finds the rankings and the amounts—you still have to retrieve the CITY, INDUSTRY, and CATEGORY columns, plus you have to re-sort everything by CATEGORY within INDUSTRY, within RANK, and within CITY. In other words:

```
    ORDER BY city, rank. industry, category;
```

Far too much work! More SQL code means more likelihood of errors. More complexity is always more difficult to tune and more complex for the optimizer to handle properly. Oracle SQL analytical functions and syntax elements are data warehouse tuning methods in themselves, simply because they exist.

Figure 9.6
Executing analysis without the OVER clause and analytics.

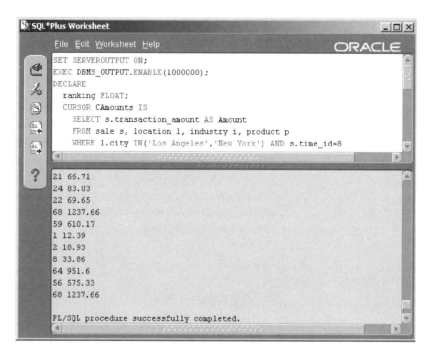

The Windowing Clause

The windowing clause logically slides a window across a data set and has a start and end point, creating a mobile subset of rows within a row set returned by a query. This window can be moved across the row set during processing, allowing processing between rows within the window as it moves.

- **ROWS or RANGE**. An analytical function aggregates all rows in the partition. ROWS specifies the width of the window in rows and RANGE a logical offset.

- **BETWEEN . . . AND . . .** Sets a start and end point for a window.

- **UNBOUNDED PRECEDING or UNBOUNDED FOLLOW-ING**. An unbounded window implies that the start and end of the window are not restricted and thus the window starts at the first row of a partition or terminates at the last row of a partition, respectively.

- **CURRENT ROW.** This option specifies a window as starting or ending according to the ROW or RANGE specification options.

- **<expression> PRECEDING or <expression> FOLLOWING.** Applies an expression to start or end points of the window.

Figure 9.7 shows an example using the windowing clause. The total adds up the current row plus the two preceding and two following rows. Can this be done with regular Oracle SQL? Probably yes, but with great difficulty and enormously complex SQL code.

Figure 9.7
Using a moving window.

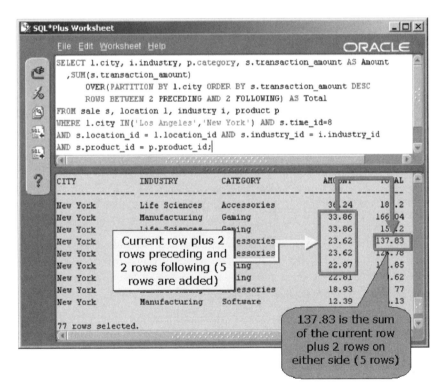

Figure 9.8 attempts to provide further explanation for the windowing clause, summing up the current row, two preceding, and two following rows. Note how in the last column on the right that the total for row 6 consists of the sum of the amounts for rows 4, 5, 6 (the current row), 7, and 8. The only exception to this rule is where preceding or following rows do not

exist in the data set. The rows represented in Figure 9.8 are the last 8 rows returned by the query of 77 rows in Figure 9.7. The first total (last total in the report) of 54.13 is a sum of only rows 1, 2, and 3. This is because there are no rows preceding row 1 and, thus, only the current row and the two following rows are included in the total.

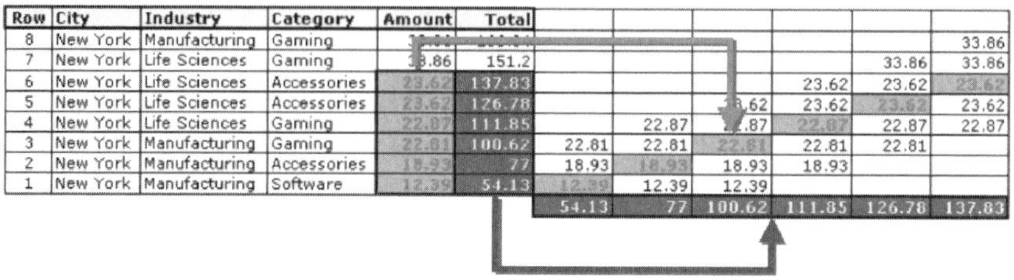

Figure 9.8
Explaining the moving window in Figure 9.7.

Row	City	Industry	Category	Amount	Total							
8	New York	Manufacturing	Gaming									33.86
7	New York	Life Sciences	Gaming	3.86	151.2						33.86	33.86
6	New York	Life Sciences	Accessories	23.62	137.83					23.62	23.62	23.62
5	New York	Life Sciences	Accessories	23.62	126.78				.62	23.62	23.62	23.62
4	New York	Life Sciences	Gaming	22.07	111.85			22.87	.87	22.07	22.87	22.87
3	New York	Manufacturing	Gaming	22.81	100.62	22.81	22.81	22.81	22.81	22.81	
2	New York	Manufacturing	Accessories	18.93	77	18.93	18.93	18.93	18.93		
1	New York	Manufacturing	Software	12.39	54.13	12.39	12.39	12.39			
						54.13	77	100.62	111.85	126.78	137.83	

Note: The row numbers have been deliberately reversed in Figure 9.8, where row 77 becomes row 1 and so on. This is to facilitate easier understanding for you, the reader.

The sheer complexity of tuning a query like that shown in Figure 9.8 into a straightforward Oracle SQL or PL/SQL coded query is simply mind boggling. I don't even want to think about it. It's just way too scary!

Figure 9.2 shows a cumulative aggregation. A cumulative aggregation is where each value is added to the total of all preceding values, for each row. The result is a running total as rows are returned. Figure 9.7 shows a moving or sliding aggregation that contains two rows on both sides of a central moving row, as the row set is passed through. Thus, the aggregation for each row contains the aggregation of five rows around the moving row. Figure 9.8 effectively demonstrates a centered aggregate.

Note: Windows on row sets allow calculations across rows by access to more than one row in a table at once, as do many of the functions described in this chapter. The result is access to more than one row in a single table at once without using two queries or a self join. This helps performance!

9.4.2 The WITH Clause

The syntax for the WITH clause is shown in Figure 9.9.

Figure 9.9
WITH clause syntax.

Cannot nest WITH clause inside another WITH clause subquery

Subquery factoring clause

```
[ WITH <query> AS ( <subquery> ) [, ... ] ]
SELECT ... FROM <query> , ... ;
```

```
WITH <query> AS (<subquery>)
, WITH <query> AS (<subquery>)
, WITH <query> AS (<subquery>)
, ...
```

The WITH clause, also known as the subquery factoring clause, allows an in-memory preprocessed creation of multiple row sets. These preprocessed row sets can then be passed directly into a controlling query, which can use, the preprocessed WITH clause query results. Effectively, the WITH clause can be used as a substitute for poorly performing queries utilizing temporary tables and set operators, such as UNION. The easiest way to explain the purpose of the WITH clause is by demonstrating. This is a basic query joining a number of tables:

```
SELECT l.city, i.industry, p.category
, SUM(s.transaction_amount) AS Amount
FROM sale s, location l, industry i, product p
WHERE l.city IN('Los Angeles','New York')
AND i.industry IN('Life Sciences','Manufacturing')
AND p.category LIKE '%a%'
AND s.time_id=8
AND s.location_id = l.location_id
AND s.industry_id = i.industry_id
AND s.product_id = p.product_id
GROUP BY l.city, i.industry, p.category;
```

Let's begin by joining the three smallest dimensions. Obviously, there is nothing to join on so we get a Cartesian Product, a little like a star query:

```
SELECT l.city, i.industry, p.category
FROM location l, industry i, product p
```

```
WHERE l.city IN('Los Angeles','New York')
AND i.industry IN('Life Sciences','Manufacturing')
AND p.category LIKE '%a%';
```

Now let's keep the TIME_ID=8 filter and retrieve the appropriate row from the TIME dimension:

```
SELECT time_id FROM TIME
WHERE month#=1 AND quarter#=1 AND year#=2002;
```

Now let's plug the first two queries into a WITH clause and join them together, again a Cartesian Product. However, only a single row is retrieved from the TIME dimension:

```
WITH ACTIVEMONTH AS (
SELECT time_id FROM TIME
WHERE month#=1 AND quarter#=1 AND year#=2002)
   , DIMENSIONS AS (
SELECT l.city, i.industry, p.category
FROM location l, industry i, product p
WHERE l.city IN('Los Angeles','New York')
AND i.industry IN('Life Sciences','Manufacturing')
AND p.category LIKE '%a%')
SELECT * FROM ACTIVEMONTH NATURAL JOIN DIMENSIONS;
```

Note: In the script above the two WITH clause subqueries have been assigned names.

Now we can join the four dimensions to the large fact table:

```
WITH ACTIVEMONTH AS
(
SELECT time_id FROM TIME
WHERE month#=1 AND quarter#=1 AND year#=2002
),
DIMENSIONS AS
(
SELECT l.location_id, i.industry_id, p.product_id
,l.city, i.industry, p.category
```

```
FROM location l, industry i, product p
WHERE l.city IN('Los Angeles','New York')
AND i.industry IN('Life Sciences','Manufacturing')
AND p.category LIKE '%a%'
)
SELECT d.city, d.industry, d.category
, SUM(s.transaction_amount) AS Amount
FROM ACTIVEMONTH a, DIMENSIONS d , sale s
WHERE s.location_id = d.location_id
AND s.industry_id = d.industry_id
AND s.product_id = d.product_id
GROUP BY d.city, d.industry, d.category;
```

The WITH clause can sometimes be effective in breaking down complex Oracle SQL coding into smaller, more easily manageable, understandable, and tune-able parts.

Note: Higher coding granularity usually leads to coding simplification but can result in poor performance.

In attempting to utilize the WITH clause to resolve something without using a PL/SQL script, as shown in Figure 9.6, we might want to do something, such as in the following script. However, for the RANK function the expression parameter must be a constant. Since the WITH clause contains a variable value returning subquery, the following script will produce an error:

```
WITH amounts AS (
SELECT s.transaction_amount AS Amount
    FROM sale s, location l, industry i, product p
    WHERE l.city IN('Los Angeles','New York')
AND s.time_id=8
    AND s.location_id = l.location_id
AND s.industry_id = i.industry_id
    AND s.product_id = p.product_id
)
SELECT RANK(amounts.amount) WITHIN GROUP
    (ORDER BY s.transaction_amount) "Rank"
FROM sale s, location l, industry i, product p, amounts
WHERE l.city IN('Los Angeles','New York')
AND s.time_id=8
```

```
AND s.location_id = l.location_id
AND s.industry_id = i.industry_id
AND s.product_id = p.product_id;
```

If we did something a little simpler, such as a SUM aggregation, then the WITH clause could be useful, but perhaps still not as effective as using real analytical capabilities by utilizing the OVER clause, as shown by the query in Figure 9.10. In Figure 9.10, we are retrieving all summary aggregations whose summation is greater than 1% of the total aggregation for the entire SALE fact table.

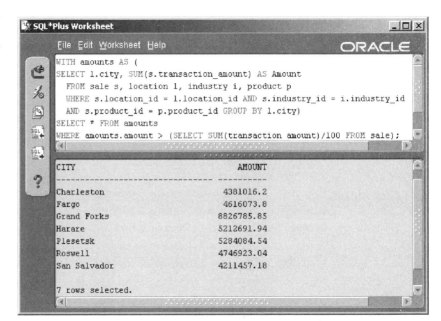

Figure 9.10
Example use of the WITH clause.

9.4.3 CASE and Cursor Expressions

CASE and cursor expressions allow CASE statements and typecasted cursor executions to be embedded into queries.

CASE Expressions

A CASE statement can be used as an inline expression within a SQL query, similar to an IF-THEN-ELSE programming construct. Figure 9.11 shows the syntax for embedding CASE statements into SQL code, as embedded expressions.

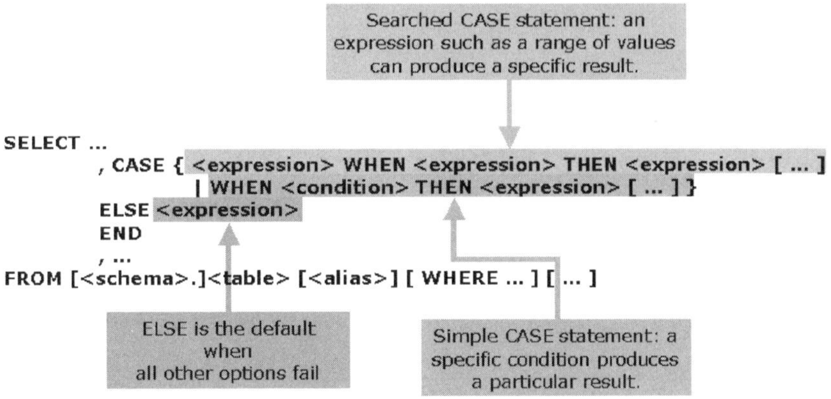

Figure 9.11
*Inline CASE
statement syntax.*

Embedded CASE statements can be used to replace the messier coding of the DECODE function. Both CASE statements and the DECODE function are useful for replacing multiple queries merged together using a UNION set operator. There are two types of CASE statements:

- **Simple CASE Statement**. A simple CASE statement contains a single condition with multiple possible expressional options.

```
SELECT region_id,
     CASE region
     WHEN 'North America' THEN 'N. America'
     WHEN 'South America' THEN 'S. America'
     WHEN 'Central America' THEN 'C. America'
     ELSE NULL END
FROM region WHERE region IN
('North America','South America','Central America');
```

- **Searched CASE Statement**. A searched CASE statement contains a condition for each of multiple WHEN clauses.

```
SELECT region_id,
     CASE
WHEN region='North America' THEN 'N. America'
     WHEN region='South America' THEN 'S. America'
     WHEN region='Central America' THEN 'C. America'
     ELSE NULL END
FROM region WHERE region IN
('North America','South America','Central America');
```

In examining CASE statement performance, the first query below, using the UNION operator, is replaced by the subsequent query using a CASE statement:

```
SELECT region_id, 'N. America' AS Region
FROM region WHERE region='North America'
UNION
SELECT region_id, 'S. America'
FROM region WHERE region='South America'
UNION
SELECT region_id, 'C. America'
FROM region WHERE region='Central America';
```

The next query, using the CASE statement, is three times more efficient than the one above using the UNION operator. This is because the query above reads the REGION table three times, as opposed to the CASE statement querying the REGION table once in the query below:

```
SELECT region_id,
    CASE region
    WHEN 'North America' THEN 'N. America'
    WHEN 'South America' THEN 'S. America'
    WHEN 'Central America' THEN 'C. America'
    ELSE NULL END
FROM region WHERE region IN
('North America','South America','Central America');
```

The other option is to use CASE statements as a replacement for the DECODE function. Using CASE statements is supposedly more efficient. Coding a CASE statement is certainly much more simplistic; however, the performance improvement factor is possibly debatable. The two examples in Figure 9.12 demonstrate that the CASE statement is no more efficient than using the DECODE function. At least, in this case it is not.

CASE statements are also much more powerful syntactically with respect to UNION operators and the DECODE function. The following example uses a searched CASE statement where each test applies validation of a different expression:

Figure 9.12
*CASE statement
versus DECODE
function.*

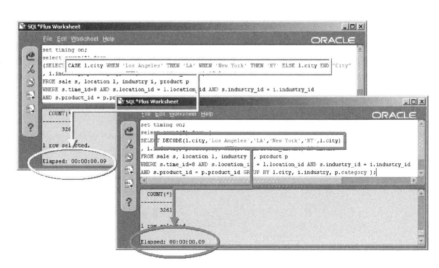

```
SELECT l.city, i.industry, p.category
, SUM(s.transaction_amount) AS Amount,
CASE
  WHEN SUM(s.transaction_amount)
< 500 THEN 'Negligible'
  WHEN SUM(s.transaction_amount)
BETWEEN 500 AND 9999 THEN 'Minimal'
  WHEN SUM(s.transaction_amount)
BETWEEN 10000 and 19999 THEN 'Good Revenue'
  ELSE 'Star Client'
END AS Value
FROM sale s, location l, industry i, product p
WHERE l.city IN('Los Angeles','New York')
AND i.industry IN('Life Sciences','Manufacturing')
AND p.category LIKE '%a%'
AND s.time_id=8
AND s.location_id = l.location_id
AND s.industry_id = i.industry_id
AND s.product_id = p.product_id
GROUP BY l.city, i.industry, p.category;
```

Building the above Oracle SQL command using the DECODE function would require embedded DECODE functions and use of the SIGN function to find the range of each aggregation—a much more complex affair.

Cursor Expressions

A cursor expression simply allows the embedding of a cursor or pre-exe-cuted query within a calling query, as in the following example script:

```
SELECT R.REGION
, CURSOR(
SELECT COUNTRY FROM COUNTRY
WHERE REGION_ID=R.REGION_ID
)
FROM REGION R;
```

A query, such as the script above, effectively joins the REGION and COUNTRY tables properly, but returns each region containing all coun-tries included within each region, sorted by country within region as shown in Figure 9.13.

Figure 9.13
An example cursor expression.

9.5   **Analysis in Practice**

This section will examine some examples using analysis functions and spe-cialized analytical syntax.

9.5.1 Rankings and Ratios

Both the RANK and DENSE_RANK functions return the rank of a value within a set of values. The difference is that the DENSE_RANK function packs ranking in a sequence counting from one upwards, incremented by one. The difference is clearly shown in Figure 9.14, showing the Dense Rank column containing no gaps in the ranking sequence.

Figure 9.14
The RANK versus DENSE_RANK functions.

Figure 9.15 adds the PERCENT_RANK function, such that each rank is represented as a percentage of the rank of the highest ranked value.

Figure 9.16 adds the NTILE function to the mix where the ranked set is split into a set of five, as shown by the NTILE(5) function execution. The NTILE function can be used to divide row sets into equally divided buckets, where each bucket contains the same number of rows (or at most one more).

Figure 9.17 shows the ROW_NUMBER function assigning a unique sequential integer identifier to each row returned, according to the order of the returned row—a ranked row number sequence. The resulting query is called by a parent query, which retrieves only the 30th to 40th row numbers retrieved.

Figure 9.15
*The PERCENT_
RANK function.*

Figure 9.16
*The NTILE
function.*

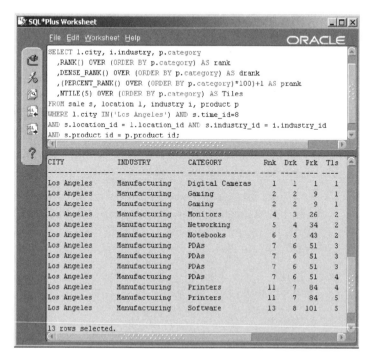

Figure 9.17
The ROW_NUMBER function.

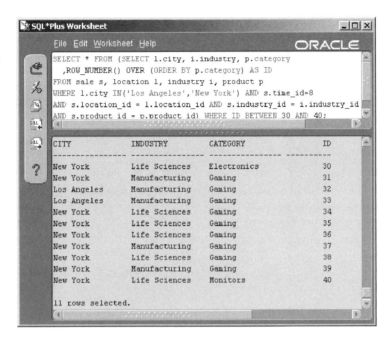

Figure 9.18 shows a restart in the ranking calculation with the introduction of the PARTITION BY clause. The rank is restarted for each separate partition. The ORDER BY clause is applied within each partition separately.

Figure 9.18
Partition a rank to restart the ranking count.

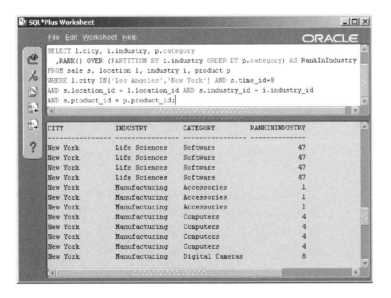

The FIRST and LAST functions operate on the first and last rows in a ranked row set. The query in Figure 9.19 finds the lowest and highest TRANSACTION_AMOUNT values for three different regions.

Figure 9.19
The FIRST and LAST functions.

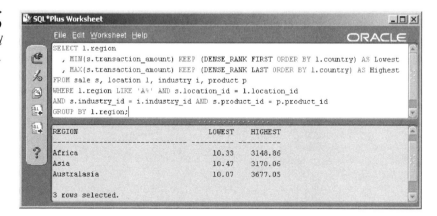

Hypothetical rankings and distributions allow the hypothetical insertion of a new row into a set of data, such that its hypothetical ranking can be assessed. These hypotheses can be performed using the RANK, DENSE_RANK, PERCENT_RANK, and CUME_DIST functions, along with the WITHIN GROUP (ORDER BY . . .) syntax. It is very simple; all you do is plug in a value to be inserted and execute the query, such as the query shown below:

```
SELECT category, price, product
, RANK(100) WITHIN GROUP
(ORDER BY price DESC) AS rank
, PERCENT_RANK(100) WITHIN GROUP
(ORDER BY price DESC) AS prank
FROM product
GROUP BY category, price, product;
```

There are many other things that can be done with ranking functions, such as reversing sorted order using DESC in the ORDER BY clause, including ranks in ROLLUP and CUBE clause calculations, even sometimes building multiple layered rankings. Simply put, a ranking tells you what is more and less important in a set of items, depending on how the ranking is decided.

The RATIO_TO_REPORT function is extremely useful. This function can be used to return a ratio of a value for a current row as compared to an aggregation of values. The aggregation can be for the entire report or a subsection of a report based on a PARTITION BY clause. Obviously, rankings can also be utilized to check for rankings of ratio to report calculations. A simple example using the RATIO_TO_REPORT function is shown in Figure 9.20.

Figure 9.20
The RATIO_TO_REPORT function.

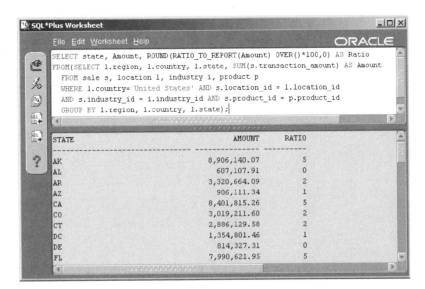

9.5.2 Lead and Lag Functionality

The LAG and LEAD functions allow for comparisons between rows in queries. The LAG functions lags behind, and the LEAD function leads ahead. In other words, the LAG function allows a reference between the current row and preceding rows, the LEAD function between the current row and subsequent rows. Figure 9.21 shows a simple example where the LAG function finds the sum in the previous row and the LEAD function the sum in the next row. Note how the last row has no LEAD result. This is because the last row does not have a next row to retrieve a leading value from.

9.5.3 Histograms

A histogram simply divides data into buckets. Histograms are often used to get a general picture of data in terms of both past and future activity. The WIDTH_BUCKET function can be used to construct a histogram with equal width buckets:

Figure 9.21
*The LAG and
LEAD functions.*

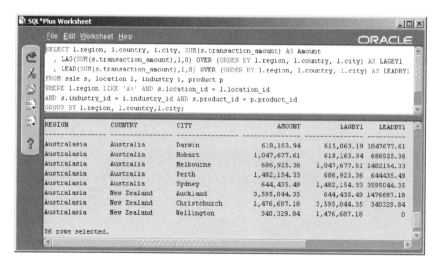

WIDTH_BUCKET(<expression>, <min>, <max>, <buckets>)

Figure 9.22 shows simple use of the WIDTH_BUCKET function to create a histogram of a row set of retrieved data set.

Figure 9.22
*Histograms with
the WIDTH_
BUCKET
function.*

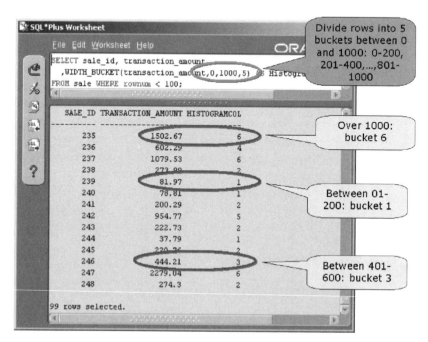

You could do something similar using CASE or IF statements. The WIDTH_BUCKET function is less prone to error than using complex coded SQL statements.

9.5.4 Other Statistical Functionality

The purpose of this book is data warehouse tuning. Statistical functions, and the demonstration thereof, essentially require an in-depth knowledge of statistics, analysis, and interpretation of statistical observations using the innumerable calculators and tools available to the expert statistician. Coverage of statistics is not the purpose of this book. However, it should be stated that use of built-in or provided statistical functionality provided with Oracle Database should perform much better than attempting to build functions and stored procedures to manually access the database in pursuit of complex statistical calculations. In other words, Oracle SQL has immense statistical capabilities—the mere fact that those capabilities are provided by Oracle SQL helps performance. Why is this the case? The programmer does not have to write the calculators.

Statistics in itself is an immensely complex and comprehensive topic. It is not necessary to describe and demonstrate the use of all available statistical functionality in this book, because knowledge of statistics is not a requirement for making a data warehouse perform better. The fact is, if you are using Oracle SQL statistical functions, you should know what those functions mean anyway—in terms of statistical interpretation. The interpretation of why a specific statistical function would be used, how it would be used, and what it means is a purely statistical matter and not a matter of making Oracle SQL perform better.

9.5.5 Data Densification

What is densification of data and why is it significant? Data stored in normalized form has as much duplication of data removed as possible. Removal of duplication achieves two objectives. First, it makes individual pieces of data easier to access as individual units. Second, it reduces I/O activity because less disk space is used. Normalized data is thus said to be stored in sparse form. Where joins between dimensions and facts contain no facts, the dimensions are densified with NULL or zero values to represent the missing facts. In other words, outer joins are used. Reports need to see information where there is no information. For instance, if there are no sales fact entries for a given day in a given country, your reports need to see a zero sales figure, rather than have the dimension for the country be missing. Densification of data is performed in Oracle SQL during query processing, using outer joins. Figure 9.23 shows an example with sparse information only. Sparse information are those rows containing nonzero amounts.

Figure 9.23
*Sparse data does
not fill in empty
rows.*

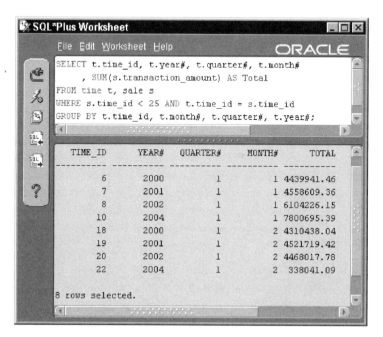

The query in Figure 9.24 forms an outer join between the two fact and dimension data sources. The result is densified data, filling in all TIME_ID values with zero total values.

This chapter has covered the implementation of detailed analysis reporting using Oracle SQL. Most important to tuning of an Oracle Database data warehouse is the implementation of built-in Oracle SQL functionality for analytical reporting, in terms of available functionality, syntax extensions, and, most importantly, using the more complex aspects of Oracle SQL to increase overall database performance.

Figure 9.24
Data densification using an outer join.

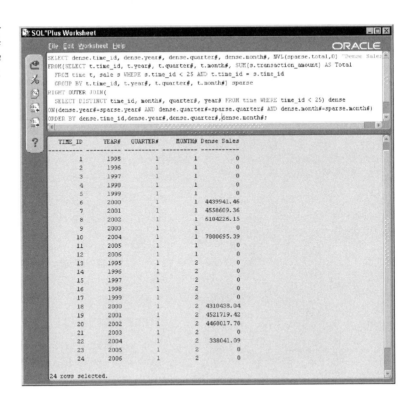

10

Modeling with the MODEL Clause

This chapter describes the Oracle SQL MODEL clause. The use of the MODEL clause is, as in previous chapters, a performance method in and of itself. The MODEL clause is the latest and most sophisticated expansion to Oracle SQL, catering for the complex analytical functionality required by data warehouse databases. Details covered in this chapter include the how and why of the MODEL clause, MODEL clause syntax, and various specialized MODEL clause functions included with Oracle SQL. The second part of this chapter analyses detailed use of the MODEL clause. Finally, some performance issues with parallel execution and MODEL clause query plans are discussed.

10.1 What Is the MODEL Clause?

The MODEL clause can be used to create spreadsheet-style output, allowing display of data into multiple dimensions or a multiple dimensional array structure. It permits calculations between rows and cells, much the same way as a spreadsheet program. The MODEL clause provides additional OLAP-type functionality and is more applicable to data warehousing, as opposed to transactional OLTP databases. However, using the MODEL clause can, in some cases, possibly reduce the number of tables in complex joins and remove the need for set operators such as UNION, INTERSECT, and MINUS to merge multiple queries together.

10.1.1 The Parts of the MODEL Clause

The MODEL clause multiple dimensional array maps query columns and rows in three separate groupings:

- **Partitions**. Partitions break MODEL clause row sets into separate physical structures. Each partition can have the application of an individual rule set. Additionally, multiple partitions allow for parallel processing and, thus, better performance.

- **Dimensions**. The cells in a MODEL clause multiple-dimensional array are defined as dimensions. Thus, all the cells in the array make up multiple-dimensional structures. These dimensions are equivalent to data warehouse dimensional entities and are synonymous with fact table dimensional foreign key columns.

- **Measuring Columns**. Essentially, measuring columns contain measured values. A measured value is the equivalent of data warehouse fact entity archived transactional entries.

Figure 10.1 shows how the MODEL clause divides dimensions and facts into partitions, dimensions, and measurements. Essentially, in Figure 10.1, the sales revenue data constitutes how the dimensions are measured. The data is also partitioned by cities, which, in relation to the MODEL clause, the sales revenues can have a separate set of rules applied to each city partition.

Figure 10.1
How the MODEL clause interprets data.

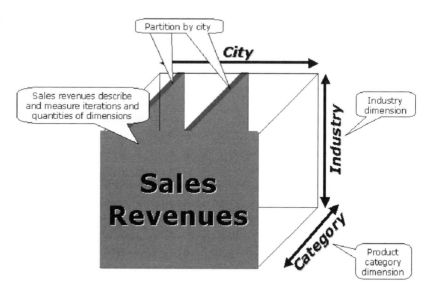

10.1.2   How the MODEL Clause Works

The MODEL clause maps facts and dimensions to a multiple dimensional array structure, potentially applying separate rule sets to individual partitions. Let's use the following query:

```
SELECT l.region, l.country, l.city, t.year#
, SUM(s.transaction_amount) AS Amount
FROM sale s, location l, time t
WHERE l.region IN ('Russian Federation','Near East')
AND t.year# IN(2003,2004)
AND s.location_id = l.location_id
AND s.time_id = t.time_id
GROUP BY l.region, l.country, l.city, t.year#;
```

The result of the query above is shown in Figure 10.2 and an equivalent spreadsheet format in Figure 10.3.

Figure 10.2

A simple query with no MODEL clause.

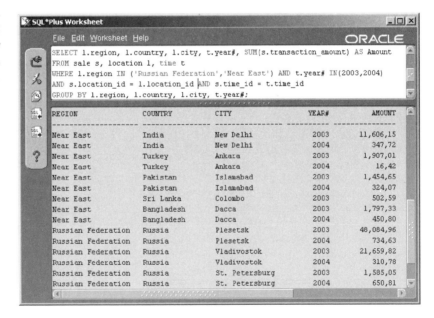

Note in Figure 10.3 that the columns containing the annual 2003 and 2004 amounts are next to each other, and not represented as separate rows, as in Figure 10.2.

Figure 10.3

*Figure 10.2 in
spreadsheet format.*

REGION	COUNTRY	CITY	2003	2004
Near East	India	New Delhi	1160615.22	34771.71
Near East	Turkey	Ankara	190700.95	1641.84
Near East	Pakistan	Islamabad	145464.89	32407.22
Near East	Sri Lanka	Colombo	50259.44	0
Near East	Bangladesh	Dacca	179733.02	45079.67
Russian Federation	Russia	Plesetsk	4808496.48	73463.34
Russian Federation	Russia	Vladivostok	2165981.7	31077.6
Russian Federation	Russia	St. Petersburg	158505.19	65081.23

Now we apply the MODEL clause in order to forecast an estimate of sales revenues in 2005 for all cities, using the query shown below. All I have done is wrap the previous query into a calling query and apply the MODEL clause to the result:

```
SELECT region, country, city, year#, amount FROM (
SELECT l.region, l.country, l.city, t.year#
, SUM(s.transaction_amount) AS Amount
FROM sale s, location l, time t
WHERE l.region IN ('Russian Federation','Near East')
AND t.year# IN(2003,2004)
AND s.location_id = l.location_id
AND s.time_id = t.time_id
GROUP BY l.region, l.country, l.city, t.year#
) s
MODEL
    PARTITION BY (region, country, city)
    DIMENSION BY (year#)
    MEASURES (s.amount amount)
    RULES(amount[2005]
=NVL(amount[2003],0)+NVL(amount[2004],0))
ORDER BY region, country, city, year#;
```

Note: The query above would very likely perform better with the aggregation in a materialized view. The materialized view should exclude the filtering that would be applied when reading the materialized view, either manually or with automatic query rewrite.

In the script above, the RULES section applies a single rule to each partition, the same rule, for all years. In other words, sales revenue amounts for both the years 2003 and 2004 are added together for each city to form a total estimated value for the year 2005, for each city. Once again, the query result is shown in Figure 10.4 and an equivalent spreadsheet format in Figure 10.5.

Figure 10.4
Applying the MODEL clause to the query in Figure 10.2.

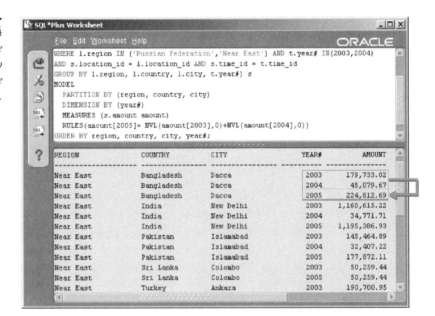

In both Figures 10.4 and 10.5, the projected 2005 total for the city of Dacca in Bangladesh is highlighted. Once again, note in Figure 10.5 that the columns containing the annual 2003, 2004, and 2005 amounts are next to each other, and not represented as separate rows as in Figure 10.4. This stresses the *spreadsheet*-like aspect of the MODEL clause.

Figure 10.5
Figure 10.4 in spreadsheet format.

REGION	COUNTRY	CITY	2003	2004	2005
Near East	India	New Delhi	1160615.22	34771.71	1195386.93
Near East	Turkey	Ankara	190700.95	1641.84	192342.79
Near East	Pakistan	Islamabad	145464.89	32407.22	177872.11
Near East	Sri Lanka	Colombo	50259.44	0	50259.44
Near East	Bangladesh	Dacca	179733.02	45079.67	224812.69
Russian Federation	Russia	Plesetsk	4808496.48	73463.34	4881959.82
Russian Federation	Russia	Vladivostok	2165981.7	31077.6	2197059.3
Russian Federation	Russia	St. Petersburg	158505.19	65081.23	223586.42

What the MODEL clause does is produce spreadsheet-like output, but as separate rows, not in a spreadsheet format. I have explained the above examples using query output and spreadsheet formats to describe the very basics of how the MODEL clause can be used.

10.1.3   Better Performance Using the MODEL Clause

How can the query presented in the previous section be rewritten without using the MODEL clause? First, all aggregated rows grouped by region, country, city, and year have to be returned. Second, a total for each city would be needed, regardless of year. Third, the two row sets would have to be merged using a UNION ALL operator. Fourth, the result would have to be resorted. The query would look something like this:

```
SELECT l.region, l.country, l.city, t.year#
, SUM(s.transaction_amount) AS Amount
FROM sale s, location l, time t
WHERE l.region IN ('Russian Federation','Near East')
AND t.year# IN(2003,2004)
AND s.location_id = l.location_id
AND s.time_id = t.time_id
GROUP BY l.region, l.country, l.city, t.year#
UNION ALL
SELECT l.region, l.country, l.city, 2005 "YEAR#"
, SUM(s.transaction_amount) AS Amount
FROM sale s, location l, time t
WHERE l.region IN ('Russian Federation','Near East')
AND t.year# IN(2003,2004)
AND s.location_id = l.location_id
AND s.time_id = t.time_id
GROUP BY l.region, l.country, l.city
ORDER BY 1,2,3,4;
```

Nasty, huh?

Figure 10.6 shows the total query plan costing estimation for the UNION and equivalent MODEL clause queries.

Figure 10.7 shows timing tests for the UNION ALL and equivalent MODEL clause queries.

Clearly the MODEL clause version of the query executes approximately twice as fast. It certainly does with my database, my tables, my data, and my

Figure 10.6
MODEL clause versus non-MODEL clause query plan cost.

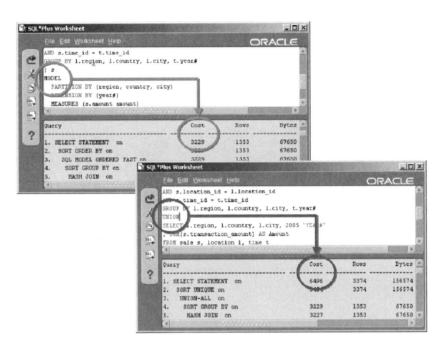

Figure 10.7
MODEL clause versus non-MODEL clause query timing.

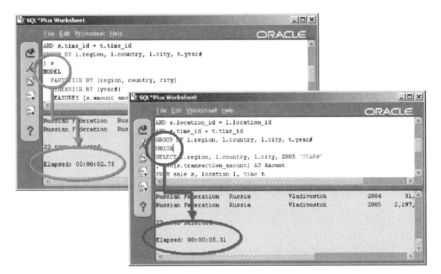

queries. This does not necessarily mean the MODEL clause will perform better under all circumstances, but it is a highly likely possibility.

10.2 MODEL Clause Syntax

The basic syntax for the MODEL clause is shown in Figure 10.8. The MODEL clause appears after every other syntax element in a SELECT statement query, even after the GROUP BY clause.

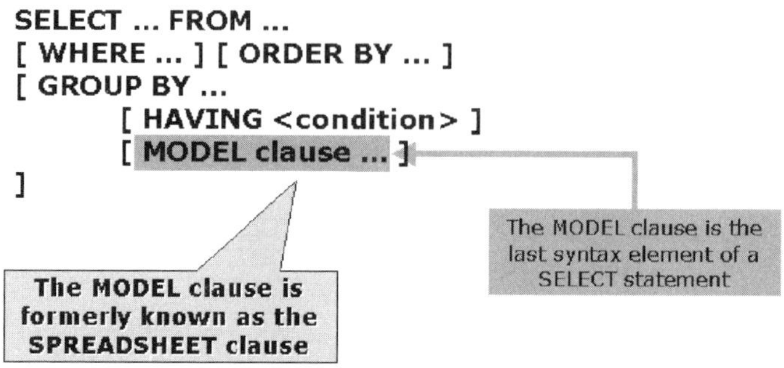

Figure 10.8
*MODEL clause
syntax location.*

```
SELECT ... FROM ...
[ WHERE ... ] [ ORDER BY ... ]
[ GROUP BY ...
       [ HAVING <condition> ]
       [ MODEL clause ... ]
]
```

The MODEL clause is formerly known as the SPREADSHEET clause

The MODEL clause is the last syntax element of a SELECT statement

Figure 10.9 shows a much more detailed syntax of the MODEL clause.

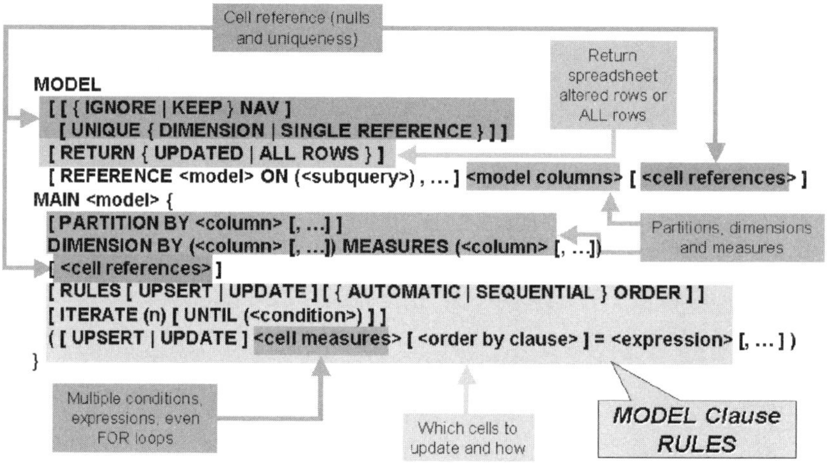

Figure 10.9
*Detailed MODEL
clause syntax.*

Cell reference (nulls and uniqueness)

Return spreadsheet altered rows or ALL rows

```
MODEL
  [ [ { IGNORE | KEEP } NAV ]
    [ UNIQUE { DIMENSION | SINGLE REFERENCE } ] ]
  [ RETURN { UPDATED | ALL ROWS } ]
  [ REFERENCE <model> ON (<subquery>) , ...] <model columns> [ <cell references> ]
MAIN <model> {
  [ PARTITION BY <column> [, ...] ]
  DIMENSION BY (<column> [, ...]) MEASURES (<column> [, ...])
  [ <cell references> ]
  [ RULES [ UPSERT | UPDATE ] [ { AUTOMATIC | SEQUENTIAL } ORDER ] ]
  [ ITERATE (n) [ UNTIL (<condition>) ] ]
  ( [ UPSERT | UPDATE ] <cell measures> [ <order by clause> ] = <expression> [, ...] )
}
```

Partitions, dimensions and measures

Multiple conditions, expressions, even FOR loops

Which cells to update and how

MODEL Clause RULES

10.2.1 Cell References

Cell reference syntax dictates treatment of NULL or missing values and unique values across MODEL clause defining columns:

```
[
[ {IGNORE|KEEP} NAV ]
      [ UNIQUE {DIMENSION|SINGLE REFERENCE} ]
]
```

- **KEEP NAV** (default). Returns NULL and missing values as NULL values.

- **IGNORE NAV.** NULL and missing values are replaced with values appropriate to returned datatypes.

- **UNIQUE DIMENSION** (default). PARTITION BY and DIMEN-SION BY columns must be unique keys. A key is not, however, necessarily indexed.

- **UNIQUE SINGLE REFERENCE.** Less restrictive than UNIQUE DIMENSION.

10.2.2 Return Rows

```
[ RETURN {UPDATED|ALL} ROWS ]
```

- **RETURN ALL ROWS** (default). Return all retrieved rows.

- **RETURN UPDATED ROWS.** Only the rows updated by MODEL clause specification rules are returned.

10.2.3 The Main Model

Columns declared in the MODEL clause are classified as being partitioning columns, dimensional columns or measure (facts) columns.

- **PARTITION BY.** Partitions break MODEL clause row sets into separate structures. Partitions are the top level of the hierarchy of the multiple-dimensional array, effectively defining the rows.

```
PARTITION BY [(]<expression> [,...][)] [alias]
```

- **DIMENSION BY.** Dimensions are the cells in the multiple-dimensional array contained within partitions declared by the PARTITION BY clause. Partition and dimension columns provide indexing into the multiple-dimensional array structure allowing reference to the measures or facts.

```
DIMENSION BY (<model column> [,...])
```

- **MEASURES**. Essentially, measuring columns contain measured values or facts. Where partition columns divide data and dimensions define data, measures are the cell referenced values containing data warehouse–type transactional fact values.

```
MEASURES (<model column> [,...])
```

Figure 10.10 shows the complete syntax of the MODEL clause.

Figure 10.10
Complete MODEL clause syntax.

```
MODEL
[ [ {IGNORE|KEEP} NAV ] [ UNIQUE {DIMENSION|SINGLE REFERENCE} ] ]
[ RETURN {UPDATED|ALL} ROWS ]
[
  REFERENCE <model> ON (<subquery>)
    [ PARTITION BY [(]<expression> [,...][)] [alias] ]
    DIMENSION BY (<model column> [,...]) MEASURES (<model column> [,...])
    [ [ {IGNORE|KEEP} NAV ] [ UNIQUE {DIMENSION|SINGLE REFERENCE} ] ]
  [, ... ]
]
[ MAIN <model>
  [ PARTITION BY [(]<expression> [,...][)] [alias] ]
  DIMENSION BY (<model column> [,...]) MEASURES (<model column> [,...])
  [ [ {IGNORE|KEEP} NAV ] [ UNIQUE {DIMENSION|SINGLE REFERENCE} ] ]
  [ RULES
    [UPSERT|UPDATE] [{AUTOMATIC|SEQUENTIAL} ORDER]
    [ITERATE (<n>) [UNTIL (<condition>)]]
    (
      [UPDATE|UPSERT] <measure column> { {[]<condition>|<expression>|<for loop>{]} [, ...] }
      [ ORDER BY ... ] = <expression>
    [, ...] )
  ]
]
<model column> = <expression> [ [ AS ] <alias> ]
```

Rules

RULES clause syntax specifies what is to change as a result of the MODEL clause, where it is changed, and how it is changed. A single RULE is essentially one expression set equal to another, of which more than a single rule can be defined:

```
<expression> = <expression>
```

The full syntax for the RULES clause is shown in Figure 10.10.

- **UPSERT** (default) **versus UPDATE**. UPSERT allows creation of values that do not exist in the row set retrieved from the database. In Figure 10.4 new rows were added to the query for the forecasted year 2005. Rows for the year 2005 do not exist in the database.

- **SEQUENTIAL ORDER** (default) **versus AUTOMATIC ORDER**. For a query MODEL clause containing multiple rules, each rule is evaluated one after the other, as opposed to an evaluation order based on dependencies, such as primary and foreign key constraint, one-to-many relationships.

  - **ITERATE(<n>) [UNTIL <condition>]**. This syntax element applies when inter-rule dependencies are ignored (SEQUENTIAL ORDER), executing all rules in SEQUENTIAL ORDER <n> times.

Assigning Cell Values

These syntax elements define what measure columns, or calculated columns, are set to, how they are set, and when they are set. This section essentially creates the new rows that are created for the year 2005 in Figure 10.4.

Cells can be changed or added to the retrieved row set, either as new cells or new rows, or both. This syntax can be implemented based on a condition, an embedded expression, or even a for loop to that iterates through multiple rows of the retrieved row set. Additionally, both single and multiple cells can be changed or added at the same time.

An ORDER BY clause can be specified to force the order in which cells in each rule are calculated. Otherwise, cells are set according to the DIMENSION BY clause column sequence.

10.2.4   **MODEL Clause Functions**

There are a number of functions specific to use with the MODEL clause. These functions apply to inter-row calculations (calculations across rows between individual cells), and can only be included as a part of MODEL clause rules:

- **CV(<dimension>)**. Returns a dimensional value or current value.

- **PRESENTNNV(<cell>, <expression>, <expression>)**. Returns one expression if a value exists, otherwise another.

- **PRESENTV(<cell>, <expression>, <expression>)**. As for PRES-ENTNNV, but allowing NULL values.

- **PREVIOUS(<cell>)**. Returns a value at the beginning of each iteration or loop.

- **ITERATION_NUMBER**. Returns a completed loop iteration sequence number or the subscript of a loop.

10.3   What Can the MODEL Clause Do?

The answer to this question is quite simple: LOTS! And the easiest way to explain all the incredible capabilities of the MODEL clause is to demonstrate by example.

The objective of this book is performance. Therefore going through all the capabilities of the MODEL clause in detail would essentially be duplicating what is already available in Oracle Database documentation. This chapter has already demonstrated that implementation of the MODEL clause in Oracle SQL code can help performance. This section will describe the MODEL clause's basic capabilities, and then a subsequent section will attempt to performance tune, and prove, and perhaps even disprove, any MODEL clause query tuning methods.

10.3.1   Materialized Views and the MODEL Clause

The first thing we should do is to make sure that we use materialized views and automated query rewrite as continual reprocessing of aggregations. Using query rewrite is generally good for performance in data warehouses. All materialized views are created with the fastest possible read options, as created in previous chapters.

Note: Materialized views are not created as partitioned in this chapter for the sake of query plan simplicity. Also, Oracle Database dimensional hierarchies are not used, since the schema utilized is a star schema and not a snowflake schema.

Materialized views are created on both SALE and PURCHASE fact tables and will be used interchangeably, if and where appropriate. As in a previous chapter the fact and dimensional tables are all joined using a single materialized view, as in the following script:

```
CREATE MATERIALIZED VIEW mv_join_sale
     PARALLEL NOLOGGING TABLESPACE mvdata
COMPRESS USING NO INDEX NEVER REFRESH
     ENABLE QUERY REWRITE
AS SELECT   s.order_amount,s.order_date
    ,s.transaction_amount,s.transaction_date
    ,s.payment_amount,s.payment_date,s.payment_text
    ,s.product_quantity,s.product_price,s.product_date
    ,l.region,l.country,l.state,l.city
    ,t.month#,t.quarter#,t.year#
    ,p.category, p.product, p.price, i.industry
FROM sale s, location l, time t, product p, industry i
WHERE s.location_id = l.location_id AND s.time_id = t.time_id
AND s.product_id = p.product_id AND s.industry_id =
i.industry_id;
```

Statistics are collected:

```
ANALYZE TABLE mv_join_sale COMPUTE STATISTICS;
```

Two further aggregation materialized views are created from the base join materialized view, and statistics are collected for both:

```
CREATE MATERIALIZED VIEW mv_revenue_by_month
     PARALLEL NOLOGGING TABLESPACE mvdata
COMPRESS USING NO INDEX NEVER REFRESH
     ENABLE QUERY REWRITE
AS SELECT year#, quarter#, month#
    ,COUNT(transaction_amount), COUNT(*)
    ,SUM(transaction_amount)
FROM mv_join_sale
GROUP BY year#, quarter#, month#;
```

```
ANALYZE TABLE mv_revenue_by_month COMPUTE STATISTICS;
```

```
CREATE MATERIALIZED VIEW mv_revenue_by_quarter
     PARALLEL NOLOGGING TABLESPACE mvdata
COMPRESS USING NO INDEX NEVER REFRESH
     ENABLE QUERY REWRITE
AS SELECT year#, quarter#
```

```
      , COUNT(month#), COUNT(transaction_amount), COUNT(*)
      , SUM(transaction_amount)
   FROM mv_join_sale
   GROUP BY year#, quarter#;

   ANALYZE TABLE mv_revenue_by_quarter COMPUTE STATISTICS;
```

Note: It is possible to create materialized views containing MODEL clause specifications along with all the standard PARTITION BY, DIMENSION BY, MEASURES, and RULES syntax specifications. MODEL clause materialized views are not used in this chapter.

One further point to note: all materialized views created for use in this chapter have been reset as NOPARALLEL. Once again, in the interest of allowing for simplistic query plans, this is the better option. Performance is a business of comparison, in this case comparing queries using the MODEL clause against those not using the MODEL clause. Parallel execution will obviously help performance, but will get in the way of this comparison process. This chapter is attempting to focus on validation of the MODEL clause, not parallel processing or Oracle Partitioning.

```
   ALTER MATERIALIZED VIEW mv_revenue_by_quarter NOPARALLEL;
   ALTER MATERIALIZED VIEW mv_revenue_by_month NOPARALLEL;
   ALTER MATERIALIZED VIEW mv_join_sale NOPARALLEL;
   ALTER MATERIALIZED VIEW mv_cost_by_quarter NOPARALLEL;
   ALTER MATERIALIZED VIEW mv_cost_by_month NOPARALLEL;
   ALTER MATERIALIZED VIEW mv_join_purchase NOPARALLEL;
```

We should also be sure that underlying tables are set in the same manner:

```
   ALTER TABLE sale NOPARALLEL;
   ALTER TABLE purchase NOPARALLEL;
   ALTER TABLE location NOPARALLEL;
   ALTER TABLE time NOPARALLEL;
   ALTER TABLE industry NOPARALLEL;
   ALTER TABLE product NOPARALLEL;
```

10.3.2   **Referencing Cells**

How are individual cells referenced in the MODEL clause, and specifically in the rules of the MODEL clause? The query executed in Figure 10.4 used a very simple rule to create a new cell, containing a sum of two other already existing cells, creating a new row for each of the unique groups declared with the PARTITION BY clause. The RULES clause in the query for Figure 10.4 looked as follows:

```
RULES(amount[2005]=NVL(amount[2003],0)
+NVL(amount[2004],0))
```

We could make the calculation a little more complex and create the projection for the year 2005 as a percentage or ratio increase based on the difference between the years 2003 and 2004:

```
RULES(amount[2005]=(
((amount[2004]-amount[2003])
 /NVL(amount[2004],1)+1)
*amount[2004])
```

And one could even have multiple rules operating on more than a single aggregation, as in the following query, returning two summary columns as opposed to one in the script shown below.

```
CREATE VIEW sales AS
SELECT l.region, l.country, l.city, t.year#
    , SUM(s.transaction_amount) AS inv
    , SUM(s.order_amount) AS ord
FROM sale s, location l, time t
WHERE s.location_id = l.location_id
AND s.time_id = t.time_id
GROUP BY l.region, l.country, l.city, t.year#;
```

Note: I have created a view (YUCK!) in order to make coding easier. Views are often used by developers to make the development process easier. Views are not good for general database performance. The reason why is because they execute a contained query, which can be refiltered when reading the view. Filtering a view does not reduce I/O activity. This can be critical to performance when there is great disparity between the numbers of rows retrieved by the view's underlying query, and the rows filtered when reading the view. Obviously, views are not a performance issue when used in a reasonable manner. The trouble is that in realistic commercial applications, views are often used inappropriately.

```
SELECT region, country, city, year#, i, o FROM sales
WHERE region IN ('Russian Federation','Near East')
AND year# IN(2003,2004)
MODEL
    PARTITION BY (region, country, city)
    DIMENSION BY (year#)
    MEASURES (sales.inv i, sales.ord o)
    RULES(
     i[2005]=(((i[2004]-i[2003])/i [2004])+1)*i[2004]
    ,o[2005]=(((o[2004]-o[2003])/o [2004])+1)*o[2004])
ORDER BY region, country, city, year#;
```

The result of the above script is shown in Figure 10.11.

Cells can be referenced in a number of ways. Methods shown above reference all cells in all rows retrieved. In the example in Figure 10.12, all amounts are set to zero where the YEAR# is greater than, or equal to, the year 2000. Also, note that new cells or rows are not added. This is called a symbolic dimension reference:

```
RULES(i[year#>=2000]=0, o[year#>=2000]=0)
```

As already shown before briefly, in Figure 10.13 it is shown that rules can access dimension values precisely, without having to refer to the name of the dimension. This is called a positional dimension reference:

```
RULES(i[2004]=0, o[2004]=0)
```

Figure 10.11
*An example
MODEL clause
query.*

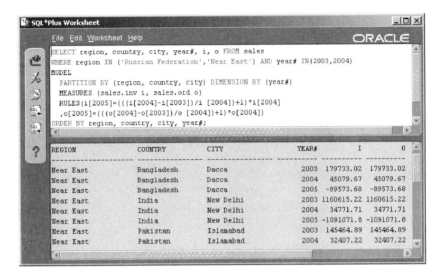

Figure 10.12
*Symbolic
dimension
references.*

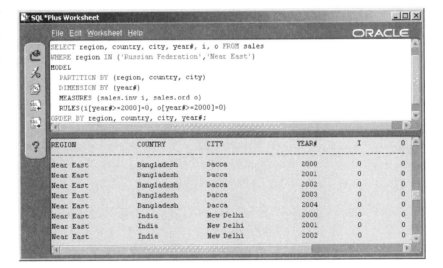

We can also create multiple-dimensional references for rules. Figure 10.14 shows that the CITY column is moved from the PARTITION BY clause to the DIMENSION BY clause, allowing direct access in rules to the CITY as well as the YEAR# dimensions.

Although this example may be somewhat uninteresting, Figure 10.15 removes all partitioned columns to the DIMENSION BY clause, allowing rules access to all four columns. Note that even though dimension columns

Figure 10.13
*Positional
dimension
references.*

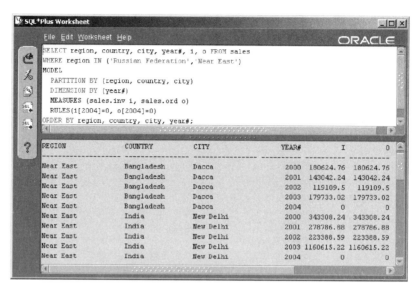

Figure 10.14
*Multiple
dimension
references.*

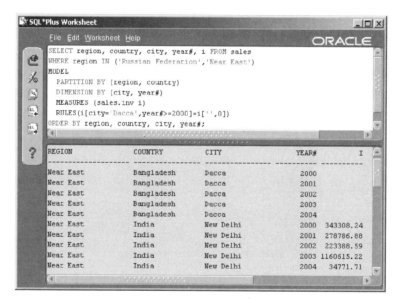

are specified as blank, that only the measure column is changed, and not the dimension columns.

Figure 10.16 shows the replacement of an exact cell value. In this case, a new cell measure and row cannot be created, since the dimension reference cannot be found.

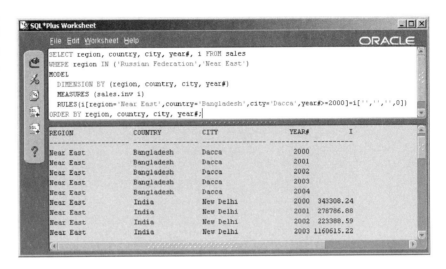

Figure 10.15
Four dimension references.

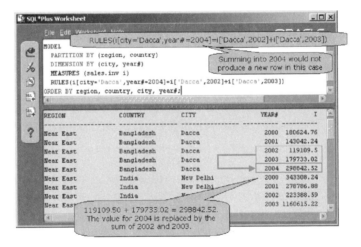

Figure 10.16
Replacing measured values.

The ANY keyword can be used as a wildcard to find any value in the form ANY or <dimension> IS ANY, as shown in Figure 10.17. Also, note the use of the OR logical operator. Filters, such as those used in WHERE clauses, can also be used, including operators such as OR and AND.

Using the CV function, as shown in Figure 10.18, allows the combination of multiple rules, such that:

```
RULES(
    i[city='Dacca',year# IS ANY]=i['Dacca',0]
    ,i[city='New Delhi',year# IS ANY]=i['New Delhi',0]
```

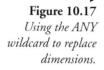

Figure 10.17
Using the ANY wildcard to replace dimensions.

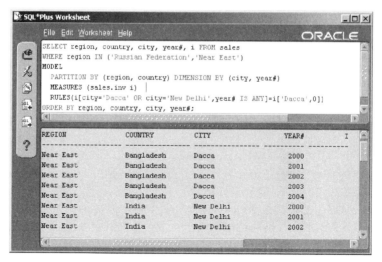

```
,i[city='Islamabad',year# IS ANY]=i['Islamabad',0]
)
```

becomes:

```
RULES(i[city IN ('Dacca','New Delhi','Islamabad')
,year# IS ANY]=i[CV(city),0])
```

Figure 10.18
Combining multiple rules using the CV function.

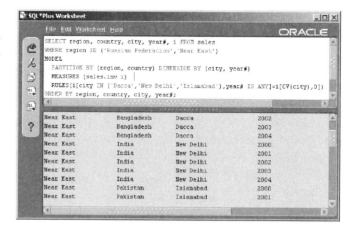

10.3.3   **Referencing Multiple Models**

The main model is the only model that can have cells inserted or updated. Reference models are read-only, but can be used to combine multiple models together with the main model. Effectively using the main model and multiple reference models, the MODEL clause can be used to merge different dimensional models together into the same query.

Chapter 2 described the details of the creation of the SALE and PURCHASE fact entities, plus four dimension entities called LOCATION, TIME, PRODUCT, and INDUSTRY. The LOCATION entity in particular is a denormalized version of the REGION, COUNTRY, STATE, and CITY entities. Figure 2.3 shows a graphical representation of these entities, repeated here in Figure 10.19 for your convenience.

Figure 10.19
Representing locations in the data warehouse.

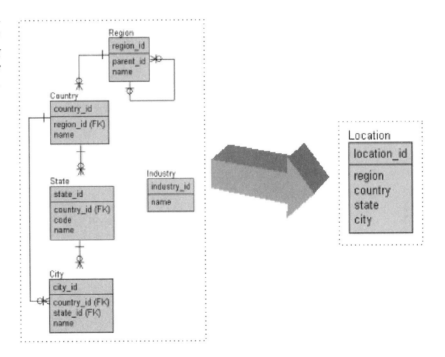

In order to demonstrate referencing of multiple models with the MODEL clause, I have added new data to the normalized entities, as shown in Figure 10.19. Figure 10.20 shows a simplified version of the REGION, COUNTRY, and CITY entities, now containing currency and population information. It is useful for demonstrating use of MODEL clause reference models with entities completely outside of the data warehouse fact dimensional structure (not in the LOCATION entity), because without the changes I could not show a true indication of multiple reference modeling using the MODEL clause. The other problem is that merging the new columns into the location entity would require updating all the fact tables, which is not helpful for data warehouse performance. So I added data outside of the established dimensional-fact entity structure created for the existing data warehouse database.

Figure 10.20
Adding dimensional data outside the data warehouse.

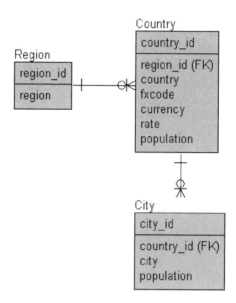

Now we can add a reference model to the MODEL clause of one of the queries we used before. The following script segments contain a single reference model. This first segment has two columns, one for USD (U.S. dollars) and another for FX (foreign exchange) calculated values:

```
SELECT region, country, city, year#, USD, FX
FROM sales
WHERE region IN ('Russian Federation','Near East')
AND year# IN(2003)
MODEL
```

The reference model is created and called *rates*. The rates reference model contains a query from the COUNTRY entity for all countries containing non-NULL-valued rates. This query is shown in Figure 10.21. Note that the reference model retrieves the name of the country and its exchange rate, dimensioned by COUNTRY and measured by RATE.

```
REFERENCE rates ON(
SELECT country, rate
FROM country WHERE rate IS NOT NULL
)
DIMENSION BY (country) MEASURES (rate)
```

Figure 10.21
*Countries with
foreign exchange
rates.*

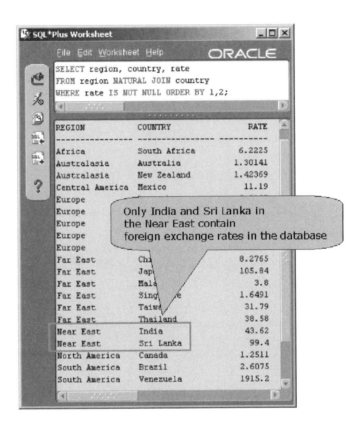

The next step is to create the actual MODEL clause itself. Since the query contains both a reference model and a main model, the main model has to be named. Values are accessed in the rules by both COUNTRY and YEAR#, so therefore the main model is dimensioned by both the COUNTRY and YEAR# columns. Note how the MEASURES clause now includes SALES view aggregate value copies for both the USD and FX columns.

```
MAIN conversion
    PARTITION BY (region, city)
    DIMENSION BY (country, year#)
    MEASURES (sales.inv USD, sales.inv FX)
```

The RULES section specifies rules for both the USD and FX columns where the rates model is referenced in the rules, in the FX column, and not in the USD column, since the USD column does not require a rate conversion calculation.

```
RULES
(
      usd[country NOT IN
('Sri Lanka','India'),2003]=
usd[CV(country),2003]
      ,fx[country IN
('Sri Lanka','India'),2003]=
usd[CV(country),2003]
*rates.rate[CV(country)]
)
ORDER BY region, country, city, year#;
```

Figure 10.22 shows the query and its result.

Figure 10.22
A reference model query.

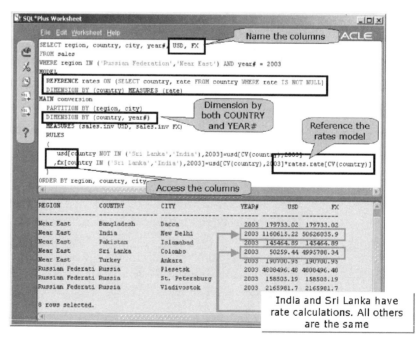

The following query contains two reference models, one for foreign exchange rates, and the second a simple column addition containing city populations. Not all cities contain population figures, as they are not all present in the database, as shown in Figure 10.23.

Figure 10.23
City populations.

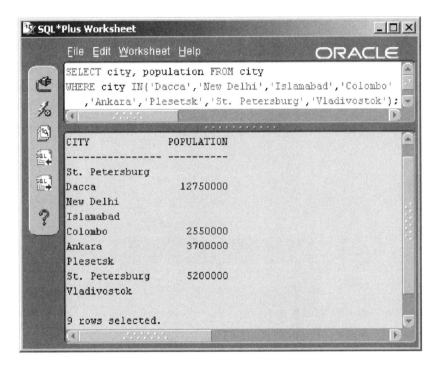

The result of the query, scripted below, is shown in Figure 10.24.

```
SELECT region, country, city, year#, USD, FX, Millions
FROM sales
WHERE region IN ('Russian Federation','Near East')
AND year# IN(2003)
MODEL
  REFERENCE rates ON
    (SELECT country, rate FROM country WHERE rate IS NOT NULL)
      DIMENSION BY (country c) MEASURES (rate)
  REFERENCE demographics ON
    (SELECT DISTINCT a.country, b.city, b.population
     FROM country a, city b WHERE b.country_id = a.country_id)
      DIMENSION BY (country c, city t) MEASURES (population)
MAIN conversion
```

```
PARTITION BY (region)
DIMENSION BY (country, city, year#)
MEASURES (sales.inv USD, sales.inv FX, 0 MILLIONS)
RULES
(
    usd[country NOT IN
('Sri Lanka','India'),ANY,2003]=
usd[CV(country),CV(city),2003]
    ,fx[country IN
('Sri Lanka','India'),ANY,2003]=
usd[CV(country),CV(city),2003]*rates.rate[CV(country)]
    ,millions
[country IS ANY,city IS ANY,year# IS ANY]=
demographics.population[CV(country),CV(city)]
)
ORDER BY region, country, city, year#;
```

Figure 10.24
A multiple reference model query.

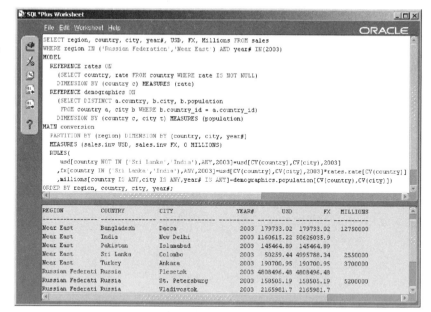

10.3.4   UPDATE versus UPSERT

The UPSERT option is the default and allows creation of new rows. UPDATE only changes column values in existing rows. Figure 10.25 shows

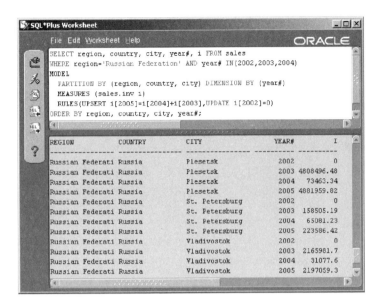

Figure 10.25
UPSERT versus UPDATE.

use of UPSERT and UPDATE, where UPSERT creates new rows for the year 2005 and UPDATE sets all amounts for the year 2002 to zero.

The obvious factor to consider with UPSERT and creating new rows is performance. Is there a performance factor when creating new rows using the UPSERT option? As can be seen in Figure 10.26, there is no apparent query plan difference between using UPSERT and UPDATE options.

Figure 10.26
UPSERT versus UPDATE query plans.

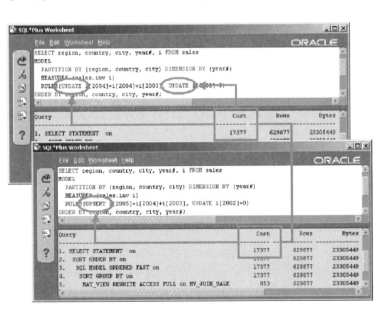

Figure 10.27 shows a very slight timing difference between using UPSERT and UPDATE options. However, the difference in execution time is so small as to probably be negligible.

Figure 10.27
UPSERT versus UPDATE timing test.

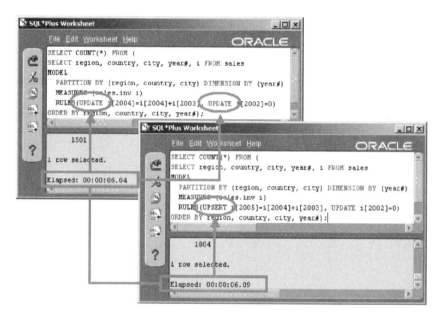

10.3.5 Loops

The MODEL clause can even use for loops to scroll through sets of rows and create multiple-dimensional cross-tabulations of all cells in a query. The example in Figure 10.28 shows 2003 and 2004 figures summed into 2005, for all countries. The MODEL clause is extremely versatile and can become highly complex.

10.4 Performance and the MODEL Clause

Even though use of the MODEL clause is a performance method in itself, there are, of course, a few ways to make MODEL clause queries perform a little better.

10.4.1 Parallel Execution

Parallel execution is an issue for performance, obviously on multiple CPU platforms, but even on single CPU platforms where multiple server processes can service a single query. The PARTITION BY clause breaks a

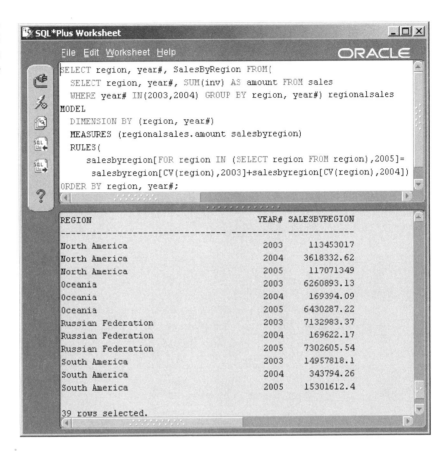

Figure 10.28
For loops in MODEL clause rules.

query into separate partitions, which can be executed against in parallel, independent of each other, because there are no dependencies between partitions. This is unlike the DIMENSION BY clause, which does establish dependencies between columns.

Executing the following two queries through EXPLAIN PLAN and timing tests yields no apparent difference. This first query partitions on three columns:

```
SELECT region, country, city, year#, i FROM sales
MODEL
    PARTITION BY (region, country, city)
    DIMENSION BY (year#)
    MEASURES (sales.inv i)
    RULES(i[2005]=i[2004]+i[2003])
ORDER BY region, country, city, year#;
```

This second query moves all partitioned columns into dimensions. There is no apparent performance difference in both query plan and timing testing:

```
SELECT region, country, city, year#, i FROM sales
MODEL
    DIMENSION BY (region, country, city, year#)
    MEASURES (sales.inv i)
    RULES
(
    i[ANY,ANY,ANY,2005]=
      i[CV(region),CV(country),CV(city),2003]
     +i[CV(region),CV(country),CV(city),2004]
    )
ORDER BY region, country, city, year#;
```

I also time-tested with following clauses shown in Figure 10.29, gradually removing columns from the PARTITION BY clause to the DIMENSION BY clause, with the last query having no DIMENSION BY clause at all, as for the previous second query above. Results are shown in Figure 10.29. In general, as fewer columns are partitioned there is a slight performance decrease. However, when all partitions are removed to dimensions, performance actually improves drastically.

Figure 10.29
MODEL clause
partition
performance
variations.

Query MODEL Options	Seconds	Performance Increase
PARTITION BY (region, country, city) DIMENSION BY (year#)	5.355	
PARTITION BY (region, country) DIMENSION BY (city, year#)	5.375	-0.4%
PARTITION BY (region) DIMENSION BY (country, city, year#)	5.650	-5.1%
	5.460	
DIMENSION BY (region, country, city, year#)	3.300	39.6%

Once again, using a single CPU box probably does not help, even though I set the PARALLEL_MIN_SERVERS parameter to two in the configuration parameter file and restarted the database to instantiate it. The restart also made sure the parameter was reset, of course.

Note: Changing the value of the PARALLEL_MIN_SERVERS parameter does not require a database restart. The ALTER SYSTEM command can be used as well.

So as a further test, all materialized views used in this chapter have previously been set to NOPARALLEL, and not PARALLEL. This could also have an effect on parallel processing of partitions. This was done in order to make query plan output more easily readable for this chapter. This will now be changed:

```
ALTER MATERIALIZED VIEW mv_revenue_by_quarter PARALLEL;
ALTER MATERIALIZED VIEW mv_revenue_by_month PARALLEL;
ALTER MATERIALIZED VIEW mv_join_sale PARALLEL;
ALTER MATERIALIZED VIEW mv_cost_by_quarter PARALLEL;
ALTER MATERIALIZED VIEW mv_cost_by_month PARALLEL;
ALTER MATERIALIZED VIEW mv_join_purchase PARALLEL;
```

I also changed all the underlying tables accordingly:

```
ALTER TABLE sale PARALLEL;
ALTER TABLE purchase PARALLEL;
ALTER TABLE location PARALLEL;
ALTER TABLE time PARALLEL;
ALTER TABLE industry PARALLEL;
ALTER TABLE product PARALLEL;
```

Setting the PARALLEL option with no value on tables and materialized views instructs Oracle Database to select a degree of parallelism for queries and DML statements:

```
degree of parallelism = number of CPUs
    + parallel threads per CPU
```

Values above are indicated from my server in Figure 10.30.

Once again, as shown in Figure 10.31, I executed the same queries a multitude of times each, with timing tests, to see if I gained any performance improvement by partitioning MODEL clause queries. As you can see in Figure 10.31, there was little difference and, once again, the best performing option by a slight margin had no PARTITION BY clause whatsoever. This is completely contrary to documented expectations.

My point here is that even though I am using a single CPU server, do not take for granted what is in Oracle Database manuals or elsewhere. In

Figure 10.30
Parallel processing configuration parameters.

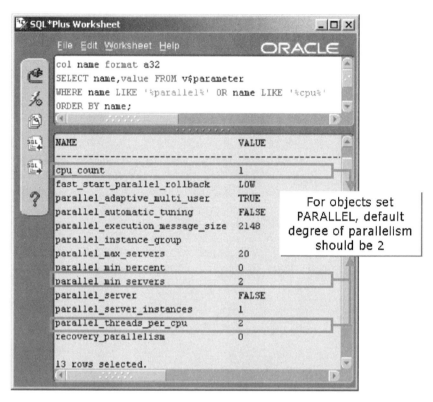

Figure 10.31
MODEL clause partition performance variations.

Query Model Options	Seconds						Performance Increase
	Test 1	Test 2	Test 3	Test 4	Test 5	Average	
PARTITION BY (region, country, city) DIMENSION BY (year#)	7.930	7.840	7.590	7.860	8.150	7.874	
PARTITION BY (region, country) DIMENSION BY (city, year#)	7.850	7.820	7.890	7.730	7.570	7.772	1.3%
PARTITION BY (region) DIMENSION BY (country, city, year#)	8.040	7.810	7.570	7.730	7.790	7.788	-0.2%
						7.811	
DIMENSION BY (region, country, city, year#)	7.810	7.760	7.750	7.850	7.650	7.764	0.6%

other words, even if you do have a multiple CPU platform with all the relevant bells and whistles, verify that parallel processing using the PARTITION BY clause performs better than without it.

Note: As well as preferably multiple CPUs, parallel processing requires enough data in a database to make it worth using. In a small database, the overhead of managing parallel processing, no matter how many CPUs are present, can outweigh its usefulness. This is acceptable and to be expected.

10.4.2 Understanding MODEL Clause Query Plans

An Oracle SQL MODEL clause query is accessed as ORDERED, CYCLIC, or ACYCLIC. Any of the three aforementioned options can be accessed as FAST. The different access methods are used by the optimizer in generating a query plan, depending on the structure of the MODEL clause RULES clause.

Figure 10.32 shows an example of an ORDERED FAST MODEL clause query where expressions on both sides of the rules are all simple cell expressions.

Figure 10.32
ORDERED FAST MODEL clause access.

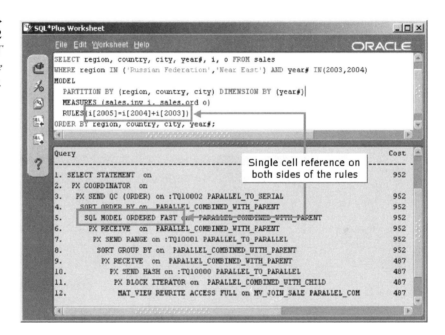

Figure 10.33 shows an example of an ORDERED MODEL clause query where expressions in the rules have multiple cell references and not single cell references, as in Figure 10.32.

Figure 10.34 shows an example of an ACYCLIC FAST MODEL clause query where the RULES clause is changed to AUTOMATIC ORDER, as opposed to the default SEQUENTIAL ORDER.

Figure 10.35 shows an example of an ACYCLIC MODEL clause query without the FAST setting because of the presence of a complex analytical function.

Figure 10.33
*ORDERED
MODEL clause
access.*

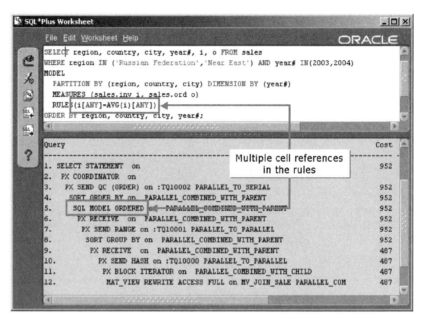

Figure 10.34
*ACYCLIC FAST
MODEL clause
access.*

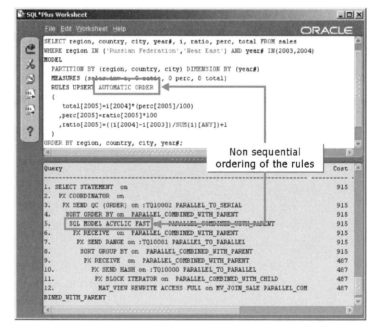

Figure 10.36 shows an example of a CYCLIC MODEL clause query, because calculations with the rules depend on each other: x depends on y, and y depends on x.

Figure 10.35
*ACYCLIC
MODEL clause
access.*

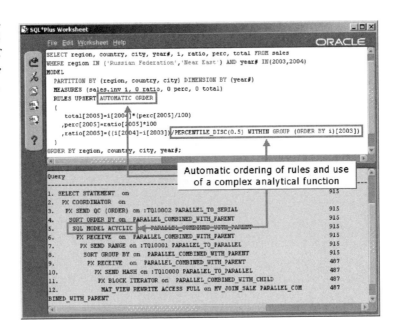

Figure 10.36
*CYCLIC MODEL
clause access.*

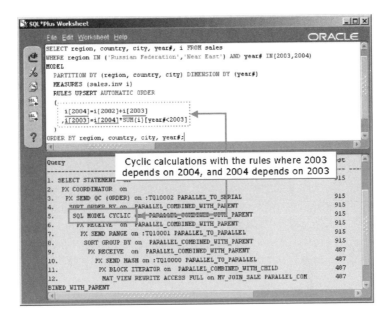

This chapter has covered many details of the Oracle SQL MODEL clause for creation of spreadsheet-like multiple-dimensional array structured reports.

The next chapter will begin the third part of this book, examining advanced and obscure topics in general—including advanced query rewrite, advanced parallel processing for data warehouses, loading data into a data warehouse, and, finally, general data warehouse architecture.

Part III

Advanced Topics

Chapter 11   Query Rewrite

Chapter 12   Parallel Processing

Chapter 13   Data Loading

Chapter 14   Data Warehouse Architecture

Query Rewrite

This chapter begins Part III of this book, expanding on previous chapters to cover more detail on query rewrite and parallel processing. Additionally, Part III includes details of data warehouse loading and general physical architecture, both as applicable to performance tuning. This chapter will cover the specifics of query rewrite in detail, rather than why it is used, and the tools used for verification. We will examine what query rewrite actually is and how its processing speed and possible use can be improved upon. So this chapter is divided into two parts. The first part explains how the optimizer query rewrites in different situations. The second part examines possibilities for improving query rewrite performance.

Chapter 4 covered query rewrite very briefly by showing how it can be implemented (ENABLE QUERY REWRITE) and by demonstrating its occurrence and relative query plan cost improvements. Chapter 4 also covered various utilities and procedures in the DBMS_MVIEW and DBMS_ADVISOR packages.

I I.I What Is Query Rewrite?

A materialized view is a physical copy of underlying data in tables. In their most efficient form materialized views are read-only objects, but they can be updated regularly, even on a real-time basis. Query rewrite occurs only using materialized views. The optimizer decides whether to rewrite a query or not, potentially replacing tables in a query with access to materialized views. Traditionally, materialized views contain aggregations of information in tables, and thus they occupy less physical space than tables. The result is less I/O activity and thus better performance. Additionally, physically separating materialized views from tables can help to reduce conflict with other activity directed at tables, such as concurrent database change activity from other applications, or general data warehouse reporting, management, and update activities.

When query rewrite occurs, the optimizer changes the objects accessed in a query from tables containing details to materialized views containing summaries of table details, even joins. Transformation of a query using query rewrite is completely transparent to the SQL programmer—unless, of course, a hint is involved.

11.1.1   When Does the Optimizer Query Rewrite?

As usual with most aspects of Oracle Database, there are various requirements and restrictions to be met for query rewrite to occur. First, the optimizer attempts to match the string of a query with the query string of a materialized view. If this first method fails, then the optimizer takes a less precise approach by comparing the constituent parts between a query and any available materialized views, comparing factors such as columns and joins, and particularly aggregations and aggregation layer content.

The most obvious factor for determining when query rewrite occurs is that a materialized view contains the correct data. A materialized view contains more detail than required can be used, although less efficiently than one containing the exact aggregation layer. On the contrary, and this is the obvious part, a materialized view that does not contain enough detail for a query because it is aggregated to a more compacted level, is not available for query rewrite of a particular query.

Note: If query rewrite fails and is a requirement then the DBMS_MVIEW.EXPLAIN REWRITE and DBMS_ADVISOR.TUNE_MVIEW procedures can be utilized to help discover why query rewrite fails.

11.1.2   What Can the Optimizer Query Rewrite?

The three obvious query types are a basic SELECT, a CREATE TABLE, or an INSERT command containing a SELECT statement. Less obvious at first glance are the individual queries separated by set operators, such as UNION. The fact is that a UNION operator represents two completely separate queries, with some restrictions, of course. Some subqueries can also be rewritten by query rewrite, such as inline views, because they are often self-contained. Subqueries can become highly complex. In general, the more complex a query, the less likely the optimizer will be able to match with a materialized view. The optimizer can only go so far.

More generally, and most sensibly, the optimizer should always select the smallest materialized view for query rewrite. In other words, if there are multiple layers of materialized views organized in a hierarchy then the most aggregated materialized view will be selected based on requiring the smallest amount of work.

11.2   How the Optimizer Rewrites Queries

This section analyzes query rewrite methods and checks made by the optimizer, followed by some special cases, including how query rewrite functions with partitioned objects. As already stated, the optimizer at first attempts to match the string of a query with the query string of a materialized view.

11.2.1   Matching Entire Query Strings

Note: Matching of strings for query rewrite is case insensitive! In other words, the case (uppercase and lowercase) is irrelevant when comparing strings, as far as query rewrite is concerned.

The following script is the DDL command for creating a materialized view called MV_SALES:

```
CREATE MATERIALIZED VIEW mv_sales
    NOPARALLEL NOLOGGING TABLESPACE mvdata
COMPRESS USING NO INDEX NEVER REFRESH
    ENABLE QUERY REWRITE
AS SELECT year#, quarter#, month#
    ,COUNT(transaction_amount)
, SUM(transaction_amount)
FROM sale s, location l, time t, product p, industry i
WHERE s.location_id = l.location_id
AND s.time_id = t.time_id
AND s.product_id = p.product_id
AND s.industry_id = i.industry_id
GROUP BY year#, quarter#, month#;
ANALYZE TABLE mv_sales COMPUTE STATISTICS;
```

The following query will match the query string in the materialized view SELECT statement exactly and, thus, a full text match occurs, as shown in Figure 11.1.

```
SELECT t.YEAR#, t.QUARTER#, t.MONTH#
    ,COUNT(s.TRANSACTION_AMOUNT)
,SUM(s.TRANSACTION_AMOUNT)
FROM sale s, location l, time t, product p, industry i
WHERE s.location_id = l.location_id
AND s.time_id = t.time_id
AND s.product_id = p.product_id
AND s.industry_id = i.industry_id
GROUP BY year#, quarter#, month#;
```

Figure 11.1
Full text match query rewrite.

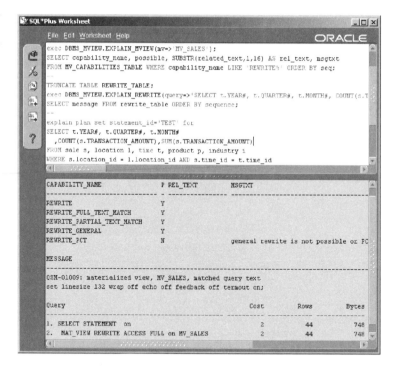

Now we can change the query deliberately to avoid a full text match and find what is called a partial text match query rewrite. Partial text query rewrite occurs when a query does not precisely match a materialized view and the match attempts starting with the FROM clause, assuming that the most likely change is to the SELECT statement expression list. The query rewrite will execute partially by using the COUNT and SUM functions to find the average (AVG). The output is the same as for Figure 11.1.

```
SELECT t.YEAR#, t.QUARTER#, t.MONTH#
, AVG(s.TRANSACTION_AMOUNT)
FROM sale s, location l, time t, product p, industry i
WHERE s.location_id = l.location_id
AND s.time_id = t.time_id
AND s.product_id = p.product_id
AND s.industry_id = i.industry_id
GROUP BY year#, quarter#, month#;
```

Another issue with missing full text query rewrite and substitution by the optimizer with a partial text query rewrite is column aliasing disparities between queries and materialized views. Changing the materialized view, as shown below, causes this problem:

```
SELECT t.YEAR# AS annual, t.QUARTER# AS quarterly
,t.MONTH# AS monthly
,AVG(s.TRANSACTION_AMOUNT) AS average
FROM sale s, location l, time t, product p, industry i
WHERE s.location_id = l.location_id
AND s.time_id = t.time_id
AND s.product_id = p.product_id
AND s.industry_id = i.industry_id
GROUP BY year#, quarter#, month#;
```

Similarly, changing the query, as opposed to the materialized view, causes partial text query rewrite as well, due to column alias name mismatches:

```
SELECT t.YEAR#, t.QUARTER#, t.MONTH#
, AVG(a.TRANSACTION_AMOUNT) AS sales
FROM sale a, location l, time t, product p, industry i
WHERE a.location_id = l.location_id
AND a.time_id = t.time_id
AND a.product_id = p.product_id
AND a.industry_id = i.industry_id
GROUP BY year#, quarter#, month#;
```

11.2.2 Matching Pieces of Queries

When the optimizer fails to match a query with a materialized view SQL string exactly, then other, less precise methods may be used. Some of these imprecise methods are join back, dimensional rollup, aggregation, and filtering.

The optimizer performs various checks between submitted queries and available materialized views in order to verify potential for query rewrite. These checks are as follows; they are generally obviously logical and do not require detailed examples:

- **Joins**. Joins can match exactly, include extra tables in a query or extra tables in a materialized view.

- **Columns**. Do required columns exist, or can they be retrieved by other means, such as by way of dimensional rollup?

- **Groups**. GROUP BY clause aggregations must match, or have more detail available, in available materialized views.

- **Aggregates**. Aggregates must be available in materialized views or be catered for adequately.

Join Back

If a materialized view does not contain all columns required by a query, the optimizer can still potentially query rewrite by executing a join back into an underlying table, joining back to the underlying table to find the column. Join back can occur when there is a functional dependency between one or more columns in the materialized view and required columns in the table, not in the materialized view. Functional dependencies are generally defined as primary keys or Oracle Database dimension objects. Let's create the materialized view, as shown below. Note the inclusion of the TIME_ID primary key column:

```
drop MATERIALIZED VIEW mv_sales;
CREATE MATERIALIZED VIEW mv_sales
     NOPARALLEL NOLOGGING TABLESPACE mvdata
     COMPRESS USING NO INDEX NEVER REFRESH
     ENABLE QUERY REWRITE
AS SELECT t.time_id, t.year#, t.quarter#, t.month#
,SUM(s.transaction_amount) AS sales
```

```
FROM sale s, location l, time t, product p, industry i
WHERE s.location_id = l.location_id
AND s.time_id = t.time_id
AND s.product_id = p.product_id
AND s.industry_id = i.industry_id
GROUP BY t.time_id, t.year#, t.quarter#, t.month#;
ANALYZE TABLE mv_sales COMPUTE STATISTICS;
```

Figure 11.2 shows a join back operation to the TIME dimension to collect the MONTHNAME column, which is not present in the materialized view shown above. The query plan clearly shows a query rewrite operation.

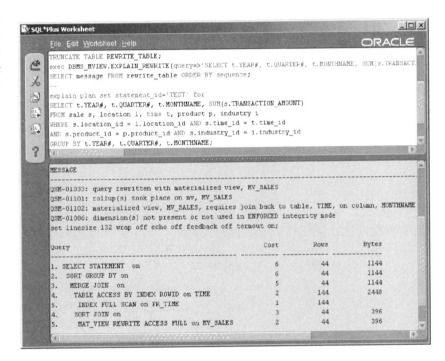

Figure 11.2
Query rewrite join back with a primary key.

Dimensional Rollups

Dimensional rollup can occur where a level of aggregation required is at a less granular detail level than is available in a materialized view, with all other necessary requirements met. Simply put, dimensional rollup allows a rollup operation up a level in a dimensional hierarchy, if the dimensional hierarchy is comprised of Oracle Database dimensional objects or even primary keys only (see Chapter 8). First, let's recreate the materialized view:

```
DROP MATERIALIZED VIEW mv_sales;
CREATE MATERIALIZED VIEW mv_sales
    NOPARALLEL NOLOGGING TABLESPACE mvdata
COMPRESS USING NO INDEX NEVER REFRESH
    ENABLE QUERY REWRITE
AS SELECT year#, quarter#, month#
    ,COUNT(transaction_amount)
, SUM(transaction_amount)
FROM sale s, location l, time t, product p, industry i
WHERE s.location_id = l.location_id
AND s.time_id = t.time_id
AND s.product_id = p.product_id
AND s.industry_id = i.industry_id
GROUP BY year#, quarter#, month#;
ANALYZE TABLE mv_sales COMPUTE STATISTICS;
```

Figure 11.3 shows an example query rewrite dimensional rollup operation where the query rolls up on the more granular materialized view, aggregating from the materialized view as opposed to the underlying tables.

A more classically demonstrative example of dimensional rollup is to recreate the materialized views generated in previous chapters. We know

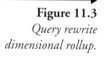

Figure 11.3
*Query rewrite
dimensional rollup.*

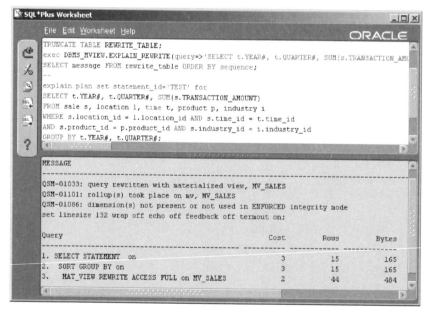

from previous chapters that the database in use for this book currently has a number of materialized views created on SALE and PURCHASE fact tables:

- **MV_JOIN_SALE and MV_JOIN_PURCHASE.** Two materialized join views join SALE and PURCHASE fact tables to all four dimensions of LOCATION, TIME, PRODUCT, and INDUSTRY.

- **MV_REVENUE_BY_MONTH and MV_COST_BY_MONTH.** These two materialized views aggregate by month from the MV_JOIN_SALE and MV_JOIN_PURCHASE materialized views.

- **MV_REVENUE_BY_QUARTER and MV_COST_BY_QUARTER.** These two materialized views do a similar task to that of the two monthly materialized views, except at a less detailed level. They aggregate by quarters rather than months. Each quarter contains three months where four quarters make up one year.

Additionally, all statistics are collected at this point, once again, plus all materialized views and underlying tables are set as NOPARALLEL in order to simplify query plans for this chapter. If PARALLEL is required at a later stage in this chapter then it will be reset for all concerned objects. At this point I will drop the MV_SALES materialized view and recreate the MV_JOIN_ SALE, followed by the less detailed MV_REVENUE_ BY_MONTH and even less detailed MV_REVENUE_ BY_QUARTER and MV_REVENUE_ BY_YEAR materialized views. These three views create a hierarchy of materialized views with a decreasing level of granularity. In other words, the aggregates are more summarized through each successive layer. Note in Figure 11.4 that there are indicators showing query rewrite and redirection of query rewrite for all the three materialized views MV_JOIN_SALE, MV_ REVENUE_BY_MONTH, and MV_REVENUE_BY_QUARTER.

Aggregation

Query rewrite can occur when aggregations are catered for in underlying materialized views. However, it appears, as in Figure 11.5, that any potential dimensional rollup using diminished granularity aggregated materialized views cannot be used in these cases. In Figure 11.5 the query rewrite is made possible from the base join materialized view MV_JOIN_SALE because MV_JOIN_SALE contains the SUM and COUNT functions on the S.TRANSACTION_AMOUNT aggregate:

Figure 11.4
Query rewrite dimensional rollup over successive hierarchical layers of decreasing granularity.

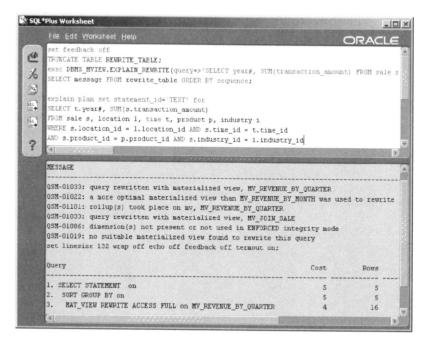

- **AVG(x) = SUM(x) / COUNT(x)**. The average is the equivalent of the mean or the sum of all values divided by the sample size. Sample size is represented by COUNT(x).

- **VARIANCE(x) = SUM(POWER((x – AVG(x)),2))/COUNT(x)**. The variance is the average squared deviation from the mean.

- **STDDEV(x) = SQRT(SUM(POWER((x – AVG(x)),2))/ COUNT(x))**. The standard deviation is the square root of the variance.

Note in the formulae above that the SUM and COUNT functions are all that is required. If either SUM or COUNT were not present in the MV_JOIN_SALE materialized view then the aggregations for VARIANCE, STDDEV, and AVG would not be catered for, and query rewrite would not occur at all. The point of Figure 11.5 is, of course, the EXPLAIN_REWRITE procedure, and not the query plan.

Filters

Filtering allows query rewrite on materialized views where a materialized view contains the rows that a query requires. If, as a result of some type of WHERE clause, HAVING clause, or IN-list filtering, a materialized view

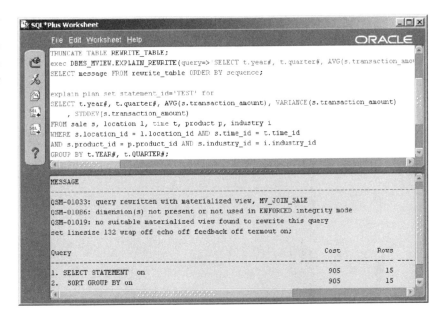

Figure 11.5
Query rewrite using aggregation constituent aggregations.

excludes a query, then, the query will not be eligible for query rewrite. Once again, I drop all materialized views in order to avoid confusion, and then create the following single materialized view with a filter restriction to only retrieve rows for the years 2001, 2002, and 2003:

```
DROP MATERIALIZED VIEW mv_sales;
CREATE MATERIALIZED VIEW mv_sales
     NOPARALLEL NOLOGGING TABLESPACE mvdata
COMPRESS USING NO INDEX NEVER REFRESH
     ENABLE QUERY REWRITE
AS SELECT t.year#, t.quarter#, t.month#
     ,COUNT(transaction_amount)
, SUM(transaction_amount)
FROM sale s, location l, time t, product p, industry i
WHERE t.year# BETWEEN 2001 AND 2003
AND s.location_id = l.location_id
AND s.time_id = t.time_id
AND s.product_id = p.product_id
AND s.industry_id = i.industry_id
GROUP BY t.year#, t.quarter#, t.month#;
ANALYZE TABLE mv_sales COMPUTE STATISTICS;
```

Figure 11.6 shows two queries. The top left query has no filter and does not match the available materialized view filter, failing to query rewrite. The bottom right query falls within the filtered scope of the materialized view and query rewrite does occur.

Figure 11.6
Filtered query rewrite.

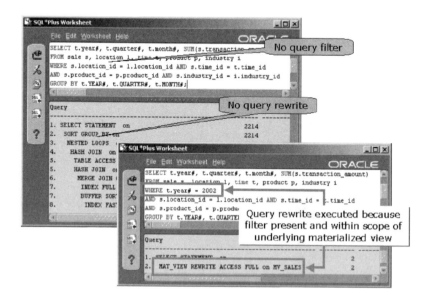

11.2.3 Special Cases for Query Rewrite

Some special cases are interesting to note:

- **Partially Stale Materialized Views**. Query rewrite can be available for a query where the fresh portion of a materialized view is that which is required by the query.
  - **Fresh Oracle Partitioning Query Rewrite**. Query rewrite is allowed on individual fresh table and materialized view partitions, as long as the fresh partitions fit query requirements and all rows in the entire partition are accessed.

Note: Partial partition queries will not query rewrite!

  - List partitions and range-list partitions are allowed, but hash partitions are not. It is likely that hash partitions are not allowed due to the explicit nondeclarative nature of row placement when using hash partitions [1]. Partition query rewrite is known as PCT query rewrite. A materialized view can include a partition marker as a replacement for a partition key. The partition marker allows specific identification of specific partitions, allowing query rewrite on those marked partitions as pruned partitions. A partition marker can identify one or more individual partitions. Once again, all rows in a marked partition must be accessed for partitioned query rewrite to occur. Also, only wholly fresh partitions can be used for query rewrite. Only fresh partitions have an available partition marker. Stale partitions will not be identifiable by a partition marker.

- **Nested Materialized Views**. The optimizer will iterate through the query rewrite process using nested layers of materialized views until the best option is found for the query, assuming all required criteria are met.

- **GROUP BY Clause Extensions**. GROUP BY clause extensions such as ROLLUP, CUBE, and GROUPING SETS clauses do allow query rewrite.

Note: The EXPAND_GSET_TO_UNION hint can be used for GROUP BY clause extension queries in order to expand a grouping set to multiple queries merged with the UNION set operator.

- **Bind Variables**. Bind variables are allowed for query rewrite as long as their respective values are not required to perform query rewrite.

- **Expressions**. Any expression is allowed as long as an underlying materialized view caters completely for the evaluation of that expression, such as SUM(x) / COUNT(x) allowing AVG(x).

- **Other Possibilities**. Inline views or FROM clause embedded subqueries allow query rewrite, as well as self joining queries, views with constraints (view constraints always match underlying tables); and UNION set operator queries allow query rewrite assuming that an underlying materialized view caters to all the required row sets.

11.3 Affecting Query Rewrite Performance

There are a number of factors possibly affecting query rewrite performance. However, as reiterated in numerous chapters throughout this book, query rewrite and materialized views are one of those factors in which their use is a tuning method in and of itself. In other words, performance tuning is accomplished simply by creating appropriate materialized views. The following is a list of potentially performance-affecting factors:

- **Statistics**. Always generate statistics and keep them up-to-date, for both materialized views and their underlying tables.

- **Constraints**. In an ideal world, it is beneficial for query rewrite, in situations such as dimensional rollup, that all constraints be fully enabled. Most significant are primary and foreign key constraints. NULL-valued foreign keys can cause possible problems. In other words, creating a properly structured data model, where primary and foreign keys represent properly implemented relations, is the best option to take. For example, the RELY constraint state allows use of nonvalidated constraint values in materialized view query rewrites. A situation like this is common, but from a purist's perspective, and for the hope of always having properly structured data, this option will not always guarantee correct results.

- **Oracle Dimension Objects**. These objects can be very useful for query rewrite performance by allowing for explicit, multiple-level, hierarchical dimensional structures.

- **Match Query Strings to Materialized Views**. This is a sensible approach, as long as the number and refresh rates of materialized views are tightly controlled. Too many materialized views can cause the same problems as too much indexing, except they will be much worse because materialized views are that much bigger than indexes.

- **Aggregates**. There are three points to make:

  - Preferably, only create materialized views with aggregates, for there is little point in duplicating tables unless creating join materialized views.

  - If not using anything other than simple aggregation functions, always include SUM and COUNT. If using more complex functions, try to include their subfunctions as well whenever possible. Frequently executed big nasty calculations, which revert to tables and avoid query rewrite altogether, completely miss the point entirely of creating potentially refresh processor-hogging materialized views.

  - By all means create aggregations with the most granularity possible, but if less detail is consistently required, consider using nested materialized views, or creating base materialized views with less granularity in the first place.

- **Expressions and Subqueries**. Create materialized views in order to precalculate complex, or very frequently executed, expressions and subqueries.

- **Outer Joins**. Personally, I have always pictured the profligate use of outer joins as a potential indication of data model entity structural problems. However, this is more likely the case in OLTP than data warehouse databases. Materialized views can include outer joins and can allow for effective query rewrite as long as inner join rows can be explicitly accessed without confusion—including primary key columns in outer join materialized views.

- **Hints**. The REWRITE and NOREWRITE hint can be used in queries to switch query rewrite on and off, respectively, for a specific query. A hint is coded as follows:

```
SELECT /* + REWRITE */ <expression list> ...
```

Always remember two things about hints:

- Hints are instructions previously being suggestions to the optimizer

- Hints are not syntax-checked. If they are erroneously typed, they will be ignored by both the SQL code parser and the optimizer.

This chapter has covered some specifics of using query rewrite and materialized views. The next chapter will examine more details of parallel processing as applicable to data warehouse databases.

11.4 Endnotes

1. *Oracle Performance Tuning for 9i and 10g* (ISBN: 1555583059)

12

Parallel Processing

This chapter will examine parallel processing. Parallel processing is most beneficial for certain types of operations in very large data warehouses, sometimes in smaller databases for a small number of operations, and rarely in OLTP or heavily concurrent transaction databases.

12.1 What Is Parallel Processing?

A process executed in parallel is, in theory, a process split into multiple, preferably independent, parts. Those independent parts are executed concurrently (at the same time) either on two separate CPUs or even by multiple server processes on a single powerful CPU. There can be dependencies between processes executed in parallel, but this type of processing tends to be constructed using specialized programming languages on specialized multiple massively parallel platforms.

Oracle Database does have some fairly sophisticated parallel processing capabilities, but these capabilities do not appear to extend into the ability to communicate between parallel executing processes at the programming level. In general, parallel processing in an Oracle Database needs three things: (1) a database large enough, and of appropriate application type, to actually be able to use parallel processing effectively; (2) spare resources in the form of multiple CPUs, CPU, memory, and I/O capacity to spare; and (3) a database requiring operations that can be executed in parallel.

Note: A database environment not being appropriate for parallel processing could be adversely affected by implementation of parallel processing.

12.1.1 **What Can Be Executed in Parallel?**

In an ideal world parallel queries are best executed on multiple CPU platforms when Oracle Partitioning [1] is being used with separate disks or RAID arrays. Generally, parallel queries are only an advantage for very large tables or in very large databases, such as data warehouses. Using parallel queries on small, highly active concurrent OLTP databases can cause, rather than solve, performance problems. Certain types of Oracle SQL can be executed in parallel:

- Any query with at least a single full table scan using SELECT, INSERT, UPDATE, and DELETE commands can be executed in parallel. Large single table scans, large joins, and partitioned index reads fall into this category. A partitioned index read implies access to local partitioned indexes, where a local index is an index created on each separate partition.

- Fast full index scans can also be executed in parallel, as can full table scans. This is because fast full index scans involve direct I/O activity. This is shown in Figure 12.7. Some specific sections within queries can be executed in parallel.

- The CREATE INDEX and ALTER INDEX REBUILD commands can be executed in parallel.

- Using the CREATE TABLE statement generated from a SELECT statement and the CREATE MATERIALIZED VIEW statement can be executed in parallel.

- Any type of mass DML operation or similar, involving INSERT, UPDATE, DELETE, and MERGE statements can be executed in parallel. This area includes not only DML operations, but also SQL*Loader parallel and parallel-direct appends.

- Moving and splitting of partitions can also be executed in parallel using the MOVE and SPLIT partition clauses.

12.2 Degree of Parallelism (Syntax)

Parallelism can be executed by the optimizer in one of two ways:

- **Object Syntax**. Settings in object syntax such as CREATE TABLE and CREATE MATERIALIZED VIEW statements.

- **The PARALLEL Hint**. Ultimately, parallelism is determined based on CPU count and how much Oracle Database *thinks* the platform can handle.

```
degree of parallelism = number of CPUs
    * parallel threads per CPU
```

Note: PARALLEL_THREADS_PER_CPU is a configuration parameter (in the configuration parameter file).

12.3   **Configuration Parameters**

The following configuration parameters can affect parallel execution performance directly, but you will want to make changes cautiously:

- **PARALLEL_MIN_SERVERS**. Causes startup of the specified number of parallel processes on database startup. Each parallel server process services a parallel execution request. This value can be increased to service more parallel requests or increase parallelism in general. However, too much parallelism can be more complex to manage than it is worth.

- **PARALLEL_MAX_SERVERS**. Limits the number of parallel processes that can be executing at any one time. Too many processes can kill system performance. This limit appears to be set at 20 for 10.1.0.2 on Windows 2000. This could be seriously overabundant, derived from CPU count and the PARALLEL_AUTOMATIC_ TUNING parameter.

- **PARALLEL_EXECUTION_MESSAGE_SIZE**. This parameter is used for parallel execution messaging where higher values give better performance, but chew up more memory in the shared pool. If a minimal configuration is exceeded by parallel processing requests, then serial processing can result.

- **PARALLEL_THREADS_PER_CPU**. This value multiplied by the number of CPUs determines the threads used in parallel execution.

When a system has spare CPU resources relative to a slow I/O subsystem then this value can be doubled or quadrupled.

- **PARALLEL_MIN_PERCENT**. Forces an error to be returned when parallel processing resources are not available as a percentage of minimum resources. Setting to zero, the default switches off the potential for throwing an error. When resources are not available, the database automatically allows sequential execution of what has been requested as a parallel operation. Setting to a nonzero value will produce an error when resources for parallel execution are limited, prohibiting serial execution of parallel requested operations.

Note: The PARALLEL_AUTOMATIC_TUNING parameter is deprecated in Oracle Database 10*g*.

Current settings for the data warehouse database used for this book are as shown in Figure 12.1.

Figure 12.1
Parallel processing configuration parameters.

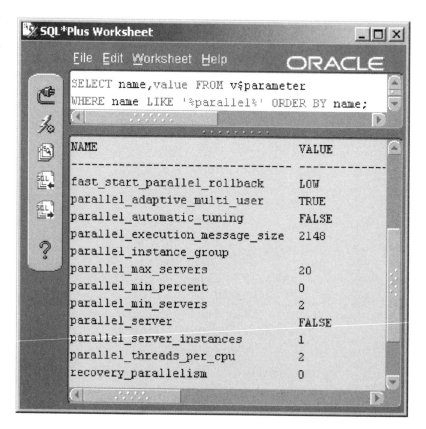

12.4 **Demonstrating Parallel Execution**

This section will cover different aspects of parallel execution, including parallel queries, indexing, subqueries, DML, and, finally, partitioning operations.

12.4.1 **Parallel Queries**

First, let's show a query plan for a serially executed query, as shown in Figure 12.2.

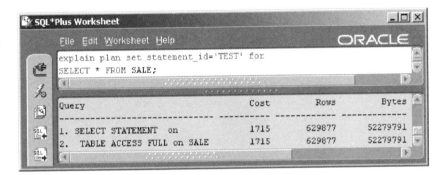

Figure 12.2
A query executed in serial.

There are two ways to execute queries against tables in parallel. The first involves the PARALLEL hint and the second involves the CREATE TABLE or ALTER TABLE statements, including the parallel clause. Figure 12.3 shows an example parallel execution.

When attempting to persuade the optimizer to execute a query in parallel, at least one table must be full table scanned. In the query shown in Figure 12.4, the LOCATION table is not filtered enough to allow index use on both tables, thus without the PARALLEL hint the SALE table would be full scanned, and thus parallel execution occurs.

The query in Figure 12.4 really does demonstrate that at least one full table scan is required for a query to be parallelized. However, it is interesting for the BROADCAST send to slaves and the double-parallel executed GROUP BY clause.

In the case of Figure 12.5, a single LOCATION row is retrieved, resulting in a small enough number of SALE rows to result in index hits on both tables in the join. The two indexes are unique and range-scanned, and there is no full table scan in use. The PARALLEL hint on the SALE table is completely ignored, being pointless for performance in comparison to the index reads. Thus, there is no full table scan and, therefore, no parallel execution.

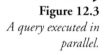

Figure 12.3
A query executed in parallel.

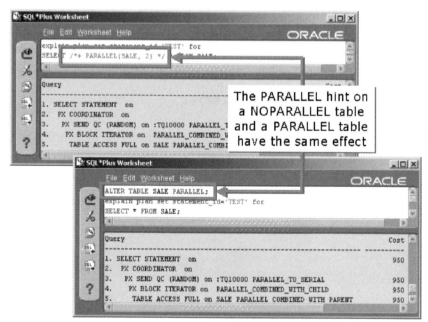

Figure 12.4
Parallel execution requires at least one full table scan.

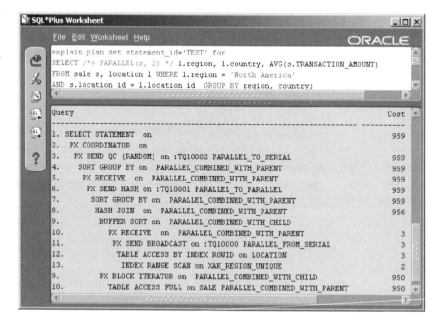

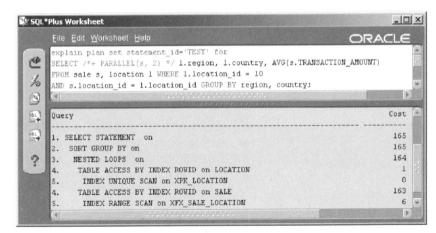

Figure 12.5
Index unique and range scans override parallel execution.

So full table scans can be executed in parallel. What about index scans? Figure 12.6 shows an ordered index scan executed in parallel.

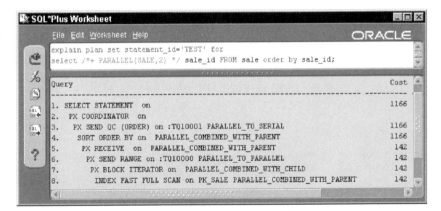

Figure 12.6
Parallel ordered index scan.

Now let's look at fast, full index scans, where an index is scanned in the physical order stored on the disk, as opposed to indexed order as determined by the ORDER BY clause, shown in Figure 12.6. Fast, full index scans get a little interesting. This first script uses the PARALLEL_INDEX hint to return a query plan with parallel execution at a cost of 256:

```
EXPLAIN PLAN SET statement_id='TEST' FOR
SELECT /*+ PARALLEL_INDEX(sale, 2) */ sale_id
FROM sale;
```

The next query will not execute in parallel using the table based PAR-ALLEL hint, even though access to the SALE_ID column will force a fast, full index scan on the primary key. However, the fast, full index scan has the same cost as before at 256. Thus, parallel execution for the previous query does not help performance at all:

```
EXPLAIN PLAN SET statement_id='TEST' FOR
SELECT /*+ PARALLEL(sale, 2) */ sale_id FROM sale;
```

In the next query specifying both table and primary key index name in the PARALLEL_INDEX hint will do the same as the first query above, executing in parallel at the nonreduced cost of 256:

```
EXPLAIN PLAN SET statement_id='TEST' FOR
SELECT /*+ PARALLEL_INDEX(sale pk_sale 2) */ sale_id
FROM sale;
```

Now this is where it gets interesting. Using the PARALLEL hint against the table, and setting the index PK_SALE to PARALLEL in the index syntax, the cost is reduced to 142, as shown in Figure 12.7.

```
ALTER INDEX pk_sale PARALLEL;
EXPLAIN PLAN SET statement_id='TEST' FOR
SELECT /*+ PARALLEL(sale, 2) */ sale_id FROM sale;
```

Figure 12.7
*Parallel fast, full
index scan.*

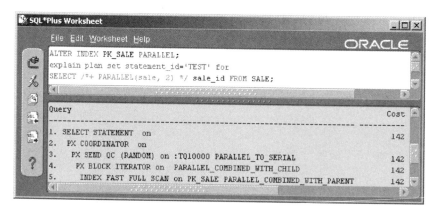

For parallel processing using partitions see Chapter 6 of this book and Chapter 17 in *Oracle Performance Tuning for 9i and 10g* (ISBN: 1555583059).

12.4.2 Index DDL Statements

The CREATE INDEX and ALTER INDEX statements can be executed in parallel. It is important to note that these commands will very likely only show a parallelized performance improvement on multiple CPU platforms. The following four scripts would produce query plans for the same CREATE INDEX statement, but without parallelism such as PARALLEL, PARALLEL 4, and PARALLEL 16. On a single CPU machine, one would expect each successive option to perform worse. According to the query plan costs this is incorrect, as costs from query plans were assessed at by the optimizer as 774, 410, 205, and 51—51 being the cost for execution with the PARALLEL 16 option.

```
EXPLAIN PLAN SET statement_id='TEST' FOR
CREATE INDEX akx_sale_1 ON sale
(industry_id, location_id, product_id, time_id)
TABLESPACE indx;

EXPLAIN PLAN SET statement_id='TEST' FOR
CREATE INDEX akx_sale_1 ON sale
(industry_id, location_id, product_id, time_id)
TABLESPACE indx PARALLEL;

EXPLAIN PLAN SET statement_id='TEST' FOR
CREATE INDEX akx_sale_1 ON sale
(industry_id, location_id, product_id, time_id)
TABLESPACE indx PARALLEL 4;

EXPLAIN PLAN SET statement_id='TEST' FOR
CREATE INDEX akx_sale_1 ON sale
(industry_id, location_id, product_id, time_id)
TABLESPACE indx PARALLEL 16;
```

Since the query plan costs looked like complete hogwash, I executed timing tests and got a sensible result. In general, the PARALLEL option (second script above) performs slightly better than the NOPARALLEL option (first script above). Also, expectedly and contrary to query plan costs, the PARALLEL 4 and PARALLEL 16 options perform poorly with PARALLEL 16, obviously performing the worst given the single CPU platform. Figure 12.8 shows a picture of parallel processes started up at two

Figure 12.8
Lots of parallel processing in progress.

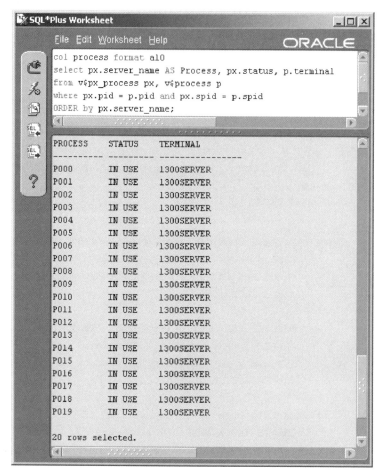

threads per parallel request—that should be 32. It is limited to 20 because PARALLEL_MAX_SERVERS is set to 20, and just as well.

12.4.3   SELECT Statement Subqueries

The following DDL and DML statements are relevant:

```
CREATE TABLE . . . AS SELECT . . .
CREATE MATERIALIZED VIEW . . . AS SELECT . . .
INSERT INTO . . . SELECT . . .
```

This also implies that many subqueries can be executed in parallel, irrespective of the parallelism of their calling queries.

Note: It is also possible to execute various parts of queries in parallel simply by the nature of those syntactical clauses. Some examples are GROUP BY, NOT IN, SELECT DISTINCT, UNION, UNION ALL, CUBE, and ROLLUP, as well as many Oracle SQL functions.

Figure 12.9 shows a CREATE TABLE statement generated using a parallel executed SELECT statement.

Figure 12.9
CREATE TABLE using a parallel SELECT subquery.

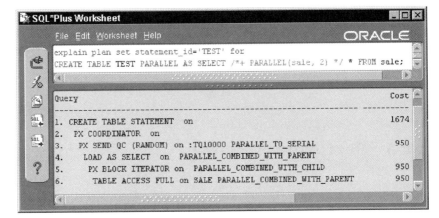

In the next example an empty table is created followed by an INSERT INTO . . . SELECT statement, where both INSERT and SELECT statements are suggested to be executed in parallel:

```
CREATE TABLE test AS SELECT * FROM sale WHERE ROWNUM < 1;

INSERT INTO /*+ PARALLEL(test) */ test
SELECT /*+ PARALLEL(sale) */ * FROM sale;
```

12.4.4   DML Statements

Mass DML operations involving all DML statements, such as INSERT, UPDATE, DELETE, and MERGE, can be executed in parallel. Partitioned tables can have UPDATE, MERGE, and DELETE operations executed against them in parallel. A nonpartitioned table having a bitmap index created from it excludes parallel processing from INSERT, UPDATE, MERGE, and DELETE operations.

> **Note:** This bitmap index restriction is lifted for Oracle Database 10*g*, Release 2.

Additionally, SQL*Loader appending loads using direct path parallel is, as it states, executed in parallel. Although, SQL*Loader can execute to load data through the SQL engine, direct path–parallel loads are appended rows and loaded to the end of tables.

12.4.5 Partitioning Operations

Many types of operations working with partitions can be executed in parallel simply because Oracle Partitioning splits tables into separate physical pieces. For parallel processing using partitions, see Chapter 6 of this book and Chapter 17 in *Oracle Performance Tuning for 9*i *and 10*g (ISBN: 1555583059).

12.5 Performance Views

Using performance views and Oracle Enterprise Manager are excellent approaches to monitoring performance of an Oracle Database data warehouse. The performance views listed below can help with monitoring parallel processing. There are many other performance views, and Oracle Enterprise Manager interfaces are always useful.

- **V$PX_BUFFER_ADVICE**. Parallel query maximum usage of SGA memory over a period of time, as shown in Figure 12.10.

- **V$PX_SESSION**. Session-level data for parallel server process.

- **V$PX_SESSTAT**. Join of V$PX_SESSION and V$SESSSTAT.

- **V$PX_PROCESS**. Contains parallel processes currently executing, similar to the V$PROCESS view. The query in Figure 12.8 joins the V$PX_PROCESS and V$PROCESS.

- **V$PX_PROCESS_SYSSTAT**. Buffer statistics as shown in Figure 12.11.

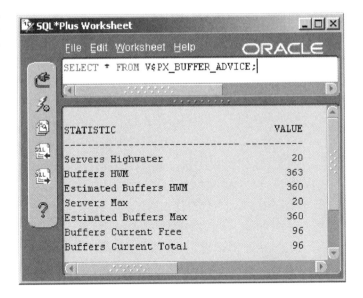

Figure 12.10
Parallelism buffer advice.

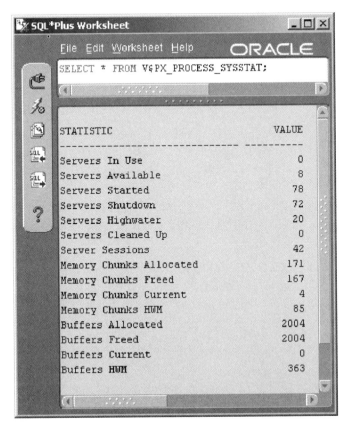

Figure 12.11
Parallel processing memory statistics.

12.6 Parallel Execution Hints

The following hints apply to parallel execution for making suggestions to the optimizer:

- **PARALLEL**[(**<table>**, **<degree>**)]. Parallelize on a table.

- **NO_PARALLEL**[(**<table>**)]. No parallelism for a table.

- **PARALLEL_INDEX**[(**<table>**, {**<index>** [, **<index>**]}, **<degree>**)]. Parallelize on an index.

- **NO_PARALLEL_INDEX**[(**<table>**, {**<index>** [, **<index>**]}, **<degree>**)]. No parallelism for an index.

- **PQ_DISTRIBUTE**(**<table>**, **<outer>**, **<inner>**). Can be used for parallel joins, and determines how joins are put together.

12.7 Parallel Execution Query Plans

The OTHER_TAG column in the PLAN_TABLE contains parallel execution details of an EXPLAIN PLAN command:

- **PARALLEL_TO_SERIAL**. Top level of parallel execution query plan.

- **PARALLEL_TO_PARALLEL**. Section of query both executed in parallel and returned to its calling parent step in the query plan in parallel.

- **PARALLEL_COMBINED_WITH_PARENT** and **PARALLEL_COMBINED_WITH_CHILD**. Parent or child operations execute both operations in parallel.

- **PARALLEL_FROM_SERIAL**. Operation in query plan showing current operation performed not in parallel but serially, and returned in parallel. Serial processing in the middle of a supposedly parallel executed query possibly indicates a problem. However, examine Figure 12.4 where the LOCATION table is accessed in serial because it is not supposed to be accessed in parallel, and does not need to be as such either.

This chapter has covered some aspects of parallel query tuning. It is important to note that there is not really much that can be done to tune parallel queries other than to verify that first, they are faster than serial processing, and second, if faster, that parallel execution is actually occurring. The two most significant factors affecting parallel processing are physical I/O partitioning and multiple CPUs. Other factors, such as minimizing logging, multiple archivers, and database writer processes, can help with parallel execution, but as with parallel processing itself, any overindulgence with resources can become difficult for the database to manage if implemented in excess. The next chapter will examine what can be done to tune loading of data into an Oracle Database data warehouse.

12.8 Endnotes

1. Chapter 17 in *Oracle Performance Tuning for 9i and 10g* (ISBN: 1555583059)

13

Data Loading

This chapter examines the loading of data into an Oracle Database data warehouse. There are various ways in which the loading process can be made to perform better. This chapter will attempt to focus on the performance aspects of what is effectively a three-step process, and sometimes even a four-step process, including extraction, transportation, transformation, and loading processes. I like to add an extra definitional step to the loading process, called transportation. Transportation methods will also be discussed in this chapter, because some methods are better and faster than others and there are some very specific and highly efficient transportation methods specific to Oracle Database.

13.1 What Is Data Loading?

Data loading for a data warehouse is essentially the process by which data is loaded into that data warehouse. Unfortunately, loading data into a data warehouse is unlikely to ever be a simple process for an innumerable number of reasons; perhaps the most significant reason is that data originates from different sources and is thus likely to differ substantially. Therefore, the loading process can be split into a sequence of steps:

1.   **Extraction**. This is the process of getting or pulling the data from a source. For example, queries against a legacy database can be used to generate flat text files.

2.   **Transportation**. A step such as this is not always an explicit requirement, but often data must be transported from one machine to another, perhaps in a specific form such as a text file or Oracle transportable tablespace, or even over a network connection.

3. **Loading**. This step loads data into a data warehouse. A load can be a straightforward, referentially acceptable load into a single table, simultaneous loads into multiple tables, or even flat files requiring post-load transformation and transformation processing. Actual load performance can be improved by placing processing requirements in previous stages, such as using transportable tablespaces to transport between two Oracle databases or preprocessing using transformation processing features external to a data warehouse database.

4. **Transformation**. This process is intended to transform or change data into a format understandable by the data warehouse and acceptable for loading, or temporary loading, into a data warehouse. The more processing that can be done during the transformation stage outside of a database using O/S (Operating System) text-parsing techniques, the less work needs to be performed by the SQL engine during or after loading. External transformation can help ultimate load performance processing.

13.1.1   General Loading Strategies

Data warehouse loading strategies are generally a single phase or many phases.

Single Phase Load

A single phase load stores all data into data warehouse target reporting tables, including any transformation processing from raw data to data warehouse structures. A single phase load can be efficient if source data is well structured, but completely disastrous for performance if data is incompatible. Processing SQL code operations and changes during data loads, because data is not properly transformed, can place a heavy performance burden on both source and target tables, plus it can also completely snooker some of the more efficient performance aspects of tools such as SQL*Loader. The presence of materialized views can complicate single phase loading even further. When are materialized views refreshed in a single phase update? Since a single phase updates all data from source to target at once, then it is likely that materialized views will need to be real-time refresh-capable. Single phase updates are not necessarily recommended for anything but the smallest of operations.

Multiple Phase Load

How are multiple phase loads implemented?

- Temporary tables in source or target database where transformation processing is executed in either or both databases
- Staging databases, which can be used in a similar manner

The objectives of multiple phase loading are twofold:

- Ease of coding and implementation when execution processes are in separate, smaller, distinct, mutually exclusive steps
- Minimized impact on concurrent activity of transactional (OLTP) databases and throughput (reporting) capability of the data warehouse

The final pushing of cleaned and transformed data into final target data warehouse tables can be performed using insertion append operations:

- The INSERT statement using the APPEND hint
- SQL*Loader DIRECT PARALLEL insertions. DIRECT PARALLEL options also append the same way as above
- Another option is building of partitions externally and then simply slotting newly built partitions in data warehouse partitioned tables as MOVE or EXCHANGE partitions

Note: Data warehouse target table deletions and appending can adversely affect reuse of space. This is because appending (direct loads) will add to the end of tables in new blocks and not reuse block space previously freed by deletions. Freed extents are obviously still freely available for conventional insertions and loads. Partitioning is slightly different for appending as well, because multiple partitions can be appended to (direct loaded) simultaneously.

An Update Window

An update window is a time period in which, will the least impact is felt by users of both source (OLTP) database and target database (data warehouse). The establishment of this window may not be strictly necessary, and may not even be possible, but it would be beneficial to user satisfaction. However, certain specific types of operations can be seriously detrimental to performance, particularly for a data warehouse subjected to constant heavy usage of a critical nature:

- Fact table loading as direct load appending, which will create new blocks (free space as a result of heavy deletion activity will not allow reuse of space freed by deletions)

Note: Any SQL processing during SQL*Loader activity completely disables parallel, direct, and appended loading.

- Reindexing on any large objects, such as tables or materialized views
- Materialized view refresh
- Any kind of processing accessing either a read-only or write changes to large data warehouse objects, such as fact tables, is inadvisable unless the post-load processing is beneficial to performance (materialized view and index maintenance)

The Effect of Materialized Views

Materialized view maintenance can be a heavy drain on performance, due to the types of operations that need to be performed and how often those operations should be performed. Bear in mind that if benefits are outweighed by maintenance processing and time requirements, then you should not use as many materialized views. Overuse of materialized views has a diverse effect on overall database performance, in the same manner as an overindulgence in creation of indexing.

Oracle Database Loading Tools

Oracle Database–included tools most often used for data warehouse construction and loading are SQL*Loader with transformation processing in O/S; processing tools such as Perl; or, in Oracle SQL coding, even PL/SQL. Other options are export (EXP) and import (IMP) utilities, DataPump EXP and IMP utilities, partitioning copies, or, finally, transportable tablespaces.

13.2 Extraction

The extraction process is the process of pulling data from a source or transactional, often OLTP, database. The trick is not to conflict with concurrent end-user requirements. In other words, do not slow down access to the source database by using an extraction method that will compromise source database performance. However, if there is a window in which the extraction process must take place, then obviously that time period restriction must also be taken into account.

13.2.1 Logical Extraction

Logical extraction implies extraction of data from a source transactional database in keeping with the existing table structure of that source database. In other words, data is extracted table by table.

- **Full Extraction**. No need to keep track of changes, because full data sets are extracted, no changes are made at the source, and no filtering occurs. Exports and even local or remote SQL query statements can be used.

- **Incremental Extraction**. Pulling data from the source database will go back to a specified point in time, for example, where source database performance may very well be affected by filtering constraints placed in an extraction query.

Note: There is an Oracle Database optional add-on called Change Data Capture, which provides automated tracking of source transactional database change activity. Other manual methods of tracking source database data changes could involve the use of timestamps or partitions (the best option, especially when using timestamped partitions). Triggers can also be a useful option, but with respect to performance, triggers are always a problematic option.

13.2.2 Physical Extraction

Physical extraction implies physically pulling data or files from a source database, not necessarily taking into account the logical and table structure of the source transactional database.

- **Online Extraction**. Pull source data from a physical, not a logical, (table) structure, such as redo logs, trigger-generated change entry tables, or even perhaps pass it through a staging database and/or staging tables in the source or target data warehouse database.

- **Offline Extraction**. Offline extraction implies the creation of some type of intermediary structure, such as flat text files, export utility files, transportable tablespaces, redo and archive log files, or even a staging database.

13.2.3 Extraction Options

Data can be extracted from a source database using a number of methods. The most basic is simply dumping data into flat text files. Otherwise there are external tables, transportable tablespaces, and the export utility, including Data Pump technology. It is also possible to read information from redo and archive log files.

Dumping Files Using SQL

We could dump one or more files from an OLTP database directly into flat text files, in a delimited form unlikely to conflict with any commonly used characters, as shown in the example below using the SQL*Plus tool:

```
SET HEAD OFF PAGES 0 COLSEP '|'
SELECT t.dte as transaction_date, o.dte as order_date
     ,lines.order_amount, lines.transaction_amount
,lines.product_quantity, lines.product_price
,lines.product_date, lines.product, lines.category
     ,cb.dte as payment_date, cb.text as payment_text
,cb.amount as payment_amount
     ,c.country, c.state, c.city, c.industry
FROM transactions t, orders o, cashbook cb, customer c
,(
     SELECT ol.order_id, ol.amount as order_amount
         ,tl.transaction_id, tl.amount as transaction_amount
         ,stock.product_quantity, stock.product_price
,stock.product_date, stock.category, stock.product
     FROM ordersline ol, transactionsline tl
     ,(
```

```
        SELECT sm.stockmovement_id, sm.qty as
product_quantity
,sm.price as product_price, sm.dte as product_date
        ,st.text as product, ca.text as category
      FROM stockmovement sm JOIN stock st
ON(st.stock_id=sm.stock_id)
           JOIN category ca
ON(ca.category_id=st.category_id)
    ) stock
    WHERE ol.stockmovement_id = stock.stockmovement_id
    AND tl.stockmovement_id = stock.stockmovement_id
) lines
WHERE t.type='S'
AND t.transaction_id = lines.transaction_id
AND o.type='S'
AND o.order_id = lines.order_id
AND cb.transaction_id = lines.transaction_id
AND c.customer_id = t.customer_id;
```

A sample of the output for the nasty-complicated join query listed above is shown in Figure 13.1.

Figure 13.1
Dumping into files using SQL.

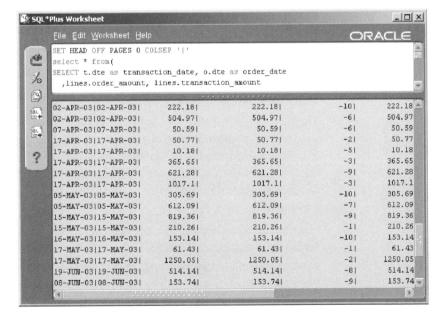

To remove the padding we could do something as shown in the following script snippet, sample output of which is shown in Figure 13.2.

```
SELECT
t.dte||'|'||o.dte||'|'||lines.order_amount||'|'||lines.transa
ction_amount||'|'||lines.product_quantity||'|'||lines.product
_price||'|'||lines.product_date||'|'||lines.product||'|'||lin
es.category||'|'||cb.dte||'|'||cb.text||'|'||cb.amount||'|'||
c.country||'|'||c.state||'|'||c.city||'|'||c.industry
```

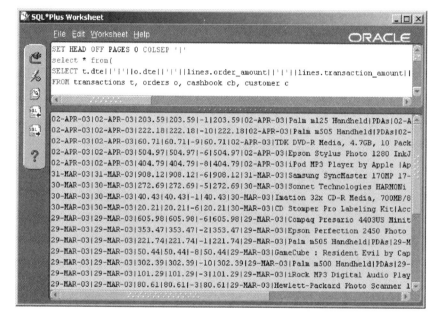

The query above is one of the queries used to pull transactional data from a custom-built OLTP database into a data warehouse database. This query is only the first stage of pulling data from OLTP database to data warehouse. Note the complexity of this query for performing the most basic functionality.

Note: Data can be copied from any accessible source database, including databases across networks using database links and even non-Oracle databases using technologies such as gateways.

Exports

Exports can be created using either the older EXP (export) utility or the updated data pump export utility (EXPDP). Data pump exports are faster, allowing for parallel execution, jobs that can be restarted, metadata filtering, and version control, among other improvements.

An EXP or export file contains specified objects from an entire database to a single schema (user) or even individual objects, such as specific tables. Exports contain both data and metadata tables, and their contents can be created in a target data warehouse using the IMP (import) utility very easily. Generally, the most efficient exports are executed as direct and in parallel. The DIRECT option allows appending to the end of files.

> **Note:** The DIRECT option creates an export file that, when reimported, can be imported as direct path loads. It is not about creation of the export file, but how rows are generated when importing again with the import utility.

Appending requires consistent versioning of rows across tables, taking all referential integrity into account. In other words, versioning implies a data snapshot, and referential integrity implies that all primary and foreign key values match for the snapshot to be valid. If either of these checks fails for any row, in any table, then the appending will fail and a direct import will not occur, requiring performance of all necessary checks to ensure versioning consistency and referential integrity between both existing and imported rows, in all tables.

Data pump exports (EXPDP) and imports (IMPDP) are much more sophisticated versions than their older import (IMP) and export (EXP) utility counterparts. Data pump technology allows for better performance and much more flexibility.

External Tables

External tables allow table data to be stored externally to an Oracle database, in the underlying operating system, in various formats. The syntax for external table creation is shown in Figure 13.3.

External tables need the creation of a directory object first, since the database needs to know where first to place, and subsequently to find, the data. So let's begin by creating a directory object for the OLTP source database:

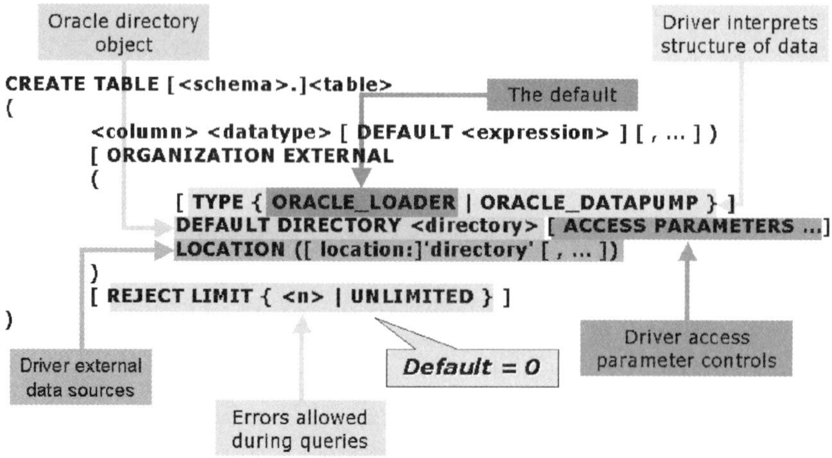

Figure 13.3
External table
CREATE TABLE
syntax.

```
Oracle directory                                    Driver interprets
    object                                          structure of data

CREATE TABLE [ <schema>.]<table>
(                                        The default
    <column> <datatype> [ DEFAULT <expression> ] [ , ... ] )
    [ ORGANIZATION EXTERNAL
    (
            [ TYPE { ORACLE_LOADER | ORACLE_DATAPUMP } ]
            DEFAULT DIRECTORY <directory> [ ACCESS PARAMETERS ...]
            LOCATION ([ location:]'directory' [ , ... ])
    )
    [ REJECT LIMIT { <n> | UNLIMITED } ]
)

  Driver external                    Default = 0       Driver access
  data sources                                       parameter controls

         Errors allowed
         during queries
```

```
CREATE OR REPLACE DIRECTORY data AS 'c:\temp\data';
```

The CREATE DIRECTORY statement above creates metadata for the directory, not the actual directory in the operating system. Make sure the directory structure is physically created on the database server machine.

Note: The CREATE DIRECTORY statement requires the CREATE ANY DIRECTORY system privilege.

Now we create a basic external table using the same query as the sub-query that was used in Figure 13.1:

```
CREATE TABLE salesext
ORGANIZATION EXTERNAL
(
    TYPE ORACLE_DATAPUMP DEFAULT DIRECTORY data
ACCESS PARAMETERS (NOLOGFILE)
    LOCATION ('salesext1.txt','salesext2.txt'
,'salesext3.txt','salesext4.txt')
)
PARALLEL 4 REJECT LIMIT UNLIMITED AS <subquery>;
```

Since four files are created, the statement above can be executed in parallel.

An empty external table can also be created using the appropriate CREATE TABLE statement, including column definitions. An INSERT . . . SELECT statement can be used to load the data into the external table. However, TYPE ORACLE_DATAPUMP, specifying the data pump driver, must be used to dynamically create or load the table using CREATE TABLE . . . SELECT or INSERT INTO . . . SELECT. The only way to load data into an external table using the ORACLE_LOADER driver is to load the rows into the text file itself—it cannot be created from within Oracle Database using Oracle SQL statements.

Table metadata must also be retrieved:

```
SET LONG 2000
SELECT DBMS_METADATA.GET_DDL(object_type=>'TABLE'
,name=>'SALESEXT',schema=>'ACCOUNTS') FROM DUAL;
```

Note: The GET_DDL procedure appears to have problems in 10.1.0.2.0.

Other Extraction Options

Other possible extraction options are redo and archive logs using log mining utilities, or even copies of physical datafiles and tablespaces using transportable tablespaces.

13.3 Transportation Methods

Transportation is the process of moving data from source (OLTP) database to target (data warehouse) database. Moving flat files or operating system–based text files is completely trivial and does not warrant explicit explanation in this book. Other methods of transportation could conceivably include copying and swapping of partitions, replication, standby databases, and even basic recovery using Recovery Manager (RMAN). However, these other transportation methods are entire topics in and of themselves, and not necessarily related as being methods of performance tuning, unless they are candidate options for implementation in their native forms. In other words, implementing replication should be primarily for the purpose of distributing data across widely spread geographical regions. Use of replicated databases could serve as a partial solution to data warehouse transportation, but not as the sole extraction, transportation, and loading method for a data warehouse.

13.3.1 Database Links and SQL

A database link is a physical connection established between two databases; it can be created from source or target databases, pointing at the other. Essentially, using a database link is really a combination of extraction and transportation processing. The following statement creates a database link in the data warehouse target database, linking into the OLTP source database:

```
CREATE DATABASE LINK oltp CONNECT TO accounts
IDENTIFIED BY accounts USING 'OLTP';
```

The statement above uses an Oracle Networking TNS (Transparent Network Substrate) network name. This requires an entry in the TNSNAMES.ORA file on the data warehouse database server machine.

Note: The CREATE DATABASE LINK statement requires the CREATE DATABASE LINK system privilege.

Data can be accessed directly from source to target database through the database link, as shown in the script below (the same example as in Figure 13.1), now including appropriate references to the database link:

```
SELECT t.dte as transaction_date, o.dte as order_date
    ,lines.order_amount, lines.transaction_amount
,lines.product_quantity, lines.product_price
,lines.product_date, lines.product, lines.category
    ,cb.dte as payment_date, cb.text as payment_text
,cb.amount as payment_amount
    ,c.country, c.state, c.city, c.industry
FROM transactions@oltp t, orders@oltp o
,cashbook@oltp cb, customer@oltp c
,(
    SELECT ol.order_id, ol.amount as order_amount
        ,tl.transaction_id, tl.amount as transaction_amount
        ,stock.product_quantity, stock.product_price
,stock.product_date, stock.category, stock.product
    FROM ordersline@oltp ol, transactionsline@oltp tl
```

```
    ,(
        SELECT sm.stockmovement_id, sm.qty as
product_quantity
,sm.price as product_price, sm.dte as product_date
            ,st.text as product, ca.text as category
        FROM stockmovement@oltp sm JOIN stock@oltp st
ON(st.stock_id=sm.stock_id)
                JOIN category@oltp ca
ON(ca.category_id=st.category_id)
    ) stock
    WHERE ol.stockmovement_id = stock.stockmovement_id
    AND tl.stockmovement_id = stock.stockmovement_id
) lines
WHERE t.type='S'
AND t.transaction_id = lines.transaction_id
AND o.type='S'
AND o.order_id = lines.order_id
AND cb.transaction_id = lines.transaction_id
AND c.customer_id = t.customer_id;
```

Note: The example above will not work in SQL*Plus as the STOCK table contains LOBs (large objects,) but the example is demonstrative of the complexities for transformation from normalized schema to star schema.

13.3.2   Transportable Tablespaces

Transportable tablespaces are a highly effective, cross-platform, operating system-independent method of transportation from source to target database. A transportable tablespace allows the placement of an entire set of datafiles belonging to a tablespace into the same tablespace name in a data warehouse. Any reprocessing can be performed on source or target databases or even an intermediary database. Transportable tablespaces can even be used to plug data into a data warehouse simply by copying and defining, much like export and import utility processing, containing both data and metadata. Properly constructed and formatted data can then be directly appended from transported tablespace inside the target database data warehouse tables, using efficient SQL processing local to the data warehouse database. Obviously, copying and swapping partitions can play a role when using transportable tablespaces, but partition exchanges are more of a loading method as opposed to a transportation method. Figure 13.4 shows the basics of using transportable tablespaces where both datafiles are copied as well as metadata structures. Metadata is copied using the export and import utilities.

Figure 13.4
How transportable tablespaces work.

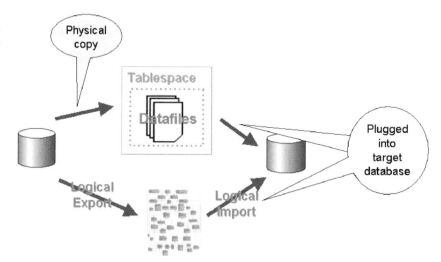

Other than data warehouse transportation performance enhancement transportable tablespaces have numerous uses, as show in Figure 13.5.

Figure 13.5
Other uses of transportable tablespaces.

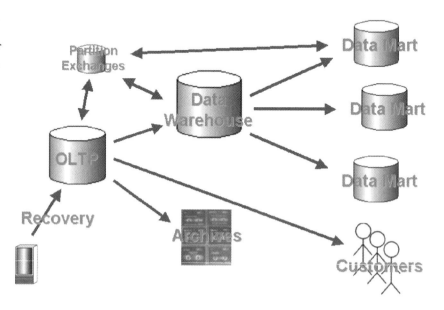

Transportable Tablespace Limitations

The downside of transportable tablespace use is a list of limitations:

- At least Oracle Database 8*i* is required

- Operating system independence can be achieved only at Oracle Database 10*g*

- Character sets have to be identical

- The Oracle Database version is not backward-compatible, but is forwards-compatible. In other words, 8*i* to 9*i* is okay, but 10*g* to 9*i* is not.

- A transportable tablespace cannot exist in a target database, so the transportable tablespace is copied across in its entirety and, thus, there is no incremental capability. Incremental capabilities can often save a lot of processing time in any type of scenario if changes are relatively minimal when updates occur.

- Materialized views require manual refresh for any transportable tablespaces to be directly accessed in a data warehouse, when no reprocessing of transported and plugged in tablespace data is performed.

Self-Containment

Tablespace sets are a requirement where transported tablespaces must be self-contained with respect to indexing, constraints, LOBs, and partitions. What we should do at this stage is create a transportable tablespace in our source database, copy it to the target database, and plug it into the target database. Once again, using a version of the query shown in Figure 13.1, the following two scripts create copies of all transaction data, both sales and purchases, in a new tablespace inside the OLTP source database:

```
DROP TABLESPACE trans INCLUDING CONTENTS;
CREATE TABLESPACE trans DATAFILE
'e:\oracle\product\10.1.0\oltp\trans01.dbf'
{SIZE 1M | REUSE} AUTOEXTEND ON
EXTENT MANAGEMENT LOCAL
SEGMENT SPACE MANAGEMENT AUTO
NOLOGGING;
```

Note: The CREATE TABLESPACE and DROP TABLESPACE statements require CREATE TABLESPACE and DROP TABLESPACE system privileges, respectively. Also, recreating the tablespace without deleting the datafile from the operating system requires replacing the SIZE option with the REUSE option.

```
CREATE TABLE trans TABLESPACE trans NOLOGGING AS
SELECT t.dte as transaction_date, o.dte as order_date
,lines.order_amount, lines.transaction_amount
    ,lines.product_quantity, lines.product_price
    ,lines.product_date, lines.product, lines.category
    ,cb.dte as payment_date, cb.text as payment_text
    ,cb.amount as payment_amount
    ,c.country, c.state, c.city, c.industry
FROM transactions t, orders o, cashbook cb, customer c
,(
    SELECT ol.order_id, ol.amount as order_amount
        ,tl.transaction_id, tl.amount as transaction_amount
        ,stock.product_quantity, stock.product_price
        ,stock.product_date, stock.category, stock.product
    FROM ordersline ol, transactionsline tl
    ,(
        SELECT sm.stockmovement_id, sm.qty as
product_quantity
            ,sm.price as product_price, sm.dte as
product_date
            ,st.text as product, ca.text as category
        FROM stockmovement sm JOIN stock st
        ON(st.stock_id=sm.stock_id)
            JOIN category ca
ON(ca.category_id=st.category_id)
    ) stock
    WHERE ol.stockmovement_id = stock.stockmovement_id
    AND tl.stockmovement_id = stock.stockmovement_id
) lines
WHERE t.dte > '31-DEC-03'
AND t.transaction_id = lines.transaction_id
AND o.order_id = lines.order_id
AND cb.transaction_id = lines.transaction_id
AND c.customer_id = t.customer_id;
```

The above query retrieves all rows in the year 2004 because of the date filter **t.dte > '31-DEC-03'**.

A self-contained tablespace implies that all objects in a transportable tablespace are not related to any objects outside of that transportable tablespace. Generally, these relationships imply referential integrity relationships between primary and foreign keys. There are no primary or foreign keys specified for the query above, so in this case it is not an issue. However, checks can be made against metadata views such as USER_TABLES and USER_INDEXES, both of which contain a TABLESPACE_NAME column.

Further checking can be performed using specialized procedures as follows, executing the following procedure as the SYS user on the source database:

```
EXEC DBMS_TTS.TRANSPORT_SET_CHECK('TRANS',TRUE);
```

Any violations of transportable tablespace self-containment can be examined using the following query, still logged in as the SYS user:

```
SELECT * FROM transport_set_violations;
```

Transporting a Tablespace

The following steps are involved in transporting a tablespace from source to target database:

- Change the source tablespace to read-only to ensure no changes can be made:

```
ALTER TABLESPACE trans READ ONLY;
```

Note: The ALTER TABLESPACE statement requires the ALTER TABLESPACE system privilege.

- The next step is to export tablespace metadata using the export utility:

```
EXP TRANSPORT_TABLESPACE=Y TABLESPACES=(trans)
TTS_FULL_CHECK=Y GRANTS=N CONSTRAINTS=N FILE=C:\TMP\TT.EXP
LOG=C:\TMP\TT.LOG
```

- When prompted for the username, enter:

```
SYS/<password>@<TNSName> AS SYSDBA
```

A successful export will look like that shown in Figure 13.6.

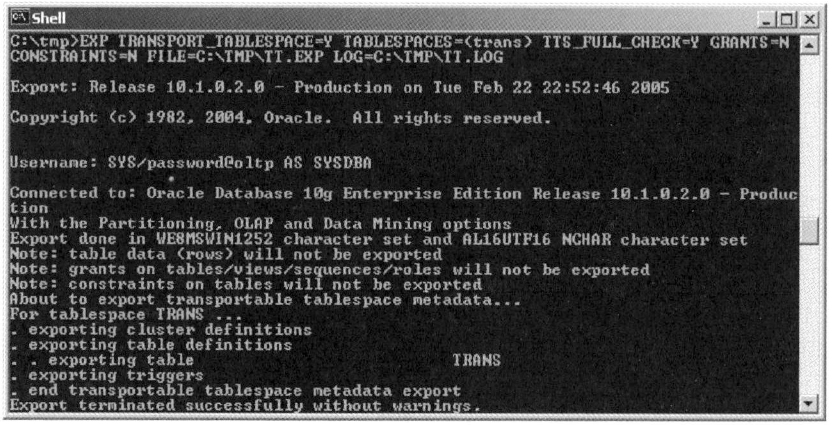

Figure 13.6
*Exporting
tablespace
metadata.*

- The next step is to copy the export file created above and the datafiles in the transportable tablespace to the target database server. Make sure datafiles are in the correct path.

Following these steps, in the loading step we can push the transportable tablespace into the target database.

13.4   Loading and Transformation

Essentially, loading data into a data warehouse is very likely to be a two-step process: loading followed by transformation processing. Loading simply plugs data into a data warehouse. Transformation changes loaded-data into a form that the data warehouse can understand, such as from a normalized 3rd normal form schema into dimensional-fact star schema for a data warehouse.

Transformation processing can be implemented both in extraction processing on a source database and after loading of a target database. Generally, transformation processing executed on a source OLTP database will hurt transactional database performance unacceptably, because concurrency requirements are completely contradictory to mass throughput processing required by transformations. Additionally, if transformation processing can hurt data warehouse performance so as to hinder usage, then a staging database can always be used to minimize impact to both source and target databases.

13.4.1   Basic Loading Procedures

Basic loading procedures involve the use of the SQL*Loader utilities or what could be called plug-ins, such as partitions, transportable tablespace, or external tables.

SQL*Loader

Going through all the details of how SQL*Loader is implemented and executed is a book in itself. This section will include only a brief summary of SQL*Loader utility detail.

SQL*Loader Performance Characteristics

The most important factor for SQL*Loader performance is that it can perform magnificently in direct path and parallel mode, and also perform equably using external tables. Direct path loads using SQL*Loader allow appending to tables. Appending implies that existing blocks are not considered when data is added, and only new blocks are used. Some situations will cause single tables, and even entire SQL*Loader executions, to execute using a conventional path load. For example, not specifying DIRECT=Y PARALLEL=Y causes conventional path loading. Additionally, any kind of SQL transformation functionality placed into SQL*Loader control files, such as TO_CHAR conversion functions, will cause direct path loading to switch to conventional path loading.

Obviously, direct path loads appending new blocks is not necessarily the best option when rows are deleted from data warehouse tables, as existing blocks will never have rows slotted into them. Your data warehouse could grow rapidly and uncontrollably in this situation.

There is one more point to be made. Direct path loading is not always possible, but is generally astronomically faster than conventional path loading, by avoiding the SQL engine. Conventional path loading is nearly always much faster than using straightforward SQL statements such as INSERT or MERGE DML statements, or even CREATE TABLE . . . SELECT DDL statements to transform and load data. Yes, I have come across companies generating SQL INSERT statements to load a database, even data warehouses. And I have even seen these INSERT statements generated using the most impractical tools for this purpose, such as Java.

Note: SQL*Loader is FAST!!! All you have to do is use it. SQL*Loader can potentially be thousands of times faster than SQL code processing for loading and even transforming data into a target data warehouse database.

SQL*Loader is not a limited utility. You can even load into a table structure, namely more than one table at once, taking all constraints into account.

Note: Do not be afraid of SQL*Loader. Its syntax and use is very comprehensive and very easy to learn.

Using SQL*Loader with external tables is as fast as direct loads. External table loads also use database parallelism and have no space issues. Additionally, using external tables automatically maintains both global and local partition indexes. The downside is that result loaded tables are external tables.

SQL*Loader Architecture

The basic architecture of the SQL*Loader utility is as shown in Figure 13.7. SQL*Loader pulls in data from input datafiles. Input data has structure applied to it using definitions found in a syntax control file. The combination of input data and definitional data defines data and structure for pushing through SQL*Loader into one or more tables in a database. In certain modes of operation, SQL*Loader can be used to create rows in tables and to maintain indexes for those new row entries, as well. In order to track the progress and success of processing, three other files can be produced. A log file describes the process of SQL*Loader loading data, including descriptions on any errors encountered. A discards file includes any rows not loaded as a result of SQL*Loader-specified filtering. A bad file includes rows that should have been loaded, but were thrown out as a result of data or structural errors.

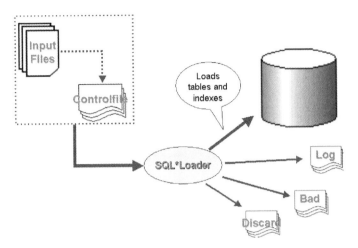

Figure 13.7
SQL*Loader
architecture.

Input Datafiles

The input datafiles provide the data to be loaded using SQL*Loader. Input datafile contents can be fixed length records, variable length records or even a single stream or string. A stream is a single string.

Input data can consist of a single datafile specified in the control file:

```
LOAD DATA INFILE 'file1.dat' INTO TABLE table1
TRUNCATE FIELDS TERMINATED BY "" TRAILING NULLCOLS

(
FIELD1 INTEGER EXTERNAL,
FIELD2 INTEGER EXTERNAL,
. . .
FIELDn …
)
```

Note: SQL*Loader control file examples in this chapter are pseudo-coded. They will not necessarily function as they appear scripted in this chapter.

or multiple datafiles specified in the control file, where each input file can specify bad and discard files:

```
LOAD DATA
INFILE 'file1.dat' BADFILE 'bad1.dat' DISCARDFILE
'discard1.dat'
```

```
INFILE 'file2.dat' DISCARDMAX n | DISCARDS n
INFILE 'file3.dat'
INTO TABLE table1
TRUNCATE FIELDS TERMINATED BY "" TRAILING NULLCOLS
(
FIELD1 INTEGER EXTERNAL,
FIELD2 INTEGER EXTERNAL,
. . .
FIELDn . . .
)
```

Input data can even be embedded into the control file:

```
LOAD DATA INFILE * INTO TABLE table1 TRUNCATE
FIELDS TERMINATED BY "" TRAILING NULLCOLS
BEGINDATA
. . .
```

The SQL*Loader Control File

The SQL*Loader control file contains a mapping between input data and the table structures into which data is to be loaded. The control file can be simple or highly complex, depending on requirements, and can contain details as described in the following sections.

Row Loading Options

Rows can be loaded as shown in the following syntax snippet:

```
LOAD DATA INFILE . . .
INTO TABLE table1 { INSERT | REPLACE | TRUNCATE | APPEND }
FIELDS TERMINATED BY "" TRAILING NULLCOLS
(
FIELD1 INTEGER EXTERNAL,
FIELD2 INTEGER EXTERNAL,
. . .
FIELDn . . .
)
```

- INSERT is the default and requires an empty target table.
- REPLACE removes and replaces all rows.

- TRUNCATE truncates all rows first and will conflict with constraints. Truncation destroys all rows without the option to rollback.

- APPEND adds to the end of files without removing existing data.

Loading Multiple Tables

Figure 13.8 clearly shows control file syntax for loading data into more than one table at once, using a single input datafile.

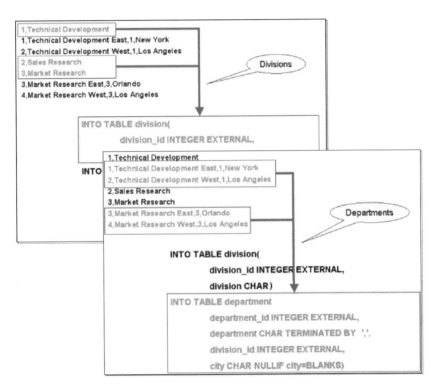

Figure 13.8
Loading more than one table.

Field Definitions

Field definitions in the control file can be defined using positioning or specific datatypes and size. The first example below splits data into separate columns using positions on each line, assuming fixed-length records of course:

```
LOAD DATA
INTO TABLE table1 TRUNCATE
(
    NAME    POSITION(001:032) CHAR(32)
```

```
TERMINATED BY WHITESPACE,
ADDRESSPOSITION(033:160) CHAR(128)
TERMINATED BY WHITESPACE,
STATE   POSITION(161:162) CHAR(2)
TERMINATED BY WHITESPACE,
BALANCEPOSITION(163:173) INTEGER EXTERNAL
)
```

This next example specifies specific values into specific places within each row, defined as having specific datatypes and lengths, but separating fields in each row by using a comma as determined by the FIELDS TERMINATED BY clause:

```
LOAD DATA
INTO TABLE table1 TRUNCATE FIELDS TERMINATED BY "," TRAILING
NULLCOLS
(
 col1 CHAR(10)
,col2 CHAR(12)
,col3 CHAR(1)
)
```

Delimiting of column values is also determined by elements in the FIELDS clause and otherwise, within the control file. The following example contains column enclosure characters regardless of length of value:

```
LOAD DATA INFILE . . . INTO TABLE table1 TRUNCATE
FIELDS
{
       ENCLOSED [ BY 'string' [ AND 'string' ] ]
     | TERMINATED BY [ WHITESPACE | 'string' | EOF ]
         [ ENCLOSED [ BY 'string' [ AND 'string' ] ] ]
} TRAILING NULLCOLS
(
FIELD1 INTEGER EXTERNAL,
FIELD2 INTEGER EXTERNAL,
. . .
FIELDn . . .
)
```

The next example also terminates columns regardless of length, or white space characters at the end of a column value:

```
LOAD DATA INFILE . . . INTO TABLE table1 TRUNCATE
FIELDS
{
      ENCLOSED [ BY 'string' [ AND 'string' ] ]
    | TERMINATED BY [ WHITESPACE | 'string' | EOF ]
        [ ENCLOSED [ BY 'string' [ AND 'string' ] ] ]
} TRAILING NULLCOLS
(
FIELD1 INTEGER EXTERNAL,
FIELD2 INTEGER EXTERNAL,
. . .
FIELDn . . .
)
```

The next example specifies both elements specified in the two previous examples:

```
LOAD DATA INFILE . . . INTO TABLE table1 TRUNCATE
FIELDS
{
      ENCLOSED [ BY 'string' [ AND 'string' ] ]
    | TERMINATED BY [ WHITESPACE | 'string' | EOF ]
        [ ENCLOSED [ BY 'string' [ AND 'string' ] ] ]
} TRAILING NULLCOLS
(
FIELD1 INTEGER EXTERNAL,
FIELD2 INTEGER EXTERNAL,
. . .
FIELDn . . .
)
```

This example prevents trimming of white space characters:

```
LOAD DATA INFILE . . . INTO TABLE table1 TRUNCATE FIELDS { . .
. }
TRAILING NULLCOLS PRESERVE BLANKS
```

```
(
FIELD1 INTEGER EXTERNAL,
FIELD2 INTEGER EXTERNAL,
. . .
FIELDn . . .
)
```

This example allows override of general syntax with specific column set-tings:

```
LOAD DATA INFILE . . . INTO TABLE table1 TRUNCATE
FIELDS { . . . } TRAILING NULLCOLS
(
        colA CHAR(10) TERMINATED BY ','
        ,colB CHAR(12) ENCLOSED BY '"' AND '"'
    ,colC CHAR(1)

)
```

And this is an example of an optional override:

```
LOAD DATA INFILE . . . INTO TABLE table1 TRUNCATE
FIELDS { . . . } TRAILING NULLCOLS
(
        colA CHAR(10) TERMINATED BY ','
        ,colB CHAR(12) OPTIONALLY ENCLOSED BY '"' AND '"'
    ,colC CHAR(1)

)
```

Dealing with NULL Values

In the following example, columns containing missing values are set to NULL:

```
LOAD DATA INFILE . . . INTO TABLE table1 TRUNCATE
FIELDS TERMINATED BY "" TRAILING NULLCOLS
(
FIELD1 INTEGER EXTERNAL,
FIELD2 INTEGER EXTERNAL,
. . .
```

```
FIELDn . . .
)
```

Load Filters

A load filter or WHEN clause can be used to discard rows from the loading process, potentially placing discarded rows in the discard file, not loading them into target database tables. In the first example below, only rows with specified values are loaded; others are ignored and placed into discards:

```
LOAD DATA INFILE . . . INTO TABLE table1 TRUNCATE
FIELDS TERMINATED BY "" TRAILING NULLCOLS
WHEN (2) = 'test'
(
FIELD1 INTEGER EXTERNAL,
FIELD2 INTEGER EXTERNAL,
. . .
FIELDn . . .
)
```

Note: The clause WHEN(2) examines the value in each record containing the string 'test' in the second column position of the datafile to be loaded.

Comparisons and conjunctions are allowed as for any standard WHERE clause filtering:

```
LOAD DATA INFILE . . . INTO TABLE table1 TRUNCATE
FIELDS TERMINATED BY "" TRAILING NULLCOLS
WHEN (colA = 'abc') AND (colB > 0)
(
FIELD1 INTEGER EXTERNAL,
FIELD2 INTEGER EXTERNAL,
. . .
FIELDn . . .
)
```

Unwanted Columns

Unwanted columns can be removed from the loading process, still loading other column values in the same row, using the FILLER clause:

```
LOAD DATA INFILE . . .
INTO TABLE table1(
    col1 CHAR(10),
    col2 FILLER CHAR(12),
    col3 CHAR(1) TERMINATED BY WHITESPACE)

TRUNCATE FIELDS TERMINATED BY "" TRAILING NULLCOLS
```

Control File Datatypes

SQL*Loader has a limited datatype set with specific commands for handling different situations for each of the various datatypes, namely strings, dates, and numbers.

- **Strings**. CHAR[(n)] and VARCHAR[(n)].
    - DEFAULTIF col1=BLANKS sets to spaces or NULL.
    - NULLIF col1=BLANKS replace with NULL.
- **Dates**. DATE, TIME, TIMESTAMP, and INTERVALs.
- **Numbers**. Numbers are externally or internally defined.
    - EXTERNAL { INTEGER | FLOAT | DECIMAL } is defined by the number loaded.
    - DEFAULTIF col1=BLANKS sets to 0.
    - NULLIF col1=BLANKS replace with NULL.
    - Non-EXTERNAL. INTEGER(n), SMALLINT, FLOAT, DOUBLE, BYTEINT, and DECIMAL(p,s).

Note: The clause BLANKS can be replaced with a literal string or number value.

Embedded SQL Statements

Including SQL statements in the control file for line-by-line application will disable direct (appending) loads, converting even individual table loads to conventional path loads, and, thus, hurting loading performance. You will not get an error, only a message in SQL*Loader output indicating a switch from direct path to conventional path load. The following example contains a column reference for COL1, a literal SQL string enclosed in double quotes for COL1 and COL2, and finally embedded functionality and a custom written function for COL2 and the TEMPERATURE columns:

```
LOAD DATA INFILE 'input.txt' INTO TABLE table1 TRUNCATE
FIELDS TERMINATED BY "," TRAILING NULLCOLS
(
 col1 CHAR(10)"UPPER(:col1)"
,col2 CHAR(12)"UPPER(INITCAP(SUBSTR(:col2,4,20)))"
,temperature FLOAT"FToC(temperature)"
)
```

SQL use is limited in SQL*Loader and has to be functionally embedded for columns on each line.

Adding Data Not in Input Datafiles

External data can be added in the following ways:

- `<column> CONSTANT <n>`
- `<column> EXPRESSION "SQL"`
- `<column> RECNUM`
- `<column> SYSDATE`
- `<column> SEQUENCE ( { COUNT | MAX | <n> } [ ,<increment> ] )`

Executing SQL*Loader

Figure 13.9 shows the syntax for the SQL*Loader utility (sqlldr.exe).

The Parameter File

SQL*Loader can utilize a parameter file to contain repeated settings, repeated for multiple loading executions of the SQL*Loader utility, as in the following example where always the same user is connected, two discards are allowed by filtering without aborting and rolling back the load, and one million errors (the maximum) are allowed without load abort. Also, direct and parallel options are specified always as a default. Conventional path loading will be reverted to automatical if direct path loading is not possible, for a specific execution of SQL*Loader, or the loading of a specific table within SQL*Loader:

```
USERID       = <username>/<password>
DISCARDMAX   = 2
ERRORS       = 1000000
PARALLEL     = TRUE
DIRECT       = TRUE
```

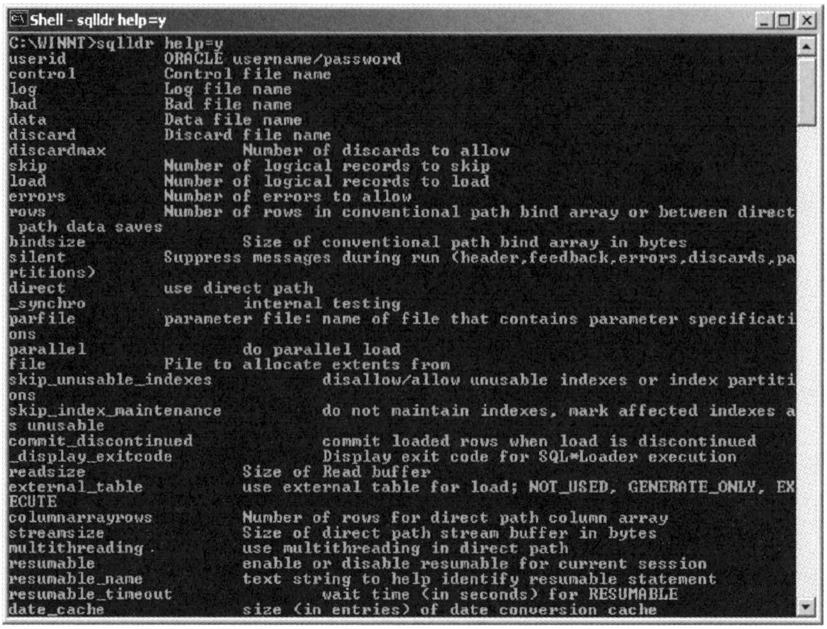

Figure 13.9
SQL*Loader
syntax.

That is really all I can tell you about SQL*Loader without going into tremendous detail.

Plug-Ins

Partitions

Partitions can be operated on specifically, such as moving, adding or exchanging of individual partitions. Therefore, if a data warehouse is to receive new data on a monthly basis, and data warehouse facts are partitioned by month, simply adding a new partition to existing fact tables can be used to perform load processing. Pseudo-syntax is as shown below, applying not only to partitions but subpartitions as well, where various restrictions apply under certain circumstances.

```
ALTER TABLE [<schema>.]<table>
{ MOVE|ADD|DROP|RENAME|TRUNCATE|SPLIT|MERGE|EXCHANGE }
{<partition> | <subpartition> };
```

The details of how these specific partition statements function is essentially syntactical in nature and, thus, not really performance tuning. The point is this:

exchanging or adding partitions, or otherwise, can present enormous performance improvements in data warehouse load processing simply because only loaded data is affected.

Note: Be sure to manage materialized view refresh and indexing, particularly bitmap indexing, when dealing with partition alteration statements.

Transportable Tablespaces

Let's import and instantiate the TRANS transportable tablespace created from the source database, earlier in this chapter. First, clear and recreate the tablespace in the target database:

```
DROP TABLESPACE trans INCLUDING CONTENTS;
```

Note: The DROP TABLESPACE statement requires the DROP TABLESPACE system privilege.

If the DROP TABLESPACE statement above is executed after copying datafiles from the source database, you will possibly get an error describing incompatibility between tablespace and datafile header. If you cannot drop the tablespace use the OFFLINE FOR DROP option (OFFLINE DROP before 10*g*) of the ALTER DATABASE statement as follows:

```
ALTER DATABASE DATAFILE '<datafile>' OFFLINE FOR DROP;
```

The statement above allows removal of the tablespace from metadata without requiring a match to the datafile header in the control file.

Plugging in a transportable tablespace has a number of steps:

- Import the metadata into the target data warehouse database using the import utility and the export metadatafile for the tablespace, copied from the source database:

```
IMP TRANSPORT_TABLESPACE=Y
DATAFILES='e:\oracle\product\10.1.0\oradata\dws\trans01.dbf'
TABLESPACES=(trans) FILE=C:\TMP\TT.EXP
TTS_OWNERS=(accounts) FROMUSER=accounts TOUSER=dws
```

When prompted for the username enter:

```
SYS/<password>@<TNSName> AS SYSDBA
```

Note: The database username (TOUSER) must exist in the target database.

A successful import will look something like that shown in Figure 13.10.

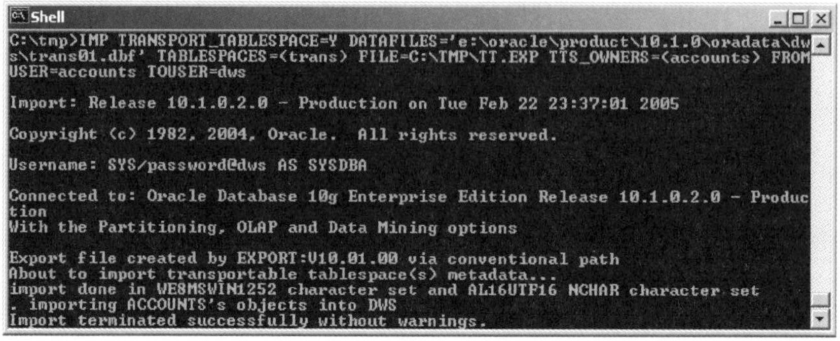

Figure 13.10
*Importing
tablespace
metadata.*

External Tables

In a previous section of this chapter, we extracted transactions using a large join from active OLTP database tables into an external table on the OLTP database. Now we can copy the external table files to the target database, build the external table metadata definition in the data warehouse, and attempt to import data into the external table in the data warehouse database. Create the directory object on the target data warehouse database:

```
CREATE OR REPLACE DIRECTORY data AS 'c:\temp\data';
```

The CREATE DIRECTORY statement above creates metadata for the directory, not the actual directory in the operating system. Make sure the directory structure is physically created on the database server machine.

Note: The CREATE DIRECTORY statement requires the CREATE ANY DIRECTORY system privilege.

Now create the external table in the data warehouse:

```
CREATE TABLE trans_ext(
  TRANSACTION_DATE        DATE
 ,ORDER_DATE              DATE
 ,ORDER_AMOUNT            NUMBER(10,2)
 ,TRANSACTION_AMOUNT      NUMBER(10,2)
 ,PRODUCT_QUANTITY        NUMBER
 ,PRODUCT_PRICE           NUMBER(10,2)
 ,PRODUCT_DATE            DATE
 ,PRODUCT                 VARCHAR2(128)
 ,CATEGORY                VARCHAR2(32)
 ,PAYMENT_DATE            DATE
 ,PAYMENT_TEXT            VARCHAR2(32)
 ,PAYMENT_AMOUNT          NUMBER(10,2)
 ,COUNTRY                 VARCHAR2(32)
 ,STATE                   CHAR(2)
 ,CITY                    VARCHAR2(32)
 ,INDUSTRY                VARCHAR2(32))
ORGANIZATION external(
TYPE ORACLE_DATAPUMP
DEFAULT DIRECTORY data
ACCESS PARAMETERS(NOLOGFILE)
    LOCATION ('salesext1.txt','salesext2.txt'
,'salesext3.txt','salesext4.txt')
) PARALLEL 4 REJECT LIMIT UNLIMITED;
```

The statement above will link the external table datafiles copied from the OLTP database to the target data warehouse database, defined as being ORACLE_DATAPUMP. It is that easy!

The Import Utility

The import utility can obviously be used to import data from source to target database, from export files created on the source database and copied to the target server, or even just accessed from the target server. Data pump technology can be used to speed up import processing.

13.4.2 Transformation Processing

Transformation processing at this stage is essentially an SQL processing function in which data is massaged from directly imported or incomplete processed data. Thus, this is essentially an Oracle SQL operation and not really appropriate for this chapter or even this book [1]. Oracle SQL transformation processing includes use of the following types of SQL functionality:

- Single and multiple table INSERT statements
- The MERGE upsert statement
- Mass UPDATE statements
- DROP and CREATE TABLE . . . AS SELECT . . . statements
- Any kind of SQL code query processing required by the target database
- PL/SQL anonymous and stored procedures
- Object-relational TABLE datatype functionality

This chapter has covered some tuning aspects of the transferring of data between OLTP transactional and data warehouse databases. The next and final chapter of this book will cover data warehouse architecture as applicable to performance tuning. Topics to be included in the next chapter include memory usage, I/O and capacity planning, and finally a brief look at OLAP and data mining technologies.

13.5 Endnotes

1.   *Oracle SQL: Jumpstart with Examples* (ISBN: 1555583237)

14

Data Warehouse Architecture

This chapter examines general data warehouse architecture and will be divided between hardware resource usage, including memory buffers, block sizes, and I/O usage. I/O is very important in the data warehouse database. Capacity planning, which is so important to data warehousing, will also be covered. The chapter will be completed with brief information on OLAP and data mining technologies.

14.1   What Is a Data Warehouse?

A data warehouse is usually intended as a tool to allow analysis on huge amounts of historical data. Historical data is often not required by an active database, such as an OLTP transactional database, as archived information conflicts with current activity. However, analysis is well suited to being carried out in data warehouses on large quantities of historical data in order to make assumptions about the future of business activities.

14.1.1   What Is Data Warehouse Architecture?

The architecture of a data warehouse as determined by underlying I/O structure, and the hardware resources available, such as memory in the database server, can greatly affect the performance of that data warehouse. Parallel processing, partitioning, and even clustering can affect how a data warehouse performs. The down side is that the more complexity is included in data warehouse architecture, then the more complex the maintenance of that data warehouse can become.

The crux of data warehouse implementation and architecture is that a data warehouse is intended for use by end users, not by the techies who build the database. The primary purpose of a data warehouse is provision of decision support reporting, preferably as accurately as possible, but within acceptable performance constraints. Decision support implies many types of forecasting, prediction, planning assistance, and *what if* analysis–type functionality. These types of reporting can be accomplished using various bells and whistles, such as OLAP utilities, data mining, advanced SQL functionality, and many available third party tools and reporting engines.

14.2 Tuning Hardware Resources for Data Warehousing

Hardware resource tuning for a data warehouse is in reality a lot easier than tuning the same for an OLTP database. The problem with an OLTP database is that it needs to be intensely shareable. Sharing even small amounts of information between a large number of people is highly complex, simply due to the necessity of a database to continually manage all aspects of high concurrency.

Data warehouse hardware resource usage tuning is actually very simple—it's all about I/O. Data warehouses typically are very large and use a lot of disk space. Coupled with high amounts of disk space usage, and the obvious result of slow response times, a data warehouse needs to access large amounts of disk space at once, or add large chunks of new information at once. Data warehouses are said to need throughput. Throughput implies a lot of information being passed into and out of the data warehouse database. Consequently, large amounts of information are constantly read from and written to disk in large chunks.

The implications of all this are very simple. I/O tuning and storage structure is much more important than minor adjustments to memory configuration parameters and changing network buffer sizes. Let's start with the easy parts and end with the complex parts.

The most efficient large data warehouses are those that have clear separation between loading and query activities. Adding new data to large tables can cause conflict with query activity reading large amounts of data, sometimes even as new data is added. In short, it is best to allow queries to be operated most of the time. Loading activity should be restricted to low query usage times. The two activities do not mix.

The importance of materialized views to data warehouses is paramount. The only issues to be careful of are incessant refresh activity that kills performance to the point that they are useless, and, as with indexes, do not create too many materialized views. More materialized views leads to more updating. Also, materialized views are physical copies and, thus, can potentially occupy huge amounts of storage space—especially if too many are created.

14.2.1   **Tuning Memory Buffers**

Memory buffers are controlled by changing configuration parameters in the database parameter file. Find values in the parameter file online by issuing the following query:

```
SELECT name, value FROM v$parameter ORDER BY name;
```

Messing with memory resource usage parameters is always a risky business. Remember that repeatedly increasing the sizes of memory buffer parameters will not help performance in general unless your system has been tampered with, your system has grown drastically in a very short period of time, or the nature of applications and database access habits have drastically altered.

Note: Drastic database growth may cause default settings to become inadequate. How does one define drastic database growth? Going from 1GB up to 250GB in one year is drastic growth; 1GB to 10GB in five years is negligible growth. Serious performance problems on a database for anything under 25GB to 50GB, even on a Windows box, makes whatever else the machine and the database are doing more than a little bit suspect.

- **PGA_AGGREGATE_TARGET**. This parameter controls automatic PGA memory management as opposed to manual memory management, discouraged in the latest versions of Oracle Database. PGA memory is available to all server processes and contains buffers for operations, such as sorts, hash joins, and bitmap operations. Parallel execution relies on these types of operations as much as serial execution does.

- **LOG_BUFFER**. I absolutely do not recommend changing this parameter. The fault of slow log writing is more often than not due to a slow I/O subsystem. Less often, the cause of log buffer problems is because the log buffer has been tampered with. Tampering implies change without forethought, without planning, or as a stab in the dark at solving a problem. Changing the size of the log buffer will make no difference to I/O performance and could possibly cause other problems. The most effective solution to redo log issues is usually something like redo log file striping, no matter how simplistic, even to the point of placing sequentially accessed redo log files on separate physical disks; or, just get a faster set of disks for redo logs. Many data warehouses don't care all that much about the log buffer, as the NOLOGGING option is often widely utilized.

Note: Changing the size of the log buffer is not harmless. Guess work tampering can cause performance problems later on.

- **DB_CACHE_SIZE**. More cache space for recently used data does not help much if the data is not reused before being aged out. Due to the high quantities of data involved in data warehouse operations, it is extremely unlikely, and I mean completely pie-in-the-sky, that reuse will occur in any manner that is useful to take advantage of in order to improve performance. A data warehouse is I/O intensive, period! Set the database buffer cache to the minimum allowed by the Oracle Database version and the operating system when using a data warehouse database. This is true unless, of course, you start using the keep and recycle pools, but still try to keep it to the bare minimum.

Note: Parallel operations do not use the database buffer cache.

- **DB_KEEP_CACHE_SIZE**. The keep pool allows semi-freezing of blocks into memory, in that they are less likely to be aged out.
- **DB_RECYCLE_CACHE_SIZE**. The recycle pool is for objects best aged out of memory as soon as possible.

14.2.2   Tuning Block Sizes

The default block size for a database can be selected on database creation. Various parameters can be set to slightly alter the way that blocks are used. The block size cannot be changed after database creation, but new tablespaces can be created with block sizes other than the default block size (DB_BLOCK_SIZE), providing that each separate block size has its individual DB_nK_CACHE_SIZE parameter settings for all nondefault block sized tablespaces.

- **DB_BLOCK_SIZE**. This one cannot be changed after database creation. Generally, the larger a data warehouse will be and the more I/O expected, the larger this value should be set. The default

size is usually 8Kb; 32Kb is not recommended, and 64Kb is not supported, even if your operating system will allow it. OLTP databases are typically set to a block size of 8K. Increase the block size to 16K for data warehouses and read-only–type databases. Block sizes of 2K or 4K are not common even for OLTP databases, except in older versions of Oracle Database.

Note: Available block sizes may vary for different operating systems.

It is an option for a data warehouse to create database blocks as large as your operating system will allow. It is not necessarily wise or intelligent to do so, though. Data warehouses tend to utilize multiple-block reads. Minimizing disk I/O is one of the most important factors in data warehouse tuning, and the more data that can be read in a single I/O, the faster your warehouse will perform. In OLTP database, smaller block size means latches for block access (tables and indexes) are held for shorter times, increasing concurrency. For data warehouse–type workloads, larger block sizes may better suit the usage profile of data.

- **DB_BLOCK_CHECKING**. Block checking can cause a performance overhead, but can help prevent data block–level corruption. Data corruption is more common when like me, you have not spent enough money on disk storage media. Use of RAID arrays makes use of parameters such as this, unnecessary.

- **DB_FILE_MULTIBLOCK_READ_COUNT**. For a large data warehouse with high I/O read activity, set multiple block reads to as high as possible, so that whenever a read occurs, multiple contiguous blocks are read at once, rather than one block at a time. Since data warehouse fact tables are generally created over time, and data warehouse read access is often performed to strict time dimensions, it is highly likely that multiple contiguous blocks reads physically conform to most, if not all, reporting and updating requirements.

14.2.3 Tuning Transactions

Changing these values could help performance where parallel execution is allowed and encouraged to increase. Once again, as with memory parameters, results could be extremely unpredictable.

- **TRANSACTIONS**. Parallel execution of DML operations executes those processes in multiple parts, effectively increasing the number of transactions equally. Increasing this parameter might help performance by allowing more concurrent transactions per server process.

- **DML_LOCKS**. Parallel processing splits transactions into pieces, thus requiring not only more transactions but consequently the potential for a higher number of concurrent DML locks.

- **ENQUEUE_RESOURCES**. Enqueue resources partially determine locking behavior.

Note: It is unwise to tamper or experiment with any configuration parameters unless you are certain of consequences to all database operations.

14.2.4   Tuning Oracle Net Services

Oracle Database uses a custom written layer of network software to interface across a network, LAN or WAN, in order to allow communication between client and server software. This network layer is called Oracle Net Services, also known as SQL*Net, Net8, and various other names in the past.

Many times I have heard that the only way to tune SQL*Net is to change the Session Data Unit (SDU) buffer size. On the contrary, there are many ways in which Net Services configuration can be adjusted, improving performance under varying circumstances. However, most of these potential adjustments are relevant to high-concurrency OLTP databases and completely irrelevant to high throughput data warehouse databases.

Tuning Net Services at the Server: The Listener

The listener is a process residing on a database server or other machine, which quite literally *listens* for database connection requests. When a request is received the listener hands off or passes on the connection to a database server process. Following is a very simple listener configuration file. This file is called LISTENER.ORA by default and is placed in the $ORACLE_HOME/network/admin directory as shown:

```
LISTENER =
  (DESCRIPTION_LIST =
    (DESCRIPTION =
```

```
        (ADDRESS = (PROTOCOL = TCP) (HOST = <hostname>) (PORT =
1521))
    )
  )


SID_LIST_LISTENER =
  (SID_LIST =
    (SID_DESC =
      (GLOBAL_DBNAME = <SID>.<xyz.com>)
      (SID_NAME = <SID>)
      (ORACLE_HOME = /oracle/ora92)
    )
  )
```

What can be done to tune or at least improve the listener under certain circumstances?

- **Listener Queue Size**. Allows a larger number of listener requests to be serviced by allowing them to wait in a queue. This will help an OLTP database, but it is unlikely to help a data warehouse. Data warehouses require a minimal number of concurrent connections but large amounts of throughput.

- **Listener Logging and Tracing**. Logging is on by default and tracing is off by default. Minimizing on tracing and logging file appends will help performance for any database type. Add the following lines to the listener configuration file:

```
LOGGING_LISTENER = OFF
TRACE_LEVEL_LISTENER = OFF
```

- **Multiple Listeners and Load Balancing**. Randomized load balancing can be created between multiple listeners, pointing at the same database. This area is again a solution for a high-concurrency OLTP database, rather than low-concurrency data warehouses.

Tuning Net Services at the Client

What can be done to tune, or at least improve, the Net Services at client machines?

- **Dedicated Versus Shared Servers**. When a user connects to a database a server process is used to service the connection. The server process can either be a dedicated or a shared server process. For a dedicated server process, the process is started up and retained for the duration of the connection. A shared server process, on the other hand, is shared indirectly between different connections through dispatcher processes. Shared server processes and dispatchers comprise what used to be called Oracle MTS or Multi-Threaded Server configuration.

  Only OLTP databases with very large concurrency requirements need to make use of shared server configuration, and then rarely. Data warehouses must use dedicated server environments. Below is a TNSNAMES.ORA configuration for OLTP and DW (data warehouse) databases:

```
OLTP =
  (DESCRIPTION =
    (ADDRESS_LIST =
      (ADDRESS = (PROTOCOL = TCP) (HOST = <hostname>)
(PORT = 1521))
    )
    (CONNECT_DATA =
      (SID = <SID>)
      (ORACLE_HOME = /oracle/product/10.1.0)
      (SERVER = SHARED)
    )
  )


DW =
  (DESCRIPTION =
    (ADDRESS_LIST =
      (ADDRESS = (PROTOCOL = TCP) (HOST = <hostname>)
(PORT = 1521))
    )
    (CONNECT_DATA =
      (SID = <SID>)
      (ORACLE_HOME = /oracle/product/10.1.0)
      (SERVER = DEDICATED)
    )
  )
```

- **The Session Data Unit Buffer (SDU)**. SQL*Net uses a buffer to contain information ready for sending over the network. The buffer is flushed to the network and sent up on request or when it is full. The larger the buffer, the more information can be sent over the network at once. SDU buffer size can range from 512 bytes up to 32KB. The default setting is operating system–dependent. The following shows a TNSNAMES.ORA configuration file with its SDU buffer size altered. Sessions containing large transactions may benefit from a larger SDU buffer size.

```
<TNSname> =
  (DESCRIPTION =
    (ADDRESS_LIST =
      (ADDRESS = (PROTOCOL = TCP) (HOST = <hostname>)
(PORT = 1521))
    )
    (SDU=1024)
    (CONNECT_DATA = (SID = <SID>) (ORACLE_HOME = /oracle/
ora81)
    )
  )
```

14.2.5 Tuning I/O

What can be done to tune I/O usage for a data warehouse. Since data warehouse activity is largely I/O activity, then I/O has the most significant impact on performance. So what is the best fundamental strategy?

First of all, stripe it. Use RAID arrays if possible. When using RAID arrays, the bandwidth is more important than disk capacity. What is bandwidth? Bandwidth is a measure of how much data can be transferred between disk and memory at once. Obviously, one should use the most up-to-date hard drive technology. Another point, which is often missed, is that in a RAID array structure, a lot of small disks will give more bandwidth than a few large disks. Why? Simple: there are more disks and therefore more busses. That makes for more bandwidth. Remember data warehouses need throughput, and disk storage is cheap. Throughput is not a measure of database size, but of how much can be processed at any given time. How fast can I/O activity be performed? How fast can the disks be read? The more disks, the more bus connections, the higher the throughput.

Mirroring has a directly negative effect on performance, because writing data involves writing to disk more than once for the same operation. However, with a data warehouse that can become very, very large, restoration and recovery in the event of a failure may take an unacceptable amount of time. If your database is down for days because you have to recover terabytes of data, your by-the-hour users might be very irritated after only a few minutes and seek similar services elsewhere. This begs the question of the need for standby database technology to avoid losing business and perhaps even bankruptcy.

Note: Above all, always capacity plan when building a data warehouse and, if possible, test I/O configuration and architectural plans before implementing with more data than you have time to handle.

Before going into details, it is important to note a few points:

- Oracle Managed Files (OMF) and Automated Storage Management (ASM) are options to consider. OMF can make Oracle Database easier to manage on a physical level. However, OMF can hurt I/O performance a little due to overhead requirements.

- In theory, data warehouses create many more indexes than OLTP databases. It is an option to separate table and index spaces, if possible. Additionally, a similar approach applies to materialized views, where materialized views and their related indexes should be separated from tables, table indexes, and each other.

Note: With regards to separating table and index spaces for a data warehouse, this approach may be invalid because of potential complexity. What is more important for a data warehouse is knowing how much I/O activity there is and how much throughput is needed overall from storage, and sizing accordingly.

- Expect a data warehouse to occupy a lot more index space than an OLTP database. It is normal. It is also normal for a data warehouse to grow, perhaps uncontrollably, but more than likely consistently. In other words, the same amount each day—just lots of it!

- Consider multiple block sized tablespaces. This is especially the case if you are considering keep and recycle pools, and particularly if the keep pool is fairly large—meaning dimensions are not trivially small tables. Quite often, a dimensional table containing dates and times can become fairly large, especially if there is subsidiary denormalized information in the same table.

- Use striping and partitioning for speed and mirroring for redundancy and fast recovery from loss.

Striping and Redundancy: Types of RAID Arrays

The RAID acronym stands for Redundant Array of Inexpensive Disks, or lots of small, cheap disks. RAID arrays, in numerous levels of sophistication and vast differences in cost (some exorbitant), can provide enormous increases in performance, loss recoverability, and reliability. There are different types of RAID architectures. RAID types used with Oracle databases are generally RAID 0, RAID 1, RAID 0+1, and RAID 5.

Note: Remember that many small disks have more bus connections and thus better bandwidth than a few large disks, resulting in, better throughput capacity.

- **RAID 0**. RAID 0 is striping. Striping is a process of splitting files into little pieces and spreading those pieces over multiple disks. RAID 0 can provide fast random read and write access performance, but nothing in the way of rapid recoverability and redundancy. RAID 0 is the most efficient method for OLTP databases, but a little dangerous. RAID 0 could possibly be insured for recoverability and availability using clustering failovers or failover standby databases for automated, instant, up to the moment replacement of service loss. RAID 0 is not appropriate for a data warehouse because it promotes random read and write access, which is conducive to highly concurrent and precise data access as for OLTP databases. However, in a RAID array with many small physical chunks split over many small disks, the small I/O chunk reads can become multiple striped chunks read in parallel, negating the disadvantage of exact reads. On the contrary, RAID 0 can be appropriate for data warehouses where large I/O executions generated by parallel slaves are broken into smaller chunks, making many disks busy simultaneously.

- **RAID 1**. RAID 1 is mirroring. Mirroring is a simple process of using multiple copies of files, making duplicate entries into multiple files every time a change is made to a file. RAID 1 can cause I/O bottle-neck problems with respect to high usage areas of disk storage, namely high usage database objects such as frequently written tables. On the contrary, read access can be extremely fast, since some highly sophisticated RAID arrays can read more than one mirror copy of a file at the same time, allowing for parallel reads. RAID 1 is potentially appropriate for sequential access for redo logs and index spaces in OLTP databases and in data warehouses. RAID 1 is not appropriate for random access of table rows from indexes using ROWID pointers. RAID 1 is possibly more appropriate for data warehouses than for OLTP databases, due to being conducive to sequential and not random access. Sequential access allows read and write of large contiguous chunks of data at once.

- **RAID 0+1**. This option combines the best aspects of RAID 0 and RAID 1, providing both striping for read and writing access performance plus mirroring recoverability and parallel read access. RAID 0+1 is not as fast as RAID 0, but it is faster than RAID 1. RAID 0 provides random access and is not applicable to data warehouses. However, this fact is very likely to be negated by high levels of striping across large numbers of small disks in a RAID array (see RAID 0 above).

- **RAID 5**. RAID 5 provides a more simplistic version of mirroring, in which only parity, rather than a complete duplicate, is provided. RAID 5 can be particularly effective in very expensive RAID array architectures, with special buffering RAM built onboard with the RAID array itself. RAID 5 is best used for sequential reading and not random write access. RAID 5 is not appropriate for OLTP databases, other than to contain log files and perhaps indexes.

The Physical Oracle Database

An Oracle database consists of a number of physical parts: datafiles (contained in tablespaces), redo logs, archived redo logs, and control files. Control files can be ignored with respect to performance, not only because more than one makes little difference but also, and more importantly, because if control files are not multiplexed and the only available control file is lost, you could be up to your neck in very deep doodoo indeed!

Oracle Database is effectively the file system layer in the operating system, plus the Oracle Instance comprised of processes and memory buffers. An active and accessible Oracle database is an Oracle database using the Oracle Instance to access Oracle database files, as shown in Figure 14.1.

Figure 14.1
*Oracle Database
and the Oracle
Instance.*

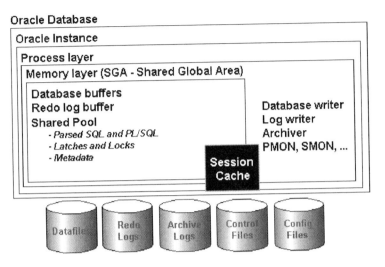

Figure 14.1 also shows different types of Oracle database files. These files are:

- **Datafiles**. Contain all physical data such as tables, indexes, database metadata, procedural code, and anything stored in the database as accessible or usable by an Oracle database user.

- **Redo Logs**. Transaction records of all database changes.

- **Archive Logs**. Historical copies of cycled redo logs, maintaining a complete history of all database change activity.

- **Control Files**. Contain pointers to all datafiles and log files used for synchronization between all of those files. Control files must be multiplexed (copied and automatically maintained).

- **Parameter File**. The configuration parameter file contains parameters that influence Oracle Database behavior.

How Oracle Database Files Fit Together

As already discussed, there are a number of different types of files at the file-system level that a running Oracle Instance uses to control and gain access to data in the database. Datafiles contain all table and index data. Redo log files contain a record of all transactions or metadata database changes. Redo logs are cyclic, such that they are reused. When a redo log file is full, it can be copied to an archive log file. An archive log file is a historical redo log file. The copied redo log file is once again ready to contain new database activity records.

The most important file in the file system structure of Oracle Database is a called the control file. The control file contains pointers to all datafiles, redo logs, and archived redo logs. The control file stores the current time state at which a particular datafile is by matching up what are called system change numbers (SCN) between datafiles and log files. An SCN is a sequential number used to synchronize changes between datafiles and redo logs. If SCN values are higher in redo logs than datafiles, then the control file knows that datafiles are older versions than they should be. Either the datafiles are recovered backups or the redo log entries, always written before datafiles, have been updated and the datafiles have not as yet been synchronized with the latest changes.

Special Types of Datafiles

Three special types of datafiles are the SYSTEM tablespace datafiles, rollback tablespace datafiles, and temporary tablespace datafiles. The SYSTEM datafile stores all the metadata, or the data about the data.

Note: The SYSAUX tablespace is created automatically along with the SYSTEM tablespace when a database is created. The SYSAUX tablespace contains options, Oracle tools, repositories, and even some types of metadata previously stored in the SYSTEM tablespace.

Rollback or automatic undo datafiles allow for undoing of certain types of previously processed, but uncommitted, transactions. Rollbacks and, to a certain extent, flashback capability cater for the multiuser ability of sessions to *snapshot* data at a specific point in time, regardless of changes made by other sessions.

Temporary datafiles allow for large sorts using disk space when memory resident sort space is used up. Figure 14.2 shows a general map of the Oracle database file system structure, plus pointer links and the flow of data between them.

Tuning Datafiles

There is little that can be done to tune datafiles. Most Oracle Database physical tuning with datafiles is performed from the tablespaces overlaying those datafiles. A datafile can have its extent growth parameter changed

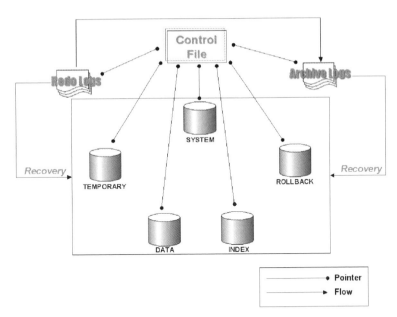

Figure 14.2
Relationships between Oracle database files.

using the ALTER DATABASE command, and Oracle Partitioning can be implemented.

Note: Any changes to datafiles, such as an extent size change using the ALTER DATABASE command, will only affect new extents, not existing extent sizes. The same applies to any block changes.

Partitioning and RAID arrays are most likely to help performance at the datafile level for data warehouses.

Tuning Redo and Archive Log Files

Tuning of redo logs and archived logs is important to Oracle database efficiency. The size of redo logs must be specified when created by a database administrator. Both the number and sizes of redo logs are important.

The more redo logs created for a database, the less likely writing of the redo logs is going to catch up with the archiving process. Let's say, for example, that your database has three small redo logs. Heavy transactional activity will rapidly switch the redo logs, but the archive process that copies redo logs to the archived log files may not be fast enough to keep up. What happens then is that all database transactional change activity halts until a redo log can be archived and recycled. A redo log will not be recycled if it has not as yet been archived. A halt will occur and effectively stop all database activity until all necessary archiving has completed and a redo log is cleared for reuse.

The same problem can occur if redo logs are too small. With high DML activity, small redo logs can result in excessive switching. A redo log file is switched from CURRENT to ACTIVE or INACTIVE when it has filled. If redo log files are too small, and a lot of switching is occurring with high transactional activity, once again the archive process may not be able to keep up, potentially temporarily halting the database.

A similar problem can occur with redo log and archiving performance when redo log files are too large. The archive process copies redo log files to archived log files. Sometimes, especially on Windows systems, very large redo log files can take so long to copy that transactional activity will once again catch up with the archive process and produce a temporary availability halt. I have seen this large file copying problem occurring on a large UNIX-based system, but only once. The redo log files were sized at 500Mb. Yes, they were half a gigabyte. The system was highly active and concurrent. It had a mixture OLTP and data warehouse activity (Yikes!) and it had enormous amounts of CPU time and space wastage as a result of terrible SQL code and bitmap indexes on transactional tables. This particular system had all sorts of problems, which I managed to resolve partially before I decided that the company was about to run out of money. I gladly accepted a better offer elsewhere. This particular company also had a history of database administrators dropping entire production databases by mistake, among other scary things. There was not really much that could be done in this situation. The fact is that someone had resized the redo logs up to a ridiculous amount in a vague trial-and-error approach, attempting to solve other problems. The result of this kind of experimentation is often further problems. Be warned! Be careful and do not change things without understanding the potential effects first. Additionally, it is also wise to record the state of a database before making changes. Simply writing down changes and making frequent backups can often help to recover from critical situations rapidly without too much downtime.

Let's get back to logging. What is the best remedy for efficient log writing and archiving of redo logs to prevent a database from halting, or perhaps worse? There is no hard and fast solution. Every database is different. Additionally, the size of the redo log buffer can have a profound effect on redo log file writes and archiving performance. There is one important thing to remember. The redo log buffer should not be the same size as the redo log files, and should generally be a very small percentage of redo log file size. In addition, recall that the redo log buffer is flushed or written to the current redo log file whenever a COMMIT or ROLLBACK is issued; the redo log buffer is partially filled to one-third full every three seconds or if the redo log reaches 1Mb.

Note: A checkpoint is a process of flushing dirty buffers from database buffer cache to disk storage. The redo log buffer is not flushed to disk when a checkpoint occurs. This is the consensus of opinion from a number of DBAs, and contrary to many Oracle software texts.

So how does the size of the log buffer affect the redo log files? The most common and most successful sizes for the redo log buffer range from 32K to 512K, and occasionally as much as 1M. I have seen many databases with problems when the redo log buffer is larger than 512K. Multiple archive processes can help to speed up archiving and alleviate pressure from elsewhere on highly active databases.

So what do we do with redo log files? How large should they be, and how many should be created? Should redo logs be duplexed? What is duplexing? Duplexing is creation of multiple redo logs, which are written from the log buffer to multiple redo log files at the same time in parallel. Duplexed redo logs are used for the sake of recoverability. Redo log duplexing is not really necessary with the more sophisticated types of RAID arrays, but it provides extra insurance. Generally, flushing of the redo log buffer to duplexed redo logs on servers with more than a single CPU has a negligible impact on performance.

How large should redo log files be, and how many should be created? The more transactional activity, the more redo logs you should have. If redo logs are continually switching, then make the redo log files larger. Do not make redo log files so large that you get a performance bottleneck when redo logs are switched and copied to archive logs. If redo logs are getting too large, either add more redo logs or perhaps try to tune other factors, such as the log buffer. In short, tuning of logging is a juggling process between multiple factors.

Another potential problem with very large redo log files is when using standby databases and passing log files over SQL*Net on a slow connection between two machines. The answer in this case would be to do something about your network connection. Changing the SQL*Net packet size can help your standby database log file transfers, but may slow network performance for small transactions. If you are operating a fast-response OLTP database through to your customers, changing packet size is not a solution.

Tablespaces

Locally managed tablespaces are the default in Oracle Database 10*g*. A locally managed tablespace has a referencing map similar to the map on the boot sector of a hard disk drive. When a file is opened on a hard disk drive, the map is accessed in order to find the address at which the file begins physically on the disk. An Oracle tablespace contains a map in the headers of datafiles describing all extents within underlying datafiles and allowing rapid access to specific addresses in those datafiles. This map of extents can either be stored in database metadata (dictionary-managed tablespace) or in a bitmap attached to the header of a datafile (locally managed tablespace). There are two different general datafile structures that can be created from a tablespace.

- **Dictionary-Managed Tablespace**. Extent and block locations are stored in database metadata. Database metadata is actually stored in the SYSTEM tablespace. Accessing data from a dictionary-managed tablespace is less efficient, because database metadata must be searched internally in the Oracle Database with SQL-type functionality in order to find addresses of data in datafiles.

Note: Dictionary-managed tablespaces are redundant.

- **Locally Managed Tablespace**. Extent and block locations are managed by, and stored in, a bitmap contained within header portions of datafiles, not elsewhere in SYSTEM tablespace metadata. Accessing the extent map of a locally managed tablespace using the file header contained bitmap is much faster than searching through database metadata to find physical addresses of data within a datafile.

Note: Locally managed tablespaces with automatically allocated extents are the default.

In the latest version of Oracle Database, all tablespaces are created as locally managed tablespaces. Conversion to locally managed tablespaces has been a gradual process in recent versions of Oracle Database. It is now safe to assume that locally managed tablespaces have been industry standard–tested and should always be used.

Note: All physical and storage parameters are inherited from datafile to tablespace and ultimately to all objects created in a tablespace. Many of these structural parameters can be overridden. Thus, a tablespace can override datafile parameters, and database objects, such as tables and indexes, can override tablespace parameters.

What are the factors that help in tuning locally managed tablespaces? Let's start with a syntax diagram for the CREATE TABLESPACE command. Certain parts are highlighted.

```
CREATE [ UNDO ] TABLESPACE tablespace
    [ DATAFILE 'file' SIZE n[K|M] [ REUSE ]
        [ AUTOEXTEND { OFF
            | ON [ NEXT n[K|M]
                [ MAXSIZE { UNLIMITED | n[K|M] } ]
]
        } ]
    ]
[ MINIMUM EXTENT n[K|M] ]
    [ BLOCKSIZE n[K] ]
    [ [NO]LOGGING ]
    [ EXTENT MANAGEMENT { DICTIONARY
        | LOCAL [ { AUTOALLOCATE | UNIFORM [ SIZE n[K|M] ] } ]

    } ]
    [ SEGMENT SPACE MANAGEMENT { AUTO | MANUAL } ]
    [
        DEFAULT [ [NO]COMPRESS ] STORAGE(
            [ INITIAL n[K|M] ] [ NEXT n[K|M] ] [ PCTINCREASE n
]
            [ MINEXTENTS n ] [ MAXEXTENTS { n | UNLIMITED } ])
    ];
```

Note: If a database is created with a locally managed SYSTEM tablespace, then dictionary-managed tablespaces cannot be created in that database. Additionally, the SYSTEM tablespace cannot be changed from local to dictionary-managed.

Now let's go through the highlighted parts of the CREATE TABLESPACE syntax.

- **Auto Extend**. Tablespaces should always be automatically extended with a specified size for the NEXT parameter. Specifying the NEXT parameter assures that datafiles grow with consistent, reusable extent sizes. If extent sizes are too small, then a large table could have so many extents to search through that performance will degrade seriously. The NEXT parameter is defaulted to the block size. Do not leave NEXT undeclared and defaulted. The block size default is usually too small. Only small static tables and indexes could have sizes for NEXT of less than 1M. For some tables, well over 1M is prudent.

  Setting MAXSIZE UNLIMITED is also sensible, because if a maximum datafile size is specified, the database will cease to function if datafiles ever reach a maximum size. It is better to extend Oracle tablespace datafiles automatically and monitor disk space usage with scripting in the operating system.

- **Minimum Extent Sizes**. This option specifies that every extent in a datafile is at least the specified size, minimizing on fragmentation.

- **Block Size**. Permanent tablespaces can be created with block sizes different to the DB_BLOCK_SIZE database block size parameter. Appropriate DB_nK_CACHE_SIZE parameters must be created in the configuration parameter file to cater for such tablespaces. Obviously, a tablespace with a smaller block size is useful to contain smaller tables. A tablespace with a larger block size is good for large tables when reading large amounts of data at once. I have personally never experimented with this aspect of Oracle 9*i* Database in a highly active production environment, but I would certainly suggest using them for storage of large objects, such as LOBs. LOBs contained within tables can be stored in a tablespace separate to the tablespace in which the table resides.

- **Logging**. Switching off logging as the default for a tablespace will increase performance in your database. However, no logging will result in no redo log entries and an unrecoverable database. Do not switch off logging for the sake of performance, unless, of course, you can recover the tablespace easily and rapidly. There is no logging for read-only tablespaces, since read-only does not allow DML command changes. Make a tablespace read-only by using the ALTER TABLESPACE command. Thus, there are no redo log entries for read-only tablespaces. Do not use NOLOGGING on read-write tablespaces unless you are prepared to lose your entire database in the event of a disaster. Individual objects in tablespaces can be forced into logging mode when other tables are not if the tablespace is set to NOLOGGING. Once again, any type of no logging setting are risky.

Note: A database setting can also be set to FORCE NOLOGGING mode, discarding logging settings at the segment level.

- **Extent Management**. Once again, the most efficient datafile structure for growth is consistent extent sizes. Differing extent sizes in datafiles will result in fragmentation and slow access times due to bouncing around a disk when searching for data. Coalescence is generally useless when trying to reclaim deleted space where extent sizes differ.

  Considering the setting of extent sizes, the more growth you have, the larger the extent size should be. I generally use 1M and larger values for very large databases or databases with high growth rates. Small objects can have smaller extent sizes, as long as the database administrator is absolutely sure that large tables or high growth rate tables will never be placed in that tablespace. Database administrators are rarely involved in the development process, and thus a database administrator is unlikely to have enough knowledge of applications to make these types of decisions.

  Keep extent sizes consistent and never less than 1M.

- **Segment Space Management**. A segment space management specification is allowed for locally managed nontemporary tablespaces. Automatic segment space management, as specified by the SEGMENT SPACE MANAGEMENT AUTO clause, eliminates the need to declare PCTUSED, FREELIST, and FREELIST GROUPS values for objects created in a tablespace. These settings are now bitmap managed automatically by Oracle Database.

> **Note:** Setting values for PCTUSED, FREELIST, and FREELIST_ GROUPS in database objects such as tables will be ignored if the containing tablespace is set to automatic segment space management.

In past versions of Oracle Database, manual free list management was usually only required for very highly concurrent active OLTP databases or Oracle RAC (Parallel Server) installations. Access to the PCTUSED parameter, on the other hand, helped immensely with tuning for performance in the following respect. The default value for PCTUSED is very low, at 40%. Any database with heavy deletion activity could have a lot of wasted space with PCTUSED set to 40%. Deleted rows are still read by full scans and can ultimately result in serious performance problems. One of the biggest problems with manually setting the PCTUSED value for a table was that it was often set based on subjective guesswork, due to a lack of understanding. Otherwise, it was simply left at the default value. Automatic management of free space resolves these issues.

BIGFILE Tablespaces

Oracle Database allows division of tablespace types for locally managed tablespaces into two categories: Smallfile tablespaces and Bigfile tablespaces. A Smallfile tablespace is the default.

> **Note:** Smallfile or Bigfile can be set as the default for the database as a whole using the CREATE DATABASE or ALTER DATABASE commands.

A Bigfile tablespace contains a single datafile, which can be up to 128 Tb for a block size of 32K. The general trend for database technology at the file structure level is fewer, larger files. Many years ago, relational databases had a single datafile for every table or index; some still do. The most advanced database engines are object databases. The most recently developed object databases generally have a single large datafile. The performance benefit of maintaining a single large file is significant. I would suggest that it is likely that Oracle Database will continue on this path of development. In a future version of Oracle Database, Bigfile tablespaces may be the default and perhaps, eventually, the only option where all physical storage structure within that Bigfile is automatically managed, transparent, and inaccessible to database administrators. Splitting files up physically using striping on a RAID array, for instance, is managed at the operating-system level and is not a requirement from within the database. Oracle Database 10*g* introduced ASM, which can implement striping managed from within the Oracle database. This hints further at less emphasis on explicit management of physical storage structures.

Avoiding Datafile Header Contention

Datafile header contention can be avoided when using locally managed tablespaces in busy Oracle installations by creating a large number of small datafiles for each tablespace. Datafile header contention is avoided since extent bitmaps attached to each datafile are not overstressed in highly concurrent environments. This is a newfangled way of doing things and is not to be confused with manual striping. It is not striping! Locally managed tablespaces have bitmaps only in datafile header blocks, much in the same way that dictionary-managed tablespaces use metadata storage (in the SYSTEM tablespace) to store extent maps. Since bitmaps compress far more than metadata storage, datafile header blocks contention under highly concurrent conditions is more likely. A symptom of locally managed tablespace contention, competing for bitmaps in this way, is buffer-busy waits on file header block class of blocks.

Now let's take a look at the different types of functions of tablespaces.

Temporary Sort Space

Temporary sort space is catered for in two ways. First, sort buffers are declared by the SORT_AREA_SIZE parameter. Second, a temporary sort space tablespace and datafile are on disk. It might make sense to size temporary sort space to a multiple of the SORT_AREA_SIZE parameter.

A temporary tablespace is specially structured for sorting and is best implemented as a locally managed tablespace. This is the syntax for creating a temporary tablespace:

```
CREATE TEMPORARY TABLESPACE tablespace
    [ TEMPFILE 'file' [ SIZE n[K|M] ] ]
    [ EXTENT MANAGEMENT LOCAL ]
    [ UNIFORM [ SIZE n[K|M] ] ];
```

Tablespace Groups

On disk, temporary space can be allocated as tablespace groups where a tablespace group can contain multiple locally managed temporary tablespaces. A tablespace group will allow spreading of SQL execution sorting across multiple temporary tablespaces, thereby potentially speeding up sorting operations. Processing is distributed. A user can be allocated a tablespace group as a temporary sort space, as opposed to just a single temporary tablespace.

Automated Undo

The automated undo tablespace was introduced in Oracle 9*i* Database. An undo tablespace automates rollback segment management so that rollback segments no longer have to be created and tuned. Many database administrators had problems tuning rollback segments. There are a number of undo configuration parameters for controlling automated undo:

- *UNDO_MANAGEMENT.* Switches automated undo on and off. Set to MANUAL to use manual rollback segments.

- *UNDO_TABLESPACE*. The name of an undo tablespace must be specified.

- *UNDO_RETENTION*. Places a time period for how much committed undo data is kept. When using the Database Configuration Assistant, default parameters for this value appear to be set to more than 10,000 for a data warehouse and less than 1,000 for OLTP databases. Documentation on this parameter is vague, and it is unclear that if this parameter is set to too short a time period that uncommitted information is overwritten. In short, Oracle Database 10*g* will try to keep undo for the UNDO_RETENTION period as long as space in the undo tablespace allows it. It is a best effort *contract*. In Oracle Database 10*g*, the default setting is 0, meaning that Oracle Database tries to keep necessary undo for ongoing queries (with a default time retention of 900 seconds).

Caching Static Data Warehouse Objects

This option is much like the keep and recycle buffer pools from a previous version of Oracle Database and applies to full table scans only. Caching will allow forcing of small static tables into the MRU (most recently used) cache and large seldom used tables into the LRU (least recently used) cache.

In a data warehouse, it might make sense to cache dimensional tables and indexes, It also might be plausible to cache foreign key indexes on fact tables.

Compressing Objects

Objects such as tables and indexes can be compressed. As for index compression, table compression tends to remove duplicate values, such as repeated foreign key indexes on fact tables. Also, note that table compression filters through to materialized views.

14.3 Capacity Planning

Capacity planning involves two main subject areas: current storage space usage and potential growth. Remember that for a data warehouse, throughput is more important than concurrent reaction time, as in an OLTP database. In other words, lots and lots of processing in the form of very large transactions, such as large updates and big reports, are the most significant factor in data warehouses.

Disk storage is now cheap and, thus, the amount of space you use is less important, perhaps, compared to how that space is used. Always allow for massive amounts of future growth by growing I/O space usage without comprising the speed with which information is accessed from disk storage, at least not too much to cause performance problems. It is an inevitability that the more data stored in a database, the longer large I/O scans will take to execute. Obviously, architectural aspects, such as partitioning, can help to alleviate this type of problem. Expect to not only cater for extreme and constant growth in a data warehouse, but also to have to actively manage data warehouse disk space usage and distribution.

Both current storage and potential growth of a database can be assessed using the same basic tools. What are those basic tools? Simple tools for capacity planning can best be explained by starting with the following question: How do we accurately assess the current physical size of an Oracle database? There are various methods. Some methods are highly accurate, but increased accuracy can hurt performance. Other methods are extremely fast, but under some circumstances can be so inaccurate so as to be rendered useless. So how do we assess the current physical size of an Oracle database? Some capacity planning methods include:

- **Datafile Sizes**. Get datafile sizes of all data containing datafiles from the operating system. This method could be the most inaccurate of all.

- **Datafile Content Sizes**. This method requires a join on the DBA_DATA_FILES and DBA_FREE_SPACE metadata views.

This method accumulates values based on what Oracle Database calls extents. Extents are the physical chunks by which an Oracle datafile is increased when more space is required. This method is totally inappropriate for an Oracle database with poor physical storage organization, particularly when the storage parameter PCTIN-CREASE is used. Most commercial Oracle databases are not properly structured in this respect. This method is more accurate than retrieval of datafile sizes from the operating system, but can result in very unreliable results.

- **The DBMS_SPACE Package**. This Oracle-provided package is utilized to sum up space used and space free at the block level, by database object name. This method adds space used at the block level and is more accurate than both of the datafile methods already listed above. However, if many blocks are partially filled, inaccuracy could be significant. For a small database this is not an issue, but a small database does not really need capacity planning anyway.

- **Statistics**. Internal Oracle optimization statistics can be generated with either a minimal or fairly heavy performance impact; the heavier the performance impact, the better the quality of the statistics. Also, generating sizing statistics for indexes requires an extra burden on performance. Use of statistics is probably the all-around most effective method for capacity planning. However, some older versions of Oracle Database and applications use rule-based rather than cost-based optimization. The simple existence of statistics can cause performance problems for rule-based tuned applications. However, the OPTIMIZER_MODE parameter in pre-Oracle 10g versions can resolve these issues at a database level. If multiple applications use the same database and these applications used a mix of rule-based and cost-based applications, then rule-based applications could have performance problems.

- **Exact Column Data Lengths**. All column lengths in all rows in all tables in a database can be counted using length functions for string fields plus fixed known lengths for all other basic datatypes. Object datatypes could be an issue using this method. This method would be the most accurate for a purely relational database (no object datatypes at all). This method will also affect performance in the extreme.

- **Oracle Enterprise Manager Capacity Planner**. The Capacity Planner package in Oracle Enterprise Manager does a lot of the work for you. It also provides lots of very nice graphical representation, automated warnings, and bells and whistles, but it will not allow predictions of database growth for the future.

Note: The Capacity Planner will not be explained specifically. Get it up and running, and it is self-explanatory.

Now let's go through each of the above listed methods for capacity assessment and planning in detail.

14.3.1 Datafile Sizes

On Solaris this would require the use of the *df –k* command, and on NT/2000, either the *dir* command and a Perl script or just a Perl script using a Perl-contained package allowing disk reads from within Perl. The script shown in Figure 14.3 could be used to validate the existence of an acceptable level of disk space available on a Solaris box. This script will indicate when disk space is reaching critical levels. Some simple adjustments to this script could be made to check current disk space results in the file DISKSPACE.LOG, with previous executions of the script stored in older log files; thus, growth rate can be estimated over a period of time.

Figure 14.3

A partial script for extracting available disk space.

```
#!/bin/ksh

panic=95
scream=99

if [ ! -d ./logs ]; then
        mkdir ./logs
fi

df -k | awk '{\
if (($1 != "Filesystem") && ($1 != "fd") && ($1 != "/proc"))\
{\
        if ($5 > scream) { print "SCREAM !!! - Disk space on",host,$1,"@",$5 }\
        else if ($5 > panic) { print "Panic - Disk space on",host,$1,"@",$5 }\
}\
}' scream=$scream panic=$panic host=$host > ./logs/diskspace.log

if [ -s ./logs/diskspace.log ]; then
        sub="Script $0 on $host detected disk space limits exceeded !!!"
        echo $sub
        mailx -s "$sub" $email < ./logs/diskspace.log
        exit 1
fi

exit 0
```

14.3.2   **Datafile Content Sizes**

The query shown in Figure 14.4 is a partial script showing a join between the Oracle performance views DBA_DATA_FILES and DBA_FREE_ SPACE. Note that this script will not amalgamate datafiles into tablespaces, but will show space used for each datafile (temporary datafiles excluded). Effectively, this query will assess database size in terms of datafile extents. Whenever an autoextensible datafile runs out of space, a new extent is automatically allocated to that datafile. For a nonautoextensible datafile, new extents have to be added manually by resizing the datafile using the ALTER DATABASE command. The DBA_DATA_FILES column BYTES shows the total size of a datafile in bytes. The DBA_FREE_SPACE column BYTES shows the BYTE size of all free extents in a datafile within a tablespace.

The consistency of extent sizes is largely dependant on settings for the storage parameter PCTINCREASE, for tablespaces, and database objects, such as tables and indexes. The important point to note about the query in Figure 14.4 is that the result of byte values in the DBA_FREE_SPACE view can be very inaccurate if PCTINCREASE is set anywhere in the database at greater than 0%. Why? A static database that has never grown in size, would not be affected by PCTINCREASE if PCTINCREASE has never been applied by the creation of a new extent. This is probably very unlikely. If many new extents are added to a datafile, it is quite possible that a new extent added could be much larger than expected. The other issue with setting PCTINCREASE greater than 0% is that empty extents, as a result of deletions, will not be reused, since new extents, created larger than old extents, will not be able to reuse old extents, which are smaller. Coalescence can help alleviate this problem, but coalescence only manages to join extents, that are physically next to each other.

In Oracle 9*i* and beyond, the PCTINCREASE parameter is largely irrelevant. The default for the CREATE TABLESPACE command is to create a locally managed tablespace. The PCT_INCREASE parameter is not set for locally managed tablespaces. The Oracle configuration parameter COMPATIBLE must be set to at least 9.0.0 for this locally managed tablespace default to take effect. Since many existing Oracle databases are pre-Oracle 9*i*, the script shown in Figure 14.4 is still relevant.

14.3.3   **The DBMS_SPACE Package**

DBMS_SPACE is an Oracle-provided package capable of summing all blocks for each database object, namely tables, indexes, and clusters. Some-

Figure 14.4
A partial script for datafile extent sizes.

```ksh
#!/bin/ksh

panic=95
scream=99

if [ ! -d ./logs ]; then
   mkdir ./logs
fi

$ORACLE_HOME/bin/sqlplus system/<password><<!
set term off echo off feedback off show off trim off trims off verify off linesize 132;
spool ./logs/tablespace.log;
SELECT    'Tablespace '||df.tablespace_name "TBS"
         ,round((sum(nvl(fs.bytes,0))/ (df.bytes)) * 100) "%Free"
         ,round(((df.bytes - sum(nvl(fs.bytes,0))) / (df.bytes) ) * 100) "%Used"
         ,round(sum(nvl(fs.bytes/1024/1024,0))) "Mb Free"
         ,round(df.bytes/1024/1024 - sum(nvl(fs.bytes/1024/1024,0))) "Mb Used"
         ,df.autoextensible "AutoExtensible"
FROM   dba_free_space fs, dba_data_files df
WHERE  fs.file_id(+) = df.file_id
GROUP BY df.tablespace_name, df.file_id, df.bytes, df.autoextensible
ORDER BY df.file_id;
spool off;
exit
!

cat ./logs/tablespace.log | grep Tablespace | grep -v grep | grep -v SQL\> | awk '{\
  if (($7 == "NO") && (int($4) > int(scream)))\
  {\
    print "SCREAM !!! - Non-AutoExtensible Tablespace",$2,"space in database",sid,"on",host,"@",$4"%"\
  }\
  else if (($7 == "NO") && (int($4) > int(panic)))\
  {\
    print "Panic - Non-AutoExtensible Tablespace",$2,"space in database",sid,"on",host,"@",$4"%"\
  }\
}' scream=$scream panic=$panic host=$host sid=$ORACLE_SID > ./logs/dbfspace.log

if [ -s ./logs/dbfspace.log ]; then
    sub="Script $0 on $host in database $ORACLE_SID detected tablespace limits exceeded !!!"
    echo $sub
    mailx -s "$sub" $email < ./logs/dbfspace.log
    exit 1
fi

exit 0
```

thing like the stored PL/SQL code shown in Figure 14.5 could be used to execute capacity planning database space usage based on used and unused blocks.

The problem with this method is that the settings of block storage parameters, such as PCTUSED, could cause an unrealistic picture of the actual size of the data. PCTUSED is defaulted to 40% for all tables and indexes. If a block has rows deleted from it, then the block will not be used until the block gets to below 40% filled. If a database has a lot of delete activity, either in many or a few large tables, this method could give very misleading results.

Another interesting DBMS_SPACE package function is the OBJECT_GROWTH_TREND function, introduced in Oracle Database 10*g*. This function describes the use of space, at a specified point in time, of a database object. It returns information about trends of growth of database objects. This function provides forecasting capabilities.

Figure 14.5
*An untested PL/
SQL script calling
DBMS_SPACE.
UNUSED_
SPACE.*

```
set serveroutput on;
create or replace procedure my_DBMS_SPACE (powner in varchar2) as
  cursor cOBJECTS is
    select decode(partitioned,'NO','TABLE','YES','TABLE PARTITION')
    as type,table_name as name from dba_tables where owner = powner
    UNION
    select decode(partitioned,'NO','INDEX','YES','TABLE PARTITION')
    as type,index_name as name from dba_indexes where owner = powner
    UNION
    select 'CLUSTER' as type,cluster_name as name from dba_clusters where owner = powner;
  total_blocks NUMBER;
  total_bytes NUMBER;
  unused_blocks NUMBER;
  unused_bytes NUMBER;
  lastextf NUMBER;
  lastextb NUMBER;
  lastusedblock NUMBER;
  used_blocks integer default 0;
  free_blocks integer default 0;
begin
  for objs in cOBJECTS loop
    dbms_space.unused_space(powner, objs.name, objs.type, total_blocks, total_bytes
      ,unused_blocks, unused_bytes, lastextf, lastextb, lastusedblock);
    used_blocks := used_blocks + total_blocks;
    free_blocks := free_blocks + unused_blocks;
  end loop;
  dbms_output.put_line('Used = '||to_char(used_blocks)||', Free = '||to_char(free_blocks));
exception when others then
  dbms_output.put_line('test '||sqlerrm(sqlcode));
end;
/
exec my_dbms_space;
```

14.3.4   Statistics

Before discussing how we can use statistics to capacity plan, let's go over
how we can gather statistics. There are two methods of gathering Oracle
database statistics:

- **The ANALYZE Command**. Can be used to collect optimizer statistics and will be deprecated in a future version of Oracle.

- **The DBMS_STATS Oracle Provided Package**. Collects optimizer
  statistics and can be executed in parallel on a multiple CPU system
  for better performance.

Using the ANALYZE Command

The command shown below will create optimizer statistics for all rows in a
specified table:

```
ANALYZE <table> COMPUTE STATISTICS;
```

A more efficient, but less accurate, form of the same command estimates the values for statistics by sampling 1064 rows from the specified table. Note the optional SAMPLE clause allowing specification of percentage or number of rows:

```
ANALYZE <table> ESTIMATE STATISTICS [SAMPLE {1-99%|<rows>];
```

Estimating statistics is much better for performance, but potentially much less accurate than computing all the statistics. Accuracy of estimating statistics depends largely on the size of the database object.

The ANALYZE command can be used to generate statistics for tables, indexes, and clusters.

The DBMS_STATS Package

Statistics can be generated and have all sorts of other things done with them in various ways, using the DBMS_STATS package. For the purposes of capacity planning, the most important aspect of the DBMS_STATS package is that of gathering statistics. Statistics can be gathered for indexes and tables, and even for a whole schema or an entire database. The commands below can be used to gather statistics for a single table and a single index:

```
EXEC DBMS_STATS.GATHER_TABLE_STATS('<owner>', '<table>');

EXEC DBMS_STATS.GATHER_INDEX_STATS('<owner>', '<index>');
```

DBMS_STATS is faster at generating statistics than the ANALYZE command.

Using Statistics for Capacity Planning

Calculating the number of blocks or the byte size for a table using statistics is simple. After statistics have been generated query the USER_TABLES metadata view with a query as shown:

```
SELECT table_name, num_rows, blocks
,blocks*<db_block_size> AS BYTES
FROM USER_TABLES;
```

We could find the DB_BLOCK_SIZE (database block size), when logged in as SYS or SYSTEM, by executing the query:

```
SELECT value FROM v$parameter WHERE name='db_block_size';
```

Note: The block size for a segment is not necessarily the database default block size, because tablespaces can have block sizes not the default block size. The DBA_TABLESPACES and USER_SEGMENTS metadata views contain more specific block sizes.

Then re-execute the above query as:

```
SELECT table_name, num_rows, blocks
,blocks*(
SELECT value FROM v$parameter
WHERE name='db_block_size') AS BYTES
FROM USER_TABLES;
```

You could then add up the size of all tables in a specified schema, assuming you have generated statistics for all tables in that schema by executing the following query, say with DB_BLOCK_SIZE at 8192 bytes or 8K:

```
SELECT SUM(BLOCKS*8192) AS BYTES
,SUM(BLOCKS*8192)/1024/1024 AS MB
FROM USER_TABLES;
```

So now we know how to utilize statistics to find the size of all your data. Other objects that could be analyzed and summed up would be objects such as indexes and clusters. Since clusters are rarely used we will ignore them. Indexes on the other hand are generally more numerous in number than tables. It is often found that the total byte size of all indexes in a schema can be larger than that of all tables. We could estimate the size of indexes based on an assumed table to index ratio, but that would be inaccurate.

The INDEX_STATS Oracle performance view is the only view that can be used to calculate an exact size for an index. Generation of data into the INDEX_STATS view requires use of the ANALYZE INDEX <index> VALIDATE STRUCTURE; command.

A simple method of assessing index size is to use index statistics generated by the ANALYZE INDEX command or the DBMS_STATS.GATHER_INDEX_STATS procedure; the USER_INDEXES view will contain the resulting statistics. The query shown below will retrieve a vague estimate of size for an index:

```
SELECT INDEX_NAME, LEAF_BLOCKS, BLEVEL
, DECODE(BLEVEL,0,1,1,1,LEAF_BLOCKS/BLEVEL) AS BRANCH_BLOCKS
, (LEAF_BLOCKS
+DECODE(BLEVEL,0,1,1,1,LEAF_BLOCKS/BLEVEL))*8192 AS BYTES
FROM USER_INDEXES
WHERE INDEX_TYPE = 'NORMAL'
ORDER BY BLEVEL;
```

Columns in the USER_INDEXES metadata view mean as follows:

- **BLEVEL**. BLEVEL is the depth of a BTree index from root block to leaf blocks. How many branches does the index have? BLEVEL ranges from 0 to 2. This means that an index can have a depth of 0, where the root and leaf block are the same. In other words, there is only one block in the index. When an index has a level of 1 it means it has one root block, all pointing off to many leaf blocks. Essentially, the size of the root block is one block, which for a large index is negligible within total space used. For BLEVEL value of 2, the index has one root block, one layer of branch blocks, and a layer of leaf blocks. Calculating branch blocks when BLEVEL is 2 is more or less impossible using a method like this. Even though a BTree index is actually a binary tree index, an Oracle Database BTree index is not actually a binary tree. A binary tree implies that every branch has only two possible branches. Oracle Database BTree indexes have more than one possible branch.

- **LEAF_BLOCKS**. This gives the total number of leaf blocks in an index.

Note: This applies to BTree indexes (WHERE INDEX_TYPE = 'NORMAL'). The compression and clustering of values (order of index values between blocks and rows) of a BTree index will make a difference to space usage. These queries assume all tablespaces are default database block size, and in this case 8K (8192 bytes). Use DBA_TABLESPACES or USER_SEGMENTS to find individual tablespace block sizes.

To reiterate for clarity, use of the DECODE function in the above query can be explained as:

- **BLEVEL=0**. The root and leaf are the same and, thus, the index occupies only one block.

- **BLEVEL=1**. The root is the only branch block and, thus, one block is added.

- **BLEVEL=2**. Leaf blocks are added to the total as divided by 2, assuming that an Oracle Database BTree index can only have two child branch options at most. This is not true, of course, making this query a guess at space usage.

Obtain a "guesstimate" total size of all indexes in a schema by executing a query like this:

```
SELECT
SUM((LEAF_BLOCKS
+DECODE(BLEVEL,0,1,1,1,LEAF_BLOCKS/BLEVEL))*8192) AS BYTES
,SUM((LEAF_BLOCKS
+DECODE(BLEVEL,0,1,1,1,LEAF_BLOCKS/BLEVEL))*8192)/1024/1024
AS MB
FROM USER_INDEXES;
```

Dividing the number of leaf blocks in an index by its branch level value is a bit of a guess as far as assessing size. For very large indexes, it would be sensible to validate this by executing the ANALYZE INDEX <index> VALIDATE STRUCTURE; command for that particular index and then executing the query shown below to get a better perspective on the actual size of that index:

```
SELECT NAME,BR_BLKS+LF_BLKS,USED_SPACE AS BYTES FROM
INDEX_STATS;
```

The two queries shown below produce summaries of current database storage capacity for objects within a schema. Both queries list byte, megabyte, and gigabyte sizes. This query lists sizes for all tables in a schema:

```
SELECT TABLE_NAME
    ,BLOCKS*8192 AS BYTES
    ,ROUND(BLOCKS*8192/1024/1024) AS MB
    ,ROUND(BLOCKS*8192/1024/1024/1024,1) AS GB
FROM USER_TABLES;
```

This query shows sizes for all indexes in a schema for each table:

```
SELECT TABLE_NAME
    ,SUM((LEAF_BLOCKS
+DECODE(BLEVEL,0,1,1,1,LEAF_BLOCKS/BLEVEL))*8192) AS BYTES
    ,ROUND(SUM((LEAF_BLOCKS
+DECODE(BLEVEL,0,1,1,1,LEAF_BLOCKS/BLEVEL))*8192)/1024/1024)
AS MB
    ,ROUND(SUM((LEAF_BLOCKS
+DECODE(BLEVEL,0,1,1,1,LEAF_BLOCKS/BLEVEL))*8192)
/1024/1024/1024,1) AS GB
FROM USER_INDEXES GROUP BY TABLE_NAME;
```

Note: Obviously, the table and index queries could be joined.

14.3.5 Exact Column Data Lengths

This method of calculating the physical size of a database involves measuring the lengths of all columns, of all rows in all tables, and indexes in the database. This method should be the most accurate, but it is a real killer for performance. How accurate do you want to get? This method does border on the ridiculous. However, if you are doing a migration from a non-Oracle database, such as PostGres, and your database is very small, how else would you be able to predict expected capacities? The simple fact is the smaller your database is, and the larger you expect it to get in the future, the more accurate your capacity planning has to be. This type of scenario is common in startup companies, where an initial (prototype) database is minuscule. These types of environments usually expect unimaginable growth. Sometimes these companies are correct—admittedly not very often, but it does happen. In a situation like this, a method such as this would apply.

In describing this approach to capacity planning it is best to keep things simple. Thus, we will stick to simple datatypes; no binary objects or other such nasty, unpredictable things. If nonsimple datatypes have to be included, then they have to be included, and factored into the calculations.

The simple datatypes in an Oracle database and their respective lengths are as follows. Note that some datatypes make things simple for use because their actual physical lengths are fixed. Also, some datatypes are automatically converted to more general datatypes when applied to columns in tables. Not a very efficient use of space, but that is something *invented* by relational database vendors such as Oracle Corporation many years ago.

This method may seem complicated, but it is actually very simple. Variable length simple datatypes in Oracle Database 10*g* are the VARCHAR2 datatypes and NUMBER datatypes with no precision specified. The LENGTH function gets VARCHAR2 datatype string length (LENGTHB returns a bytes semantic and might be slightly more accurate). NUMBER datatypes, without precision, can be measured using the VSIZE function. All other simple datatypes have fixed lengths.

I created the following table:

```
CREATE TABLE ATABLE(
    rnum INTEGER,
    vc1 VARCHAR2(4000) DEFAULT '0123456789',
    vc2 VARCHAR2(4000) DEFAULT '012',
    c1 CHAR(2) DEFAULT 'ab',
    c2 CHAR(10) DEFAULT 'abc',
    n1 NUMBER DEFAULT 100,
    n2 NUMBER(10) DEFAULT 101,
    n3 NUMBER(12,4) DEFAULT 103.1234,
    f1 FLOAT DEFAULT 1.23334,
    si1 SMALLINT DEFAULT 0,
    si2 SMALLINT DEFAULT 100,
    i1 INTEGER DEFAULT 0,
    i2 INTEGER DEFAULT 222,
    d1 DATE DEFAULT SYSDATE,
    t1 TIMESTAMP DEFAULT SYSDATE);
INSERT INTO ATABLE(rnum) VALUES(1);
COMMIT;
```

Now we can examine the column length specifications of the table we have just created by selecting the appropriate columns from the

Figure 14.6
*Querying the
USER_TAB_
COLUMNS view.*

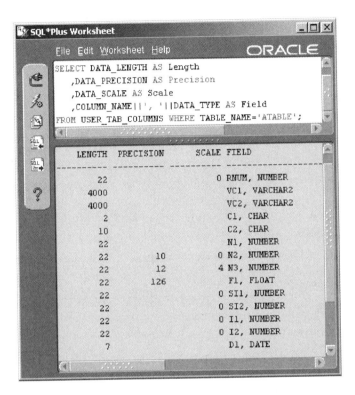

USER_TAB_COLUMNS Oracle metadata view. The result is shown in Figure 14.6.

In Figure 14.6, all the data lengths are shown for each type of datatype contained in the table created by the script shown previously.

The resulting calculation simply needs to multiply the number of rows in each table with the sum of the lengths of its datatype–defined column lengths, as shown in Figure 14.6. Adjustment is required for VARCHAR2 datatypes and NUMBER columns with no precision, by applying the appropriate functions to the column values. This is why this method can seriously hurt performance. Index sizes can be assessed simply by multiplying table rows again by the sum of the lengths of the columns for all indexes created on each table. Indexes can be erroneous, due to NULL values not being stored in indexes in some cases. However, most modern databases use object front-end applications. These types of applications tend to avoid use of composite keys for anything but many-to-many join resolution entities; these entities usually contain integers in their key values, which are never NULL values.

That's capacity planning. Oracle Enterprise Manager Capacity Planner is a useful tool. Unfortunately at the time of writing this book, using Oracle Database 10.1.0.2, the database control service for Enterprise Manager was refusing to function at all on my Windows 2000 box.

14.4　**OLAP and Data Mining**

What is OLAP? OLAP stands for Online Analytical Processing. What's that? Well, first of all, there are MOLAP and ROLAP. MOLAP is multiple-dimensional OLAP, and ROLAP is Relational OLAP. MOLAP generates cubic or multiple-dimensional cross-tabulations from relational data. ROLAP utilizes not only relational tables but also dimensional hierarchies, such as with Oracle Dimension objects.

Data mining allows for analysis of data in a database for comprehensive predictive results.

Oracle Database provides add-on optional packages covering OLAP and data mining functionality. Note that a lot of OLAP type functionality is provided by the latest built-in additions to Oracle SQL queries.

OLAP and data mining are not really Oracle Database tuning, but as with many other topics presented in this book, they are perhaps a means or set of tools to performance tune. However, these tools are provided for Oracle Database as separate packages and, thus, their detailed coverage is too much for this book.

This chapter has covered some tuning aspects of general data warehouse architecture. It is the final chapter in this book. I hope you have enjoyed reading it as much as I have enjoyed writing it.

New Data Warehouse Features in Oracle Database 10g

- The MODEL clause is new allowing for a complex spreadsheet, like multiple dimensional calculations. See Chapter 10.

- SQLAccess Advisor offers improved access to advisory information previously catered for by the DBMS_ADVISOR package. This tool is not covered in this book and is delayed until the release of Oracle Database 10.2, in a future edition of this book, or another Oracle Database tuning title.[1]

- DBMS_ADVISOR.TUNE_MVIEW provides advice for materialized views in terms of fast refresh and query rewrite.

- Materialized view refresh capabilities are improved for refresh, including nested refresh capability.

- Query rewrite is improved.

- Index organized tables can now be partitioned.

- The Oracle SQL DML MERGE statement is enhanced.[2]

- Oracle Managed Files (OMF) provides automation of underlying datafiles, redo log files, archive redo log files, and control files. Automatic Storage Management (ASM) manages the disks as well, as an additional extension to OMF. OMF will simplify management, but is reputed to hurt performance.

A.1   Endnotes

1.   Chapter15 in *Oracle SQL: Jumpstart with Examples* (ISBN: 1555583237)

2.   *Oracle Performance Tuning for 9i and 10g* (ISBN: 1555583059)

B

Sample Schemas

Container Tracking Schemas

The normalized relational form of the container tracking schema is shown in Figure B.1.

The dimensional-fact form of the container tracking schema is shown in Figures B.2 and B.3. Figure B.2 shows facts for voyages of containers and Figure B.3 shows damage sustained to containers. In both Figures B.2 and B.3, fact tables are shaded and dimension tables are not.

Demographics Schema

Two demographics schemas were used in this book, the first is shown in Figure B.4. The second version, shown in Figure B.5, is a slightly enhanced version containing population and foreign exchange information.

Inventory-Accounting Schema

The schema in Figure B.6 represents the original normalized version of the OLTP database schema from which the data warehouse schema was created. The data warehouse schema is shown in Figure B.7.

Sample Schemas

Figure B.7 shows the data warehouse schema, containing two fact table star schemas.

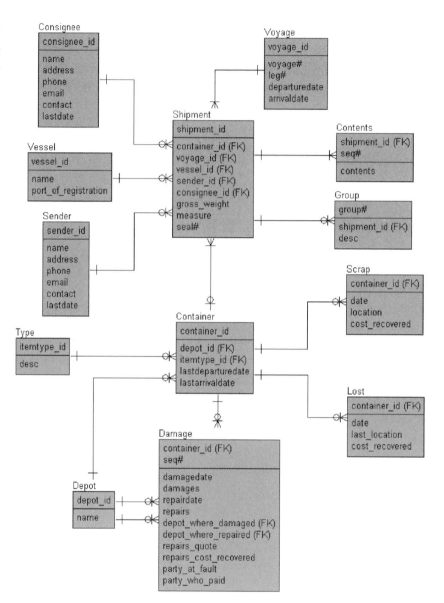

Figure B.1
The relational model container tracking schema.

Figure B.2
Container voyages dimensional-fact tracking schema.

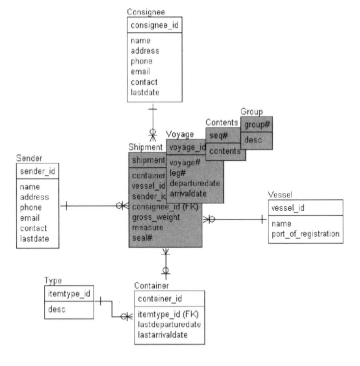

Figure B.3
Container damage dimensional-fact tracking schema.

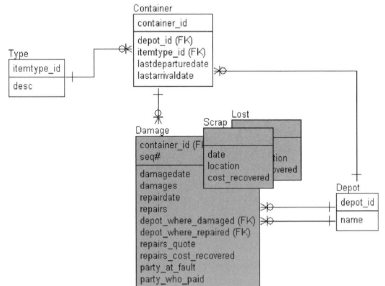

Figure B.4
*Demographics for
the locations
dimension.*

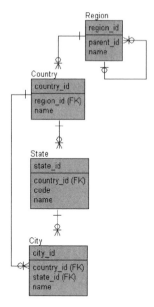

Figure B.5
*Enhanced
demographics.*

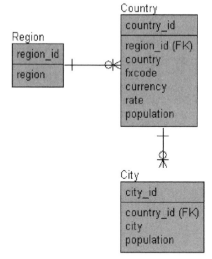

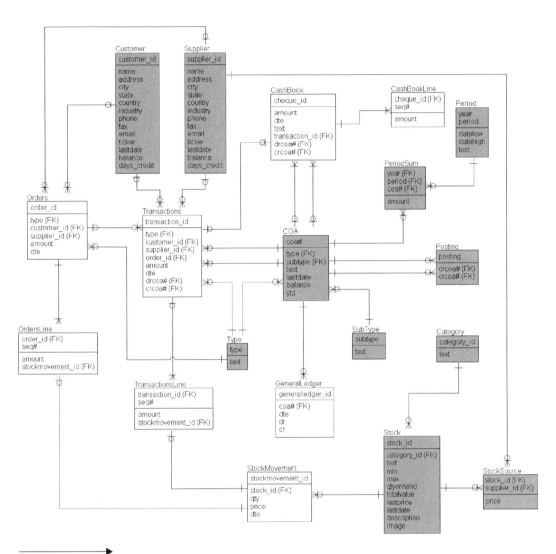

Figure B.6   *OLTP transactional normalized schema.*

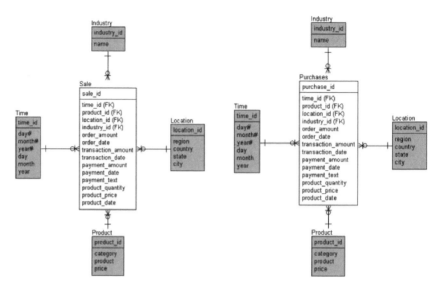

C

Sample Scripting

All relevant schema scripts can be found from a simple menu on my web site at the following URL, along with many other goodies including my resume:

```
http://www.oracledbaexpert.com/oracle/
OracleDataWarehouseTuning/index.html
```

I have also added datafiles for fast loading of a database on my web site. Datafiles are too large to include in this text.

C.1 EXPLAINP.SQL

```
set linesize 132 wrap off echo off feedback off termout on;

spool ./explainp.log;

--
--explain plan set statement_id='TEST' for
--<SQL Statement;>
--

COL Query FORMAT a64 WRAP ON;
COL Pos FORMAT 990;
COL Cost FORMAT 999999990;
COL Rows FORMAT 99999999990;
COL Bytes FORMAT 999999999990;
COL Sort FORMAT 990;
COL IO FORMAT 9990;
COL CPU FORMAT 9990;
```

```
--COL Cost FORMAT 990;
--COL Rows FORMAT 99990;
--COL Bytes FORMAT 999990;
--COL Sort FORMAT 999990;


SELECT      TRIM(LEVEL)||'. '||LPAD (' ', LEVEL -
1)||operation||' '||options||' on '||object_name||'
'||other_tag||' '||TRIM(TO_CHAR(partition_start))||'
'||TRIM(TO_CHAR(partition_stop)) "Query"
         ,cost "Cost"
         ,cardinality "Rows"
         ,bytes "Bytes"
         --,search_columns "SC"
--       ,decode(level,1,0,position) "Pos"
--       ,temp_space "Sort"
--       ,io_cost "IO"
--       ,cpu_cost "CPU"
FROM     plan_table
WHERE    statement_id = 'TEST'
CONNECT BY prior id = parent_id AND prior statement_id =
statement_id
START WITH id = 0 AND statement_id = 'TEST'
ORDER BY id;


delete from plan_table where statement_id='TEST';
commit;


spool off;


set echo on feedback on;
```

C.2   Create Tablespaces

```
CONNECT SYS/password@DW AS SYSDBA


--
--Primary tablespaces
--


CREATE TABLESPACE DATA DATAFILE 'F:\ORACLE\PRODUCT\10.1.0\
ORADATA\DWS\DATA01.DBF' SIZE 250M AUTOEXTEND ON EXTENT
MANAGEMENT LOCAL SEGMENT SPACE MANAGEMENT AUTO NOLOGGING;
```

```
CREATE TABLESPACE INDX DATAFILE 'E:\ORACLE\PRODUCT\10.1.0\
ORADATA\DWS\INDX01.DBF' SIZE 125M AUTOEXTEND ON EXTENT
MANAGEMENT LOCAL SEGMENT SPACE MANAGEMENT AUTO NOLOGGING;


CREATE TABLESPACE OBJECTS DATAFILE 'C:\ORACLE\PRODUCT\10.1.0\
ORADATA\DWS\OBJ01.DBF' SIZE 25M AUTOEXTEND ON EXTENT
MANAGEMENT LOCAL SEGMENT SPACE MANAGEMENT AUTO NOLOGGING;


alter tablespace system nologging;
alter tablespace sysaux nologging;
alter database default tablespace data;


--
--Materialized view tablespaces
--


CREATE TABLESPACE MVDATA DATAFILE 'F:\ORACLE\PRODUCT\10.1.0\
ORADATA\DWS\MVDATA01.DBF' SIZE 500M AUTOEXTEND ON EXTENT
MANAGEMENT LOCAL SEGMENT SPACE MANAGEMENT AUTO NOLOGGING;


CREATE TABLESPACE MVINDX DATAFILE 'E:\ORACLE\PRODUCT\10.1.0\
ORADATA\DWS\MVINDX01.DBF' SIZE 250M AUTOEXTEND ON EXTENT
MANAGEMENT LOCAL SEGMENT SPACE MANAGEMENT AUTO NOLOGGING;


--
--Partitioning tablespaces
--


CREATE TABLESPACE PDATA1 DATAFILE 'D:\ORACLE\PRODUCT\10.1.0\
ORADATA\DWS\PDATA101.DBF' SIZE 10M AUTOEXTEND ON EXTENT
MANAGEMENT LOCAL SEGMENT SPACE MANAGEMENT AUTO NOLOGGING;


CREATE TABLESPACE PDATA2 DATAFILE 'E:\ORACLE\PRODUCT\10.1.0\
ORADATA\DWS\PDATA201.DBF' SIZE 10M AUTOEXTEND ON EXTENT
MANAGEMENT LOCAL SEGMENT SPACE MANAGEMENT AUTO NOLOGGING;


CREATE TABLESPACE PDATA3 DATAFILE 'F:\ORACLE\PRODUCT\10.1.0\
ORADATA\DWS\PDATA301.DBF' SIZE 10M AUTOEXTEND ON EXTENT
MANAGEMENT LOCAL SEGMENT SPACE MANAGEMENT AUTO NOLOGGING;


CREATE TABLESPACE PINDX1 DATAFILE 'D:\ORACLE\PRODUCT\10.1.0\
ORADATA\DWS\PINDX101.DBF' SIZE 10M AUTOEXTEND ON EXTENT
MANAGEMENT LOCAL SEGMENT SPACE MANAGEMENT AUTO NOLOGGING;
```

```
CREATE TABLESPACE PINDX2 DATAFILE 'E:\ORACLE\PRODUCT\10.1.0\
ORADATA\DWS\PINDX201.DBF' SIZE 10M AUTOEXTEND ON EXTENT
MANAGEMENT LOCAL SEGMENT SPACE MANAGEMENT AUTO NOLOGGING;

CREATE TABLESPACE PINDX3 DATAFILE 'F:\ORACLE\PRODUCT\10.1.0\
ORADATA\DWS\PINDX301.DBF' SIZE 10M AUTOEXTEND ON EXTENT
MANAGEMENT LOCAL SEGMENT SPACE MANAGEMENT AUTO NOLOGGING;
```

C.3   GENERATE.SQL

```
CONNECT SYS/password@DW AS SYSDBA
@CREATEUSER.SQL
@schemaDimsDW.sql
@sequencesDimsDW.sql
@dataDimsDW.sql
@schemaFactsDW.sql
@sequencesFactsDW.sql
@dataFactsOLTP.sql
@dataFactsDW.sql
```

C.3.1   CREATEUSER.SQL

```
SPOOL log/CREATEUSER.LOG;
create user dws identified by dws
default tablespace data temporary tablespace temp
quota unlimited on data quota unlimited on INDX quota
unlimited on objects;
grant connect,resource,unlimited tablespace,query
rewrite,create materialized view,advisor,create dimension to
dws;
SPOOL OFF;
```

C.3.2   SCHEMADIMSDW.SQL

```
spool log/schemaDimsDW.log;


--
--Stock, industry and locations are static for all databases
--The accounts database simulation creates only orders,
transaction, cashbook entries,
--stock movements and general ledger entries - new static data
is never introduced. Thus
--the DW assumes static data is never altered
--
```

```
CREATE TABLE Industry(
     industry_id NUMBER NOT NULL
    ,industry VARCHAR2(32) NOT NULL
    ,CONSTRAINT PK_Industry PRIMARY KEY(industry_id) USING
INDEX TABLESPACE INDX
    ,CONSTRAINT XAK_Industry_Name UNIQUE(industry) USING
INDEX TABLESPACE INDX
) TABLESPACE DATA;

CREATE TABLE Location(
     location_id NUMBER NOT NULL
    ,region VARCHAR2(32)
    ,country VARCHAR2(32)
    ,state VARCHAR2(32)
    ,city VARCHAR2(32)
    ,CONSTRAINT XPK_Location PRIMARY KEY(location_id) USING
INDEX TABLESPACE INDX
    ,CONSTRAINT XAK_Region_Unique
UNIQUE(region,country,state,city) USING INDEX TABLESPACE INDX
) TABLESPACE DATA;

CREATE TABLE Product(
     product_id NUMBER NOT NULL
    ,category VARCHAR2(32)
    ,product VARCHAR2(128)
    ,price NUMBER(10,2)
    ,CONSTRAINT XPK_Product PRIMARY KEY(product_id) USING
INDEX TABLESPACE INDX
    ,CONSTRAINT XAK_Product_Unique UNIQUE(product) USING
INDEX TABLESPACE INDX
) TABLESPACE DATA;

--
--THIS IS THE ORIGINAL FORM OF THE TIME ENTITY WHICH
--WAS CHANGED DURING THE WRITING PROCESS
--


--
--Oracle date formatting
--
--
--HH24 - hour of day 1-24
```

```
--
--D-day of week 1-7
--DD-day of month 1-28/30/31
--DY- abbrev name of day
--DAY-name of day padded to 9 chars
--
--W-week# of month
--IW-week# of year
--
--MM-month #
--MON-abbrev month
--MONTH-month name to 9 chars
--
--Q-quarter#
--
--YYYY-4 digit year
--

CREATE TABLE Time(
         time_id NUMBER NOT NULL
        ,hh24# NUMBER NOT NULL
        ,dayofweek# NUMBER NOT NULL
        ,dayofmonth# NUMBER NOT NULL
        ,dyabbrev CHAR(3) NOT NULL
        ,dayname CHAR(9) NOT NULL
        ,weekofmonth# NUMBER NOT NULL
        ,weekofyear# NUMBER NOT NULL
        ,month# NUMBER NOT NULL
        ,monabbrev CHAR(3) NOT NULL
        ,monthname CHAR(9) NOT NULL
        ,quarter# NUMBER NOT NULL
        ,year# NUMBER NOT NULL
        ,CONSTRAINT PK_Time PRIMARY KEY (time_id) USING INDEX
TABLESPACE INDX
) TABLESPACE DATA;

spool off;
```

C.3.3 SEQUENCESDIMSDW.SQL

```
spool log/sequencesDimsDW.log;
```

```
create sequence industry_seq start with 1 increment by 1
nomaxvalue nocycle;
create sequence location_seq start with 1 increment by 1
nomaxvalue nocycle;
create sequence product_seq start with 1 increment by 1
nomaxvalue nocycle;
create sequence time_seq start with 1 increment by 1
nomaxvalue nocycle;
spool off;
```

C.3.4 DATADIMS.SQL

```
spool log/dataDimsDW.log;
```

Sample data only (see http://www.oracledbaexpert.com/oracle/
OracleDataWarehouseTuning/index.html).

```
insert into industry values(1,'Aerospace and Defense');
insert into industry values(2,'Automotive');
insert into industry values(3,'Chemicals');
insert into industry values(4,'Communications');
insert into industry values(5,'Consumer Goods');
. . .
```

Sample data only (see http://www.oracledbaexpert.com/oracle/
OracleDataWarehouseTuning/index.html).

```
. . .
insert into location values(130,'North America','United
States','','Guam');
insert into location values(131,'North America','United
States','','Midway');
insert into location values(132,'North
America','Greenland','','Godthab');
insert into location values(133,'North
America','Greenland','','Thule');
insert into location values(134,'North
America','Canada','','Burlington');
insert into location values(135,'Europe','Northern
Ireland','','Belfast');
```

```
insert into location values(136,'Europe','Slovak
Republic','','Bratislava');
insert into location
values(137,'Europe','Yugoslavia','','Belgrade');
insert into location
values(138,'Europe','Scotland','','Edinburgh');
insert into location values(139,'Europe','United
Kingdom','','London');
insert into location values(140,'Europe','United
Kingdom','','Ascension Island');
insert into location values(141,'Europe','United
Kingdom','','Diego Garcia');
. . .
```

Sample data only (see http://www.oracledbaexpert.com/oracle/
OracleDataWarehouseTuning/index.html).

```
insert into product values(1,'PDAs','Sony CLIE S360
Handheld',205.86);
insert into product values(2,'Printers','Epson Stylus Photo
820 InkJet Printer',115.08);
insert into product values(4,'Printers','Epson Stylus C80
Color Inkjet Printer',171.78);
insert into product values(6,'Printers','Epson Stylus C40UX
InkJet Printer',61.98);
insert into product values(7,'Printers','Epson Stylus C60
Inkjet Printer',103.56);
. . .
```

Sample data only (see http://www.oracledbaexpert.com/oracle/Oracle
DataWarehouseTuning/index.html).

```
insert into time values(1,1,'Jan','January',1,1995);
insert into time values(2,1,'Jan','January',1,1996);
insert into time values(3,1,'Jan','January',1,1997);
insert into time values(4,1,'Jan','January',1,1998);
insert into time values(5,1,'Jan','January',1,1999);
insert into time values(6,1,'Jan','January',1,2000);
insert into time values(7,1,'Jan','January',1,2001);
insert into time values(8,1,'Jan','January',1,2002);
insert into time values(9,1,'Jan','January',1,2003);
```

```
insert into time values(10,1,'Jan','January',1,2004);
insert into time values(11,1,'Jan','January',1,2005);
insert into time values(12,1,'Jan','January',1,2006);
insert into time values(13,2,'Feb','February',1,1995);
. . .


--
--This script created the contents of the original TIME table
--

declare
    i integer;
    d date default '01-JAN-2000';
    noofyrs integer default 7;
begin
    for i in 0..(24*365*noofyrs) loop
        d:=d+1/24;
        insert into time
        (
            time_id
            ,hh24#
            ,dayofweek#
            ,dayofmonth#
            ,dyabbrev
            ,dayname
            ,weekofmonth#
            ,weekofyear#
            ,month#
            ,monabbrev
            ,monthname
            ,quarter#
            ,year#
        )
        values
        (
            time_seq.nextval
            ,TO_NUMBER(TO_CHAR(d,'HH24'))
            ,TO_NUMBER(TO_CHAR(d,'D'))
            ,TO_NUMBER(TO_CHAR(d,'DD'))
            ,INITCAP(TO_CHAR(d,'DY'))
            ,INITCAP(TO_CHAR(d,'DAY'))
```

```
            ,TO_NUMBER(TO_CHAR(d,'W'))
            ,TO_NUMBER(TO_CHAR(d,'IW'))
            ,TO_NUMBER(TO_CHAR(d,'MM'))
            ,INITCAP(TO_CHAR(d,'MON'))
            ,INITCAP(TO_CHAR(d,'MONTH'))
            ,TO_NUMBER(TO_CHAR(d,'Q'))
            ,TO_NUMBER(TO_CHAR(d,'YYYY'))
        );
        commit;
    end loop;
exception when others then
    dbms_output.put_line('TIME table error:
'||SQLERRM(SQLCODE));
end;
/



--
--Generate statistics
--
analyze table industry compute statistics;
analyze table location compute statistics;
analyze table product compute statistics;
analyze table time compute statistics;
```

C.3.5   SCHEMAFACTSDW.SQL

```
spool log/schemaFactsDW.log;

drop table sale;
drop table purchase;

CREATE TABLE Sale(
    sale_id NUMBER NOT NULL
    ,time_id NUMBER NOT NULL
    ,product_id NUMBER NOT NULL
    ,location_id NUMBER NOT NULL
    ,industry_id NUMBER NOT NULL
    ,order_amount NUMBER(10,2)
    ,order_date DATE
    ,transaction_amount NUMBER(10,2)
    ,transaction_date DATE
```

```
    ,payment_amount NUMBER(10,2)
    ,payment_date DATE
    ,payment_text VARCHAR2(32)
    ,product_quantity NUMBER
    ,product_price NUMBER(10,2) --price at the time
    ,product_date DATE
    ,CONSTRAINT PK_Sale PRIMARY KEY (sale_id) USING INDEX
TABLESPACE INDX
    ,CONSTRAINT FK_Sale_Time FOREIGN KEY (time_id)
REFERENCES Time
    ,CONSTRAINT FK_Sale_Product FOREIGN KEY (product_id)
REFERENCES Product
    ,CONSTRAINT FK_Sale_Location FOREIGN KEY (location_id)
REFERENCES Location
    ,CONSTRAINT FK_Sale_Industry FOREIGN KEY (industry_id)
REFERENCES Industry
) TABLESPACE DATA NOLOGGING;
CREATE INDEX XFX_Sale_Time ON Sale(time_id) TABLESPACE INDX
NOLOGGING;
CREATE INDEX XFX_Sale_Product ON Sale(product_id) TABLESPACE
INDX NOLOGGING;
CREATE INDEX XFX_Sale_Location ON Sale(location_id)
TABLESPACE INDX NOLOGGING;
CREATE INDEX XFX_Sale_Industry ON Sale(industry_id)
TABLESPACE INDX NOLOGGING;

CREATE TABLE Purchase(
     purchase_id NUMBER NOT NULL
    ,time_id NUMBER NOT NULL
    ,product_id NUMBER NOT NULL
    ,location_id NUMBER NOT NULL
    ,industry_id NUMBER NOT NULL
    ,order_amount NUMBER(10,2)
    ,order_date DATE
    ,transaction_amount NUMBER(10,2)
    ,transaction_date DATE
    ,payment_amount NUMBER(10,2)
    ,payment_date DATE
    ,payment_text VARCHAR2(32)
    ,product_quantity NUMBER
    ,product_price NUMBER(10,2) --price at the time
    ,product_date DATE
```

```
        ,CONSTRAINT PK_Purchase PRIMARY KEY (purchase_id) USING
INDEX TABLESPACE INDX
        ,CONSTRAINT FK_Purchase_Time FOREIGN KEY (time_id)
REFERENCES Time
        ,CONSTRAINT FK_Purchase_Product FOREIGN KEY (product_id)
REFERENCES Product
        ,CONSTRAINT FK_Purchase_Location FOREIGN KEY
(location_id) REFERENCES Location
        ,CONSTRAINT FK_Purchase_Industry FOREIGN KEY
(industry_id) REFERENCES Industry
) TABLESPACE DATA NOLOGGING;
CREATE INDEX XFX_Purchase_Time ON Purchase(time_id)
TABLESPACE INDX NOLOGGING;
CREATE INDEX XFX_Purchase_Product ON Purchase(product_id)
TABLESPACE INDX NOLOGGING;
CREATE INDEX XFX_Purchase_Location ON Purchase(location_id)
TABLESPACE INDX NOLOGGING;
CREATE INDEX XFX_Purchase_Industry ON Purchase(industry_id)
TABLESPACE INDX NOLOGGING;

spool off;
```

C.3.6   DATAFACTSDW.SQL

These tables have millions of rows and are provided on my web site as a
download in various forms.

```
spool log/dataFactsDW.log;
analyze table sale compute statistics;
analyze table purchase compute statistics;
spool off;
```

Sample data only (see http://www.oracledbaexpert.com/oracle/
OracleDataWarehouseTuning/index.html).

```
insert into sale values(1,6,57,39,12,530.87,'18-JAN-
00',530.87,'18-JAN-00',4185.15,'18-JAN-00','Sales Invoice
53186',-10,530.87,18-JAN-00');
insert into sale values(2,6,12,39,12,163.25,'18-JAN-
00',163.25,'18-JAN-00',4185.15,'18-JAN-00','Sales Invoice
53186',-2,163.25,18-JAN-00');
```

```
insert into sale values(3,6,91,39,12,170.01,'18-JAN-
00',170.01,'18-JAN-00',4185.15,'18-JAN-00','Sales Invoice
53186',-1,170.01,18-JAN-00');
insert into sale values(4,6,62,39,12,33.8,'18-JAN-
00',33.8,'18-JAN-00',4185.15,'18-JAN-00','Sales Invoice
53186',-9,33.8,18-JAN-00');
```

. . .

Purchase table is similar to Sale table.

C.3.7 SEQUENCESFACTSDW.SQL

```
spool log/sequencesFactsDW.log;
create sequence sale_seq start with 1 increment by 1
nomaxvalue nocycle;
create sequence purchase_seq start with 1 increment by 1
nomaxvalue nocycle;
spool off;
```

C.4 Normalized Dimensions

```
spool log/schemaNormalize.log;

create sequence region_seq start with 1 increment by 1
nomaxvalue nocycle;
create sequence country_seq start with 1 increment by 1
nomaxvalue nocycle;
create sequence state_seq start with 1 increment by 1
nomaxvalue nocycle;
create sequence city_seq start with 1 increment by 1
nomaxvalue nocycle;

CREATE TABLE Region(
     region_id NUMBER NOT NULL
    ,region VARCHAR2(32)
    ,CONSTRAINT XPK_Region PR1MARY KEY(region_id) USING INDEX
TABLESPACE INDX
) TABLESPACE DATA;

CREATE TABLE Country(
     country_id NUMBER NOT NULL
    ,region_id NUMBER NOT NULL
```

```
    ,country VARCHAR2(32)
 ,FXCODE CHAR(3)
 ,CURRENCY VARCHAR2(32)
 ,RATE FLOAT(126)
 ,POPULATION NUMBER
    ,CONSTRAINT XPK_Country PRIMARY KEY(country_id) USING
INDEX TABLESPACE INDX
    ,CONSTRAINT FK_Country_Region FOREIGN KEY (region_id)
REFERENCES Region
) TABLESPACE DATA;
CREATE INDEX XFX_Country_Region ON Country(region_id)
TABLESPACE INDX;


CREATE TABLE State(
    state_id NUMBER NOT NULL
    ,region_id NUMBER NOT NULL
    ,country_id NUMBER NOT NULL
    ,state VARCHAR2(32)
    ,CONSTRAINT XPK_State PRIMARY KEY(state_id) USING INDEX
TABLESPACE INDX
    ,CONSTRAINT FK_State_Region FOREIGN KEY (region_id)
REFERENCES Region
    ,CONSTRAINT FK_State_Country FOREIGN KEY (country_id)
REFERENCES Country
) TABLESPACE DATA;
CREATE INDEX XFX_State_Region ON State(region_id) TABLESPACE
INDX;
CREATE INDEX XFX_State_Country ON State(country_id)
TABLESPACE INDX;


--
--NB. State remove from City table
--
CREATE TABLE city(
    city_id NUMBER NOT NULL
    ,region_id NUMBER NOT NULL
    ,country_id NUMBER NOT NULL
    --,state_id NUMBER
    ,city VARCHAR2(32)
,POPULATION NUMBER
    ,CONSTRAINT XPK_City PRIMARY KEY(city_id) USING INDEX
TABLESPACE INDX
```

```
    ,CONSTRAINT FK_City_Region FOREIGN KEY (region_id)
REFERENCES Region
    ,CONSTRAINT FK_City_Country FOREIGN KEY (country_id)
REFERENCES Country
    --,CONSTRAINT FK_City_State FOREIGN KEY (state_id)
REFERENCES State
) TABLESPACE DATA;
CREATE INDEX XFX_City_Region ON City(region_id) TABLESPACE
INDX;
CREATE INDEX XFX_City_Country ON City(country_id) TABLESPACE
INDX;
--CREATE INDEX XFX_City_State ON City(state_id) TABLESPACE
INDX;
```

Sample data only (see http://www.oracledbaexpert.com/oracle/
OracleDataWarehouseTuning/index.html).

```
insert into region values(1,'Africa');
insert into region values(2,'Asia');
insert into region values(3,'Australasia');
insert into region values(4,'Caribbean');
insert into region values(5,'Central America');
insert into region values(6,'Europe');
insert into region values(7,'Far East');
. . .
```

Sample data only (see http://www.oracledbaexpert.com/oracle/
OracleDataWarehouseTuning/index.html).

```
insert into country values(1,1,'Algeria','DZD','Algeria
Dinars',,30081000);
insert into country
values(2,1,'Angola','AOA','Kwanza',,12092000);
insert into country values(3,1,'Benin','','',,5781000);
insert into country
values(4,1,'Botswana','BWP','Pulas',,1570000);
insert into country values(5,1,'Burkina
Faso','','',,11305000);
insert into country
values(6,1,'Burundi','BIF','Francs',,6457000);
insert into country values(7,1,'Central African
Republic','','',,3485000);
```

```
insert into country values(8,1,'Congo','','',,49139000);
insert into country
values(9,1,'Djibouti','DJF','Francs',,623000);
insert into country values(10,1,'Equatorial
Guinea','','',,431000);
. . .
```

Sample data only (see http://www.oracledbaexpert.com/oracle/ OracleDataWarehouseTuning/index.html).

```
insert into state values(1,125,'BC');
insert into state values(2,125,'NS');
insert into state values(3,125,'ON');
insert into state values(4,125,'QB');
insert into state values(5,127,'AK');
insert into state values(6,127,'AL');
insert into state values(7,127,'AR');
. . .
```

Sample data only (see http://www.oracledbaexpert.com/oracle/ OracleDataWarehouseTuning/index.html).

```
insert into city values(1,125,'Vancouver',2200000);
insert into city values(2,125,'Halifax',);
insert into city values(3,125,'Ottawa',1150000);
insert into city values(4,125,'Toronto',5150000);
insert into city values(5,125,'Montreal',3600000);
insert into city values(6,125,'Quebec City',);
insert into city values(7,127,'Anchorage',);
insert into city values(8,127,'Fairbanks',);
insert into city values(9,127,'Juneau',);
insert into city values(10,127,'Kenai',);
. . .

analyze table region compute statistics;
analyze table country compute statistics;
analyze table state compute statistics;
analyze table city compute statistics;

spool off;
```

D

Syntax Conventions

Syntax diagrams in this book will utilize what is known as Backus-Naur Form syntax notation convention. Backus-Naur Form has become the de facto standard for most computer texts. Oracle SQL is used to describe the notation.

- **Angle brackets: < . . . >.** Angle brackets are used to represent names of categories (substitution variable representation). In this example <table> will be replaced with a table name in a schema as shown.

```
SELECT * FROM <table>;
```

Becomes:

```
SELECT * FROM ARTIST;
```

Note: Angle brackets are generally not used in this book unless stated as such at the beginning of a chapter.

- OR: |. A pipe or | character represents an OR conjunction meaning either can be selected. The asterisk (*) and curly braces ({}) are explained further on. In this case all or some columns can be retrieved, some meaning one or more.

```
SELECT { * | { <column>, … } } FROM <table>;
```

- Optional: [. . .]. In a SELECT statement a WHERE clause is syntactically optional.

```
SELECT * FROM <table> [ WHERE <column> = … ];
```

- **At least one of:** { . . . | . . . | . . . }. In this example the SELECT statement retrieval list must include an asterisk (*), retrieving all columns in a table, or a list of one or more columns.

```
SELECT { * | { <column>, … } } FROM <table>;
```

Note: This is a not precise interpretation of Backus-Naur Form where curly braces usually represent zero or more. In this book curly braces represent one or more iterations, never zero.

Sources of Information

The author of this book can be contacted at the following email addresses:

    oracledbaexpert@earthlink.net
    info@oracledbaexpert.com

Oracle Technology Network at http://technet.oracle.com or http://otn.oracle.com is an excellent source for entire Oracle reference documentation sets.

Metalink at http://metalink.oracle.com is also excellent and a source of current information from support calls, questions and answers placed by both Oracle users and Oracle support staff. The information on this site is well worth the Oracle licensing fees required.

Search for a term such as "free buffer waits" in search engines, such as http://www.yahoo.com. Be aware that not all information will be current and some might be incorrect, therefore, verify on Oracle Technet. If no results are found using Yahoo then try the full detailed listings on http://www.google.com.

Try http://www.amazon.com and http://www.barnesandnoble.com, among other bookseller web sites, where many Oracle titles can be found.

Other titles by the same author:

- *Oracle 9i: SQL Exam Cram 2* (1Z0-007) (ISBN: 0789732483).

- *Oracle SQL: Jumpstart with Examples* (ISBN: 1555583237).

- *Oracle Performance Tuning for 9i and 10g* (ISBN: 1555583059).

- *ASP Scripting* (ISBN: 1932808450).

- *Oracle Performance Tuning* (ISBN: 1932808345).

- *Oracle Database Administration Fundamentals II* (ISBN: 1932072845).

- *Oracle Database Administration Fundamentals I* (ISBN: 1932072535).

- *Introduction to Oracle 9i and Beyond: SQL & PL/SQL* (ISBN: 1932072241).

Schema scripts can be found from a simple menu on my web site at the following URL, along with many other goodies including my resume: http://www.oracledbaexpert.com/oracle/OracleDataWarehouseTuning/index.html

Software accreditations:

- Microsoft Word, Powerpoint, Excel, Win2K

- ERWin

- Paintshop

- Oracle Database 10*g* and Oracle Database 9*i*

Index

1st normal form, 4
2nd normal form, 4, 5
3rd normal form, 4–5, 6
   query optimization, 44
   schemas, 44
4th normal form, 5
5th normal form, 6

Abstraction, 12
Aggregated materialized views, 128
Aggregations, 46–47, 327–28
   application of, 115
   cumulative, 262
   fast refresh requirements, 93–94
   GROUP BY clause, 169
   GROUP BY clause extensions, 215–47
   HAVING clause, 169–70
   joins and, 97
   physical space, 80
   precalculation, 80
   processing, 80
   query rewrite performance and, 332–33
   single table, 101
Aliases, 188
ALTER DIMENSION statement, 123
ALTER INDEX statement, 343
ALTER MATERIALIZED VIEW [LOG]
     statements, 90, 91
Alternate indexing, 53–54

defined, 53
disadvantages, 54
excessive, 54
need for, 53
See also Indexes; Indexing
ALTER TABLESPACE statement, 367
Analysis, 46–47
Analysis reporting, 249–79
   analytical functions, 253–56
   categories, 251–53
   data densification, 252
   defined, 249
   equiwidth histograms, 252
   first and last, 252
   frequent itemsets, 252
   hypothetical ranks and distributions, 252
   inverse percentiles, 252
   lag and lead, 251
   linear regressions, 252
   moving windows, 251, 261–62
   objective, 249
   performance and, 251
   in practice, 270–79
   rankings, 251
   specialized expressions, 252
   specialized statistical functions, 253
   specialized syntax, 256–70
Analytical functions, 253–56
   aggregation, allowing analysis, 256
   lag and lead, 255

ranking, 255
statistical, 253–54
statistical distribution, 254–55
summary, 253
Angle brackets (<...>), 447
Anti comparison condition, 173
Anti-joins, 41, 180
ANY wildcard, 299, 300
Appending, 353
direct load, 354
space reuse and, 353
Archive logs
defined, 397
tuning, 399–402
See also Redo logs
Attributes, 12
Automated undo tablespace, 408

Bitmap indexes, 40, 58–61
block level locking, 60
cardinality, 58, 74
composite column, 60
data distribution and, 73
experimentation, 43
hint compatibility, 41
illustrated, 59
on individual nonunique columns, 74
NULL values and, 61
overflow, 60
performance, 60
restrictions, 60–61
structure, 74
using, 43
See also Indexes
Bitmap join indexes, 61, 70–73
defined, 61, 70
star transformation query and, 70–73
See also Indexes
Bitmaps, 8
Blind variables, 331

Block sizes, tuning, 388–89
BTree indexes, 46, 50, 55–58
ascending, 56
attributes, 55
building, 52
compressed composite column, 58
descending, 56
fact-dimensions join, 63
function-based, 57
internal structure, 56
reverse key value, 58
sorted, 57
types of, 56–58
unique, 56
unsorted, 57
See also Indexes
Buffer busy waits, 199
Business processes, 21

Capacity Planner, 410–11, 422
Capacity planning, 409–22
Capacity Planner, 410–11, 422
datafile content sizes, 409–10, 412
datafile sizes, 409, 411
DBMS_SPACE package, 410, 412–14
defined, 409
exact column data lengths, 410, 419–22
methods, 409–11
statistics, 410
CASE statement, 266–69
DECODE function vs., 269
defined, 266
embedded, 267
searched, 267
simple, 267
syntax, 267
UNION operators and, 268
Cell references, 288–89, 295–300
Classes, 12
Clusters, 46, 75–77

creating, 76
defined, 8
tables, 76
Collections, 12
Columns, 324
    composite key, duplicating, 28
    duplication into child entities, 9
    exact data lengths, 410, 419–22
    frequently/infrequently accessed, 9
    measuring, 282
    MODEL clause, 289–91
    SELECT clause, 164
    summary, in parent entities, 9
    unwanted, 377–78
Comparison conditions, 172–75
    anti, 173
    equi, 173
    EXISTS set membership, 174
    grouping, 175
    IN set membership, 174
    LIKE pattern matching, 173
    range, 173
Composite groupings, 243–45
    defined, 243
    to filter aggregates, 244
    See also Groupings
Composite indexes, 51
    reading with/without matching WHERE
        clause, 167
    too few columns in, 167
    See also Indexes
Composite partitioning
    defined, 140
    types of, 140
    uses, 142–43
    See also Partitioning
Concatenated groupings, 245–46
Conditions comparison, 172–75
Constraints
    with dimensions, 123–24
    foreign key, 41, 51

query rewrite performance and, 332
    referential integrity, 45
Container tracking schema, 13–15
    entities, 14–15
    illustrated, 14
    inventory-accounting, 425, 429
    sample, 425, 426–27
Control file, 372–79, 396
    adding data, 379
    data types, 378
    defined, 372, 397
    embedded SQL statements, 378–79
    field definitions, 373–76
    load filters, 377
    loading multiple tables, 373
    NULL values and, 376–77
    row loading options, 372–73
    unwanted columns, 377–78
    See also SQL*Loader
CREATE DIMENSION statement, 117–23
    attribute clause, 122–23
    defined, 117
    dimension join clause, 120–22
    extended attribute clause, 123
    hierarchy clause, 119–22
    level clause, 117–19
CREATE DIRECTORY statement, 360, 382
CREATE INDEX statement, 343
CREATE MATERIALIZED LOG
    statement, 88–90
    SEQUENCE clause, 90
    syntax, 89
    WITH clause, 89–90
CREATE MATERIALIZED VIEW
    statement, 82–88
    BUILD DEFERRED option, 88
    BUILD IMMEDIATE option, 88
    CACHE option, 88
    ENABLE QUERY REWRITE clause, 85–
        87
    NOLOGGING option, 88

ON PREBUILT TABLE option, 87
PARALLEL option, 88
REFRESH clause, 82–85
syntax, 83
TABLESPACE option, 88
USING INDEX option, 88
CREATE TABLESPACE statement, 366, 403
privileges requirements, 366
syntax, 404–6
CREATE TABLE statement, 144–50
hash partition, 147–48
list partition, 146–47
with parallel SELECT subquery, 345
range-hash partition, 148–49
range-list partition, 149–50
range partition, 144–46
CREATEUSER.SQL, 434
Cross joins, 180
CUBE clause, 222–25
defined, 216
equivalence expressions, 230–31
execution speed, 229, 230
materialized views and, 235, 236
multiple-dimensional summaries, 222
multiple dimensions, 225
performance and, 223–25
restricting, 215
syntax, 223
totals, 224
Cumulative aggregation, 262
Cursor expressions, 270
CV function, 299, 300

Data
adding, not in input datafiles, 379
marts, 13
mining, 422
retention time, 27
separation, 9

Database links, 362–63
creating, 362
data access, 362–63
defined, 362
Database memory health, 210, 211
Database samples, this book, xvi
Data Definition Language (DDL), 82
Data densification, 252, 277–79
defined, 277
with outer join, 279
performance, 278
DATADIMS.SQL, 437–40
DATAFACTSDW.SQL, 442–43
Datafiles, 397, 398–99
content sizes, 409–10, 412
defined, 397
header contention, 407
sizes, 409, 411
tuning, 398–99
types, 398
Data loading, 351–84
extraction, 351, 355–61
loading step, 352
multiple phase load, 353
procedures, 369–83
single phase load, 352
steps, 351–52
strategies, 352–54
tools, 354
transformation, 352, 368–84
transportation, 351, 361–68
update window, 354
Data Manipulation Language (DML), 43
operations, 158
statements, 345–46
Data models, 3–29
data warehouse, 13–29, 34–37
demographics, 31–32
dimensional, 15–21
inventory-accounting, 32–33
object, 10–13

object-relational, 13
relational, 4–10
Data warehouse data model, 15–29
   business processes, 21
   design basics, 21–29
   dimensional, 15–21
   dimension entities, 22–24
   dimension identification, 22
   dimensions, 35–36
   fact building, 22, 36–37
   fact entities, 24–27
   fact identification, 34–35
   granularity, 21–22
   granularity data model, 35
   object data model vs., 12–13
   referential integrity and, 28
   surrogate keys and, 27–28
   See also Data models
Data warehouses
   architecture, 385–422
   capacity planning, 409–22
   data modeling, 3–29
   dimensional data outside, 302
   implementation, 385
   indexing, 49–77
   index space, 394
   I/O intensive, 50
   location representation, 301
   managing, 28–29
   origin/history, ix–x
   performance issues, 95–96
   relational model vs., 10
   sample schema, 425, 430
   tuning, xi–xii, 31–47
   tuning hardware resources for, 386–409
DBMS_ADVISOR package, 108–9
DBMS_ADVISOR.TUNE_MVIEW, 423
DBMS_MVIEW package, 104–8
DBMS_SPACE package, 410, 412–14
   defined, 412–13
   functions, 413

DBMS_STATS package, 415
DECODE function, 269
Demographics data model, 31–32
Demographics schema, 425, 428
Denormalization, 7–10
   data warehouse schema and, 20–21
   defined, 7
   forms, 9–10
   process, 38
   See also Relational data model
DENSE_RANK function, 271
DETERMINES clause, 132
Dimensional data model, 15–21
   defined, 15–16
   illustrated, 16
   snowflake schema, 19–20
   star schema, 17, 18–19
   See also Data models
Dimensional rollups, 325–27
   occurrence, 325
   query rewrite, 326
   See also Rollups
DIMENSION BY clause, 289, 297
Dimension entities, 21, 22–24
   location, 23
   normalized, 19
   product, 23
   TIME, 22, 125–26
   types, 22–24
Dimension hierarchies, 117, 119–22
   multiple, 122
   options, 121
Dimension objects, 113–36
   benefits, 114–16
   defined, 113
   drawbacks, 116
   hierarchies, 44
   join back using, 132–36
   metadata, 124
   performance and, 125–36
   performance improvement, 116

query rewrite performance and, 332
rollup using, 127–31
syntax, 116–24
uses, 8, 44, 113
Dimension references, 298–99
four, 299
multiple, 298
positional, 298
Dimensions, 24
building, 35–36
constraints with, 123–24
DETERMINES clause, 132
identifying, 22, 35–36
level, 117–19
MODEL clause and, 282
normalized, 118, 443–46
product, 22
single-level, 39
state, 124
time, 22
validation, 123
Direct loader log, 84
Drill down, 115
into latches, 207
Oracle Enterprise Manager for, 209
wait event, 212
DROP DIMENSION statement, 123
DROP MATERIALIZED VIEW [LOG]
statements, 90–91
DROP TABLESPACE statement, 366
Dumping files, 356–58
Dynamic sampling, 187

Embedded SQL statements, 378–79
Equi comparison condition, 173
Equiwidth histograms, 252
Event parameters, 195
EXISTS set membership, 174
EXPDP utility, 359
EXPLAIN PLAN, 128, 129, 134, 135, 191

differences, 130
execution, 127
illustrated, 127
partitioning, 153–54
EXPLAIN.SQL, 431–32
Exports, 359
EXP utility, 359
External tables, 359–61
CREATE TABLE statement, 360
defined, 359
empty, creating, 361
Extraction, 355–61
defined, 351
dumping files, 356–58
exports, 359
external tables, 359–61
full, 355
incremental, 355
logical, 355
offline, 356
online, 356
options, 356–61
physical, 355–56
See also Data loading

Fact entities, 24–27
attribute types, 26
foreign key constraints, 41
granularity, 26–27
multiple, 21
PURCHASE, 37, 38
remote, 41
SALES, 37, 38
star schema, 18–19
TIME, 37
types, 25
Facts
building, 22, 36–37
defined, 26
identifying, 34–35

Fact tables
    characteristics, 25
    illustrated, 25
    loading, 354
Filtered query rewrite, 330
Filters, 328–30
First and last, 252
FIRST function, 274
Foreign key constraints, 41, 51
Foreign key indexes, 51
Frequent itemsets, 252
FROM clause, 331
Full partition-wise joins, 155–57
Function-based BTree index, 57
Functions
    aggregation, allowing analysis, 256
    grouping, 216, 232–35
    indexing, 171–72
    lag and lead, 255
    in queries, 171
    ranking, 255
    statistical, 253–54
    statistical distribution, 254–55
    summary, 253
    using, 170–72

GENERATE.SQL, 434–43
    CREATEUSER.SQL, 434
    DATADIMS.SQL, 437–40
    DATAFACTSDW.SQL, 442–43
    SCHEMADIMSDW.SQL, 434–36
    SCHEMAFACTSDW.SQL, 440–42
    SEQUENCESDIMSDW.SQL, 436–37
    SEQUENCESFACTSDW.SQL, 443
Global indexes, 141, 146
Granularity, 21–22
    access, 115
    defined, 26
    fact entities, 26–27
    identifying, 35

level, 27
GROUP BY clause, 79, 169
    results, 169
    sorting, 170
GROUP BY clause extensions
    aggregation using, 215–47
    defined, 215
    grouping combinations, 242–47
    materialized views and, 235–42
    in nested materialized views, 243
    query rewrite and, 331
    reasons for use, 215–16
    See also CUBE clause; GROUPING SETS
        clause; ROLLUP clause
GROUP_ID function, 234–35, 236
GROUPING function, 232–34
Grouping functions, 216, 232–35
    GROUP_ID, 234–35, 236
    GROUPING, 232–34
    GROUPING_ID, 234, 235
    uses, 232
GROUPING_ID function, 234, 235
    single number return, 241
    using, 242
Groupings, 242–47
    combining, 242–47
    composite, 243–45
    concatenated, 245–46
    hierarchical cubes and, 246–47
GROUPING SETS clause, 225–32
    aggregates filtering, 229
    defined, 216
    equivalence expressions, 230–31
    execution speed, 229, 230
    functions, 225–27
    performance and, 227–32
    processing behind, 230
    syntax, 227
    unspecified totals prevention, 228
    See also GROUP BY clause extensions
Groups, 175, 324

sets, creating, 227–32
tablespace, 407–8

Hard parse, 185
Hash joins, 181–82
Hash partitioning
    CREATE TABLE syntax, 147–48
    defined, 140
    uses, 141–42
    See also Partitioning
HAVING clause, 169–70, 216
Hierarchical cubes, 246–47
Hints, 187–91
    bitmap index compatibility, 41
    change index scans, 189–90
    change joins, 190
    change table scans, 189
    changing queries/subqueries, 190–91
    classifying, 188
    influence the optimizer, 189
    parallel execution, 348
    parallel SQL, 190
    query rewrite performance and, 333
    as suggestions, 191
    syntax, 187–88
    use of, 42, 187
Histograms, 275–77
    defined, 275
    with WIDTH_BUCKET function, 276–
        77
Hypothetical ranks and distributions, 252

Idle events, 196–99
IMPDP utility, 359, 383
Indexes
    bitmap, 58–61
    BTree, 46, 50, 52, 55–58
    composite, 51, 167
    defined, 49

foreign key, 51
global, 141, 146
local, 141
non-BTree, 50
partition, 61, 140–41
rebuilding, 52
removing during batch uploads, 52
skip scan, 168
storage parameters, 88
structures, 55
types, 54–61
using, 183
Indexing, 46, 49–77
    alternate, 53–54
    basics, 49–54
    decision, 55
    effective, 76
    function-based, 171–72
    NULL values and, 51
    partition, 140–41
    referential integrity, 51–53
Index organized tables (IOTs), 8, 46, 75–77,
        423
    creating, 75
    defined, 61
    rebuilds, 75
Information sources, 449–50
Inheritance, 12
IN set membership, 174
Intersections, 179
INTERSECT operator, 176
Inventory-accounting data model, 32–33
    defined, 32–33
    illustrated, 33
    sample schema, 425, 429
    See also Data models
Inverse percentiles, 252
I/O, tuning, 393–409

Join back, 324–25

defined, 132
with dimension objects, 132–36
manual, 134
query rewrite, 133, 325
Join materialized views, 94–97
benefits, 94
dropping/recreating, 111
query rewrite with, 128
See also Materialized views
Joins, 179–84, 324
aggregations and, 97
anti, 180
creating, 179–81
cross, 180
efficient, 179
fast refresh requirements, 97
hash, 181–82
inefficient, 180
intersections, 179
nested loop, 181
outer, 180, 279
partition-wise, 155–57
queries, pre-creating, 96–97
query rewrite on, 110
range, 179
self, 179
sort merge, 182–83
tuning, 179, 183–84

KISS rule, 163

Lag and lead, 251, 255
LAG function, 275, 276
LAST function, 274
LEAD function, 275, 276
LIKE pattern matching, 173
Linear regressions, 252
List partitioning
CREATE TABLE syntax, 146–47

defined, 140
query rewrite and, 330–31
uses, 141
See also Partitioning
Load filters, 377
Local indexes, 141
Logical extraction, 355
Logical operators, 175
Low cardinality, 40

Matching
entire query strings, 321–23
pieces of queries, 324–30
Materialized view logs, 83
altering, 90, 91
creating, 88–90
dropping, 90–91, 110
entries, 88–89
purging, 108
requirement, 88
Materialized views, 8, 79–112
access, 81
in aggregation precalculation, 80
aggregations/filtering, 91–94
altering, 90, 91
analyzing, 102–9
benefits, 80–81
CUBE clause and, 235, 236
defined, 41, 79
dropping, 90–91
existing, registering, 87
explaining, 105–6
faster, 109–12
fast refresh, 83
formats, 91
GROUP BY clause extensions and, 235–42
importance to data warehouses, 386
join, 94–97
in LRU list, 88

maintenance, 354
managing, 102–9
MODEL clause and, 292–94
nested, 98–101
ON COMMIT, 84
ON DEMAND, 84
ORDER BY clause, 102
overuse, 101
partially stale, 330
partitioned, 81, 151–52
performance gains, 109
potential pitfalls, 81–82
querying with/without, 135
reading, 79
refresh, 80, 82, 423
refresh incremental changes, 83–84
requirements, 45
ROLLUP clause and, 235, 238–39
set operator, 98
statistics computation, 111
storage space, estimating, 105
syntax, 82–91
types of, 91–102
uses, 45
verifying, 104
MEASURES clause, 290
Memory buffers
    control, 387
    log size, 388
    tuning, 387–88
Metadata
    dimension objects, 124
    partitioning, 158–59
    tablespace, exporting, 368
    tablespace, importing, 382
Metadata views, 102–4
    illustrated, 103
    USER_BASE_TABLE_MVIEWS, 103
    USER_MVIEW_AGGREGATES, 104
    USER_MVIEW_ANALYSIS, 104

    USER_MVIEW_DETAIL_RELATI
        ONS, 104
    USER_MVIEW_JOINS, 104
    USER_MVIEW_KEYS, 103
    USER_MVIEW_LOGS, 103
    USER_MVIEW_REFRESH_TIMES,
        103
    USER_MVIEWS, 103
    USER_REGISTERED_MVIEWS, 103
    USER_TUNE_MVIEW, 104
Metalink, 449
Methods, 12
MINUS operator, 176
Mirroring, 394, 395–96
MODEL clause, 281–316, 423
    ACYCLIC, 313, 314, 315
    applying, 284, 285
    cell references, 288–89
    columns, 289–91
    complete syntax, 290
    creating, 303
    CYCLIC, 313, 314, 315
    defined, 281
    detailed syntax, 288
    DIMENSION BY clause, 289
    dimensions, 282
    functioning, 283–86
    functions, 291–92
    illustrated, 282
    for loops, 308
    materialized views and, 292–94
    MEASURES clause, 290
    measuring columns, 282
    ORDERED, 313, 314
    parallel execution, 308–12
    PARTITION BY clause, 289
    partition performance variations, 310, 312
    partitions, 282
    parts, 281–82
    performance and, 286–87, 308–16

query plan, 313–15
query plan cost, 287
query timing, 287
referencing cells, 295–300
referencing multiple models, 301–6
return rows, 289
SEQUENTIAL ORDER, 291
spreadsheet-like aspect, 285
syntax, 288–92
syntax location, 288
UPSERT vs. UPDATE option, 291, 306–8
Moving windows, 251, 261–62
   explaining, 262
   using, 261
Multiple-dimensional OLAP (MOLAP), 422
Multiple phase load, 353

Nested loop joins, 181
Nested materialized views, 98–101
   executing ROLLUP through, 239
   GROUP BY extensions in, 243
   query rewrite with, 129, 331
   tricks, 99
   See also Materialized views
Nested subqueries, 175, 184
Net Services
   defined, 390
   tuning, 390–93
   tuning at client, 391–93
   tuning at server, 390–91
Normalization, 4–6
   1st normal form, 4
   2nd normal form, 4, 5
   3rd normal form, 4–5, 6, 44
   4th normal form, 5
   5th normal form, 6
   See also Relational data model
Normalized dimensions, 443–46
NTILE function, 271, 272

NULL values
   bitmap indexes and, 61
   control file and, 376–77
   indexing and, 51

Object data model, 10–13
   abstraction, 12
   attributes, 12
   classes, 12
   collections, 12
   data warehouses vs., 12–13
   inheritance, 12
   many-to-many relationships, 11
   methods, 12
   multiple inheritance, 12
   objective, 10
   specialization, 12
   types and, 11
   See also Data models
Object-relational data model, 13
Objects
   compressing, 409
   dimension, 19
   static, caching, 408
Online Analytic Processing (OLAP), 422
Online Transaction Processing (OLTP)
     databases, ix, 7
   data warehouse database separation, x–xi
   demographics data model, 31–32
   environments-sessions, 200
   fast turnaround requirement, x
   inventory-accounting data model, 32–33
   pulling transactional data from, 358
   static entities, 33
   surrogate keys, 7
Operators
   logical, 175
   set, 98, 176
Optimizer, 183, 185–91
   capabilities, 185

defined, 185
hints and, 187–91
methods, 185
query rewrite determination, 320
query rewrite methods, 321–31
statistics, 186–87
Oracle Database
10g new features, 423
10g tools, 191–92
defined, 396–97
as file system layer, 396
index types, 54–61
loading tools, 354
Oracle databases
archive logs, 397, 399–402
datafiles, 397, 398–99
elements, 396
files, 397–98
physical, 396–402
redo logs, 397, 399–402
Oracle Enterprise Manager
Capacity Planner, 410–11
performance views and, 346
Wait Event Interface and, 209–12
Oracle Managed Files (OMF), 394, 423
Oracle SQL, 46–47
execution, 184–91
optimizer, 183, 185–91
parser, 184–85
Oracle Technology Network, 449
ORDER BY clause, 102, 257, 291
Organization, this book, xii–xvi
Outer joins, 180, 279, 333
OVER clause, 256–62
defined, 256
ORDER BY clause, 257
PARTITION clause, 257–60
partitioning in, 258
sorting in, 258
syntax, 256–57
windowing clause, 260–62

Parallel index scans, 341–42
fast, full, 342
ordered, 341
Parallelism
buffer advice, 347
degree, 336–37
execution types, 336
Parallel processing, 8, 46, 139, 308–12, 335–49
against multiple partitions, 154
configuration parameters, 312, 337–38
defined, 137, 335
demonstrating, 339–46
DML statements, 345–46
hints, 348
index DDL statements, 343–44
memory statistics, 347
partitioning and, 143–44
partitioning operations, 346
performance gains, 143
performance views, 346–47
queries, 336
query plans, 348–49
SELECT statement subqueries, 344–45
Parallel queries, 339–42
execution methods, 339
full table scan, 340
illustrated, 340
See also Parallel processing; queries
Parameter file, 397
Parser, 184–85
Parses, 185
Partial partition-wise joins, 157
PARTITION BY clause, 289, 295
PARTITION clause, 257–60
Partitioned materialized views, 151–52
Partitioned tables, 144–52
Partition indexes, 140–41
defined, 140

types, 141
See also Indexes
Partitioning, 46, 395
  benefits, 46, 138–39
  composite, 140
  defined, 8, 137
  EXPLAIN PLANs, 153–54
  hash, 140
  list, 140
  materialized views, 81
  metadata, 158–59
  methods, 139–43
  method use, 141–43
  operations, 346
  in OVER clause, 258
  parallel processing and, 143–44
  physical, 138
  range, 140
  range-hash, 140
  range-list, 140
  tricks, 158
  tuning queries with, 153–57
Partition keys, 140, 142, 151
Partition markers, 152
Partitions, 380–81
  adding, 158
  composite, 148–50
  creating, 139
  dropping, 158
  exchanging, 158
  hash, 147–48
  indexes, 61
  list, 146–47
  merging, 158
  MODEL clause and, 282
  moving, 158
  pruning, 139, 142, 154–55
  range, 144–46
  range-hash, 148–49
  range-list, 149–50
  separating, 137

  splitting, 158
  truncating, 158
Partition-wise joins, 155–57
  full, 155–57
  partial, 157
  See also Joins
PERCENT_RANK function, 271, 272
Performance
  analysis reporting and, 251
  bitmap indexes, 60
  CUBE clause and, 223–25
  data warehouse issues, 95–96
  dimension objects and, 125–36
  GROUPING SETS clause and, 227–32
  MODEL clause and, 286–87, 308–16
  parallel processing and, 143
  query rewrite, 86–87, 331–33
  ROLLUP clause and, 217–22
  SQL*Loader, 369–70
  views, 103
Performance views, 103
  Oracle Enterprise Manager and, 346
  parallel processing, 346–47
  V$EVENT_HISTOGRAM, 209
  V$EVENT_NAME, 193, 194, 196
  V$FILE_HISTOGRAM, 209
  V$LATCH_NAME, 207
  V$SESSION_EVENT, 200, 201
  V$SESSION_WAIT, 196, 202, 206, 207
  V$SESSION_WAIT_CLASS, 209
  V$SYSTEM_EVENT, 192, 293
  V$SYSTEM_WAIT_CLASS, 209
  Wait Event Interface, 192
Physical extraction, 355–56
Plug-ins, 380–83
  external tables, 382–83
  partitions, 380–81
  transportable tablespaces, 381–82
Positional dimension references, 298
Pseudocolumns, 176–78
  ROWID, 177–78

ROWNUM, 178
PURCHASE fact entity, 37–38
  defined, 37
  illustrated, 38

Queries
  3rd normal form, 44
  comparing, 67
  filtered, 92
  filtered and aggregated, 92
  functions in, 171
  join, 96
  matching pieces of, 324–30
  MODEL clause, 286–87
  no MODEL clause, 283
  parallel, 339–42
  parent, 271
  reference model, 304–5
  ROLLUP clause, 222
  serial execution, 339
  star, 40, 62–69
  strings, matching, 321–23
  with/without materialized views, 135
Query rewrite, 45, 319–33, 423
  with aggregation, 329
  blind variables and, 331
  defined, 79, 85, 319
  determination, 320
  dimensional rollup, 326
  executing through nested materialized
    views, 239
  explaining, 106–7
  filtered, 330
  fresh partitioning, 330–31
  full text match, 322–23
  GROUP BY clause extensions and, 331
  improving, 112
  join back, 133, 325
  with join materialized view, 128
  on joins, 110

  matching pieces of queries, 324–30
  matching query strings, 321–23
  methods, 321–31
  with nested materialized views, 129, 331
  occurrence, 320
  performance, affecting, 331–33
  performance, improving, 86–87
  query types, 320–21
  requirement, 80
  restrictions, 86
  special cases, 330–31
  verifying, 86
Query tuning, 163–212
  basic, 163–84
  parallel processing with partitions, 154
  with partitioning, 153–57
  partition pruning, 154–55
  partition-wise joins, 155–57
  tools, 191–212

RAID
  array structure, 393
  defined, 395
  RAID 0, 395
  RAID 0 + 1, 396
  RAID 1, 395–96
  RAID 5, 396
Range comparison condition, 173
Range-hash partitioning
  CREATE TABLE syntax, 148–49
  defined, 140
  uses, 143
  See also Partitioning
Range joins, 179
Range-list partitioning
  CREATE TABLE syntax, 149–50
  defined, 140
  query rewrite and, 330–31
  uses, 143
  See also Partitioning

Range partitioning
    CREATE TABLE syntax, 144–46
    defined, 140
    uses, 141
    See also Partitioning
Ranking functions, 255, 271–75
Rankings, 251, 274
RATIO_TO_REPORT function, 275
Recovery Manager (RMAN), 361
Redo logs
    buffer, 401
    defined, 397
    large, 400, 401
    number of, 399
    size, 400
    small, 400
    tuning, 399–402
Reference models, 302
    multiple queries, 306
    queries, 304
Referencing multiple models, 301–6
Referential integrity, 6–7
    data warehouse design and, 28
    defined, 6
    enforcement, 7
    foreign keys, 51, 54
    primary keys, 51, 54
Refresh, 80, 82
    fast requirements, 93–94
    incremental changes, 83–84
    manual, 107–8
REFRESH clause, 82–85
Registration, 108
Relational data model, 4–10
    container tracking schema, 14
    data warehouses vs., 10
    denormalization, 7–10
    normalization, 4–6
    referential integrity, 6–7
    See also Data models
Relational OLAP (ROLAP), 422

Resources, 449–50
Return rows, 289
Reverse key value BTree index, 58
ROLLUP clause, 217–22
    defined, 216
    example, 218
    executing through nested materialized
        views, 239
    materialized views and, 235, 238–39
    partial queries, 241
    performance and, 217–22
    queries, 222
    query plan without, 238
    restriction, 215
    syntax, 217
    two-dimensional structures, 217
    UNION ALL, 223
    See also GROUP BY clause extensions
Rollups
    aggregation calculation, 246
    dimensional, 325–27
    with dimension objects, 127–31
    without ROLLUP clause, 221
ROWID pseudocolumn, 177–78
ROW_NUMBER function, 271, 273
ROWNUM pseudocolumn, 178
RULES clause, 290

SALE fact entity
    defined, 37
    illustrated, 38
    star query, 66
SCHEMADIMSDW.SQL, 434–36
SCHEMAFACTSDW.SQL, 440–42
Schemas, 425–30
    container tracking, 425, 426, 427
    data warehouse, 425, 430
    demographics, 425, 428
    See also Snowflake schemas; star schemas
Schema scripts, 431–46

create tablespaces, 432–34
  EXPLAIN.SQL, 431–32
  GENERATE.SQL, 434–43
  location, 431
  normalized dimensions, 443–46
SELECT statement
  columns in, 164
  subqueries, 344–45
Self joins, 179
SEQUENCE clause, 90
Sequences, 176–77
  as counters, 176–77
  in integer identifier creation, 176
SEQUENCESDIMSDW.SQL, 436–37
SEQUENCESFACTSDW.SQL, 443
SEQUENTIAL ORDER clause, 291
Session Data Unit (SDU) buffer, 393
Session layer, 199–206
  defined, 192
  V$SESSION_WAIT, 202
  V$SYSTEM_EVENT, 200, 201, 203
  See also Wait Event Interface
Session-level events, 200
Sessions
  hooking wait events to, 204
  identifier (SID), 204
  SQL code for, 205
Set operators, 98, 176
Single phase load, 352
Snowflake schemas, 19–20
  defined, 43
  in dimension organization, 21
  duplication removal, 43
  illustrated, 19, 114
  star schemas vs., 37–44
  See also Dimensional data model
Soft parse, 185
Sorting
  GROUP BY clause, 170
  in OVER clause, 258
Sort merge joins, 182–83

Specialization, 12
Specialized expressions, 252
SQLAccess Advisor, 423
SQL*Loader, 354, 369–80
  architecture, 370–71
  control file, 372–79
  executing, 379–80
  input data files, 371–72
  parameter file, 379–80
  performance characteristics, 369–70
  speed, 370
  syntax, 380
SQL*Net, 390–93
SQL*Plus tool, 356
SQLTrace, 191
Star queries, 40, 62–69
  defined, 62
  fact table foreign key constraint indexes, 51
  with heavy filtering, 69
  illustrated, 67
  problems with, 62–69
  running, 65
  SALE fact table, 66
  See also Queries
Star schemas, 39–43
  defined, 17, 39
  efficiency, 39
  fact entities, 18–19
  illustrated, 17, 20, 114
  multiple, 21
  snowflake schemas vs., 37–44
  SQL joins and, 39
  See also Dimensional data model
Star transformation queries, 42, 69–73
  bitmap join indexes, 70–73
  cost, 69
  dimension filtering, 67
  illustrated, 70
  multiple single column bitmaps, 73
  occurrence, 69

problems with, 73–75
Star transformations, 40–43
Statistical distribution functions, 254–55
Statistical functions, 253–54, 277
Statistics, 186–87, 410
    with ANALYZE command, 414–15
    for capacity planning, 415–19
    with DBMS_STATS package, 415
    defined, 186
    dynamic sampling, 187
    query rewrite performance and, 332
    realistic, 186
STATSPACK, 191
Striping, 395
Subqueries
    for efficiency, 174–75
    nested, 175, 184
    query rewrite performance and, 333
    SELECT statement, 344–45
Subquery factoring clause, 263
Summary functions, 253
Super aggregates, 216
Surrogate keys, 7, 52–53
    data warehouse design and, 27
    defined, 52
    duplicating, 27–28
    uses, 52
Syntax conventions, 447–48
System aggregation layer
    defined, 192
    idle events, 196–99
    illustrated, 193
    V$EVENT_NAME view parameter
        columns, 193–95
    See also Wait Event Interface

Tables
    appending, 353
    compression, 87–88
    deletions, 353

    external, 359–61, 382–83
    fact, 25, 354
    highly filtered, 183
    partitioned, 144–52
Tablespaces, 402–9
    auto extend, 404
    automated undo, 408
    BIGFILE, 406–7
    block size, 404
    dictionary-managed, 402
    extent management, 405
    groups, 407–8
    locally managed, 402
    logging, 404–5
    metadata, exporting, 368
    metadata, importing, 382
    minimum extent sizes, 404
    multiple block sized, 394
    segment space management, 405–6
    SYSTEM, 404
    temporary sort space, 407
    transportable, 363–68, 381–82
TIME dimensional entity, 22, 125–26
    hierarchy, 126
    illustrated, 125
TKPROF, 191
Transactions, tuning, 389–90
Transformation, 368–84
    defined, 352, 368
    loading procedures, 369–83
    processing, 369, 383–84
    SQL functionality, 384
    See also Data loading
Transportable tablespaces, 363–68, 381–82
    defined, 363
    functioning, 364
    importing, 381–82
    limitations, 365
    plugging into, 381
    self-containment, 365–67
    transportation steps, 367–68

uses, 364
See also Tablespaces
Transportation, 361–68
    database links, 362–63
    defined, 351, 361
    tablespaces, 363–68
    See also Data loading
Tuning, 31–47
    3rd normal form schemas, 44
    archive log files, 399–402
    bitmap join indexes, 45
    block sizes, 388–89
    datafiles, 398–99
    hardware resources, 386–409
    I/O, 393–409
    joins, 179, 183–84
    materialized views, 45
    memory buffers, 387–88
    methods, 37–47
    Net Services, 390–93
    query, 153–57
    query, tools, 191–212
    redo log files, 399–402
    referential integrity constraints, 45
    star queries, 40–43
    transactions, 389–90

UNION ALL operator, 176, 231–32
UNION operator, 176
UPDATE vs. UPSERT, 291, 306–8
    illustrated, 307
    query plans, 307
    timing test, 308
    See also MODEL clause

Views
    defined, 8, 53
    inline, 331
    metadata, 102–4

    not using, 41
    performance, 103
    secondary processing on, 53
V$ performance views, 191

Wait Event Interface, 192–212
    defined, 192
    improvements, 208–9
    Oracle Enterprise Manager and, 209–12
    performance view sections, 192
    session layer, 199–206
    system aggregation layer, 192–99
    third layer and beyond, 206–8
WHEN clause, 377
WHERE clause
    filtering matching index, 166
    filtering on table only, 165
    filtering with, 164–69
    index use with, 166
    multiple column filters, 166–69
    reading composite index with/without
        matching, 167
    ROWNUM restriction, 178
    uses, 164
WIDTH_BUCKET function, 276–77
Windowing clause, 260–62
WITH clause, 89–90, 262–66
    example use, 266
    purpose, 263
    subqueries, 264
    syntax, 262–63
    variable value, 265